North Carolina
Civil War
Monuments

NORTH CAROLINA CIVIL WAR MONUMENTS
An Illustrated History

Douglas J. Butler

McFarland & Company, Inc., Publishers
Jefferson, North Carolina, and London

All photographs are by the author unless otherwise indicated.

LIBRARY OF CONGRESS CATALOGUING-IN-PUBLICATION DATA

Butler, Douglas J., 1954–
North Carolina Civil War monuments :
an illustrated history / Douglas J. Butler.
    p.   cm.
Includes bibliographical references and index.

ISBN 978-0-7864-6856-0
softcover : acid free paper ∞

1. North Carolina — History — Civil War, 1861–1865 —
Monuments. 2. United States — History — Civil War, 1861–
1865 — Monuments. 3. Soldiers' monuments — North
Carolina. 4. War memorials — North Carolina. I. Title.
E573.4.B87 2013   973.7'6 — dc23   2013008601

BRITISH LIBRARY CATALOGUING DATA ARE AVAILABLE

© 2013 Douglas J. Butler. All rights reserved

*No part of this book may be reproduced or transmitted in any form
or by any means, electronic or mechanical, including photocopying
or recording, or by any information storage and retrieval system,
without permission in writing from the publisher.*

Front cover: Soldier statue detail, Randolph County Confederate
monument, Asheboro, North Carolina. Soldier figure manufactured by
W. H. Mullins Company, Salem, Ohio; monument erected by the
Blue Pearl Granite Company, Winston-Salem, North Carolina.
Dedicated September 2, 1911 (photograph by the author).

Manufactured in the United States of America

*McFarland & Company, Inc., Publishers
Box 611, Jefferson, North Carolina 28640
www.mcfarlandpub.com*

To One Nation Under God

Table of Contents

Acknowledgments	ix
Preface	1
Introduction	3

Section I : Early Commemoration, 1865–1895

1. Gathering the Fallen	7
2. Memory	21
3. New Ground	33
4. A Capital Celebration	42

Section II : Evolving Commemoration, 1896–1918

5. "To the Confederate Soldier"	55
6. Monumental Day	66
7. The Daughters	80
8. Financing	99
9. Dedication Day	112
10. Soldier Statues	127
11. Monument Companies	141
12. Poetry and Prose	153
13. Women of the Confederacy	166
14. Across the Chasm	175

Section III : Expanding Commemoration, 1919–1961

15. New Expressions	188
16. Hard Times	200
17. The Centennial Nears	213

Appendix A. North Carolina Confederate Monuments 221
Appendix B. North Carolina Union Monuments 229
Chapter Notes 231
Bibliography 251
Index 253

Acknowledgments

Historical research, especially a compilation covering an entire state, can be daunting. Source material, in large measure, determines a work's reliability and usefulness, and while preparing *North Carolina Civil War Monuments*, I have been aided by individuals and organizations throughout North Carolina.

Even in this Internet era, most primary source material is not (at least yet) available online. Libraries remain its chief repository, and I thank the many librarians and archivists who assisted in searching vertical files, facilitated reviewing microfilmed newspapers, and guided me to unpublished manuscripts and reliable local histories. Others photocopied or emailed documents in my absence, significantly expanding the breadth of material available for my research.

Ashe County Public Library, my home library, has been particularly helpful. I especially thank Kim Grindrod and Sarah Spanburgh for obtaining numerous hard-to-find references through inter-library loans, guidance in searching online texts and databases, and providing computer assistance during manuscript preparation.

In addition to thorough research, clear communication and effective photography enhance nearly any history, especially one concerning a subject based on visual imagery and symbolism. Ramelle Pulitzer of the Hawthorne Gallery and Jane Lonon of the Ashe County Arts Council provided guidance and encouragement in preparing the exhibition that formed the photographic basis of this work. The Blue Ridge Writers Group, meeting monthly, listened as this text evolved, giving collegial support and advice as I sought to "breathe life" into this historical narrative. And I thank Dr. Al Corum of the Writers, who not only read the manuscript in its entirety but reviewed it with a scholarly eye and offered valuable advice.

Family support is vital as well, especially when a project extends for years and involves portions of many vacations. My mother has been a steady source of encouragement and, although legally blind, read and reviewed the manuscript, offering suggestions, critiquing ideas, and helping refine its presentation.

And a special thank you to Sheryl, for enduring many chilly mornings as I waited, with camera and tripod, for that "perfect light"; for reading and re-reading chapter drafts, offering constructive criticism and advice; and providing steady encouragement as the manuscript progressed from concept to reality.

I also wish to thank my fellow North Carolinians. While photographing and researching, I traveled more than 10,000 miles within the Tarheel State. These journeys renewed my appreciation of our state's rich history, its varied natural beauty, and the kindness and friendliness of our citizens, memories that, for me, will be as enduring as those sought by earlier generations through monuments of bronze and stone.

Preface

Some books seem destined to be written. *North Carolina Civil War Monuments* is one such work. Nearly two decades ago, noting controversies surrounding Confederate monuments, my late father suggested that I photograph these commemorations "before they might be moved." My photographic interests at that time, however, were of landscapes, wildlife, and mountaineering—and I was just beginning to document indigenous cultures, work that would garner numerous awards. Yet his suggestion seemed reasonable, and when I encountered a monument, which wasn't often, given my love of natural environments, I took a quick, and often uninspired, snapshot.

Inherent curiosity, however, soon prompted closer examination of these memorials. I read the inscriptions, looked closely at the sculpted symbolism, and noted details of the soldier figure. These monuments were not a defiant call for the "South to rise again," nor were they a standard artistic form. Instead these varied commemorations often expressed sorrow and grief through complex symbolism and a rich selection of poetry and prose.

Gradually I began searching for monuments and photographing them more carefully, documenting each memorial in its setting then highlighting details, often with a large telephoto lens. By 2009, I had photographed most of the state's Civil War monuments and, with support from a North Carolina Regional Art Project grant, organized a traveling interpretative photo exhibition. The following year, the North Carolina Humanities Council sponsored my accompanying lecture as a "Road Scholar" presentation.

At lectures and exhibitions people often asked, "Are you going to write a book?" Knowing the variety and complexity of North Carolina's Civil War commemorations, I was initially reluctant. The photo exhibit and accompanying text outlined the basic history of these monuments; a full-length work without images, however, might fail to convey the artistic range of these commemorations. As a result, I chose a format that includes both the history of these monuments as well as at least one photo of each.

How many Civil War monuments are located in North Carolina? The answer depends on one's definition of "monument." Monument, memorial, and (physical) commemoration will be used interchangeably in this book, yet determining which structures to include is not easy. Nearly everyone would agree that an infantryman of stone or bronze atop a prominently placed granite shaft is a monument. But what of a similarly sited and inscribed plaque bolted to a rock? Or an installation honoring soldiers of a single military unit? Or one celebrating a well-known individual? And does size, form, or location matter?

This book includes 109 North Carolina Civil War monuments erected across the state between the Confederate surrender in 1865 and the beginning of the Civil War centennial in 1961. Sometimes termed "soldiers' monuments," these commemorations honor many troops, not one individual or a single event. One hundred one are Confederate monuments; eight are Union memorials, including one honoring African American troops.

This total is based on the following criteria:

(1) A monument must *predominantly* honor *all* members of a group: the dead, veterans, a regiment or company, a demographic cohort, or one county's soldiers.
(2) Size, cost, or form does not matter. Commemorative intent, judged largely by inscription, although subjective, is the sole criterion.
(3) Location is not a determinant.
(4) Cemetery monuments honoring an entire group are included, individual gravestones are not.
(5) Subsequent commemorative additions including plaques and decorative gates placed on or near existing memorials, while generally noted, are not tallied separately.
(6) Commemorations of individuals, however prominent, or documentation of battles or specific events, are not included. Neither are historical markers such as the state-sponsored black-on-silver metal signs.
(7) Out-of-state memorials, even if sponsored by North Carolinians, are not included.

Even the best definition, however, fails to delineate all eventualities, and readers may disagree with decisions. To mitigate concerns, well-known but otherwise excluded monuments will be mentioned briefly, especially if they help clarify North Carolina's commemorative history.

The book is arranged in three sections reflecting North Carolina's changing commemorative milieu. "Early Commemoration" begins following Confederate surrender in 1865 and extends through the 1895 state monument unveiling in Raleigh. "Evolving Commemoration," details the most prolific monument-building period, 1896 to 1918, and, due to the large number of installations, is arranged thematically. The final segment, "Expanding Commemoration," discusses post–World War I memorialization and, like the first section, is presented chronologically.

Any compilation, however, even of decades-old monuments, can never be guaranteed as complete. Additional Civil War memorials, especially in cemeteries, are occasionally reported, and despite painstaking effort and diligence in preparation of this work, including "on-the-ground" searches, other monuments meeting defined criteria may exist.

Many challenges confront a researcher documenting a broad yet locally based movement. Primary sources, notably contemporaneous newspaper accounts, are referenced if available. Regional lore, including recently published local histories, unless well-documented, are cited less frequently and generally used only in the absence of other data or if they provide exceptional insight.

Meticulous care has been taken in the research, writing, and photography. While citing thousands of details and hundreds of sources covering an entire state over the course of a century, errors may have slipped in. If any have — and I trust they are few — it is my sincere hope that they will not detract from the readability or usefulness of this book, yet for errors of any magnitude, I offer my apology and accept full responsibility.

Introduction

Defeat. Total, unequivocal. Defeat with devastation, material and economic.

Complete defeat—as well as total victory—was, in 1865, new to the citizens of the now-reunited United States of America.

As spring warmed to summer, Confederate capitulations mounted: Lee at Appomattox; Johnston near Durham; Martin in the Appalachians; Smith in Texas. The southern Confederacy was dead.

Southern confidence, as well as its armies, lay shattered. Nineteenth-century Americans widely believed that God had blessed, even ordained, the United States as the world's "beacon of hope." Eight decades of national expansion seemingly testified to this fact.

But in 1861 this divine order was put to the test as both sides claimed the mantle of the chosen, "true" Americans defending the principles of Washington, the ideals of Jefferson, and upholding the nation's founding truths. Four years later, any pretense of Southern invincibility was gone, shattered by Northern industrial might and crushed by a military strategy that smashed Confederate armies and destroyed civilian resources.

Throughout eleven Southern states, defeat was complete. Stunned men and women turned from war to face an insecure and frightening future.

Survival demanded that work be done—and soon. As the citizens of North Carolina, an overwhelmingly agrarian state, acknowledged the changed reality, crops needed to be planted. As Tarheels learned of their governor's arrest, houses and barns and fences needed repair. As the full realization of freedom for thousands of once-enslaved African Americans was felt, so too was the reality that fully one-quarter of North Carolina's adult white male population had perished during four years of civil war. And as federal forces settled in for a dozen years of military occupation, the wartime loss of livestock and draft animals, feed and forage, tools and implements cast a specter of starvation across the state.[1]

And then there were the dead. While North Carolina was largely spared from major engagements during the first three years of war, its hospitals and prisons suffered mortality rates which frequently exceeded those on the battlefield. In 1865 bloody fighting came to North Carolina when William Sherman's blue-coated army pushed north toward Raleigh and George Stoneman's 6,000 mounted "raiders" cut an arc of destruction through the mountains and Piedmont.[2]

Crude, hastily dug graves—Union and Confederate—dotted North Carolina's landscape. Often little more than shallow excavations covered with mounds of dirt, these interments were frequently made by retreating troops or opposing forces. Some were marked with a simple board, the decedent's name scrawled in pencil with barely legible letters on untreated pine. More often, the grave was unmarked save for an unadorned rock at the end of a dirt mound.

The Union dead would be tended with honor: catalogued, moved, and properly reburied. Congress and the victorious federal government would see to that. But in 1865, the Confederate dead had no champion; the southern national government was gone, state authorities were unable to meet the needs of the living, and many Northerners viewed the just-defeated region's dead not as fallen warriors but as disgraced traitors.

¶

In North Carolina the Civil War had been internally divisive, at times degenerating into "a war within a war." The first vote to authorize a secession convention narrowly failed in February 1861. Only after President Lincoln's April demand for 75,000 troops to suppress the "rebellion," and after Virginia made it clear that it too would secede, did North Carolinians vote to join the Confederacy, five months after South Carolina left the Union.[3]

Once committed, however, the Tarheel State gave fully to the fight for Southern independence. Nearly ninety percent of the state's white male population between the ages of fifteen and fifty — 125,000 men in all — fought for the Confederacy. More than 40,000 never returned, having been killed in battle, succumbing to wounds, or dying from disease. Thousands more hobbled back as amputees, returned with devastating psychological problems, or struggled with alcoholism or the "soldier's disease" — morphine addiction.[4]

North Carolina was nearly torn apart during the four-year conflict. Federal forces seized the barrier islands soon after hostilities began then pushed inland to New Bern and Plymouth by the spring of 1862, blocking water routes and occupying much of the state's northeastern corner. In the Piedmont, site of the strongest Confederate sentiment and defenses, Quakers nevertheless stirred dissension while Northern sympathizers proved to be capable saboteurs.

Farther west, in North Carolina's foothills and mountains, Unionists, draft-dodgers, and deserters created a lethal mix of renegades and criminals who demanded attention from Confederate military units, bringing instability and fear to areas untouched by the Federal army. Discord deepened as the war dragged on, and by 1865, efforts were under way to join North Carolina's mountain counties with eastern Tennessee, creating a new state and re-entering the Union as West Virginia had done two years earlier.[5]

By the time large-scale fighting came to North Carolina during the war's final months, the Federal strategy of "total war" — the defeat of enemy armies coupled with destruction of industrial and agricultural capacity as well as the civilian will to resist — had been perfected. Sherman burned Fayetteville, then after being slowed at Bentonville, pushed toward Raleigh. Meanwhile, as Lee retreated toward Appomattox, General George Stoneman's massed cavalry swept east from Tennessee in a month-long spree of pillage and ruin.

Stoneman met almost no resistance in North Carolina and accomplished little militarily. He did succeed, however, in terrorizing and embittering the civilian population by wrecking bridges and rail lines, ransacking food supplies, and torching county courthouses, burning decades of vital documents, including property deeds, in the process.

As Confederate armies crumbled, defeated men straggled home carrying parole papers promising safe passage through Union forces as well as rations from military supply depots. Once home, however, there was little time to rest or recuperate.

Spring planting was already late as southern resistance collapsed. Food shortages were widespread and the state's labor force severely disrupted. Large planters faced an exodus of newly freed slaves from sprawling agricultural operations, while North Carolina's small farmers, the vast majority of whom were non-slaveowning whites, coped with the war-related deaths or disabilities of family members.

No script existed for rebuilding a defeated region or reuniting a fractured nation. The war's leading Federal architects — Lincoln, Grant, and Sherman — had relentlessly prosecuted the armed struggle but sought a conciliatory peace, Lincoln famously calling for "malice toward none and charity for all," while Sherman's original surrender terms at Bennett Place were so lenient as to be rejected by superiors in Washington, D.C.

But with Lincoln's assassination less than one week after Appomattox, hopes for a conciliatory reunification vanished. Angry Northern politicians intensified demands for harsh retribution, calling for curtailment of Southern rights and demanding that former Confederate leaders stand trial for treason. Charity succumbed to military occupation.

Amidst such chaos and devastation, it would have seemed nonsensical to imagine a future filled with grand celebrations of the now-defeated Confederacy. Throughout human memory, victors had been honored, the defeated forgotten. Just as history is largely written by winners, so too had monuments been raised by, and for, the triumphant. Yet less than twelve months after Appomattox, despite military occupation, grass-roots efforts arose across the South to care for — and honor — the region's dead. Diverse, spontaneous, and led by an unlikely demographic, these activities filled a critical need and led, perhaps unintentionally, to the Confederate memorial tradition.

SECTION I
EARLY COMMEMORATION, 1865-1895

1. Gathering the Fallen

Dr. Joseph Huske, rector of St. John's Episcopal Church in Fayetteville, North Carolina, began the ceremony. On a spring day in 1865, in the "back part of the cemetery, overlooking Cross Creek, a very pretty situation, with room for all," thirty Confederate soldiers would be laid to rest, men who had died weeks earlier attempting to defend the city and its Confederate arsenal from Sherman's legions.[1]

Sherman stayed in Fayetteville just long enough to torch the arsenal and many downtown buildings and to demolish vital transportation links before resuming his march north toward Goldsboro and Raleigh. When the main Federal force left on March 14, thirty Confederate troops lay dead, many hastily interred in shallow graves scattered throughout the city.[2]

Within "days" according to most accounts — and almost certainly before General Joseph Johnston's surrender of Southern forces to Sherman on April 26, 1865 — Ann Kyle, a nurse and founding member of Fayetteville's Soldiers' Aid Association, met with Mayor Archibald M. McLean to discuss care of the fallen. Kyle, wife of Captain Jesse Kyle of the Fifty-second North Carolina Regiment, and McLean selected a site in the back of Cross Creek, Fayetteville's most prominent cemetery. With the help of unidentified townspeople, Kyle raised funds for coffins then the women of the Soldiers' Aid Association "placed our brave Southern Men in their last resting place."[3]

Accounts do not relate the date of this "proper" burial, a dignified Christian service, and no mention is made of other memorial activities. Afterwards, however, Kyle suggested that the women meet the next day to discuss raising funds for an appropriate monument to mark the graves.

In the spring of 1865, Fayetteville lay decimated by the war. Yet the city's women, contemporaneously with the Confederate surrenders at Appomattox and Bennett Place, sought a permanent monument to honor the fallen soldiers and serve "as an evidence of womans [sic] loyalty, perseverance, and fidelity" to the Confederate dead.[4]

Fund-raising would be challenging. In a region with a now-worthless paper currency, in a state that would soon repudiate its wartime debts, and in an area losing an enslaved labor force once worth millions of dollars, the women turned to Maria Spear, a seamstress and educator for more than fifty years. Spear suggested utilizing domestic handicraft skills to create an intricately patterned silk quilt that could be raffled to finance the monument.[5]

The women met every Friday evening, sewing "into each square ... loving thoughts and prayers for our 'loved and lost.'" Work progressed slowly, however. On May 27, 1867, Spear, who had moved to Chapel Hill, inquired as to the quilt's progress. Two years after the project had begun, the textile remained unfinished. By August, however, the incomplete quilt had been shipped to Spear who lamented in an undated letter, "When I saw the Quilt this evening, I felt overwhelmed, how I am to get it done, I don't know."[6]

The aging seamstress, nevertheless, completed the work by late November, and less than one month later, on December 10, 1867, an advertisement for the upcoming raffle was published in the *Fayetteville News*. The silk textile reportedly was magnificent. "Every one [sic] who has seen the quilt," Spears wrote, "decides that it is the handsomest one they ever beheld."[7]

The ladies hoped to sell one thousand chances at a dollar apiece. The quilt would be displayed in Wilmington; sales would ultimately extend from Chapel Hill throughout eastern North Carolina, yet after six months, just $300.00 had been realized. In May 1868, the women ended sales and conducted the raffle. Martha Lewis, of Tarboro, who purchased her ticket from Maria Spear before the quilt had been completed, held the winning entry.

As with most North Carolina Civil War monuments, documentation provides little insight into the process by which Fayetteville's women selected the sculptor, the memorial's style, and its inscriptions. A monument, as a work of art, should relate a unified message through form, symbol, and prose, and the ladies turned to George Lauder, a prominent local stonemason, to carve and install the work. Lauder placed a slightly tapering octagonal shaft of white Italian marble atop a sculpted square of identical stone then set both upon a boldly striated marble base. Inscriptions chosen by the women adorn each face of the square block making this memorial the most verbose of North Carolina's early Confederate commemorations.

North Carolina's first Confederate monument. Cumberland County, 1868. Erected three-and-one-half years after Appomattox, this octagonal shaft of Italian Carrara marble is located in Fayetteville's Cross Creek Cemetery.

Dedicated December 30, 1868, and widely considered North Carolina's first Civil War memorial, Lauder's creation is a modest structure. Topped with a white metal cross, the memorial rises barely a dozen feet above a small earthen mound and is comparable in size and style with contemporaneous memorials marking graves of prominent individuals.

"IN MEMORY OF THE CONFEDERATE DEAD," is inscribed in capital letters on the monument's front face. On the right panel, the ladies selected the dedication, "WOMAN'S record to the HEROES in the dust." Quotes from Theodore O'Hara's ode, "Bivouac of the Dead"—penned following the 1847 battle of Buena Vista to honor Americans slain in the Mexican War and words that would be widely used on subsequent North Carolina Civil War memorials—mark the monument's remaining sides. "On Fame's eternal camping ground/Their silent tents are spread," followed by "Rest on embalmed and sainted dead!/ Dear as the blood ye gave," fill the back panel, while a later quatrain,

> Nor shall her glory be forgot
> While Fame her record keeps,
> Or honor points the hallowed spot
> Where valor proudly sleeps,

is inscribed on the left face below "Erected Dec. 30, 1868." The sculptor carved his surname into the monument's base, the only inscription outside the memorial's nearly flawless white surfaces.

The monument has no sculpted images, yet distinct fonts add clarity and visual impact. The front panel to the Confederate dead, the word "heroes" on the right, and the dedication date are deeply chiseled with easily read, unadorned capital letters. O'Hara's poem is inscribed in a gracefully slanted style, letters embellished with serifs giving the words a softer appearance yet one that is less easily read. The word, "Woman's," atop the right panel employs a third font, an ornate script with multiple serifs, executed in capitals.

Each font has visual and symbolic merit. The block letters are read easily in nearly any light. "Woman's," in bold yet elaborately enhanced script, coupled with the plainly carved "heroes," literally and symbolically contrast the monument's dual constituencies, while O'Hara's words necessitate careful reading, prompting contemplation.

Right panel detail. An elaborately carved "Woman's" and a large inscribed "Heroes" denote the sponsors, and honorees, of the state's first Confederate monument. Cross Creek Cemetery, Fayetteville.

There is no record of any dedication ceremony or civic celebration following the 1868 installation. This marble shaft, however, would soon become a focal point of Confederate commemoration. As military occupation eased and memorialization spread, cemeteries became centers of such activity. This monument to the Confederate dead, erected through the efforts of Fayetteville's women, would, on future Memorial Days, be surrounded with mounds of flowers and draped with strands of garland.

And the quilt? Mrs. Lewis gave the magnificent textile to former Confederate president Jefferson Davis. In an 1870 letter thanking Lewis, the former leader cited the pleasure of being "associated with tenders [sic] memories of the noble women of our land." The quilt would eventually return to Davis' wartime residence, today part of the Museum of the Confederacy's collection housed beside the Confederate White House in Richmond, Virginia.[8]

The Civil War dead presented a problem. As Southern armies capitulated throughout the spring of 1865, shallow, poorly marked soldier burials — Union and Confederate — dotted the American landscape. More than 600,000 men — two percent of the population of the United States — had perished during four years of fighting. Most lay buried far from home in makeshift graves unbefitting for soldiers who died honorably. Some remains were beneath the sod of well-known battlefields; others had been massed in burial trenches near hospitals or prisons, while thousands more lay scattered throughout the former Confederacy, crudely interred victims of unnamed clashes that rarely rate a historical footnote.

The shallow graves — some marked with a crudely lettered name scrawled in pencil on a slab of pine, others unnoted save for a disturbed mound of earth above the surrounding terrain — violated Victorian sensibilities. Remains might be scavenged by animals, plowed up by farmers, or looted by relic-seekers. A nation's dead deserved better.

Grieving relatives also wanted information. How had their loved one died? Where was he buried? And had he experienced a "good death" — struck down while bravely confronting the enemy then, surrounded by loyal comrades, speaking final words of valor and familial love? And would he receive a "proper" burial, with appropriate religious ceremonies and dignity worthy of the cause for which he fell?

The dead had to be cared for. But their number was overwhelming. Death on an industrial scale was new to America.

Within months the victorious federal government devised a plan; by the spring of 1866, Congress funded the concept through a national appropriation. Soldiers directed by the U.S. Army Quartermaster General fanned out across the "states lately in rebellion," searching, sometimes farm-to-farm, for graves of Union soldiers. Once located, however, contemporary embalming techniques coupled with advanced decomposition rarely allowed remains to be repatriated from distant locales. Instead private contractors, generally paid $8 per corpse, exhumed and transported the dead to one of the newly established "national" cemeteries, most of which were located near major battlefields or former prison camps.[9]

There the deceased would be re-interred with the same standardization and efficiency that had guided the Northern war effort. Each grave, including those of soldiers unable to be identified, would be identical. All would be of equal importance regardless of the decedent's military rank, and each would be marked with a regulation white headstone listing name, rank, unit, and date of death — or the single word, "Unknown." And following a pattern established in 1863 at the battlefield cemetery in Gettysburg, burials would be separated by state with additional sections allotted for the "Unknowns" and, if needed, for African Americans. The latter — officially named the United States Colored Troops (USCT) — would be grouped by race instead of state yet otherwise receive the same respect as white soldiers.[10]

Forty-one such cemeteries, including four in North Carolina, would be established by the federal government across states of the former Confederacy in the years immediately after Appomattox. Soldiers would be laid to rest with proper military and religious honors in sites that would receive perpetual care from a government that could also provide detailed information to next-of-kin. Soon, however, these cemeteries were embellished, resulting in a symbolic prominence greater than that of merely a resting place for the dead. Massive stone walls encircled carefully groomed grounds; two-story brick and stone lodges provided housing for on-site superintendents; and above all, the Stars and Stripes flew from a lofty flagpole, announcing a Federal presence — and reminding all of a Federal victory.[11]

But the Southern dead were not welcome inside these fortress-like compounds. Congressional action prohibited the use of public monies to preserve, protect, or even identify fallen Confederates. "The nation condemns our dead," the *Richmond Daily Examiner* fumed on May 5, 1866. "They are left in deserted places to rot into oblivion."[12]

One year after Appomattox, as the federal government tallied and re-interred its fallen, the Confederate dead had no such champion. The Southern national government was gone; state governments, often led by former Unionists with little sympathy for ex–Confederates, were nearly bankrupt. Most gatherings of men were prohibited by occupying military authorities, leaving few resources to care for, much less honor, the Confederate dead.

Southern troops were still "Rebels" in the eyes of many Northerners, and it appeared that few would be re-interred with dignified ceremonies such as the one conducted by the Reverend Huske and the Fayetteville women. Instead the scattered mounds of dirt marked with decaying wooden headboards might, in the words of Henry Ward Beecher, remain "dishonored graves."[13]

An unlikely demographic, however, would fill this void. As in Fayetteville, Southern white women, many of them elite and upper class, launched grass-roots efforts to care for the Confederate dead. Many had belonged to wartime Soldiers' Aid Societies nursing sick and injured Southern troops, sewing garments, packing supplies, and even raising funds for armaments. Now watched carefully by occupying military authorities but facing fewer restrictions than men, these women turned their energy and considerable organizational skill to cataloging and re-interring the Confederate dead.[14]

Nearly all of these locally based, independent groups took the title of Ladies' Memorial Association (LMA), modified by the locality's name. Their number was modest, estimated by Carolyn Janney as between seventy and one hundred across the South and fewer than a dozen in North Carolina, yet these Ladies had a profound influence, assuming in the absence of federal or state help, a semi-official role locating and identifying Southern dead, obtaining perpetual-care cemetery sites, then re-interring the deceased. Years before monuments to the Confederate dead were widely raised in Southern cemeteries, and decades before similar memorials appeared across Southern courthouse lawns, these Ladies were busy meeting basic human needs — caring for the dead and aiding grieving relatives — services provided for the Union dead by the federal government but denied Confederates.[15]

Many early local leaders, like Fayetteville's Ann Kyle, were wives of former Confederate officers. These women generally enjoyed a wide range of social contacts; their husbands were similarly well-connected through political and commercial interests, relationships that provided business acumen and fund-raising opportunities. Each LMA, however, remained locally based throughout the nineteenth century. While members certainly communicated between groups, and newspapers across the South reported the Ladies' memorial deeds and carried fund-raising appeals, no national organization coordinated or directed these women's activities for nearly four decades.[16]

Without a defined agenda and with different local needs as well as resources, these groups varied widely cross the South. In Richmond, Virginia, well-organized LMAs transferred thousands of war dead, preserved some of the Confederacy's most hallowed sites, funded iconic shrines, and kept detailed minutes that have been extensively studied by historians. The Ladies in nearby Petersburg — one of the few LMAs still in existence — similarly established a Confederate cemetery that would hold thousands then restored Blandford Church, adding Tiffany windows and creating one of the South's most beautiful commemorations.

North Carolina, among the poorest states of the former Confederacy, faced different challenges. Prior to 1865, few major battles had been fought on Tarheel soil. This relative safety led to the establishment of numerous military training camps, prisons, and hospitals, sites with mortality rates rivaling those on battlefields. The number of Southern war dead interred within North Carolina was probably no greater than in neighboring states, but the Tarheel State lacked the fund-raising aura provided by well-known battles or prominent leaders. Instead local efforts — by individuals, LMAs, and mixed-gender groups — were launched in the months after Appomattox. Few are as well-documented, and none as large, as those managed by the Virginia Ladies, yet these efforts demonstrate a widely based resolve to care for and honor North Carolina's Confederate dead.

Raleigh's women are the state's best-documented and most-studied LMA. Formed May 23, 1866, as the Wake County Ladies' Memorial Association, the group was "composed of the wives, widows, mothers, and daughters of Confederate soldiers." Little fighting occurred in the immediate Raleigh area, and the modest number of Confederate dead, many of whom had succumbed while at Pettigrew Hospital, were laid to rest in the Rock Quarry Cemetery southeast of town. Miss Sophia Partridge — a schoolteacher described by Catherine Bishir as "the moving spirit behind the LMA," as well as its first secretary — guided the wartime effort, making sure that "boards with their names were placed at the head of their graves."[17]

The state's capital seemed fortunate; other locales struggled to find suitable sites for the Confederate dead. Some North Carolina cities owned municipal cemeteries, but in others, private organizations operated the "cities of the dead." Although later acclaimed among the most revered Southern sites, locations for soldier remains and mass graves seemed difficult to obtain, at least as donations.

On November 17, 1866, New Bern's city council deeded a central plat in the city's municipally owned Cedar Grove Cemetery to the local Ladies' Memorial Association. The donation to establish this mass burial of sixty-eight Confederates, however, barely passed, approved by a 4–2 vote. In Wilmington, privately owned Oakdale Cemetery Company gave land to that city's LMA for a mounded common grave that would eventually hold the remains of 367 Southern soldiers. Yet the donation did not occur until December 15, 1867, two-and-one-half years after Appomattox.[18]

In High Point, W. G. Barbee, owner of the Barbee House, a downtown hotel used as a Confederate hospital from September 1863 until the war's end, gathered the fifty dead from his facility which had been "buried in fence corners and back yards here and there over High Point," and had the bodies transferred in 1867 — apparently at his own expense — to the "extreme Southeast corner of [High Point's] Oakwood Cemetery." Neatly re-interred in five parallel rows with markers denoting each individual's grave, all but four of the decedents are identified, one of the highest percentages in the state.[19]

Just north of High Point, the Greensboro Ladies' Memorial Association, formed in 1866, purchased land beside the Methodist Church Cemetery on Ashe Street. Assisted by the Eclectic Club, a mixed-gender literary society formed two years after the Ladies, the groups re-interred nearly three hundred Confederate remains in trench graves, including 234 victims of the Bentonville fight who died after being evacuated to Greensboro following battlefield wounds.[20]

Raleigh's good fortune, however, did not last. In 1867, federal authorities seized the graveyard along today's Rock Quarry Road for a "national cemetery," ordering the expulsion of the Confederate dead. Yet the Raleigh women were not totally unprepared. In May 1866, at the first meeting of the nascent Ladies, President Nancy Haywood Blount Branch, widow of Confederate General Lawrence O'Bryan Branch, appointed "three men to explore suitable locations for a Confederate cemetery." The trio reported the following month about the deteriorating conditions at Rock Quarry where identifying headboards had been defaced and occupying military authorities had begun burying Union dead alongside Confederates. A new cemetery was needed, the three concluded, and the Southern dead should be transferred to the new site.[21]

Civic leader Henry Mordecai, owner of a large tract of land blocks from the state Capitol, ultimately offered the LMA "as many acres of my land as is needed for such a sacred purpose." But the land was "covered with native oaks and pines and was full of gulches," unfit for immediate burials. The Ladies went to work, raising funds and clearing the site. Former Confederate General Thomas Clingman, Mrs. Henry Burgywn (mother of the Twenty-sixth North Carolina's "Boy Colonel" killed at Gettysburg), and Mr. P. F. Pescud, who later penned a history of the Raleigh LMA, would, among others, each contribute one hundred dollars to the cemetery fund. Others gave more modest amounts; women could become "life members" with a $1 donation. But by early 1867, site preparation had exhausted available monies, and the Ladies were forced to turn to "their friends in the legislature" for $1,500 to complete their "labor of love." On February 14, with the state house galleries overflowing with Raleigh's Ladies, the appropriation was unanimously approved by both legislative chambers.[22]

Less than one week later, the Ladies were notified by military authorities that "Confederate soldiers buried at the Rock Quarry Cemetery must be removed immediately to make room for the Federal Dead." A more strident demand arrived days later threatening, according to Behan, that "if our dead were not removed in twenty-four hours their remains would be thrown in the public road." Issued by "the man in charge of the Federal cemetery," a "wretch sent by the authorities at Washington City," this decree inflamed an already tense situation in the occupied capital. Cooler heads would prevail, and the order of "this said Nero" was soon overturned by the post commandant with a severe rebuke.[23]

By the end of March 1867, the Rock Quarry Confederate dead had been transferred through the efforts of the Ladies and Captain George M. Whiting, a former Confederate infantry officer who directly oversaw the project. Nearly all Confederate remains from elsewhere in Wake County were also re-interred at the new site — today's Oakwood Cemetery — considered by most historians including Gaines Foster to be the South's first true Confederate cemetery.[24]

As dogwoods bloomed two years after Southern surrender, Wake County's Confederate dead had been gathered and laid to rest in what would become one of the city's most honored locations. But the Ladies took little time to rest. Despite the tense military situation, the women turned their attention to activities that would dominate Confederate commemoration for much of the next century, formulating plans for the capital's second Memorial Day, to be held on May 10, 1867, and consider a monument to honor the more than five hundred Southern dead that lay in their new cemetery.

On March 12, 1866, less than a year after Appomattox, the *Columbus* (Georgia) *Times* published a letter from Mrs. Charles Williams and Lizzie Rutherford. The pair, members of Columbus' Ladies' Memorial Association, proposed "dedicating, at least one day in each year to embellish their [the Confederate dead] humble graves with flowers." April 26, the anniversary of General Joseph Johnston's surrender at Bennett Place, near Durham, North Carolina, was suggested as the date.[25]

Months after the cessation of hostilities, even a memorialization by women was not without risk. In the spring of 1866, however, under the more lenient Presidential Reconstruction, the first "Decoration Day"—later renamed Memorial Day—was accomplished peacefully. By the next spring, in the wake of November's Congressional elections and subsequent imposition of much harsher Reconstruction terms, memorial activities faced increased scrutiny and, in some places, greater danger.

In North Carolina—where May 10, the anniversary of General Thomas J. "Stonewall" Jackson's death, quickly became the preferred memorial date—military authorities in New Bern curtailed that city's ceremonies. A procession through the streets by the LMA was banned. A less public event organized by the Ladies, laying the cornerstone of the Confederate mausoleum in Cedar Grove Cemetery, was nevertheless allowed to be "conducted according to the publicized program."[26]

In Raleigh, less than three months following the Rock Quarry Cemetery debacle, an even tenser situation existed. "Indeed the threat was made [by Federal military authorities]," according to a published 1904 account written by the Raleigh women, "that if the Ladies' Memorial Association, chiefly women and children did form a procession, it would be fired upon without further warning." No procession formed that day, but in an early act of civil disobedience testing the limits imposed by the military decree, "loyal and devoted women gathered in groups of not more than two or three at different street corners, each one bearing their crosses and wreaths ... closely followed by a Federal officer, to see that no procession was formed." Throughout the city, "there were no exercises of any kind, not even a prayer," according to the report, "and it demanded some courage and independence ... to fulfill this poor duty to the dead."[27]

The (Raleigh) *Sentinel* concurred that no public procession or "formal display" was allowed. The paper added, however, as in New Bern, a cemetery observance did take place. "Between five and six hundred deeply moved and interested spectators," the *Sentinel* reported on May 13, 1867, gathered at Oakwood Cemetery for a short service that included a prayer by a former Confederate chaplain, a hymn by a men's choir, and a brief oration from the *Sentinel*'s editor, Confederate veteran Seaton Gales.[28]

Gales spoke of the defeated Confederacy, "whether right or wrong, [that] was inexpressibly dear to our hearts," and of those who had defended it. Turning to a still unfilled commemorative hope, he conceded, "We may not build for them lofty monuments of marble or of bronze—for we are poor," but spoke of the Ladies' "holy task"—remembrance. Concluding, the editor urged those present to "Go scatter those flowers, which so aptly prefigure the brightness of the resurrection morn!"[29]

The *Sentinel*'s editor was perhaps unaware of plans already under way for monuments honoring the Confederate dead. Maria Spear and the Fayetteville ladies were finishing up their fund-raising quilt. In Averasboro, "two years after the close of the War," a decorative iron fence surrounding Chicora Cemetery was erected by the Smithville (Cumberland County) Memorial Association. Funds for the fence, likely the earliest physical Confederate commemoration in North Carolina, came from "people of the neighborhood and nearby communities," as well as "generous contributions ... from South Carolina," the native state of many of the fifty soldiers buried in the small battlefield plot. Businessmen assisted too; the owners of the steamers *Hurt, Halcyon,* and *North Carolina* all were publicly thanked by the Association for "freighting the fence free of all charge."[30]

In 1872, half a decade after Gales' 1867 acknowledgement that no "lofty monuments" had been raised "for we are poor," five such commemorations honoring the Confederate dead stood across the Tarheel landscape: Fayetteville (1868); Hoke County (circa 1870); Raleigh (1870); Wilmington (1872); and Averasboro (1872). Not all were "lofty"—and records reveal fund-raising was uniformly difficult—yet all were erected through local efforts.

Three of these early monuments are located within a twenty-mile radius encircling Fayetteville; the dead who they honor fell resisting Sherman's advance. Fayetteville's Cross Creek Cemetery monument, detailed earlier, is widely considered the state's first, dated December 30, 1868. Shortly thereafter—evidence suggests 1870 but the exact date remains uncertain—a white marble obelisk was placed atop a mass grave fifteen miles northwest of Cross Creek. Inscribed with just two words, "CONFEDERATE SOLDIERS," this four-foot-tall shaft marks a common grave estimated to contain as many as thirty men. There is no record of funding source or of any dedication ceremony for this monument in the Long Street Presbyterian Church cemetery. Today the shaft has weathered to a dull gray while the church sits empty, both cemetery and building now part of the Ft. Bragg Military Reservation.

The Confederate Dead. Hoke County, c. 1870. This simple marble obelisk marks a mass grave in the cemetery of the Long Street Presbyterian Church, seen in the background. The plaque is a recent addition.

The third monument of this localized triad is located in Chicora Cemetery on Averasboro Battlefield, twenty miles northeast of Fayetteville. This five-foot-high square shaft of native sandstone—"a handsome one for its time," according to Smith—was funded by the Smithville Memorial Association, who five years earlier had erected the decorative fence encircling the cemetery. But the monument's May 10, 1872, dedication was an elaborate affair, revealing a marked evolution of Confederate commemoration.[31]

"A large assembly of people—more than five hundred in number—gathered at Chicora Cemetery," according to an account cited by Smith, "to witness memorial ceremonies and the erecting of a monument in honor and memory of the Confederate dead there buried." A procession formed in a "nearby grove," then "marched to the cemetery." The Rev. D. D. McBryde gave a "most appropriate" prayer; the "Masonic fraternity laid the foundation stone of the monument with all the dignified ceremonial [sic] of the order;" and the "ladies covered the graves with flowers and evergreens, and with sweet voices and most touching pathos, sung the songs of the 'lost cause.'"[32]

Averasboro Battlefield. Harnett County. A small monument, "In Memory of Our Confederate Dead Who Fell Upon That Day," is the centerpiece of the battlefield's Chicora Cemetery. Fence erected 1867; monument dedicated May 10, 1872.

Following the ceremony, an event conducted with the "utmost decorum," the procession reformed and returned to the shady grove. There the "Hon. Thos. C. Fuller, the most distinguished citizen in our Congressional district," delivered the address from "a stand covered with flowers and evergreens," that had been erected "for the occasion." "Nowhere [sic] in the South," the report concludes, "has there been more attention paid to the Confederate dead than in this neighborhood."[33]

Although diminutive by later standards, this monument, funded "from the same source as those for the fence," is extensively inscribed on all sides. "In Memory of our Confederate Dead Who Fell Upon That Day," marks the memorial's south-facing panel. "The Hearts That Were True to Their Country and God, Shall Report at the Grand Reveille," is inscribed on the right. The back panel quotes from Horace's *Odes*:

"Dulce et Decorum est Pro Patria Mori" (It is sweet and fitting to die for one's country), while on the left "Battle of Averasboro March 16, 1865," announces the engagement that claimed the soldiers' lives.[34]

Not all of North Carolina's early Confederate monuments were small. Two of the state's oldest memorials — one of marble, the other of marble, granite, and bronze — were more elaborate creations. In Raleigh, weeks after Seaton Gales' Memorial Day speech noting the lack of such commemoration, the Wake County LMA renewed efforts for a memorial in Oakwood Cemetery. Two years later, however, the Ladies still lacked sufficient funds. The money was "inadequate to the erection of a monument," President Branch conceded in 1869, before adding, "not to its commencement." Giving her "humble opinion," the LMA leader thought it "would be judicious," to begin the monument, hoping that once begun, "it would have a tendency to stimulate and arouse persons to action." In a pattern that would be emulated numerous times — occasionally with embarrassing results — the monument was begun. Branch's plan worked; the following year a modified marble obelisk set upon a complex base of carved marble blocks was complete.[35]

Surprisingly little is written in any of the Ladies' accounts regarding this memorial with no documentation of any dedication ceremony. The obelisk, its corners leveled with angled cuts, rises from a base that includes twelve flat panels. Only two of these lower surfaces, however, are engraved. "In Memory of our Confederate Dead," above "Erected A. D. 1870," is inscribed on a north-facing panel, while to the right, facing west, a verse penned by George M. Whiting, the former infantry captain who managed the transfer of the Confederate dead from Rock Quarry Cemetery reads:

> Sleep! warrior, sleep! the struggle,
> The battle cry is hushed,
> Our standards have been lowered,
> Our blooming hopes been crushed.
> Sleep! for thy name is cherished
> By the bravest and the best,
> And soldier's hearts and woman's love
> Are with thee in thy rest.

Whiting's body lies among those he helped transfer, after dying in 1870 from tuberculosis, contracted while a POW following his capture at Gettysburg.[36]

The monument's most impressive feature is a bas-relief carved at the base of the obelisk just above Whiting's poem. A shield with a single star surrounded by the detritus of war and a defeated nation — fallen flags, broken cannon, an abandoned drum, a partial stack of cannonballs, and sheathed swords — extends outward from the shaft's otherwise smooth surface. Through eloquent words chiseled in a graceful font, and with symbols of strife scattered around an intact shield adorned with a single boldly cut star, a firm message is conveyed on the monument's west face: the war has been lost; the Confederacy's defeat is complete; and the nation has been re-united.

The obelisk is otherwise unadorned as are the ten remaining panels of the base. The work is signed, "King & Whitelaw Ral," on an inscribed rectangle beside the south base. The asymmetric inscriptions placed at a 90-degree angle with multiple bare faces give an unfinished "feel" to the work, as if its creators expected future engravings. Oakwood Cemetery has been the scene of numerous subsequent projects from the repatriation of North Carolina's Gettysburg dead in 1871 to the interment of sediment containing human remains from the CSS *Hunley* recovery in 2000, yet the monument's other surfaces remain blank.[37]

Oakwood Cemetery. Raleigh, 1870. Funded by the Wake County Ladies' Memorial Association, this marble monument marks Oakwood Cemetery's Confederate section.

In Wilmington, North Carolina's most populous city during the Civil War and throughout much of the nineteenth century, a new style of monument was raised to the Southern dead on Memorial Day, 1872. A soldier at parade rest, musket in hand, the weapon's stock resting at his feet, gazes watchfully from atop a marble and granite base in the city's Oakdale Cemetery. Forged by Maurice J. Power (1838–1902) at the National Fine Art Foundry in

New York from a design by William Rudolph O'Donovan (1844–1920) of Virginia, Wilmington's bronze is not only the state's first soldier statue, but represents — artistically and culturally — evolving commemorative themes.

At first glance this figure may appear much like the dozens of sculpted, stamped, and forged infantrymen standing watch from granite pillars on courthouse lawns throughout the Tarheel State. There are, however, subtle but important differences.

Wilmington's soldier is outfitted wearing a small cape over an officer's frock coat, signifying higher military rank; later courthouse soldiers would be nearly universally depicted as privates in simple, tight-fitting uniforms. The frock coat, however, (sometimes termed a great coat), as well as the small cape, represents transitional artistic conventions. Pre Civil-War American sculpture favored classical forms, often depicting subjects in flowing robes or Roman togas. The antebellum South looked to Europe for art and design, and the region's elite favored Greek and Roman elements. A realistically cast soldier statue was a break with that past, but the figure's cape and coat reflect continuing influences from that era.[38]

Two classically styled bronze plaques, also by Power and O'Donovan, embellish the monument's shaft. A bust of General Robert E. Lee encircled with a star-studded wreath fills the front panel, while a similar image of General Thomas J. "Stonewall" Jackson is at the back. "TO THE CONFEDERATE DEAD," the memorial's sole inscription, is boldly cut below Lee's profile.[39]

The monument was dedicated with an elaborate ceremony on May 10, 1872, the same day Smithville's Association was dedicating its memorial at Chicora Cemetery at Averasboro. The events, although separated by one hundred miles, were remarkably similar. Cadets of the Cape Fear Military Academy led a procession from downtown Wilmington to Oakdale. The day's orator and chaplain came next followed by the women of the Ladies' Memorial Association who, with the help of "many other donations and sacrifices of our citizens," had made this monument possible. Townspeople and Confederate veterans — in stark contrast to later events in which former soldiers were accorded places of prominence — brought up the rear.

Two original odes penned for the ceremony and put to music lent a somber air to the event. The day's speaker, former Confederate Major Charles W. McClammy, praised the antebellum South, a time when, "No gleaming bayonet had usurped the place of law! No remorseless tyrant had done violence to the plain and primitive principles of liberty." He spoke too of the men who had shed their blood on the "altar of freedom" for the Southern cause, 367 of whom lay beneath a nearby prominence topped with the new memorial.[40]

But the elegantly attired bronze officer atop the burial mound and the medallions honoring the Confederacy's two greatest generals may represent more than just evolving sculptural styles. In 1872, the Southern elite had yet to regain their pre-war dominance, political and economic power lost after Appomattox and with the end of slavery. Depictions of bold leaders — military officers, wealthy planters, eloquent statesmen — hearkened back to when a select few controlled the drivers of commerce and state. In North Carolina, as throughout the South, these men would regain much of that influence. But the struggle would not be easy nor would their success be permanent.

North Carolinians, in the immediate post-war years, had come together for a common, easily understood goal: to gather their fallen, rebury their dead, and provide comfort and closure to grieving relatives. By 1872, these basic human needs had largely been met. As Tarheels celebrated Memorial Day that year, and as the state's fourth and fifth Confederate monuments were dedicated, competing visions of Civil War memory — not only between

Oakdale Cemetery. Wilmington, 1872. North Carolina's first soldier statue stands atop Oakdale Cemetery's Confederate Mound, a mass burial of 367 bodies. Remains were interred in a rosette pattern with feet toward the monument and heads outward.

Northerners, African Americans, and ex–Confederates — but among Southern whites themselves, were being advanced.

The need to care for a region's dead, a task the Federal government refused to undertake, had, perhaps unintentionally, unified a defeated people and formed a nexus of Confederate memorialization. A New South was emerging, however, one that would compete with the Old. Differing ideas of Confederate memory and tradition would be part of that struggle.

2. Memory

On Monday, May 11, 1885, the people came. By railroad and steamer, by horse, carriage, and on foot. From Kinston, from Smithfield, even from as far as Morehead City, North Carolinians poured into New Bern, congregating into a "dense throng" around a decorated speaker's stand at the New Bern Academy. Old veterans came too, bringing with them a pair of regimental battle flags, the scarred ensign of the Forty-eighth North Carolina and the banner of the Sixty-seventh, the latter borne by a one-armed ex–Confederate.[1]

Twenty years after Appomattox, the Ladies of New Bern would today dedicate an eighteen-foot-high shaft of Rutland blue marble topped with a life-sized sculpted soldier honoring the Confederate dead. More Cavalier than yeoman farmer, the great coat-clad figure standing picket duty had been carved by the "best workman" in Carrara, Italy, "after a design expressly for this monument." Fund-raising, however, had taken nearly two decades.

The ceremony did not begin beside the veiled statue in Cedar Grove Cemetery but three blocks away in the shade beneath a "beautiful grove of elms" at the historic Academy. A choir opened the event then a prayer was offered by the Reverend Y. W. Shields. Following the invocation, Clement Manly introduced the day's featured speaker, Captain Hamilton C. Graham, a native Tarheel from Halifax County now practicing law in Alabama.

The New Bern Ladies' Memorial Association had invited this former Confederate officer to speak about the life of General James Johnston Pettigrew, an eastern North Carolinian killed shortly after Gettysburg whose command included some of the state's most celebrated regiments. Part tribute, part historical lecture, part political theater, Graham's nearly hour-long oration followed a style typical of late-nineteenth century Confederate Memorial Day speeches.

Graham also spoke of New Bern's Confederate dead, "noble soldiers" to whom the monument would be dedicated. Citing a theme that dominated Tarheel memorialization, he declared that, "of the great men of this civil war history will take care. The issues were too high, the struggle too famous ... for them to be forgotten." But of the dead, our state "will never forget them. She will speak of them in a whisper if it must be, but in tones of love that will live through all these dreary days ... and the South ... if die she must will murmur with her latest breath the names of the 'Confederate Dead.'"

After the captain finished, Chief-Marshall E. M. Duguid organized the crowd into a procession. The Silver Cornet Band led Confederate veterans, citizens, and schoolchildren

Confederate monument. Cedar Grove Cemetery, New Bern. The unveiling ceremony concluded with "the great assembly united in singing the doxology." May 11, 1885.

three blocks to Cedar Grove, where at a grassy mound near the center of the cemetery, the group gathered around the veiled monument.

"Tenting on the Old Camp Ground," performed by the choir, opened the dedicatory program. Reverend L. C. Vass, former Confederate chaplain, current pastor of New Bern's First Presbyterian Church, and husband of the LMA's vice president, then addressed the crowd. The clergyman provided few details about the two-decades-long struggle to commission and erect the monument, challenges probably well-known to most in attendance.

Vass instead paid tribute to the late Mrs. E. B. Daves, the LMA's recently deceased long-time president, who for eighteen years led fund-raising efforts but died days before

Soldier detail. New Bern, Craven County, 1885. The soldier was carved by the "best workman" in Carrara, Italy, "after a design expressly for this monument."

the monument's unveiling. Vass spoke too of the "honor to celebrate the fame of the noble." Referring to cemeteries as "cities of the dead," he spoke of memorials to "those whose name and fame we will not willingly let die." But the minister talked of reconciliation as well, citing that "evil passions are beginning to be laid to rest, and friend and foe are joining in admiring true courage and devotion to duty."

As his wife prepared to pull the cord and unveil the monument, the clergyman concluded with a flourish, "let these shot-torn battle flags wave their salute ... and let us cherish ever, and proclaim the virtues of our Confederate brothers, soldiers, patriots."

The crowd's reaction upon first viewing the memorial was not recorded in the published report. However, the text concluded, "in memory of God's kind providences, the great assembly united in singing the doxology—'Praise God from whom all blessings flow,'" before covering the graves with beautiful flowers.

New Bern's dashing marble figure, dedicated in 1885 with an elaborate ceremony in North Carolina's colonial capital, was only the second Confederate monument erected in the state since 1872. Following the twin unveilings in Wilmington and Averasboro on May 10 of that year, no Confederate memorials were raised for more than a decade; only a towering, federally funded obelisk to the Union dead in Salisbury National Cemetery (c. 1876) had been added to North Carolina's commemorative landscape.

Like many cultural trends, this hiatus had multiple causes. Certainly the Panic of 1873, a financial calamity that ushered in a six-year-long national economic depression, played a major role. But hard times were not new to post–Civil War North Carolina. With the demise of the Confederacy, southern paper currency became worthless; with ratification of the Fourteenth Amendment in 1868, state wartime debts were annulled making bonds worthless as well. Yet despite such hardships, five monuments to North Carolina's Confederate dead had been raised during the seven years after Appomattox.

Political change accompanied the decade's economic turmoil. Federal military occupation eased, especially after northern Democrats gained power in the 1874 elections. The following year North Carolina held a constitutional convention—its third since 1865—adopting thirty amendments and strengthening the power of conservative Democrats and their mostly white constituency. Public school segregation was codified; interracial marriages were banned; and authority was centralized with the state legislature, limiting Republican power in the west and African American influence in the east.[2]

The election of 1876 brought further Democratic gains. Zebulon B. Vance, North Carolina's popular Civil War–era governor, was returned to the state's top executive post, completing the state's "Redemption"—the return of conservative whites and ex–Confederates to power. Reconstruction was in its final throes and would officially end months later as part of the national compromise following that November's disputed presidential election. Yet even in this less restrictive political environment, seven years would pass before the next Confederate monument dedication.

More importantly perhaps than economics or politics, the primary goal of the Ladies' Memorial Associations, one nearly universally supported in North Carolina, had been realized. By 1872 the Confederate dead had been gathered from the state's battlefields and skirmish sites and reinterred in established cemeteries with "proper" Christian burials. The fallen had been cared for, a responsibility fulfilled.

No consensus existed, however, in North Carolina or across the eleven states of the former Confederacy, as to what commemorations should follow. While Mrs. Daves struggled for nearly two decades to fund a cemetery monument in New Bern, memorialization of a defeated cause competed with charity for the living. Confederate widows, orphans, soldier-amputees, and the disabled all sought much-needed assistance. In addition Southerners were sharply divided as to how—or if—a lost war should be acknowledged.[3]

Historical consensus building, creating what social scientists term "useable memory," can be a contentious process. Groups and cultures may concur on widely held principles, but some facets of collective memory might take decades to develop, or perhaps may never be fully realized. From 1872 until the early 1900s, North Carolina's Confederate memorial tradition assumed varied forms as citizens sought to honor the dead, care for the living, and preserve dignity.[4]

Personal and societal memory is a basic but complex attribute of our humanity. Reflective processing — recalling, sorting, analyzing, and learning from events — is possibly unique to our species. Individuals create memory by consciously or subconsciously assigning degrees of significance to recollections. But not all occurrences are remembered; many are jettisoned as insignificant, while others are repressed as too painful.

Confederate monument. Willowdale Cemetery, Goldsboro, Wayne County. Dedicated in 1883, this was the first Confederate monument erected in North Carolina since 1872. The soldier, of sandblasted zinc and bronze, was manufactured by the Philadelphia White Bronze Company.

Confederate monument. Riverside Cemetery, Smithfield, Johnston County. Dedicated May 10, 1887.

Societies, from nation-states to private groups, similarly create memory. Consensus is formed by actively selecting the people and events to publicly remember, deciding how to interpret and celebrate the past, and choosing what might best be "forgotten." Leaders and great deeds are often honored. So too are "independence" or "founding" dates, major triumphs, and pivotal successes, while missteps, failure, and defeat often are ignored.

Resulting commemorations may take many forms with varying degrees of permanence. Some are fleeting; parades, commendations, and symbolic presentations are ephemeral. Street or place names, plaques, and historical markers while longer-lasting can nevertheless be changed quickly or easily dismantled. Holidays and "official" calendars — civic, religious,

Confederate monument. Green Hill Cemetery, Greensboro. The three hundred bodies under this monument were relocated from a prior reburial in Greensboro. Most of the soldiers died from wounds suffered at Bentonville. Dedicated June 3, 1888.

and organizational — although intangible, are another powerful expression of collective memory, one that reflects changing public perception as the significance of commemorative dates wax and wane, molded by evolving opinion.[5]

Monuments and sculpture, especially large public installations, are among humanity's most enduring forms of acknowledgement. Although costly and challenging to erect, these structures are unequaled in longevity. As with other forms of commemoration, however, these works are most effective when perceived as created through broad consensus, endorsed by "all," or at least most of the population. And since memory—personal as well as societal—is malleable, celebrations and physical memorials need continuing support to remain relevant. Just as personal values evolve over a lifetime, so too are events re-interpreted across generations in an on-going process, a conversation between present and past.

There was no commemorative tradition to guide the citizens of the former Confederacy in how to honor a defeated army or fallen nation. Some religions and a few secular groups acknowledged martyrs, defeats, and massacres, but no nation or region had widely commemorated a lost war.

For the majority of North Carolinians, personal grief and daily survival dwarfed thoughts of long-term memorialization during the years immediately after Appomattox. Forty thousand dead—one of every four adult white male North Carolinians—was the state's reality. Sons. Brothers. Fathers. Husbands. But these men had also been merchants, artisans, farmers, and laborers, the economic backbone of families and communities statewide. Grief and its stages—denial, anger, bargaining, depression, and finally acceptance—would cast a shadow across the state for decades.

While disagreements about commemorating a lost war simmered among editors, former leaders, and the Southern elite, a more fundamental struggle played out between African Americans, Unionists, and former Confederates, with each group promoting their vision of antebellum and Civil War memory while vying for political power and economic dominance. Roiled by wartime loss, economic and social instability, and rapid political swings, consensus, even among white Southerners, would not be easily or quickly realized.

While few records of nineteenth century deliberations exist, patterns and styles of North Carolina commemoration reveal a complex struggle to shape a memorial consensus. If physical commemorations were to be erected, who should be honored? Leaders? The dead?

"A Generous Foe." Willowdale Cemetery, Goldsboro, Wayne County, 1883. Northern businessmen contributed nearly one-third of this monument's $992 cost, acknowledged with this inscription.

War heroes? Foot soldiers? And where should these structures be located? Cemeteries or spaces of the living? Should monuments be sited near courthouses, on town commons, in street intersections, or at similarly prominent locations such as train stations? And who should pay — or at least lead fund-raising efforts — to make these monuments a reality and attain a broad-based consensus?

For nearly a quarter century after Appomattox, all of North Carolina's Civil War monuments were placed in cemeteries, in sections reserved for the Confederate wartime dead or, more frequently, atop mass graves of the unknown. But locating memorials exclusively in "cities of the dead" was not a pattern uniformly shared across the South.

Civic-space monuments — on courthouse lawns, in street intersections, or other heavily trafficked "spaces of the living"— appeared contemporaneously in other Southern states. In Bolivar, Tennessee, citizens erected a shroud-draped obelisk in front of the county courthouse perhaps as early as 1868, making this monument the Confederacy's first civic-space sculpture and one of the South's oldest memorials.[6]

South Carolina had an early and prominent civic-space memorial tradition, as well. The Confederacy's first monument — a marble shaft engraved with, among other images, an uprooted palmetto tree — was erected during the summer of 1867 in Cheraw's St. David's Episcopal Church cemetery while Federal forces occupied the state. The soldiers would remain for nearly a decade, but within months of their departure a monument to the Confederate dead would be raised on the state Capitol grounds in Columbia.[7]

Virginia, with its aristocratic tradition, took another commemorative tact. Elite white women and well-connected former army officers sought to lead region-wide commemorations of the Confederacy. As in North Carolina, locally based Ladies' Memorial Associations led in tending the Confederate dead. But across Virginia, site of many of the War's bloodiest battles, the number of corpses and the cost of reburial were overwhelming. The women catalogued tens of thousands of Southern dead, recording the place of death, name and rank if known, and site of final interment, invaluable details as families throughout the South sought information about missing soldiers. To support their efforts, Virginia's Ladies requested and received region-wide financial assistance including appropriations from other state legislatures.[8]

After the dead were reburied in formal cemeteries, Virginians hoped to continue leading a regional memorial tradition. The Old Dominion had produced the wartime South's most revered leaders — Robert E. Lee, Thomas J. "Stonewall" Jackson, and J. E. B. Stuart — and within the state's borders lay many of the Confederacy's most hallowed sites including the former national capital. But internal friction developed between commemorative groups, and regional support ebbed. Despite national fund-raising efforts, thirteen years would pass between Robert E. Lee's death in 1870 and the unveiling of Edward Valentine's "Recumbent Lee," a marble sarcophagus marking the general's grave in Lexington. Fund-raising for the sculptures lining Richmond's Monument Avenue, the center of Confederate memorial tradition, would take even longer. The first of these famed bronzes — also honoring Lee — was dedicated in 1890; the fifth and last to a Confederate hero would not be completed until 1929.

Financing North Carolina's monuments proved equally daunting. As icons of commemorative consensus, memorials need at least the *perception* of having been created with broad-based public support. Across late nineteenth-century Europe, with its tradition of state-sanctioned art, governments imposed an "official" version of national memory through, among other methods, erection of public sculpture. In the United States, however, in the

Confederate monument. Elmwood Cemetery, Charlotte. Funded by the Ladies' Memorial Association. Dedicated June 10, 1887.

post–Civil War era as well as today, official art—and similar efforts conceived and underwritten by a single individual—are generally viewed with disdain. Memorials funded through civic groups or by citizen donations (commonly termed subscriptions during the late-nineteenth and early-twentieth centuries) are more readily accepted as reflecting community opinion.[9]

Throughout North Carolina local groups, often with minimal funding, sought to assist the War's survivors or honor the conflict's dead. In Greensboro, the Eclectic Club, a literary society founded in 1869 that included both men and women, assisted the local Ladies in moving the Confederate dead to mass trench graves adjoining the Methodist Church on Ashe Street. Established for "social and literary improvement," the club met in members' homes for book discussions and, from "time to time"—including once "when Vance was the speaker and the old courthouse the scene"—sponsored public lectures "from prominent men."

In addition to its literary activities, the club maintained an ongoing role in Confederate memorialization. The *Greensboro Patriot* on May 11, 1871, reported that the group had "provided a wreath to be placed (by the day's speaker, Judge Dyer) on the Confederate graves," for Memorial Day activities. Two years later, the society underwrote a lecture at the Benbow House, with proceeds "devoted" to the organization's "Lee Memorial Fund."[10]

The following decade, assisted by an otherwise unidentified "Confederate committee,"

Confederate monument. Maplewood Cemetery, Kinston, Lenoir County, c. 1892. This marble obelisk marks a mass grave containing forty-four Confederate unknowns.

the Eclectic Club helped move the soldiers' remains a second time, from the soon-to-be-abandoned church graveyard to a plat purchased by the literary group in the city's newly created Green Hill Cemetery. There on June 3, 1888, atop the massed remains of three hundred Confederates, the Greensboro Ladies in a solemn ceremony removed the veil covering a bronze soldier statue upon a granite plinth. Greensboro's Confederate dead, most of whom had been transported to the city following wounds received at the battle of Bentonville, had been laid to their final rest.[11]

Further east, the Goldsboro Rifles—an elite group of businessmen and Confederate descendants—assisted by the town mayor, two surgeons, a judge, and ex–Confederate army officers, sought to erect a monument atop the state's largest Confederate mass grave, a mound containing the remains of eight hundred soldiers in that city's Willowdale Cemetery. The effort succeeded, and on May 10, 1883, a life-size zinc-bronze statue atop a shaft of Quincy Granite—a memorial fabricated by the Gaddess Brothers Steam Marble Works of Baltimore, Maryland, for a cost of $992.00—was dedicated.[12]

"Eight Hundred Rest Here" is inscribed in block letters on the monument's front panel, just below the similarly styled, "In Memory of the Confederate Dead 1861–1865." The right panel credits the Rifles' role erecting the memorial and its dedication date, on the left a widely quoted excerpt from Theodore O'Hara's "Bivouac of the Dead," the poem featured by the Fayetteville women on their 1868 monument. Chiseled into the back panel are the enigmatic words, "A Generous Foe Contributed to the Erection of this Memorial."

No sources name specific individuals, but this generous foe, also referred to as "Northern Friends," most likely were New York wholesalers supplying Goldsboro businesses. The Northerners sponsored a three-day bazaar — a sale of donated goods and services that was a popular late-nineteenth century fund-raising method — that netted $316.00, nearly one-third of the monument's final cost. Additional contributions came from local citizens, the Neuse Lodge 6–100 F, and the city of Goldsboro, monies sufficient to complete the project debt-free.[13]

Other locales did not have such generous benefactors. In Smithfield, twenty-five miles northwest of Goldsboro, "admirers and fellow citizens" of the Confederate dead raised funds for a marble obelisk placed on a small mound in the midst of soldiers' graves in Riverside Cemetery. Dedicated May 10, 1887, the monument's lone embellished face is inscribed, "To the Soldiers of the Southern Confederacy Who Sacrificed Their Lives in a Cause Which Though Lost, Will Always Remain Near to Their Countrymen." A pair of downward-pointing crossed and sheathed swords is shallowly engraved above these words.

Two more cemetery memorials would be added to North Carolina's commemorative landscape before the decade was over. In Charlotte, a tall granite obelisk set upon a multi-tiered base in the Confederate section of Elmwood Cemetery was unveiled by the Ladies' Memorial Association on June 10, 1887, while in Kinston, a modest obelisk of marble honoring the Confederate dead was placed by townspeople atop a mass tomb of forty-four Confederate Unknowns in Maplewood Cemetery.

A third monument, a granite shaft set beside the Pamlico River in 1888, would extend Confederate sculpture into the state's northeastern corner. This memorial to the Confederate dead, however, would expand more than geographic distribution; it would introduce major changes — artistically and culturally — to North Carolina's commemorative tradition.

3. New Ground

Nine monuments to the Confederate dead stood in Tarheel cemeteries when, on May 10, 1888, the Ladies' Memorial Association of Washington, North Carolina, unveiled a granite shaft topped by a carved soldier on the north bank of the Pamlico River. Located on a slight rise beside the intersection of Water and Monumental Streets, this nine-foot-tall granite likeness of a Confederate infantryman atop a thirty-foot-tall column gazed across the water from a perch so high as to reportedly be the first structure seen as boats approached from Pamlico Sound.[1]

Daniel Fowle, a native of the city who later that year would be elected governor of North Carolina, was the day's featured speaker, while F. H. Busbee, Grandmaster of Masons, officiated the ceremony. Undoubtedly present that day was fellow Beaufort County resident Thomas M. Allen, a former Confederate captain who had enlisted at Washington on June 3, 1861. A member of Company E (Southern Guards), Fourth North Carolina Infantry, Allen rose from sergeant to captain during the ensuing two-and-one-half years. Wounded three times and taken prisoner twice, the soldier spent more than half his military service as a POW, housed in at least six Federal prison sites. Imprisonment, however, did not seem to derail his military career. While incarcerated in 1862, the North Carolina native was promoted to first lieutenant; following exchange and subsequent recapture at Gettysburg, Allen was elevated to captain during his second confinement.[2]

During the summer of 1864, however, midway through his second captivity, this well-traveled prisoner was taken by Federal forces to Morris Island, South Carolina, to be used as a human shield. Part of a carefully chosen group of Confederate officers — later acclaimed across the South as the "Immortal 600" — these men were confined in front of Battery Wagner, one of a series of Federal artillery bastions laying siege to Charleston. On what one survivor described as "an immense plain of white sand, which, being heated by the rays of a Southern sun, makes sufficient heat to cook an egg," the six hundred prisoners were penned for forty-five days in a 1.5-acre stockade exposed not only to South Carolina's summertime heat, but also to Confederate artillery shells aimed at the Federal cannon behind the enclosure.[3]

The men received starvation rations: three moldy, maggot-infested hardtack crackers daily supplemented with two ounces of spoiled horse meat and a small serving of weak broth. Fragments of artillery shells rained down on the captives. Remarkably, however, none of the prisoners perished from artillery fire. The Union guards were not as lucky.

Confederate monument. Oakdale Cemetery, Washington, Beaufort County. North Carolina's first civic-space Confederate memorial was dedicated May 10, 1888, on the banks of the Pamlico River. Ten years later it was moved to Oakdale Cemetery atop a mass grave. Rededicated May 10, 1898.

"One shell," a survivor recalled, "exploded immediately over us, but most of the fragments missed the pen, and killed a number of negroes composing the guard."[4]

After more than six weeks of being "continually filled with the prospect of instant death," Allen and the others were moved to Fort Pulaski, a Federal prison near Savannah, Georgia. But the atrocities did not end. At the new site, the six hundred endured weeks of "retaliation rations"— spoiled cornmeal and soured onion pickles — fed in retribution for

Captain Thomas M. Allen. Oakdale Cemetery, Washington. A member of the "Immortal 600," Beaufort County resident Thomas Allen was the model for this soldier figure atop Washington's Confederate monument.

reported conditions at the Andersonville, Georgia, and Salisbury, North Carolina, Confederate prisons. As cold weather set in, the men were moved to a third coastal impoundment, there to spend the winter denied heat, firewood, or warm clothing.[5]

Allen survived the ordeal; forty-six others did not. Released July 1865, three months after Appomattox, the captain returned to Washington, married, then relocated to the nearby Beaufort County town of Aurora, apparently residing there the rest of his life. But in the 1880s, as the Ladies of Washington raised $2,250.00 for what would be North Carolina's first civic-space Civil War monument, Allen was chosen again, selected as the model for the sculpted soldier that would top a granite shaft honoring the Confederate dead.[6]

It is not clear through what process, or why, Allen was chosen. He was not the only local officer imprisoned as part of the Immortal 600; two others from Washington are listed among the 111 North Carolinians who endured the same Federal brutality.[7]

In Beaufort County, as throughout North Carolina, the war and its aftermath had taken a toll. Sixteen years after the monument's dedication, Washington LMA secretary Margaret Arthur Call described how, in 1865, the town lay as "a blackened ruin." But as "prosperity began to smile," she wrote, the townspeople wanted a monument to those "who live in fame, but not in life."

Aided by "young ladies and gentlemen" and by Major Thomas J. Sparrow, whom Call described as "the father of the Memorial Association in our city," "merchants and citizens responded liberally," making the memorial to the Confederate dead a reality. Yet despite successful fund-raising and "the busy hum of the Confederate Soldier's hammer," which slowly turned "defeat to prosperity," the aging writer was melancholy as she recalled the war's human toll: "We sing no loud oratories of victory, we celebrate no national jubilees, we sing of our great suffering in a low minor strain. We wreathe no graves with victor's laurels, but mournfully mingle the laurels with cypress and deck their last resting place."[8]

Washington's monument to the Confederate dead was not only North Carolina's first civic-space Civil War memorial, it also inaugurated a more realistic style in the state's commemorative art. Likely carved by a local stonecutter, an individual who did not sign the work and whose identity is today unknown, this heroic-sized (larger-than-life) figure not only is modeled after a local veteran, but more accurately depicts the uniform and accoutrements of a typical Confederate infantryman than previous Tarheel sculptures.

Gone is the "great coat," a widely used mid-nineteenth century artistic convention hearkening back to classical depictions of toga-clad Romans. North Carolina's three previous soldier statues — and a fourth which would be dedicated in Greensboro later in 1888 — had been cast as wearing these garments. But few soldiers owned such formal attire.

Instead the sculptor depicted Allen as a rank-and-file infantryman who could represent any — or all — of the estimated 125,000 North Carolinians who served in the Confederate army. Portrayed wearing a well-fitted uniform, clothing less likely to be snagged by branches and undergrowth lining narrow roads and scattered across backcountry battlefields, the figure has no backpack, just a bedroll looped across his torso and accoutrements near his waist.

While generalizations about Civil War clothing and gear can be risky, several characteristics help differentiate "Billy Yank" statues from "Johnny Rebs." Even these distinctions, however, can be suspect, as sculptors and monument committees frequently placed aesthetics and technical feasibility above detailed accuracy. Artistic freedom, however, came with a price. Jokes and accusations persist yet today in several North Carolina counties that a "Yankee soldier" mistakenly stands guard over the county courthouse.

Across the Confederacy, uniform styles varied widely through the four years of fighting. In 1861 as the first companies — units numbering approximately one hundred men and led by a captain — left for the front, many sported distinctively designed and sometimes flamboyant outfits supplied by state authorities or local benefactors. Varied uniforms, however, made differentiating friend from foe difficult, and as opposing forces prepared for a prolonged struggle, factories on both sides ramped up production, manufacturing standardized uniforms by the tens of thousands.

Blue remained the color of Federal clothing, but gray, today synonymous with Confederate forces, was not the only hue worn by Southern troops. Butternut was widely used as well and, like gray, easily differentiated from Northern blue. But colors cannot be permanently depicted on monuments. Commemorative identification instead is often accomplished through an oval belt buckle or cartridge box plate stamped with the letters "CS"—Confederate States. Such insignias, however, can be small, often barely noticeable without binoculars.

Headgear, bedrolls, and backpacks are more apparent differences between Union and Confederate soldier statues. While Captain Allen's likeness is topped with a tall, debonair hat more typical of a Wall Street financier than a Confederate infantryman, most Southern troops wore "slouch hats," fully brimmed head coverings with little shape, similar to hats used by hikers and tourists today. Often brought by soldiers from home, slouch hats not only shaded the ears and face but shed rain as well.

Confederate monument. Oakwood Cemetery, High Point, 1899. Centerpiece of a small Confederate plot with fifty neatly aligned graves, this memorial was sponsored by the Guilford Council No. 23, Junior Order United American Mechanics.

Federals meanwhile were issued *kepis*, smartly formed caps with sloping tops and rigid bills, derived from headgear worn by U.S. troops during the Mexican War.

Marching and sleeping gear varied also. Northern soldiers typically carried a tightly rolled blanket atop a rigid backpack. In contrast, Southerners seldom wore a backpack, utilizing instead a haversack, a large pouch similar to a modern purse slung across the chest and held closely to the waist with a belt. The Confederate's blanket was rolled inside a rubber ground cloth, an 1844 invention of Charles Goodyear, which kept the blanket dry while marching as well as preventing nighttime ground dampness from chilling the soldier.[9]

As the war dragged on and shortages worsened, many soldiers, especially Confederates, "customized" their gear with items captured from opposing forces or taken from the dead. This mixing of gear not only made the portrayal of a standard Confederate soldier chal-

Bentonville Battlefield. Johnston County. Sponsored by the Goldsboro Rifles, this marble monument, according to its inscription, honors "about 360 unknown Confederate dead [who] are buried here." There is no archeological evidence, however, of graves beneath this memorial; that number may represent the estimated dead over the entire battlefield. It was dedicated March 20, 1895, the thirtieth anniversary of the battle; former South Carolina governor Wade Hampton delivered the oration. It is inscribed October 10, 1894, the originally planned dedication date.

lenging, it led in part to the difficulty of identifying the dead, with survivors sometimes unable to ascertain for which army the deceased had fought.

But Washington's carved soldier is distinctly Southern. Allen is portrayed carrying a blanket and ground cloth looped across his torso; CS is stamped prominently on his belt buckle. The soldier stands at attention, gazing straight ahead, a rifle in his right hand, the butt resting on a tree stump. This stump, while structurally broadening the statue's support base, also serves as a metaphor denoting a shortened life.

Representations such as broken shafts or severed trees were commonly used to symbolize early death or tragically ended lives, and these motifs would have been familiar to contemporary observers. Near Gordonsburg, Tennessee, a fractured cylinder of stone stands where Meriwether Lewis, of Lewis and Clark fame, succumbed to a gunshot wound. Even children's graves featured similar themes; a flat-topped stump surmounted with a resting lamb, representing innocence, often denotes a child's burial.

Visual symbolism, particularly in monumental and funereal art, reached a zenith during the Victorian Age. Classical Greek and Roman images were used as well as contemporary representations. A prominently carved laurel wreath — an ancient symbol of victory — topped the 1876 Union obelisk in Salisbury's National Cemetery. In Cheraw, South Carolina, the Confederacy's first monument (1867) featured an uprooted but otherwise intact palmetto tree beneath the still-defiant words, "Fallen but not dead." Twenty years later, citizens of Smithfield, North Carolina, selected more submissive iconography; a pair of crossed, downward-pointing sheathed swords — weapons of war put to rest — were carved on the front panel of that city's obelisk to the Confederate dead.

Imagery, however, served more than a decorative role. Illiteracy remained high, especially across the rural South, and depictions of furled banners, stacked rifles, and broken flagstaffs graphically relate the Confederacy's demise. Whether the severed tree behind Captain Allen's figure represents soldier deaths, the death of the Confederacy — or both — will probably never be known. But it is a depiction employed in subsequent North Carolina Confederate monuments.

Symbols of defeat, death, and ultimately acceptance would proliferate with improved tools and stonecutting techniques in the twentieth century, but North Carolina's most enigmatic symbolism remains New Bern's 1885 monument, the dashing Cavalier featured in the previous chapter. A single cannonball rests near that figure's right foot. Behind the leg, positioned similarly to the tree stump beside Captain Allen, a smooth cylindrical object extends unobtrusively from the carving's base upward beneath the figure's great coat. A small square block is carved in relief near the object's base. Close inspection reveals the form to be an upright, dismounted cannon barrel of marble, complete with priming hole, the weapon's muzzle hidden beneath the soldier's coat.

While Washington's memorial to the Confederate dead introduced new artistic styles to North Carolina, its civic-space location, a first for the state, represents this commemoration's greatest cultural impact. Early monuments, although in publicly accessible and often publicly owned cemeteries, were seldom seen by citizens on a daily basis. The Confederate dead had been cared for; grief, perhaps still too overwhelming to acknowledge on a daily basis, had been compartmentalized — at least commemoratively — to the cities of the dead.

North Carolina was relatively late extending Confederate memorialization into civic spaces. Citizens of Tennessee, South Carolina, and Virginia erected such monuments at least a decade prior to Washington's 1888 unveiling. Yet there is no evidence of any serious, earlier attempt to raise a similar memorial in the Tarheel State.[10]

A brief overview of North Carolina's political and cultural environment suggests possible reasons for delay. Despite providing large numbers of Confederate troops, North Carolinians remained sharply divided during and after the war. The state's first call for a secession convention had been narrowly rejected; internal divisions — often with deadly confrontations — continued in many counties throughout the conflict, leaving legacies of hatred that would last into the twentieth century. In addition, the Tarheel State produced few Confederate generals or government leaders whose achievements might be widely acclaimed. The most important influence upon the state's commemorative mood, almost certainly lay in the war's human toll, claiming the lives of one of every four Tarheel soldiers.[11]

Processing grief takes time, the interval often proportionate to the magnitude of loss. Siting monuments in less-prominent cemetery locations may have been more than symbolic; such placements were politically expedient and psychologically more tolerable than erecting centrally located reminders.

While none of North Carolina's nineteenth-century monuments featured the defiance of Cheraw's "Fallen but not dead" inscription, the state's first monument, in Fayetteville's Cross Creek Cemetery, did refer to the dead as "heroes," an appellation that would not be inscribed on another Tarheel memorial for nearly four decades. Thereafter, as denial and anger of grief's early stages faded to sadness and depression, most North Carolina memorials—including Washington's civic-space commemoration—were carved with little more than the phrase "To the Confederate Dead." Another decade-and-a-half would pass—and with it most of the generation who had endured the "troubles of the '60s"—before a more robust Confederate celebratory tradition would emerge.

Washington's tall shaft topped with Captain Allen's likeness would not remain overlooking the Pamlico River. Transportation patterns changed; river traffic declined, and a newly constructed train station made the monument's once-prominent location less significant. Ten years after its erection, North Carolina's first civic-space Civil War monument was disassembled, moved just over a mile to Oakdale Cemetery, and there reconstructed atop a mass burial of unknown Confederate troops.[12]

Captain Allen, like many soldiers who endured severe wartime deprivation, lived a long life, surviving until 1911. He was fifty-eight years old when the monument was re-dedicated on May 10, 1898, ten years to the day after its original unveiling.[13]

Confederate commemoration evolved significantly during that decade. Five North Carolina monuments honoring the Southern dead had been unveiled, three in civic locations. In 1892 the Memorial Association—a group of "Veterans and Patriotic Women of [Cabarrus] County"—raised the state's first *permanently* sited civic-space monument, an inscribed shaft of darkly striated marble topped with a smooth sphere, on the courthouse lawn in Concord. Four years later in Windsor, Bertie County Confederate veterans

North Carolina's first *permanent* civic-space Confederate monument. Cabarrus County courthouse grounds, Concord. Dedicated May 5, 1892.

funded a granite monument topped with a kepi-wearing, great coat-clad soldier in a park beside the courthouse. And in Raleigh, following heated debate and challenging fund-raising, a towering monument on the west lawn of Capitol Square was unveiled before a crowd of 30,000 on May 20, 1895. Three decades — and more than a generation after Appomattox — North Carolina's Confederate memorialization was moving from the "cities of the dead" into "spaces of the living."[14]

4. A Capital Celebration

On May 20, 1895, Alfred Moore Waddell addressed an estimated 30,000 people gathered on the Capitol grounds in Raleigh for the unveiling of North Carolina's monument to the Confederate dead, the state's grandest Confederate celebration to date. "One thousand [visitors] Saturday," the Raleigh *News and Observer* trumpeted on Monday, May 20, while "about one thousand came in by the afternoon trains yesterday" and "five hundred more" arrived via the Seaboard "Last night at 10 o'clock." On dedication-day morning, "The station looked like a small city," the paper reported, with such crowds proving "that love of brave men has not waned, and that honoring noble martyrs and love of country are as dominant in the North Carolinian's heart [today] as in the Revolution or the War Between the States."[1]

Scores of notable North Carolinians attended the dedication including Governor Elias Carr and at least two of his predecessors. Featured guests included three Confederate widows: Mrs. General "Stonewall" Jackson; her sister, Mrs. General D. H. Hill; and Mrs. General Lawrence O'Bryan Branch, dressed in black, the color she wore since the death of her brigadier-general husband, killed by a Federal sharpshooter in 1862. Miss Julia Jackson Christian was present also. Outfitted in white with pink ribbons in her hair, the seven-year-old granddaughter of General Thomas J. "Stonewall" Jackson would pull the cord to unveil the monument.[2]

The weather was "ideal," according to the *News and Observer*. "The sun never shone more beautifully, and the birds never sung sweeter." Ashley Horne, a Confederate veteran and prominent Johnston County businessman who would later singlehandedly fund North Carolina's monument to the Women of the Confederacy, helped organize the parade's carriages. The three Confederate widows and Miss Christian, accompanied by former Confederate General William R. Cox of Edgecombe County, rode in the first carriage. Four prominent women occupied the second, while "His Excellency Governor Elias Carr, Col. A. B. Waddell [sic], the orator of the day, and Rev. Bennett Smedes, who was to deliver the opening prayer," were assigned to the third.[3]

Waddell's selection as featured orator might seem unusual given the dignitaries present. The well-known Wilmington attorney, however, according to historian William Powell, possessed a "polished eloquence and commanding stage presence." In addition, Waddell was a leading advocate for the state's Confederate commemorative movement, having proclaimed, in an 1885 Memorial Day speech to Raleigh's LMA, that the period of mourning after the war should be over, as was the economic hardship often cited to excuse the paucity

4. A Capital Celebration

North Carolina monument to the Confederate Dead. Raleigh, 1895. Photograph taken on May 20, 2011, the 150th anniversary of the state's secession.

of Tarheel monuments. While acknowledging the importance of cemetery monuments, the former lieutenant colonel declared that the Confederate dead deserved civic memorials to reflect "a sentiment alike jealous of the honor of North Carolina, and tenderly grateful to her heroic sons."[4]

Seven years later in 1892, Captain Octavius Coke helped organize the North Carolina Monumental Association (NCMA), a group of socially prominent men and women closely allied with the Wake County LMA. The Wake LMA, whose early membership also included men, had created Raleigh's Oakwood Cemetery, re-buried the area's Confederate dead, and, in 1870, raised that city's first Confederate monument (Chapter 1). The NCMA now undertook an equally ambitious goal, attempting to raise $25,000.00 — equivalent to nearly two-thirds of a million dollars today — for a Capitol-grounds monument honoring the state's Confederate dead.[5]

Despite an economic depression, the NCMA, in May 1894, placed the monument's cornerstone beside the state capitol at the head of Hillsborough Street, the city's most prominent thoroughfare. In a ceremony attended by "thronging thousands," and timed to coincide with two notable state anniversaries — the adoption of the purported Mecklenburg Declaration of Independence on May 20, 1775, and the state's secession on the same date in 1861 — the stone was set, and within it, a box filled with Confederate relics and contemporary items.[6]

Yet the NCMA did not have sufficient funds to complete the monument. A year of political tumult and fund-raising challenges ensued, but by May 20, 1895, the completed monument was ready for unveiling. "A Perfect Day," the *News and Observer* crowed. "It was another such day as in 1776," the paper reminded readers, that "the sturdy folk of Mecklenburg adopted the famous Declaration of Independence," adding, "The same spirit of love of freedom that animated the men of 1776, is still fresh in the hearts of the people."[7]

Waddell's dedication-day oration expanded on this theme, emphasizing similarities between America's war for independence and the South's failed bid for a separate nation. The former Confederate officer linked North Carolina's actions, and those of her soldiers, with beliefs of the founding fathers and the nation's core principles, not sectional strife. "In the hour allotted ... in discharging this duty," Waddell told the crowd, "Let no man say ... I am digging up sectionalism, and trying to revive the animosities of the past." Yet the speaker reminded listeners "that for thirty years past, my countrymen, my kinsmen and my friends have been pilloried before the world as ignorant, barbarous, cruel traitors and rebels, who ... sought to destroy the best government under the sun and deluged a continent in blood."[8]

The *News and Observer* declared the speech "A Masterly Defense of the Cause for Which They Fought — In History's Clear Light." Fellow Wilmingtonian and business leader James Sprunt effused, "You were first in the hearts of your countrymen ... the eloquent words of your masterful address on probably the last occasion of such public honours to the Lost Cause will be repeated from generation to generation."[9]

Like many North Carolinians, Waddell had, at first, opposed the state leaving the Union, not because secession was believed illegal, but because it was considered unwise. Advocating for the Unionist cause in 1860, Waddell supported the Constitutional Union Party, serving as an alternate delegate at its national convention, and purchasing and editing the *Wilmington Herald* to spread his views. But when war came, Waddell joined the Third Cavalry (renamed the Forty-first North Carolina Regiment), attaining the rank of lieutenant colonel before illness forced his resignation.[10]

Thirty years after Appomattox, the former officer provided Raleigh's dedication-day throng a lengthy legal justification for the right of secession, concluding that Southern states' "allegiance was not given to any government, but to the Constitution of the United States, and they never violated it." In equally spirited remarks, Waddell denied that defense of slavery prompted North Carolina's action. "It was an institution, guaranteed and protected by the Constitution," the speaker declared. "The South did not go to war for slavery ... it was the *occasion*, not the cause of the war [italics in original text]."[11]

Waddell then described the Confederate soldier as a man who "had always loved the Union ... but he loved his State more." Detailing hardships faced, and the valor displayed, by North Carolina troops, the Tarheel native nevertheless insisted that if these virtues "constituted his only claim to admiration, he would be but an ordinary figure on the page of history." Instead Waddell asked, "Did they prove themselves worthy of their Revolutionary sires?" linking again the state's struggle for Southern nationhood with her earlier fight for American independence."[12]

Waddell's answer did not come from "the testimony of any commanding officer ... not even to the utterance of the stainless Lee, in the last agonies of Appomattox: 'God bless old North Carolina.'" Instead the affirmation was chiseled into the monument's shaft, "First at Bethel, Last at Appomattox," words that the orator used to detail North Carolinians' efforts on behalf of the failed Confederacy.[13]

Perhaps surprisingly, given the occasion, Waddell also reiterated his 1885 lament as to the lack of monuments, claiming, "The Old North State. She boasts not: she never did of any of her achievements ... never preserved the memorials of them, which other people are

Back panel detail, state monument. An early, abbreviated version of the North Carolina "Rebel Boast" is inscribed into the back of the main shaft.

careful to keep of their own." Instead, the former officer declared that North Carolinians have "been content to substitute for them a sacred shrine in her own heart."[14]

"Stand then, bronze image of him who wore the gray!" Waddell commanded in closing, before contrasting the metallic representation with the flesh-and-blood Confederate soldier. "Not more enduring is thy granite base than the love on which he [the Confederate soldier] rests. Thou art a triumph of Art; he was God's gift to his country. Thou shalt perish; but he shall live forever in the hearts of his people."[15]

Monuments and collective memory, according to many historians, represent a conversation between present and past. "A land without monuments is a land without memories," the North Carolina Monumental Association reminded citizens as the Raleigh-based organization struggled to fund the state Confederate memorial. Collective memory, however, involves more than just present and past — or even the future — addressing also a society's current psychological needs and its political realities.

North Carolina's monument to the Confederate dead, raised thirty years after Appomattox, was not the first Southern effort to erect a Capitol-grounds Confederate memorial. Florida raised a state monument in 1874; South Carolina followed four years later. But North Carolina's attempt, one which would be funded largely through state monies, came during a particularly contentious political era and brought psychological and societal issues to the fore.[16]

The Honorable Thomas W. Mason, addressing thousands gathered for the ceremonial placement of the commemoration's cornerstone on May 22, 1894, barely hinted at the political firestorm raging across the state and throughout the South, forces that would lead to his defeat in a Senate bid later that year. The barrister from Northampton County instead focused on unifying themes of honor and memory before turning to a question that had undoubtedly dogged Tarheel memory for three decades.[17]

"Shall we say of the Confederate soldier that he died in vain?" Mason asked midway through his speech. The orator had spoken of heroism and sacrifice, citing the North Carolina soldier's "treasure of his blood." With "a military population of one hundred fifteen thousand men," Mason told the crowd, North Carolina recruited "an army of one hundred twenty five thousand men," and "Forty thousand two hundred seventy-five sons of North Carolina gave their lives to the Confederacy," statistics likely well-known to his audience and numbers that would become a standard feature of many twentieth-century dedication speeches.[18]

"Shall we stand above his grave and declare that all was lost but honor?" Mason asked. "Shall we say of his mighty struggle that it has no higher meaning than defeat?" Questioning whether the Confederate dead had died in vain, a subject rarely broached in commemorative speeches, touched the deepest levels of a people's grief. Actions of the Ladies' Memorial Associations had assured that Southern soldier burials would not be, in the words of Henry Ward Beecher, "dishonored graves." But although not dishonored, had these deaths — nearly one-third of a generation of North Carolina's white men — been in vain?

Southern writers and poets were among the first to address this question. Father Joseph A. Ryan, the South's most popular poet, opined in the "Deathless Dead:

> They bore the flag of a
> Nation's trust
> And fell in a cause
> Though lost, still just
> And died for me and you,

lines that, decades later, would be inscribed into Iredell County's Confederate monument (Statesville, 1906). The "Lost Cause" mantra, an ill-defined rationale still hotly debated today, was also advanced, in part as explanation for a national fratricide, in part for political gain, and in part to meet a people's need to believe that the War had been waged for a "cause," however nebulous, worthy of sacrifice.

Standing beside the state Capitol, where thirty-three years earlier a battery of cannon had fired signaling North Carolina's secession from the United States, Mason offered reasons for the "death and passion" of the Confederate soldier. "Men may be lifted up" through the "example of his devotion to the memory of his fathers," the former Confederate captain and aide-de-camp to General Robert Ransom told the throng, reassuring them that, even in defeat, Confederate soldiers' heroism and dedication to duty would inspire future generations.

Mason then equated the sacrifices of the state's Confederate soldiers with those of an earlier Tarheel generation who had died to free America from England, introducing a theme that would also be featured at the monument's dedication the following year. "If they did not die in vain who fell at Moore's Creek Bridge, at King's Mountain, at Guilford, at Germantown ... then their sons did not die in vain who fell at Bethel, at Manassas ... at Gettysburg, and on every field, where they sealed, with their blood the covenant made with their fathers that this should be a Union of sovereign States ... limited by the letter of the written compact."[19]

"For this covenant they died," Mason declared, not for "the lost cause of a dead Confederacy, but ... the vital cause of a living Union, its soul and strength, its only hope of future life."[20]

"The Confederate soldier has not died in vain," the orator twice proclaimed as he concluded his speech and briefly alluded to national political issues. "Elsewhere in our Union there is trouble. Social disorder vexes the soul of the patriot." But "you have been brave in peace as you have been strong in war," Mason declared of the Confederate soldier, men of all classes sharing a bond of sacrifice. "You have lifted North Carolina up in your arms and made her as true to our Union as the bride is true to her marriage vows. By your patience, peace and hope and order are ours."[21]

While Mason largely sidestepped controversy and emphasized a common heritage among white voters, Raleigh's newspapers vividly detailed a politically divided state debating Confederate commemoration and its societal implications. The *News and Observer* and its new editor, Josephus Daniels, spoke for the state's Democratic establishment, praising former Confederate soldiers and lauding efforts of Raleigh's women to raise a shaft honoring the Confederate dead.

The *Caucasian*, meanwhile, edited by Marion Butler, echoed Populist sentiments and became a forceful voice for North Carolina's Fusionist movement, a powerful political coalition of poor white farmers, African Americans, and Republicans. In 1895, Butler opposed further state monies for the Capitol-grounds monument, insisting instead that funds would be better spent on public schools.[22]

Not only did the *Caucasian's* editor oppose the supplemental appropriation, but wrote that "it is not at all certain that any monuments ought to be built on either side to perpetuate the memories of our unnatural civil war. The sooner the rancors and hates of that unhappy struggle are forgotten by both North and South," Butler added, echoing the views of many Southerners, "the better it will be for the whole country."[23]

These divergent opinions reflect North Carolina's volatile political climate in the 1890s.

Any pretense of Democratic hegemony was crumbling as poor whites — subsistence farmers, tenants, and factory workers, many of whom were former Confederate soldiers — became increasingly disillusioned with state Democratic leadership viewed as beholden to railroad, banking, and industrial interests. Many of the disaffected turned to the Populist Party, a nationwide third-party movement espousing "progressive" ideals benefiting farmers and laborers.

With the easing of Reconstruction and "restoration" of Democratic Party power early in the 1870s, former Confederate officers came to dominate North Carolina's political and business leadership, while ex-enlisted men often endured lives of physical toil. Veterans' reunions, monument dedications, and memorial events brought former soldiers and officers together in a shared Confederate heritage, but economic strains were dividing the men politically. Similar stresses were occurring throughout the South, but in North Carolina these forces would result in loss of Democratic Party control.

In 1894, North Carolina's Populists joined with Republicans and African Americans, forming a "Fusionist" coalition and nominating a common slate of candidates. Stunning victories followed. Republican Marion Butler, outspoken editor of the *Caucasian*, defeated Democrat Thomas Mason for the U.S. Senate, while Fusionists, including five African Americans, swept to power in the state legislature. (African Americans retained widespread voting rights in North Carolina until a constitutional amendment, adopted through a statewide vote in 1900, effectively disenfranchised most blacks).

In the midst of political turmoil, and as the nation endured an economic depression, the North Carolina Monumental Association strove to erect a state monument honoring the Confederate dead. The timing may have been more than coincidental. Fund-raising efforts, as well as the monument's ultimate design, reached across social classes and the political chasm, emphasizing unity and the shared bond of Confederate sacrifice.

The NCMA, formed in 1892, was a formidable organization. Founders included many of Raleigh's most prominent men and women. The association's first president, Nancy Branch Jones, was the daughter of the Wake County LMA's founding president, providing a symbolic link and enhancing cooperation between the commemorative groups. In addition, ninety-six vice presidents, one from each of the state's then-established counties, provided the NCMA a statewide presence. Yet despite these advantages, fund-raising progressed slowly.[24]

Within months, the organization realized that private donations would be inadequate for the grand memorial they hoped to erect, and, early in 1893, the NCMA appealed to the state legislature for funds. The predominantly Democratic legislature responded "enthusiastically," appropriating $10,000.00 while mandating that the shaft be made of North Carolina stone and that the monument stand on Capitol Square.

The following spring, the NCMA, using a tactic successfully employed by President Jones' mother a quarter-century earlier to fund the Oakwood Cemetery monument, staged an elaborate ceremony, placing the monument's cornerstone beside the state capitol. The event had the trappings of a full-scale dedication. On Monday evening, May 21, 1894, a "Grand Confederate Concert" was held at the Metropolitan Hall, enjoyed by a "'Standing room only'" crowd, according to the (Raleigh) *News-Observer-Chronicle.*

The next morning a procession, including the governor, Committee of Arrangements, the Fayetteville Light Infantry, Confederate veterans, and "Ladies Monumental Society," made its way from the intersection of Cabarrus and Fayetteville Streets to Capitol Square. There the "exercises" were called to order by Governor Elias Carr. The "Old North State" was sung "by one hundred voices," followed by an invocation, multiple hymns and speeches including the featured oration by Thomas Mason, and the "Announcement of contents of Corner-stone," a recitation of the relics and contemporaneous keepsakes placed within the monument.[25]

But hopes that a grand ceremony and a highly visible yet incomplete commemorative shaft would spur sufficient contributions, proved optimistic. Just $5,000.00 had been raised through private donations by the end of 1894, and, in February 1895, the NCMA again appealed to the legislature, requesting a $10,000.00 loan to complete the memorial for a planned May 20 unveiling.

The legislature to which the NCMA turned for help, however, had changed. The Democratic majority of 1893 had been replaced with one that was "overwhelmingly Fusionist" according to Allen W. Trelease. Yet the NCMA hoped that its presence might carry the day.[26]

Throughout the morning of February 23, 1895, the day the "Confederate Monument Bill" would be considered, "The Senate galleries were constantly filling with ladies," the *News and Observer* reported, with "members of the Monumental Association attending in a body." When debate began at noon, "the galleries were crowded to their utmost capacity with the ladies and they filled the lobbies on floor [sic] of the Senate."[27]

The debate, reported by the *News and Observer*, provides insight into contemporaneous arguments for and against such commemorations. Senator Moody of Haywood County "championed the bill in the strongest and ablest speech he has made this session," asserting that "Monuments, statues and paintings are the greatest educators." Senator Mitchell of Bertie County praised the North for "honoring and keeping fresh the memory of their great men" through monuments before summarizing supporters' key points: "Money invested in stone is not wasted. It is the best educational instrument and the best instructor in patriotism."[28]

Opponents pressed their case, too. Senator Black of Mitchell County "wanted the money to go to public schools." Senator Mewhorne added the warning that "Egypt, Babylon and Rome were monument building countries, but because they neglected the education of their children they perished." Senator Marshall of Surry County was more circumspect, speaking of his "great sympathies for the soldiers." But when asked by a colleague, "'Have you got $10,000.00 worth?' He had not." Neither had Senator Paddison, who added that "the people were too poor to pay their taxes and he could not therefore support the proposal," while "Mr. Parsons, of Hyde [County], thought all the arguments for the monument were pure sentimentality and gust."[29]

"28 To 8!" the *News and Observer* headline announced the following day. "No Money For Monuments," a subtitle read above bold print declaring "The Little Band Made a Heroic Fight for the Memory of Their Comrades, But Were Outnumbered — The Floor and Galleries Packed With the Flower of Raleigh's Women." Within two weeks, however, the NCMA would have its money.[30]

Race loomed large in this unlikely turn of events. While race relations are seldom far from the surface of Southern politics, they were rarely mentioned during Tarheel Confederate monument-building efforts. In 1895, however, this issue was blatantly used to procure funds for the state Confederate monument. "Shame, Shame, Shame!" the front-page *News and Observer* headline read on February 24, the day after the monument bill's defeat. Yet the measure's downfall was reported on page two; the "Shame," the "General Assembly's Infamy," was, according to the paper, adjourning out of respect for Frederick Douglass, the African American leader who had died four days earlier.[31]

"Miscegenation Endorsed," a *News and Observer* headline had declared two days earlier on February 22, reporting the adoption of a resolution by "Crews, colored, of Granville [County]," that the House "adjourn in respect to the memory of the deceased." Douglass had married a white woman, and the paper used a marital analogy in attacking the Fusionist coalition, "Fusion is a marriage of two parties having no principles in common. The endorsement of the miscegenation leader is the legitimate heir of this union."[32]

The following day, as the Senate debated the monument bill, the *News and Observer* labeled the House adjournment "The Climax of Infamy," one that "has created a sensation in every part of the country." Terming the state's political shift a "revolution," the paper declared the House action "a logical sequence to the other acts of this Legislature."[33]

In this charged atmosphere, on February 24, the *News and Observer* juxtaposed the monument bill's defeat with the House adjournment, closely timed but otherwise unrelated events. In an editorial cartoon directly above the "Shame" headline, Raleigh's women are shown around an unfinished monument base inscribed, "To the Confederate Dead," begging legislators, "Let us teach posterity that patriots die not in vain. A land without monuments is a land without memories. Lend us your means to commemorate the virtues of our fallen dead." To the right, legislators gather around the coffin of "Fred Douglas [sic]," appearing to ignore the women while the caption reads: "It is not your dead, but our Fred over whom we weep. 'Bear with us; our hearts are in the coffin there with Caesar, and we must pause till they come back to us.'"[34]

The attack worked superbly. Within four days, Republican Senator Hiram Grant, a Union veteran from Wayne County who had been officially excused from the earlier vote, introduced a measure calling for a direct appropriation, not a loan, to finish the Confederate monument. Heated rhetoric ensued with one opponent maintaining "to build a monument to the Confederate dead could not rectify the mistake of that adjournment," while another "thought our duty was to the living and not to the dead." Yet within ten days, the measure became law, and the *News and Observer* trumpeted, "Blue and Gray join in honoring the Confederate dead," as well as "And the Women Win."[35]

Politics, race, a generation's grief, and the need to forge collective memory all shaped the commemorative milieu in which the NCMA operated. The monument's design, illustrated in the *News-Observer-Chronicle* the day the cornerstone was placed, reflects stylistic changes ushering in a more-inclusive Tarheel commemoration, likely in response to the societal and economic forces straining the political landscape.[36]

Four of the state's five earliest soldier statues — Wilmington (New Hanover County, 1872), Goldsboro (Wayne County, 1883), New Bern (Craven County, 1885), and Greensboro (Guilford County, 1888) — depict figures clad in great coats, a form hearkening back to the Roman toga but also an item worn almost exclusively by high-ranking officers. The fifth figure, while not wearing a great coat, was modeled after a former Confederate captain (Washington/Beaufort County, 1888 — Chapter 3). The three bronzes of the Raleigh monument, however, sculpted by Ferdinand von Miller II, whom the *News and Observer* described as the "finest sculptor in bronze living" and cast in Bavaria, Germany, depict rank-and-file troops, a representation new to the Tarheel State.[37]

Also new was the use of multiple figures, an infantryman atop the granite pillar and an artilleryman and a cavalryman flanking the base, representing the army's three branches. While multiple troops would prove an aberration, likely due to cost, depictions of a single rank-and-file soldier, often described as a "Confederate private," would almost immediately, and nearly universally, supplant the great-coated figure.

4. *A Capital Celebration* 51

Artilleryman, state monument. Three figures, one for each branch of the army, celebrate the role of the common soldier. This bronze is on a lower pedestal, left of the main shaft.

A common soldier of bronze, not an elite officer, would stand beside the state capitol. Similar representations — of zinc or cast bronze, of stamped sheet-metal, marble, or granite — would follow, placed atop pillars of stone at courthouses and prominent intersections across the state in what historian Catherine Bishir terms a "sculptural reversal of hierarchy," emphasizing common values and shared cultural experience while promoting social and political unity across classes of whites. Surviving veterans, many disgruntled with the state's political leadership, would now be celebrated through icons of stone and metal and be praised by leaders, eventually returning in large numbers to the Democratic fold.[38]

Sociological considerations were likely far from veterans' minds as they boarded trains

Artilleryman detail, state monument. Sculpted by Ferdinand von Miller II and cast in Bavaria, Germany, all three bronzes feature exquisite detail.

for Raleigh in mid–May 1895. To encourage attendance, the Southern Railway priced tickets at one cent per mile, "not only from all stations in North Carolina, but also from all stations between Richmond and Danville, Virginia," the *News and Observer* reported. The reduced fares were wildly successful, for although extra trains were added, there remained "not enough railroad accommodation for the unexpected swell of people."[39]

"The soldiers came in companies and as individuals — the glorious remnant of a glorious army," the paper effused. Upon arrival, the Governor's Guards met the men and "escorted them to the military headquarters ... where they were conveniently and comfortably quartered." "From Alleghany to Currituck they came ... three thousand of the old veterans," the *News and Observer* proclaimed, some with "only one leg or an empty sleeve," descriptions of maimed men repeatedly used by the Southern press, while others had "scarred bodies and shattered health from exposure on the battle-field."[40]

Julian Carr (cousin of Governor Elias Carr), a wealthy industrialist and future national commander of the United Confederate Veterans, led Durham's contingent, "an even thousand" strong, and also served as the event's "Commander in Chief of the Veteran Brigade." Carr supplied Durham's men with a float — "a handsome, black draped car with the inscription 'In memoriam — Durham county's Legion [sic]' 'Faithful unto death, Raleigh, May 20.'" — as well as "the wreaths, the flags, the badges, and enabled the band to get in proper shape." "Too much credit cannot be given him," the *News and Observer* concluded, "for the result of which our people are all proud."[41]

Raleigh prepared for a throng several times the size of its population. Under a headline, "There Must be Food for an Immense Crowd," the *News and Observer* urged citizens "to have prepared extra food, and to be ready to furnish as many meals as possible on Monday, either for pay or free, as they prefer." Jones' Warehouse offered to feed any veteran on May 20, "with the best that we have." Wake County veterans assisted as well; "Mr. G. B. Alford of Holly Springs [brought] the largest ham, which weighed thirty-six pounds," while soldiers brewed coffee in a forty-gallon pot.[42]

Hucksters, businessmen, and city officials also prepared. Unauthorized souvenirs competed with "official" items. "The Committee of Arrangements are aware," the *News and Observer* reported two days before the unveiling, that "other badges [ribbons] are being sold upon the street." While the committee denied any "desire to interfere," a description of the genuine item was provided, emphasizing that others lack the "authorized imprimatur of the Association." After the event, however, official ribbons were easily obtained; J. D. Riggan advertised in the *News and Observer* on May 22, "Received the official badges of the Ladies' Monumental Association yesterday. Call and secure one," at any of five locations including a cigar store and a toy store.[43]

Others found opportunity as well. S. D. Berwanger, "High Art Clothiers" who boasted of "the best and largest stock of Men's and Boy's Wearables," offered visitors "space for your baggage while here," with the "promise that you will not be worried about buying." Attendees, however, apparently spent freely. "'Our visitors were not penurious,'" one prominent businessman told the *News and Observer*, while estimates of "the

Dedication-day ribbon. Raleigh, 1895. Some ribbons were to identify program participants; others were sold as souvenirs (courtesy Lon Ellis, Raleigh, North Carolina).

amount left in Raleigh by those who came to the unveiling" ranged from fifty to one-hundred thousand dollars. And although the city incurred added expense — police, for example, at "four dollars for one extra man" — the crowd was so orderly "that there was but one arrest."[44]

A "Show of Humanity ... Filled the City on Monument Day," the *News and Observer* boasted. The governor and two of his predecessors attended. So did United States Senator Marion Butler, the *Caucasian* editor who had opposed monument funding one year earlier and doubted that "any monuments should be built," as well as Captain Thomas Mason, the Northampton County jurist who had delivered the keynote address at the cornerstone placement before losing the Senate contest to Butler. Three Congressmen, a dozen newspaper editors, and scores of elected officials were there too — as was G. B. Alford, the former Confederate officer from Holly Springs (Wake County) who had delivered the thirty-six pound ham and would, in 1923, singlehandedly fund that town's Confederate monument.[45]

Social events complemented the public ceremony. Mrs. E. A. Moffitt gave a lunch in honor of Mrs. "Stonewall" Jackson. The parlors were "draped in the Confederate colors," the *News and Observer* reported, while "white lillies [sic] and red roses adorned the table." Attendees included Mrs. Josephus Daniels, wife of the *News and Observer* editor; Mrs. Walter Clark, wife of the state's most prominent Civil War authority (Chapter 9); and Mrs. Henry A. London, a future U.D.C. state president.[46]

The Charles F. Fisher Camp #309, United Confederate Veterans, met also, adopting resolutions of "heart felt thanks" for "the great honor that has been done to our fallen comrades by the Ladies' Monumental Association," and thanking Raleigh's citizens for "the splendid hospitality with which they have greeted and entertained the old soldiers." An "Unveiling German" at the Capital Club, "a Brilliant Social Function," closed the day's events. "Dancing commenced at 11:30 o'clock [sic]," the *News and Observer* reported, "and ceased at an early hour," while at its "height one hundred couples probably was [sic] on the floor with many prominent spectators banked around the wall."[47]

Yet the day's highlight was performed not by a gray-bearded veteran or a society matron but by a seven-year-old girl. Julia Jackson Christian, granddaughter of revered Confederate General "Stonewall" Jackson, rode with her grandmother in the lead carriage; the widow was dressed "in mourning," according to the *News and Observer*, while the youngster, outfitted in white with pink ribbons in her golden hair, was "merry in the childish welcome of the soldiers she loves both by the force of inheritance as well as by rearing."[48]

Grandmother and child shared the stage, symbolically linking decades of memorializing the state's 40,000 Confederate dead with a future that would commemorate surviving veterans as well. When Colonel Waddell finished his oration, Miss Christian stepped forward to unveil the monument. The seven-year-old had been selected for this prominent role, not only because of her elite pedigree, but also to represent a generation too young to have personally experienced the war or Reconstruction. These sons and daughters of aging Confederate veterans and war-era women would soon need to assume the commemorative mantle from their mothers and grandmothers if, in the closing words of Waddell, the Confederate soldier would "live forever in the hearts of his people."[49]

The unveiling went flawlessly. Miss Christian tugged at the cords holding the shroud. The covering broke free, and in front of 30,000 people, the cloth floated down "like the garments of Elijah," revealing North Carolina's completed Confederate monument.[50]

SECTION II
EVOLVING COMMEMORATION, 1896–1918

5. *"To the Confederate Soldier"*

"I may have begged too hard and been a little offensive," Colonel Sidney Vance Pickens declared in *The* (Hendersonville) *Western North Carolina Times*. "I will not beg any more," he promised, "but leave the men and women to determine whether they will have any part in this last tribute to the Confederate soldier."[1]

The year was 1903. The United Daughters of the Confederacy had formed nine years earlier, and North Carolina's division was six years old, but the group's efficient monument-building enterprise was just beginning. In Hendersonville, county seat of Henderson County, a committee of private citizens led by an ambitious yet sometimes outspoken lawyer wished to erect a marble obelisk honoring the Confederate soldier.

Bordering South Carolina and stretching from North Carolina's western piedmont to the crest of the Pisgah Mountains exactly one mile above sea level, Henderson County would have seemed an easy location to fund and construct a monument honoring the aging men who had fought for the Confederacy. Politically less divided during the Civil War than the mountain regions to the north and west, 1,700 Henderson men had taken up arms for Southern independence.

Christopher G. Memminger, Confederate Treasury Secretary (1861–1864) had lived here. So too had George A. Trenholm, Memminger's successor. For decades Low Country planters had summered here, escaping the heat, mosquitoes, and "swamp fevers" of Charleston and the South Carolina coast.[2]

Protected on two sides by steep mountains, with good transportation routes to South Carolina and a greater distance from Union forces than nearly any location in the Confederacy, Henderson County was one of the safest Southern sites during the Civil War. Memminger even proposed that the Confederate national capital be relocated here, and throughout the war coastal planters sent families, as well as slaves, here for protection.[3]

But in 1903, thirty-eight years after Appomattox, fund-raising was progressing slowly. The proposed monument, modest even by standards of the day, would be smaller than many contemporary personal and family memorials in nearby cemeteries. Barely two hundred dollars had been raised by June 12.

Contributions and social events continued through the summer with progress duly noted in the *Times*. M. C. Byers gave fifty cents, as did W. T. Bryson. A "summer visitor" donated five dollars. And Mrs. Hatch hosted a lawn party, netting an apparently disappointing ten dollars. "We believe," the committee wrote, "but for the rain the effect would

"To the Confederate Soldier." Hendersonville, 1903. North Carolina's first monument to honor *all* Confederate soldiers stands today beside the old Henderson County courthouse.

have been a great social and financial success." Undeterred, the missive ended by asking, "Who will be next for a lawn party? Don't all speak at once."[4]

Fund-raising accelerated during the next three weeks; twelve citizens contributed sums ranging from fifty cents to one dollar, and on July 28, through the "kindness of Mr. Young and the Orchestra of the Imperial," the committee achieved a "splendid success," raising seventy-one dollars from a gala night of entertainment.[5]

Ten days later, the committee reported that the monument's base had been cut from "beautiful gray Granite," donated by Dr. and Mrs. Ransieur from a quarry on their "home place." On August 21, the *Times* listed forty-eight additional contributors, with amounts ranging from Mrs. Barnett's ten cents to Mr. Smith's twenty-two dollars. Thirty-four more people would give the following week.[6]

With the fund nearing four hundred dollars, the gray marble obelisk was cut, the square base engraved and plans made for the memorial's dedication. The public was invited, especially "friends and contributors to the monument," as were Sunday school classes and city employees. However, the unveiling must have been envisioned as a predominantly local affair, for the date depended upon the weather. If, according to the *Times*, at 3:00 P.M., Tuesday August 25, it was "too rainy," the dedication would be postponed and take place on "the first pretty afternoon thereafter, Sunday excepted."[7]

August 25 was hot and dry, one of the year's warmest days according to the newspaper, but a "large number of persons attended the exercise." There was a prayer by Reverend Egerton, music by the Board of Trade band, a reading of the veteran's roll of honor, and finally the keynote speech by Colonel Pickens, the monument committee's treasurer, who just two-and-one-half months earlier had publicly apologized for his behavior while also expressing discouragement about the pace of fund-raising.[8]

Following Pickens' remarks and Mayor Williams' formal acceptance on behalf of the city of Hendersonville, nine young girls drew back a ceremonial curtain, unveiling the monument. The twenty-foot-tall memorial — an unadorned lightly striated gray marble obelisk atop a square granite base inscribed front and back with "To the Confederate Soldier" — was located in the town's most prominent location, mid-intersection of Main and Chestnut Streets just southeast of the county's recently constructed Victorian courthouse. Total cost: $432.45.[9]

The challenges faced by Colonel Pickens and his committee reflect western North Carolina's troubled wartime legacy as well as the evolving nature of Confederate memorialization. The state's mountain and foothill counties had been late developing a sculptural Civil War commemorative tradition; thirty years passed between the dedication of the state's first monument in Fayetteville's Cross Creek Cemetery and the 1898 unveiling of the Zebulon Vance memorial in Asheville's Pack Square.

Yet even this seventy-five-foot-tall obelisk of rough-cut granite blocks in downtown Asheville is not a true "soldiers'" monument. Funded largely by philanthropist George W. Pack, the memorial not only honors a single individual, but celebrates more than Vance's wartime service as a Confederate colonel and North Carolina's Civil War-era governor.[10]

Except for a small Masonic notation at the base, no additional words or symbols save for "VANCE," incised in block letters on each of the structure's four sides, embellished the original. No mention was made of specific achievements or offices held during the Buncombe County native's four decades of public service, and until 1938, no hint was present as to Vance's Confederate-era record.

The monument's dedication, although held on Confederate Memorial Day, May 10, 1898, had few airs of a Confederate celebration. The only musical selection reported by name in the *Asheville Citizen* was a medley, combining strains of "Yankee Doodle," "Tenting on the Old Camp Ground," and "Dixie." Governor Robert C. Taylor of Tennessee, the day's featured speaker, told of Vance's wit and character, "He was as honest as Davis, humorous as Lincoln, eloquent as Daniels." Yet Taylor devoted a mere half sentence to Vance's service as North Carolina governor during "the great war," with multiple paragraphs detailing his service as U.S. Congressman and Senator. Even when Taylor spoke briefly of the failed

Southern nation, that Vance was "as true to the hopes that perished at Appomatox [sic] as Gordon and Forrest," he immediately added, "and afterwards as loyal to the Union as Wheeler and Lee who now wear the blue."[11]

For forty years the monument remained unadorned, sited at the west end of Pack Square where it remains today. In 1938, however, the Asheville Chapter, United Daughters of the Confederacy, added a bronze plaque above the west face inscription, citing Vance's service as "Confederate Soldier, War Governor, U.S. Senator, Orator, Statesman."

At the beginning of the twentieth century, no public monument west of Charlotte honored North Carolina's Confederate dead, paid tribute to its soldiers, or included the word "Confederate." In 1903, however, a flurry of monument building began in and around Asheville that introduced new themes, symbolism, and honorees to the state's commemorative landscape. Six of the thirteen monuments that would be raised across North Carolina between 1903 and 1905 were within a twenty-five-mile radius of Asheville, and each featured a unique or tradition-expanding feature.

In Candler, North Carolina's first monument honoring a single military unit, Company I, Twenty-fifth North Carolina Regiment, was dedicated on January 1, 1903; in nearby Asheville, the state's first monument sponsored by the Daughters of the Confederacy was erected that same year; while in August, twenty miles south, Colonel Pickens and the citizens of Hendersonville unveiled the state's first monument honoring all Confederate soldiers. Two years later, Asheville further expanded Tarheel commemorative tradition, dedicating three courthouse-lawn monuments on a single day, an event detailed in the next chapter.

That nearly forty years had passed between Confederate surrender and the region's first monument to those soldiers, speaks of the conflict's divisiveness across the foothills and mountains of western North Carolina. Secession had little support among area citizens prior to South Carolina's shelling of Fort Sumter and President Lincoln's subsequent demand for troops to quell the "Rebellion." There were few large plantations and relatively few slaves in these western counties, and perhaps most importantly, yeoman farmers throughout the region retained a deep loyalty to the ideals and principles of the United States, liberty achieved with the blood of these people's ancestors eight decades earlier at Kings Mountain and Guilford Court House.

Once committed, however, western North Carolina, like the rest of the state, gave fully to the Southern cause, with many counties supplying troop numbers in excess of their 1860 voting populations. Yet with the exception of the months immediately following secession on May 20, 1861, loyalties remained divided, and a "war within a war" smoldered throughout the region.[12]

Madison County endured some of the worst violence. Tensions steadily increased between the largely pro–Confederate region around the county seat of Marshall, not far from Vance's birthplace in Weaverville, and the more mountainous, pro–Union area bordering Tennessee. On January 8, 1863, a band of raiders led by Unionist John Kirk conducted a "salt raid" in Marshall, seizing nearly fifty bushels of the scarce commodity. Although the brash guerrilla leader hailed from Tennessee, many of his accomplices were residents of Shelton Laurel, a mountain valley near the state line. After taking the salt, vital for meat preservation, raiders attacked the home of Colonel Lawrence Allen, commanding officer of the Sixty-fourth North Carolina Regiment, harassing his wife and stealing blankets from his three sick children, two of whom died shortly thereafter.

Retaliation was quick and brutal. Thirteen men and boys, Confederate deserters as well as adolescents as young as thirteen, were taken prisoner from Shelton Laurel. Few likely

Company I, 25th N.C. Regiment. Buncombe County, 1903. This marble obelisk, in Candler's Montmorenci Methodist Church cemetery, is the state's oldest commemoration honoring a single military unit.

had participated in the raid, but on January 19, without trial, the captives were lined up and, under orders by Lieutenant Colonel James A. Keith of the Sixty-fourth, executed in an atrocity that stunned Confederate authorities.[13]

Other mountain counties experienced clashes as well. In Ashe, the state's northwesternmost county, "Approximately 1200" men joined Confederate forces, according to a twenty-first century courthouse plaque, while a significant number, although "less than

100," fought for the Union. Violence flared here as well. On June 17, 1864, Lieutenant Isaac Wilson, a Confederate officer on home furlough, was shot and killed as he plowed his field near the county's southwestern border. Retribution was again swift. A Unionist neighbor suspected in the murder was summarily hanged the next day, and an alleged accomplice was killed fleeing to Tennessee.[14]

Volunteers from Henderson and Transylvania Counties in the state's southern mountains joined Northern forces, too. Although numerical estimates of these troops vary widely, two monuments — a 1985 memorial in Etowah (Henderson County) and a 2008 inscribed granite slab just twenty feet from Colonel Pickens' relocated 1903 monument to the Confederate soldier — have been raised in honor of these Union men.[15]

Violence also affected the northwestern Piedmont. Yadkin County was the scene of a shootout between Confederate militia and bushwhackers holed up in the Bond School House on February 12, 1863, a firefight that left two dead on each side and renegades scattered across an area that, according to one local resident, "is so disloyal."[16]

Reconciliation following such neighbor-on-neighbor violence would take decades; public-space commemoration would take even longer. By 1965, one century after Appomattox, only seven of North Carolina's twenty-one mountain counties had monuments to Confederate soldiers or the Southern dead. Even across the western Piedmont, just over half the counties — eight of thirteen — had erected such commemorations prior to the Civil War centennial.[17]

Of the seven mountain counties that had raised Confederate monuments by 1965, five were part of the state's southern border or lay within one county of that line. These political units form a contiguous arc extending from South Carolina north through Asheville, Candler, and Waynesville then southwest to the Georgia line. To the north and west of these jurisdictions, none of North Carolina's nine other counties bordering Tennessee would dedicate civic-space Civil War memorials prior to the end of the twentieth century. (The two "mountain" counties not part of this commemorative arc that erected Confederate monuments are Caldwell (Lenoir, 1910) and Burke (Morganton, 1918). Both include some of the highest peaks in the Blue Ridge, yet most of their population and land area, as well as their courthouses, are located east of the foothills, and both are closely linked through trade and transportation with North Carolina's largest cities.)[18]

Commemorative variation occurred in the Piedmont as well, again reflecting internal wartime conflicts. North and west of Winston-Salem, where pockets Unionist sentiment prevailed deep, no civic-space memorial to the Confederacy or its troops had been raised by 1965, while further south, all but Polk County (Columbus) had erected such monuments.[19]

That Confederate commemoration in western North Carolina would be centered near Asheville should not be surprising. The region's most populous city, like neighboring Henderson County, was a favorite summertime retreat for affluent Charlestonians. Following early Confederate defeats along the Atlantic coast, plantation owners and their slaves fled, many retreating to North Carolina's southern mountains. Other planters, fearing impressment of slaves by Confederate authorities, or liberation by Union armies, sent their human property to the Asheville area for safety; by 1862, refugees, black and white, swelled the region's population and strained its already tenuous food supply.[20]

In addition to Treasury Secretary Memminger, so many prominent Confederates resided in and around the area that an army unit, Company E, Sixty-fourth North Carolina Regiment, was stationed at the Woodfield Inn near Flat Rock (Henderson County) in 1864. That regular troops, not militia or home-guard, would be deployed, spoke of the increasingly precarious situation. "A gang of bushwhackers, escaped Yankee prisoners and renegades," had been on the loose, according to the *Asheville Citizen*, "committing murder and robbery in the region."[21]

Company E saw little action, but received commemorative recognition nine decades later. On October 18, 1959, the *Asheville Citizen* reported that Dr. C. C. Crittenden, director of the State Department of Archives and History, would be at the Woodfield Inn to "discuss the importance of the company." Following his remarks, a commemorative plaque honoring Company E would be unveiled by the grandchildren of Captain B. T. Morris, the unit's commanding officer. The United Daughters of the Confederacy, represented by state president Mrs. E. A. Anderson of Charlotte, would be there as well, yet little else is known about this commemoration, and repeated attempts to locate this plaque have been unsuccessful.[22]

Topography and economic development also played roles in greater Asheville's rise to commemorative prominence and perhaps to its varied styles of remembrance. Through much of North Carolina the Blue Ridge and southern Appalachian Mountains are bounded on the east by a steep escarpment, a rugged obstacle that, for decades, curtailed travel between mountain regions and the rest of the state. While this escarpment made travel between Asheville and the east difficult, a broad valley from South Carolina to the city's 2,200-foot elevation provided easy passage, making the city a gateway to neighboring communities and forging commercial and cultural ties that undoubtedly shaped the region's commemorative response.

By the late nineteenth century, the region was becoming more than a summer retreat for Low Country planters. Tourism was increasing, and the 1895 completion of George W. Vanderbilt's Biltmore, the nation's largest private residence, further enhanced Asheville's reputation. The nearly four-acre chateau was designed by architect Richard Morris Hunt; Frederick Law Olmsted, noted landscape architect and creator of New York City's Central Park, planned the grounds, while Gifford Pinchot and Dr. Carl A. Schenck, the "Fathers of American Forestry," managed Vanderbilt's nearly 125,000 wooded acres. Intellectual and national leaders followed. Vanderbilt hosted Edith Wharton and Henry James. Presidents William McKinley, Theodore Roosevelt, and Woodrow Wilson visited also.[23]

Since commemorative planners seek large audiences, Asheville's increasing prominence made for an excellent memorial venue. A private grave marker, however ornate or elegant, will seldom receive more than a handful of visitors; cemetery memorials, exemplified by North Carolina's earliest Civil War monuments, will attract a larger yet mostly local crowd. But a civic-space memorial, especially sited along a main thoroughfare or central public space, can garner a daily audience of thousands. Growing affluence, increased visitation, and public spaces ideal for commemorative display, helped make greater Asheville the scene of a brief but intense Confederate memorial florescence.

All three of western North Carolina's 1903 memorials are modest obelisks. The earliest, "Erected Jan. 1, 1903," according to its front panel inscription, is located near the back of the Montmorenci United Methodist Church Cemetery in Candler. Approximately fifteen feet tall, this monument was "erected by private subscription" from "good souls who put up the money," according to W. T. Rogers, in the September 1909 *Confederate Veteran*. Other sources, however, including a 1907 article in the same periodical, state that Captain Augustus Buckingham Thrash, the company's third and final commanding officer, single-handedly funded the memorial.[24]

One hundred seventy names, every soldier who served at any time in Company I,

Twenty-fifth North Carolina Regiment, from when it was "organized at Hominy Baptist Church, July 22, 1861," according to the monument's inscription, until the unit "surrendered at Appomatax [sic] April 9, 1865," are carved in a uniform font and arranged, irrespective of rank, in (mostly) alphabetical order. Five names, however, are engraved more prominently. Four are company officers, cited a second time in a larger, raised font. Three of these men had served as company captain; the fourth had been "promoted to adjutant of the regiment." The fifth name, W. G. Candler, is not on the company roster, but is credited on the monument by whom, "This land [was] donated to Co. I 25th N.C. Vol."[25]

The monument is "a beautiful shaft of East Tennessee marble," according to the *Confederate Veteran*. Above the signature, "Erected by G. W. Sellers and Sons Newport, Tenn.," a shallowly carved flag of unusual design and proportion curves gracefully down the obelisk's front panel. Attached to a similarly carved vertical staff, the banner's upper corner features a small motif of the Confederate battle flag. Yet the rest of this partially furled banner is massively elongated, three to four times wider than a standard flag, with three stripes extending its length. Though awkwardly joined with the battle insignia, the broad bands likely represent the two red and one white stripe of the "Stars and Bars," the Confederacy's earliest, and most widely used, national flag. This commingling of designs is probably unique in North Carolina, and this monument's depiction of a large, intact Confederate flag, although modified, is one of the state's earliest.[26]

There is no record of any dedication ceremony for this privately funded monument, and although burial plots were offered to company soldiers, only a handful of Confederate graves are near this monument.

A dozen miles east, a second obelisk, also unveiled in 1903, stands beside two rows of Confederate graves in Asheville's Newton Academy Cemetery, one of the city's oldest burial grounds. "Erected By the Asheville Chapter Daughters of the Confederacy," this monument, according to its inscription, is dedicated "To the Confederate Dead, Buried In This Cemetery."

Little is known about this memorial. "Unveiled 1903," carved beneath the dedication, would make this monument the first erected in North Carolina by the United Daughters of the Confederacy. Yet the sponsoring organization is the Daughters of the Confederacy, not

Confederate monument. Newton Academy Cemetery, Asheville, Buncombe County, 1903. This obelisk, erected by "the Asheville Chapter Daughters of the Confederacy," may be North Carolina's oldest U.D.C.–sponsored monument.

the *United* Daughters of the Confederacy, or U.D.C., monikers more frequently used by the prominent women's group. Nor is this monument included in Smith's *North Carolina's Confederate Monuments and Memorials*, a text published in 1941 by the North Carolina U.D.C. from reports submitted by the organization's local chapters, including one from Asheville. Neither is it included in Ralph Widener's 1982 nationwide compilation of Confederate monuments, a work aided by photo submissions from both U.D.C. and Sons of Confederate Veterans' members.[27]

The obelisk has no engraver's signature or manufacturer's mark; three of its four sides remain blank. The back panel, however, is polished, as is the front, suggesting that additional inscriptions might have been planned. The dedication, "To the Confederate Dead, *Buried in this Cemetery*" (italics added), is also unusual. Contemporaneous North Carolina monuments are nearly always inscribed with phrases such as "The Confederate Dead," "Our Confederate Dead," or to the dead of a county, implying broader commemoration than just to soldiers buried nearby. Maybe Asheville's Daughters selected an awkward phrase, but for a city's first Confederate monument, and one that remained in relative obscurity, this wording is highly atypical.

Crossed flags. Newton Academy Cemetery, Asheville, Buncombe County, 1903. An uncommon symbolic depiction pairs a Confederate battle flag with a stylized North Carolina state flag on this obelisk.

Another unusual feature of this monument is a pair of small highly polished, unfurled flags carved in relief directly above the inscription. A Confederate battle flag is crossed with a stylized North Carolina state flag, the latter depicted with one star and a single date, May 20, the date of the purported Mecklenburg Declaration of Independence in 1775 and the state's secession in 1861.[28]

By selecting the banner of the Confederacy's most successful fighting force, the Army of Northern Virginia, Asheville's Daughters honored both the army and the short-lived nation for which their fathers and grandfathers had fought. And by depicting the North Carolina flag with a single date, May 20, these women linked the state's Revolutionary War heritage with its later attempt to establish a Southern nation, a theme emphasized by Colonel Waddell and Judge Mason in Raleigh nearly a decade earlier (Chapter 4).

Twenty miles south of Asheville, Colonel Pickens and his committee — perhaps a "committee of one"— had an even more profound effect on Tarheel Confederate commemoration. On August 25, 1903, when nine young girls unveiled the region's third Confederate memorial, the state's commemorative landscape expanded dramatically.

Fund-raising had been difficult, and the modest memorial had just a single four-word phrase carved into opposite sides of the base, "To the Confederate Soldier." The Confederate Soldier. Not exclusively the Southern dead, not members of a single company, but the Confederate Soldier. The men who had fought — and lost — now honored with an obelisk in the middle of the town's busiest and most prominent intersection.

Newspaper accounts do not report the crowd's reaction upon first seeing the monument, nor did editors proffer comment as to the memorial's merits. Public acceptance, perhaps, can best be judged by the monument remaining mid-intersection for more than two decades, despite becoming a traffic hazard. When the obelisk was eventually relocated to the courthouse grounds in 1925, the move was accomplished only after receiving "the approval of the Daughters of the Confederacy and the Confederate veterans."[29]

There was not a statewide embracing of this expanded commemorative tradition, however, and regional variation ensued. In 1904, two monuments were dedicated, both in eastern North Carolina. On May 10, Chowan County (Edenton) unveiled its memorial to "Our Confederate Dead 1861–1865," while five months later, Edgecombe County (Tarboro) dedicated its statue on the village green "In Honor of the Confederate Soldiers of Edgecombe County. 'Defenders of State Sovereignty.' 1861 C.S.A. 1865."

During the next five years, twelve additional Civil War monuments would be dedicated in North Carolina civic spaces. Three of the six memorials erected along or east of present-day Interstate 85 honored the Confederate dead, while all but one of the six western sculptures were dedicated to Southern soldiers or, in Shelby (1907), the more inclusive "Confederate Heroes of Cleveland County 1861–1865," the first use of that appellation since the Fayetteville women carved the term onto the state's first monument nearly four decades earlier.[30]

Why the state's western third, the region most conflicted during the war, would honor all Confederate soldiers, while the rest of North Carolina, with more widespread support of Southern goals, dedicated many of its monuments to the dead is not entirely clear. Both themes are egalitarian, one honoring all soldiers regardless of rank, the other similarly commemorating the deceased. Nor had the state's regions differed greatly in human loss; the percentage killed from western North Carolina was as great as or greater than in the east, although western fatalities often occurred farther from home.

In 1965, only one "western" county — Forsyth (Winston-Salem), in the northwestern Piedmont — had a civic-space monument devoted primarily to the Confederate dead, a memorial erected by the U.D.C. in 1905. Across eastern North Carolina, however, especially in the coastal plain, monuments to the Confederate dead remained common through much of the twentieth century, including commemorations in Pitt County (Greenville, 1914), Currituck County (Currituck, 1923), Pamlico County (Bayboro, 1940), and Jones County (Trenton, 1960).[31]

Few documents detail deliberations as groups designed monuments and selected symbols and prose. One possible explanation for this persistent regional variation, however, is that eastern North Carolina's commemorative tradition was born of the necessity to care for massed graves of Confederate soldiers who had perished locally during the conflict. Hospitals, training camps, and supply depots had been established here, a short yet "safe" distance from Virginia's bloody battlegrounds, and wherever troops congregated, death from infection and disease followed. Coupled with nearby battlefield losses, more than a dozen mass graves — common burials containing the remains of twenty or more troops — and Confederate cemeteries, groups exclusively of individually interred remains of Southern soldiers, are located along and east of today's Interstate 85.

To the west, although Confederate graves are numerous, deceased soldiers are almost always interred among relatives and non-combatants, often in family or church cemeteries. Attempts at communal soldier burials in this region, including Captain Thrash's offer of gravesites beside his 1903 monument in Candler, rarely succeeded. Indeed the two rows of Confederate headstones beside the Daughters' monument in Asheville may represent western North Carolina's largest such burial.

Communal graves, especially of unknowns or decedents without nearby relatives, generally necessitate shared maintenance responsibility. While family and church members could care for individual soldier interments across western North Carolina, Ladies' Memorial Associations led in tending massed burials across the central and eastern parts of the state. For three-and-one-half decades, these women cared for the Southern dead, and as the LMAs and their aging members yielded commemorative leadership to the U.D.C. early in the twentieth century, many of these Ladies continued with influential advisory roles within the new group.

Tradition, however, may have slowed adoption of newer commemorative themes. For many older women, care of the Confederate dead had been a cause, while the region's sculptural tradition as well as its Memorial Day activities similarly focused on the honored fallen. Across central and eastern North Carolina, these "women of the '60s," as well as local custom, probably shaped the beliefs of the rising generation of commemorative leaders who would guide the region's United Daughters of the Confederacy.

In western North Carolina, meanwhile, no sculptural commemorative tradition existed prior to the twentieth century, and when the region's first monuments were erected, efforts were led, not by older Ladies steeped in memorial tradition, but by aging veterans and younger women. The men undoubtedly wished to honor comrades; younger women, many of whom had not personally experienced the conflict, likely wanted to commemorate fathers, grandfathers, and uncles, aging soldiers whom they knew personally and were dying at a rapid rate. Without the guidance or constraints of an established commemorative tradition, and somewhat isolated from the rest of the state, groups and individuals across western North Carolina explored new memorial themes, expanding Tarheel commemoration and, temporarily, making this region the state's memorial leader.

6. Monumental Day

November 8, 1905, dawned cold and raw in Asheville. A "chilly breeze from the north" swept from the mountains across Pack Square, a blocks-long park in the city's center. By noon, 1,500 people gathered at the Square's southeastern corner near the Buncombe County courthouse, where three veiled forms, monuments to county Confederate heroes, awaited unveiling.[1]

"Monumental Day," would be a grand celebration of Asheville's, Buncombe County's, and North Carolina's Confederate heritage. For the first and only time in state history, multiple Civil War monuments would be dedicated in a single event. The governor would be here, delivering the keynote speech. The state auditor was to attend also, to assist the Asheville Chapter, United Daughters of the Confederacy, in presenting Crosses of Honor to Southern veterans. Colonels and captains, choirs and ministers would be here as well, each with a role in the day's ceremony.

This event, however, was not Asheville's first Confederate commemoration. Although western North Carolina had, for decades, lagged behind the rest of the state in establishing a monumental tradition, a towering obelisk, the exact height of the state monument to the Confederate dead in Raleigh, dominated the western end of Pack Square. Dedicated on May 10, 1898, in front of the then-current courthouse, the seventy-five-foot-tall granite shaft honored North Carolina's Civil War-era governor, Zebulon B. Vance, a Buncombe County native. Asheville's Daughters of the Confederacy had raised a monument as well; in 1903, the women erected a modest obelisk to the Confederate Dead in Newton Academy Cemetery, one of the city's oldest graveyards (Chapter 5).[2]

Monumental Day, however, would expand Asheville's Confederate celebration. More than one man, albeit the area's most well-known native son, and more than the Southern dead, however venerated they might be, would receive acclaim. Buncombe's aging veterans would join the pantheon of Confederate heroes.

The event was carefully planned. Some in the crowd sported six-and-one-half-inch-long ribbons imprinted with a multicolored, unfurled Confederate battle flag above "Monumental Day/Asheville, N.C./November 8, 1905," serving to identify program participants. The *Asheville Citizen* urged, in its November 8 morning edition, "that flags be displayed" and that "places of business be closed at noon and that all citizens attend the unveiling exercises." North Carolina governor Robert B. Glenn was to deliver the keynote address, the paper reported, "to Honor the Memory of the Brave Men Who Carried the Cross Barred Flag Furtherest in Battle Line."[3]

6. Monumental Day

"Farthest at Chickamauga." Asheville, 1905. This marble monument beside the Buncombe County courthouse was sponsored by veterans of the Sixtieth North Carolina Regiment, whose valor at Chickamauga became part of the Tarheel "Rebel Boast."

The soldiers who advanced the Southern banner farthest at Chickamauga, the Sixtieth North Carolina Regiment, were mostly Buncombe County men; six of the unit's ten companies had been recruited locally. The regiment fought in the war's western theater — Murfreesboro, Vicksburg, Jackson, Chickamauga — before attempting to halt Sherman's advancing forces at Resaca and Kennesaw Mountain, Georgia, and finally at Bentonville, North Carolina. But it was the Sixtieth's charge at Chickamauga, an attack that "about noon on Sept. 20, 1863," reached "the furthest point attained by Confederate troops in that famous charge," according to the monument's front inscription, which brought fame to the unit and became part of North Carolina's "Rebel Boast."[4]

The governor, and nearly all those assembled, knew of these deeds. "It was the blood of the Sixtieth Regiment," Colonel James M. Ray would remind the throng, "that had bought the right to a place for this monument." That location was prime real estate, in front of a stately six-columned portico, the courthouse's main entrance.[5]

Two smaller memorials flanked the sculpture to the Sixtieth. A marble obelisk honoring Thomas L. Clingman, Confederate brigadier general, United States representative and senator, and namesake of the highest summit in the Smoky Mountains, stood shrouded near the courthouse's northwestern corner, while a similarly covered marble block, honoring Colonel William Burton Creasman, commander of the Twenty-ninth North Carolina Regiment, stood near the building's northeastern edge.

But weather forced a change of plan. Unveilings would be conducted outdoors as scheduled, but other activities would take place inside the courthouse. The first monument unveiled was a modest sculpted marble block inscribed "W. B. Creasman/Colonel/Twenty-ninth N.C. Regt./C. S. A." Grandchildren of the unit's soldiers did the honors. At the opposite end of the courthouse, members of the R. E. Lee Chapter, Children of the Confederacy, uncovered that group's sponsored memorial, a marble obelisk honoring General Thomas L. Clingman. Then, as the choir of the Sixtieth Regiment sang "with touching effect," "In the Sweet Bye and Bye," the crowd watched as "eight little girls," grandchildren of regimental soldiers, pulled ribbons attached to a white drape covering the central sculpture and "the monument was disclosed for all to see."[6]

The white marble memorial, manufactured by Cherokee Marble Works, sculptors of all three commemorations, was unlike any previous Tarheel monument. With 680 words, dates, and initials carved on four panels, each five feet high, the state's most verbose memorial to date not only detailed the Sixtieth's military service as well as Buncombe County's contribution to the Southern cause, but served also as historical record, political defense, and public proclamation of North Carolina's contribution to the Confederate effort, a theme no previous county memorial had broached.

"NORTH CAROLINA," in massive, ornate letters dominates the lower front panel while a stylized "NC" is carved in relief high on each lateral side. Two flags,

Monumental Day ribbon. This ribbon was possibly worn by a U.D.C. member for identification; an otherwise identical example substitutes "Unveiling — Girls for Creasman Monument Grandchildren of 29th N.C. Regiment" for the Asheville Daughters text (courtesy Lon Ellis, Raleigh, North Carolina).

"the staves gracefully crossed" according to the *Citizen*, adorn the front face. But the carved banners, unlike commemorative representations elsewhere in the state, pair the familiar "crossed-barred" Confederate battle flag with a modified state flag, the latter inscribed, May 20, 1775, the date of the purported Mecklenburg Declaration of Independence.[7]

Atop the structure, twenty-five feet above the ground, a carved Minie ball rests atop a sculpted pine log, the former representing the infantry, to which the Sixtieth belonged, the latter symbolizing the unit's native state. At the bottom of the back panel, below a recitation of Buncombe County colonels, units, and troop enrollments are the words, "Was at Bethel June 10, 1861, first land engagement, and at Bentonville March 19–21, and Appomattox April 9, 1865, the last two!"

After the children ceremoniously removed each monument's covering, activities moved indoors. The crowd, however, was so large, according to the *Citizen*, "that they filled all seats and standing room, the gallery and adjoining halls, so that many could not come within the sound of the speakers' voices."[8]

Detail, Buncombe County Confederate monument. Asheville, 1905. A carved Minie ball rests on a sculpted pine log; "NC," in stylized script, is inscribed within the triangle.

The choir of the Sixtieth sang "America," "with every one [sic] standing," according to the *Citizen*. Dr. A. S. Whitaker offered an "appropriate prayer," then Colonel James M. Ray, acting commander of the Sixtieth at Chickamauga, announced that "a collection would be taken up in the nature of an offering in a church," with proceeds helping complete payment for the Clingman and Creasman memorials. The Sixtieth's monument, according to the Colonel, had been paid in full "by that regiment's members, their descendents and the addition of the granite base given by Mr. P. S. Henry."[9]

Captain J. P. Sawyer of Asheville then introduced North Carolina's governor. "We meet today," the former Confederate officer said, "to do honor to the heroes of the greatest army that ever fought the battles of this world." The crowd concurred, with the *Citizen* adding the word "Applause" in parentheses after the captain's words.[10]

Governor Glenn received similar plaudits when, early in his remarks, he referred to the struggle for Southern independence as "that glorious cause for which my father died." In a concise yet eloquent summary of contemporary Confederate commemoration four decades after Appomattox, the state's chief executive spoke of "three ends to be attained [from the day's address]: The commemoration of glorious deeds; the speaking of kind words to those who survive, and the teaching of youth what it is to be true patriots."[11]

"There never has been, there never will be more heroic men than those who wore the gray," the governor said, "and of these men none were more noble, more brave, more true than the boys of North Carolina." Defending the state's position in a burgeoning controversy with Virginia, Glenn reminded the throng that "the first settlement in this country was on Roanoke Island in this state"; that during the American Revolution "it took a King's Mountain and a Guilford Court House [North Carolina] to make a Yorktown [Virginia]"; and that although North Carolina was "the last [state] save one to enter the Union we were the last save one to leave it; and though so late in seceding, we were first in battle at Bethel."[12] The governor extolled the heroism of the Sixtieth, detailing engagements including that notable advance at Chickamauga, driving the enemy back "Yard by yard, inch by inch," and winning fame by "advancing furtherest [sic] on that bloody field." "You deserve the right," Glenn said, "to put on your monument 'First at Bethel, fartherest [sic] at Chickamauga and Gettysburg, last at Appomattox.'"[13]

Glenn then asked if Buncombe's other soldiers had also done "their duty." His affirmative response profiled Zebulon Vance, Generals Thomas L. Clingman and Robert B. Vance, the former governor's brother, as well as the names and statistics chiseled into the monument's back panel: eighteen colonels from Buncombe County; twenty-one and one-half companies recruited locally; and 2,810 Confederate troops enlisted from an 1860 "voting

Manufacturer's signature, Buncombe County Confederate monument. Cherokee Marble Works manager S. C. Brinks sculpted all three monuments unveiled on Asheville's Monumental Day, November 8, 1905.

population" of just 1,830. "I bow before you today, old veterans," Glenn said in tribute, "as grander and nobler men than I can ever hope to be."[14]

The governor spoke too of those "even braver and nobler" than the aging warriors. "What part did the women take?" Glenn asked. "Old soldiers don't you remember those sweet women who attended you in the field hospitals and cheered the dying soldier as his soul ascended to his God? I bow before the grandest and the purest and the best women God ever gave to any land."[15]

To "cheers and great applause," the governor concluded by citing eternity and the South's greatest chieftain, "If a tear can be shed in heaven, it will be shed by Robert E. Lee if his Buncombe men cannot join him in heaven. You were immortals here, will you not be immortals there?"[16]

After four "little girls" presented chrysanthemums to Glenn, Locke Craig, a former state representative from Asheville and a future North Carolina governor, accepted the monument on behalf of the county commissioners. Craig thanked the women, the Daughters of the Confederacy, Children of the Confederacy, and Mr. P. S. Henry, before closing with "an eloquent tribute to the soldiers."[17]

The next event was to have been the presentation of Crosses of Honor to Buncombe's aging veterans. Awarding of these medals, bestowed by the United Daughters of the Confederacy for honorable service in the Confederate military, was an increasingly important aspect of many monument dedications. But Dr. B. F. Dixon, state auditor of North Carolina, who had been scheduled to make an address then assist the Daughters during the ceremony, had been "left by the train at Raleigh," according to the *Citizen*. Colonel Ray, instead, had to inform the veterans and gathered crowd that the crosses "would be distributed informally at later dates."[18]

The formal event concluded with a benediction by Bishop A. Coke Smith then the Daughters retired to their "camp room" to serve "refreshments." With the three just-unveiled memorials, sculptures that had "occupied" Cherokee Marble Works and its manager, S. C. Brink, "for the past three months," according to the *Citizen*, Asheville stood at the forefront of North Carolina Confederate commemoration with five Confederate monuments. Three honored individuals, the only civic-space commemorations outside of Raleigh's Capitol Square dedicated thus far to individual Confederates, while another of the city's memorials made the strongest defense to date for North Carolina's role in the Civil war.[19]

It is fitting that Asheville's Monumental Day served as venue for Governor Robert B. Glenn's spirited defense of North Carolina's role in the short-lived Confederate States of America. State allegiance was more pronounced through the nineteenth and early twentieth centuries than today, and as the new century dawned, aging veterans wrote their final, and what they hoped would be definitive, recollections of the war.

Like any history, however, especially of a conflict setting a nation against itself, memories subject to forty years of self-reflection are open to question. Just as regions and races advanced differing interpretations of the Civil War and its aftermath in an ongoing struggle to forge a collective national memory, Southerners similarly argued amongst themselves about the conflict. Political factions, states, and even counties sought credit and shifted blame as each struggled to accept changed circumstances while seeking economic opportunity and renewed influence.

The organization of Civil War armies helped foment some post-war squabbles. Confederate infantry regiments, one thousand men each at full strength, had nearly all been organized and identified by state. Likewise most of the one hundred men comprising each of a regiment's ten companies had been, especially early in the war, recruited from a common locale. Identifying with a specific region, companies often chose colorful identifying monikers in addition to assigned alphanumeric designations. North Carolinians marched off as Jeff Davis Mountaineers (Company A, Twenty-sixth North Carolina Regiment), Anson Guards (Company C, Fourteenth North Carolina Regiment), and Beaufort Plow Boys (Company B, Sixty-first North Carolina Regiment), to name a few. Men lived and fought beside neighbors, friends, and relatives in perhaps the ultimate extension of peer pressure. County and state units judged each other's fighting ability, while individual bravery as well as cowardice would be reported back home, there to be known, at least in whispers, for the rest of a man's life.[20]

Regimental action could bring praise to a state and its troops while deeds by a company could bring similar plaudits locally. General Robert E. Lee, during the retreat from Petersburg shortly before the war's end, witnessed a small brigade marching smartly with obvious pride despite the army's dire circumstances. "What troops are those?" the general asked. "Cox's North Carolina brigade," an aide replied. Lee removed his hat and bowed his head. "God bless gallant old North Carolina," the beloved leader said, words that would be cherished by a state and enshrined a half century later as part of a magnificent Tiffany stained glass window in Virginia's Blandford Church, not far from where Lee's words were spoken, as well as on Rockingham County's (Reidsville, 1910) Confederate monument.[21]

There is no question that North Carolina supplied more than her share of Southern troops or that these fighters suffered a disproportionate number of casualties. However the state's wartime record — and especially its political commitment to the Confederate cause — was subject to criticism during the conflict and debate afterwards, challenges that helped forge the Tarheel commemorative response.

North Carolinians brought a contentious past into the Confederacy when, on May 20, 1861, they voted to leave the Union after refusing President Abraham Lincoln's call for troops to put down the "Rebellion." South Carolina had wasted little time seceding following Lincoln's 1860 election, voting to do so on December 20 of that year. Mississippi (January 9), Florida (January 10), Alabama (January 11), Georgia (January 19), and Louisiana (January 26) followed the next month; Texas did likewise February 1. But North Carolina, by many measures the poorest of the Southern states, vacillated.

Zebulon B. Vance, who would later command North Carolina's Twenty-sixth Regiment before being elected governor in 1862, was among the North Carolinians vigorously resisting secession. A Buncombe County native, Vance returned to Asheville following his education at the University of North Carolina. As assistant editor of the *Asheville Spectator*, Vance quickly established a reputation as an ardent Unionist, lashing out at fellow Buncombe County resident Thomas L. Clingman, calling antebellum North Carolina's longest-serving congressman "a liar and a scoundrel" and charging that the popular politician's radical Southern rhetoric and secessionist leanings were seriously threatening the Union.[22]

In 1857, at age twenty-seven, the young editor challenged Clingman for his congressional seat but suffered a crushing defeat, losing by more than a 2-1 margin. The following year, after Clingman had been appointed to a vacated Senate seat, Vance ran again, scoring a decisive victory over William Waightstill Avery, a prominent member of an elite Burke County family and, like Clingman, a vocal advocate of Southern rights.

Vance and Clingman, articulating disparate views, framed the choice faced by North

6. Monumental Day

General Thomas L. Clingman. Riverside Cemetery, Asheville. This marble obelisk, funded by the Children of the Confederacy, was unveiled in front of Buncombe County's courthouse on Monumental Day, 1905. Decades later it was relocated to Clingman's grave.

Carolinians as the nation slid toward war. But the populace was sharply divided. In the 1860 presidential election, John Breckenridge, sitting vice president and staunch proponent of Southern rights, carried the Tarheel State by a mere 848 votes. John Bell, a moderate Unionist, finished second. (The national Democratic nominee, Stephen A. Douglas, finished a distant third, while Abraham Lincoln's name did not appear on the ballot, since the fledgling Republican Party could not garner enough signatures to place his name in front of voters.)[23]

Three-and-one-half months later, after seven Southern states had left the Union and formed a new confederation, North Carolina's secession convention vote, like its 1860 presidential ballot, was almost evenly split. On February 28, 1861, the statewide call for a convention was defeated by 651 votes (50.3 percent to 49.7 percent), keeping North Carolina, at least temporarily, part of the fracturing United States.[24]

Pragmatism, as well as ideology, shaped North Carolina's decision. Although a secession convention had been rejected, Tarheels realized that Virginia's course would largely dictate North Carolina's future. If its northern neighbor left the Union, North Carolina would be forced to follow suit or be surrounded by opposing states. If the Old Dominion stayed, North Carolina could do likewise or, as the northernmost Confederate state, be the scene of a war's most intense fighting.

Virginia and Tennessee rejected secession through statewide forums early in 1861. As Abraham Lincoln took the oath of office on March 4, North Carolina was holding steadfast to Vance's counsel that "we have everything to gain and nothing on earth to lose by delay, but by too hasty action we may take a fatal step we can never retrace — may lose a heritage we can never recover."[25]

But on April 15, 1861, three days after South Carolina's shelling of the Federal garrison at Fort Sumter, the new president called for 75,000 troops, including two regiments from North Carolina, to quell the "Rebellion." Governor John W. Ellis promptly rejected the request, refusing to take up arms against another Southern state, a stand widely supported by North Carolinians.

"I was canvassing for the Union with all my strength," Vance would later write, "and literally had my arm upward in pleading for peace and the Union of our Fathers, when the telegraphic news was announced of the firing on Sumter and the President's call for seventy-five thousand volunteers. When my hand came down from the impassioned gesticulation, it fell slowly and sadly by the side of a Secessionist. I immediately, with altered voice and manner, called upon the assembled multitude to volunteer, not to fight against but for South Carolina."[26]

Vance may have taken liberty with his description — the shelling of Fort Sumter and Lincoln's call for troops were separated by three days in an era when telegraph lines spread news in seconds — but the future governor's words accurately reflect the abrupt change in Tarheel sentiment. Five weeks after Vance's hand "came down" as a Secessionist, a statewide convention voted unanimously for North Carolina to leave the Union and join the Confederacy. Unionist rhetoric all but vanished as the state prepared for war. Virginia, Tennessee, and Arkansas followed similar timelines, joining the Southern nation after rejecting Lincoln's call for troops. However, North Carolina's reticence to secede, as well as its deep internal divisions, had been noted by both Confederate and Federal leaders.

Jefferson Davis, many historians believe, never fully "trusted" North Carolina's wartime resolve despite the state's massive commitment of troops. That Vance as governor repeatedly clashed with the Confederate president over fundamental issues is incontrovertible. The North Carolina governor, according to historian William Powell, "objected strenuously" to Confederate military conscription, impressment (seizure) of private property, suspension of the writ of habeas corpus, use of Virginia officers in North Carolina, and discrimination in the appointment and promotion of North Carolinians as Confederate military officers, stands that won Vance acclaim at home but put him in conflict with officials in Richmond.[27]

North Carolina's politics and cultural milieu did little to reassure the ever-edgy Davis. In 1861, three mountain counties split over secession; Clay, Mitchell, and Transylvania counties all formed with strong Unionist sentiments. Families, communities, and churches — congregations as well as entire denominations — broke apart over slavery and politics, while nearly every aspect of the state's social fabric was severely strained as a divided people debated North Carolina's future.

The furor quieted briefly following the May 20 secession, as citizens mobilized in a patriotic frenzy for what was expected to be a short war. In an era marked by state allegiance, and now part of a new nation formed on the principle of states' rights, Tarheels poured forth to defend the Old North State. But as the war dragged on and casualties surged, divisions resurfaced. Unionism and anti-war sentiment, though subdued, had remained prevalent among Quakers, in some mountain communities, and in pockets across the northern Piedmont. With Confederate setbacks and mounting losses, dissenting voices found increasing audiences.

In 1862 Zebulon Vance, former Unionist and now popular colonel of the Twenty-sixth North Carolina Regiment, was elected governor, defeating William J. Johnston, the Confederate Party candidate by nearly a 3-1 margin. The thirty-two-year-old Vance won with the strong support of William Woods Holden, the *North Carolina Standard's* powerful editor and a leading critic of Davis, prompting accusations that the youthful colonel was a "Yankee" candidate as well as "a pliant tool of Holden," charges apparently dismissed as Vance swept to victory over Johnston, a Davis backer.[28]

Doubts about North Carolina's Confederate loyalty increased the following summer when a peace movement gained momentum across the state after Southern defeats at Gettysburg and Vicksburg. Citizens in forty North Carolina counties held public meetings criticizing the war, and concern mounted in both Raleigh and Richmond that the burgeoning unrest might lead to a statewide convention seeking North Carolina's withdrawal from the Confederacy. Holden and the *Standard* publicized and encouraged these meetings, leading to a bitter feud and eventual split with his former ally, Vance. Violence ensued. A passing Georgia regiment demolished the *Standard*'s office in Raleigh. In retaliation, Holden's supporters ransacked offices of the *State Journal*, an opposing newspaper.[29]

In 1864, Holden ran for governor as the Peace Party candidate, the main opposition to his former protégé. While Vance strongly disagreed with many national Confederate policies, he steadfastly urged North Carolinians to remain true to Southern independence. The wartime governor never doubted the legality of secession, only its wisdom, but once committed, despite numerous clashes with the Confederate president, Vance never wavered in supporting the Southern cause. "Fight the Yankees and fuss with the Confederacy," the governor repeatedly urged. Tarheels apparently agreed, re-electing Vance by more than a 4 to 1 margin.[30]

While Confederate leaders fretted over North Carolina's acrimonious debates, officials in Washington, D. C., noted the tensions as well. Federal strategists crafted plans to use the southern Appalachian Mountains with its largely Unionist population as an invasion corridor, an idea abandoned in part due to logistical difficulties. Military incursions into the state's northeastern quadrant by General Ambrose Burnside in 1861–62, however, the war's first major Federal offensive, led to the fall of Forts Ocracoke and Hatteras, the seizing of Roanoke Island, and Union control of the Pamlico Sound. New Bern, Plymouth, and Washington (N.C.) fell in rapid succession before the bulk of Burnside's forces were withdrawn to reinforce Federal armies near Richmond. But northeastern North Carolina, despite intermittent attempts to dislodge Northern troops, remained firmly under Union control for the war's duration.

The state was spared from the most intense fighting during the ensuing two-and-one-half years, but as the Confederacy began to crumble, Tarheels' early equivocation likely worked to their advantage. General William Tecumseh Sherman, marching north in 1865 after laying waste to wide swaths of Georgia and South Carolina, moderated tactics as his army moved into North Carolina. Though Yankee foragers, often called "bummers," seized food and feed for Sherman's army and its animals, and portions of downtown Fayetteville including its Confederate arsenal were burned, the wanton destruction doled out as retribution farther south largely ceased. Raleigh and much of eastern North Carolina were spared, and when surrender came near Durham in late April, the general's original terms were so lenient as to be rejected by superiors in Washington.

Wartime bickering among North Carolinians helped shape the state's commemorative response. So too would the fact that North Carolina did not have a Lee, a Jackson, a Davis, a Wade Hampton, or a Nathan Bedford Forrest to lionize after the war. Few Confederate officials hailed from the state. North Carolina could claim Zebulon Vance, the popular wartime governor; a handful of highly capable yet only regionally known generals, many of whom were cut down in battle; and 125,000 men who had fought for the Confederacy, many participating in the conflict's bloodiest battles.

Colonel W. B. Creasman. Bethel Baptist Church Cemetery, Buncombe County. This heavily-stained memorial was originally sited in front of the Buncombe County courthouse. Unveiled Monumental Day, 1905.

As Governor Glenn addressed the courthouse crowd in Asheville on Monumental Day, Vance had been twice honored with memorials. A seventy-five-foot-tall obelisk dedicated on May 10, 1898, rose in Pack Square, while a larger-than-life bronze, erected in 1900, stood beside the state Capitol in Raleigh.

But for most North Carolinians, the Confederate dead, and later the "men who wore the gray," were those to be honored. With the exception of memorials to Vance and a few smaller installations — Asheville's monuments to Clingman and Creasman which were later moved; a drinking fountain honoring Orren Randolph Smith, designer of the first Confederate national flag, in Louisburg; a plaque to General Junius Daniel in Halifax; and a 1911 statue in downtown Wilmington of Confederate Attorney General George Davis — the state's civic-space monumental tradition remained steadfastly egalitarian.[31]

This honoring of the "common

soldier" includes two works dedicated to Henry Lawson Wyatt, the Edgecombe County private killed in action on June 10, 1861—North Carolina's "First at Bethel." On August 3, 1910, the Dixie-Lee Chapter, Children of the Confederacy, a youth group affiliated with the United Daughters of the Confederacy, dedicated an ornate lighted fountain surrounded with a decorative wrought-iron fence on Tarboro's village green, not far from Edgecombe County's Confederate soldier statue. Two years later, on the fifty-first anniversary of Wyatt's death, a life-size bronze funded by the North Carolina U.D.C. was unveiled on the state Capitol grounds.

Raleigh's Wyatt memorial, sculpted by Gutzon Borglum, carver of Mt. Rushmore's presidential likenesses, and cast by the Gorham Manufacturing Company, producer of elegant silver and a leading fine-arts bronze fabricator, is one of North Carolina's most artistically accomplished Confederate commemorations. In addition to honoring a single individual, the memorial symbolically represents the Confederate private, the state's dead, as well as answering criticisms about North Carolina's war record. Wyatt's place in Tarheel Confederate memory is hard to overestimate; one proposal, published in 1892, called for the state Confederate monument to consist of "a shaft composed of 96 blocks of granite, one for each county [at that time]," and to be topped with "a bronze statue of Henry Lawson Wyatt, the first Confederate killed in State services."[32]

That a private killed in action would be among the few Confederates honored with name-specific civic-space memorials reveals how North Carolinians chose to remember the four-year-long struggle. The private, the common soldier, the war's dead, the local company, these were the men to be honored.

As a new generation of North Carolinians assumed commemorative leadership early in the twentieth century, memorialization evolved to include not only the dead but all Confederate veterans. Communal acts, however, not individual bravery, were most celebrated, however, and North Carolinians refined six claims — most of which entail loss — into the state's "Rebel Boast."[33]

The two earliest and most widely quoted statements, "First at Bethel; Last at Appomattox," are prominently inscribed on the back panel of the state monument erected on the Capitol grounds in 1895. "First at Bethel" refers not only to Private Wyatt's death, considered for more than a century as the earliest Confederate battlefield fatality, but also to North Carolina's prominent role in that victory, furnishing 800 of the 1,200 Southern troops engaged. "Last at Appomattox," recalls the final assaults by units of the Army of Northern Virginia, operations led by three North Carolina generals and carried out largely by Tarheel troops.[34]

"Farthest to the front at Gettysburg and Chickamauga," are the next most cited claims, inserted between the Bethel and Appomattox assertions. The four statements were boldly imprinted in 1901 onto the cover of the state-published *Histories of the Several Regiments and Battalions from North Carolina in the Great War 1861–'65*, cited into Asheville's 1905 courthouse-grounds monument, and repeated in countless Memorial Day orations and monument dedications throughout the state.

But the Gettysburg declaration challenged one of Virginia's most cherished claims, that its soldiers reached the Confederacy's "High-Water Mark," briefly cracking Union defenses during Pickett's Charge. Virginians led by General Lewis A. Armistead did breach Northern lines at a salient known as "The Angle," but to the Virginians' left, Tarheel regiments (and units from Mississippi) led by North Carolina General James Johnston Pettigrew, advanced farther east, literally "farther to the front," crossing eighty additional yards of exposed ground before being stopped at the base of a rock wall. While the dispute may seem academic today, North Carolina's claim, and the resulting controversy became a critical part of the state's early twentieth-century commemorative milieu.[35]

"Farthest at Chickamauga" is less controversial and frequently, though not invariably, accompanies North Carolina's Gettysburg claim. Twice on September 20, Tarheel units — the Sixtieth at noon and the Fifty-eighth Regiment later that day — held the most forward positions. Unlike Gettysburg, however, Chickamauga was a tactical Confederate victory, yet one in which the advantage was not exploited.

The final two North Carolina claims, supplying the most troops of any Southern state and suffering the highest number of dead, were well-known. The state's wartime "military population"—"all white males between the ages of 18 and 45 without regard to any physical or mental infirmity or religious scruples,"— numbered 115,369, yet the state, aided by enlistments outside this age range, enrolled 125,000 soldiers. Aspersions, however, were cast upon these men. The perceived shakiness of North Carolina's political commitment as well as its lack of high-ranking generals led to disparagement of Tarheel resolve and ability. A high "desertion" rate, often little more than temporary unauthorized absences for farming or family matters, added concerns as to soldiers' reliability.[36]

That North Carolina would need to defend its Confederate credentials, even after the collapse of the Southern nation, reflects the region's intense wartime political discourse as well as rampant second-guessing after Appomattox. Controversy and intrigue had been rife throughout the Confederate political and military hierarchies, and post-war historians vied to shift blame while rationalizing defeat. Such treatises revealed denial, anger and rationalization — stages of grief set to words — even while promoting specific locales as worthy partners in a violently re-forged United States.

In 1903, however, Judge George L. Christian, "surprised the country by questioning the claims made by North Carolina as to her record in the War for Southern Independence," according to a North Carolina Historical Commission report issued the following year. The Virginia judge not only challenged the "Rebel Boast," but did so in front of the Grand Camp of the Virginia Confederate Veterans, one of the South's most prominent veterans' groups, then detailed his charges in a pamphlet issued by the United Confederate Veterans of Virginia.

North Carolinians responded swiftly. On November 12, 1903, the State Literary and Historical Association adopted a resolution by J. Bryan Grimes, North Carolina's Secretary of State and son of the Confederate Major-General who had led the final Southern charge at Appomattox, naming seven "gentlemen" to "investigate and report upon the accuracy of North Carolina's claim as to the number of troops furnished by this state to the Confederacy and upon the merits of our claims as to 'First at Bethel, Farthest at Gettysburg and Chickamauga, Last at Appomattox.'"[37]

The "gentlemen" were Confederate veterans and some of North Carolina's most prominent citizens. Walter Clark was Chief Justice of the state Supreme Court and a noted Civil War historian; Samuel A. Ashe, former editor of the (Raleigh) *News and Observer*, was a prolific author and successful businessman; Walter A. Montgomery sat as associate justice on North Carolina's Supreme Court; William R. Bond, author, had written *Pickett or Pettigrew* (1888), supporting North Carolina's claims at Gettysburg; Edward J. Hale, editor and publisher of the *Fayetteville Observer*, had served as U.S. consul in England; A. C.

Avery, former state supreme court justice, had been dean of Trinity College (now Duke University) Law School; and Henry A. London, long-time editor of the *Chatham Record*, was president pro-tem of the North Carolina Senate.[38]

Not surprisingly, the panel found North Carolina's claims valid. Their report, *Five Points in the Record of North Carolina in the Great War of 1861–5*, maintains, "These claims were not made as a matter of boast. They were merely a statement of historical facts, amply supported.... There was no intention to assert that the soldiers from North Carolina were braver than those from our sister Southern States, but merely that the fortune of war having furnished them the occasion they were *equal to the opportunity*—only this, and nothing more [italics in original]."[39]

Beyond defending six assertions, this report provides insight, perhaps better than any other document, as to how North Carolina's leaders viewed Confederate commemoration nearly four decades after Appomattox: "But it is not to her generals and lesser officers, capable and faithful as they were, that North Carolina should turn with her greatest pride. With tacit recognition of this truth, the State has appropriately crowned the Monument raised to her gallant dead with the statue of

A PRIVATE SOLDIER

with belted cartridge box, and his faithful musket in hand, *on guard*, scanning the horizon, as in life, with ceaseless watching for the foe [italics in original]." Written by six former Confederate officers and one private, the report continues, "and North Carolina owes no greater debt than to the unshaken fidelity of him whose highest honor is that he was a North Carolina *Private Soldier* [italics in original]."[40]

7. The Daughters

On October 29, 1904, Judge Henry Clay Bourne, former colonel of the Sixth Mississippi Regiment, addressed two thousand people gathered on the town common in Tarboro, North Carolina. Described as a "silver-tongued orator" by the *Tarborough Southerner*, Bourne, according to the paper, had labored "in season and out ... to have this memorial crown the efforts of the Daughters of the Confederacy." The judge's "zeal," the report continued, resulted not only "because of the cause, but accentuated and stimulated because the good, true, loyal, and patriotic woman, who blesses him as a wife, was the leader of a devoted band of women who had made up their minds that the Edgecombe soldier should have an enduring memorial."[1]

This "devoted band," the William Dorsey Pender Chapter of the recently formed United Daughters of the Confederacy, made surprisingly quick work of erecting a monument. More than three dozen U.D.C. chapters had already formed across North Carolina when, in February 1903, Tarboro's women organized an affiliate named for Confederate Major-General William Dorsey Pender, an Edgecombe County native mortally wounded at Gettysburg. The nascent chapter "appealed to the public" for financial support in erecting a monument then worked "zealously," according to the *Southerner*, to complete the memorial, the second Tarheel civic-space commemoration largely sponsored by the fledgling U.D.C.[2]

Just thirteen months after the chapter's formation, Judge Bourne was finalizing construction details with the Cockade Marble Works of Petersburg, Virginia, "Manufacturers of Marble and Granite Monuments Crosses, Tombs and Grave Stones of every description," according to the firm's letterhead. Cockade's owner, Charles M. Walsh, writing to Bourne on March 22, 1904, promised to "put in foundation of the Soldiers Monument [sic]" before May 10, "as the Ladies would want the corner stone of their monument put in place at that time."[3]

That placement ceremony, part of Tarboro's 1904 Memorial Day activities, was an elaborate event, with many of the embellishments of a monument dedication. Members of ten Masonic lodges "formed in procession" then "proceeded to the Court House," according to an undated *Southerner* report citing Masonic records. The Daughters joined the men at the courthouse then, "headed by a band of music" and "under escort of the Edgecombe Guards," the group proceeded to the town common, a blocks-long undeveloped area filled with stately oaks, where the "foundation ... had been prepared."[4]

Judge Bourne presided over the ceremony. A "Selection by the Band" and a prayer by

7. The Daughters

Edgecombe County Confederate monument. Tarboro, 1904. Dedicated October 29, 1904, on Tarboro's village green.

W. Alexander opened the event. Mayor R. G. Allsbrook delivered the welcoming address followed by a response from Masonic Grand Master Francis D. Winston. Then, "according to the ancient usages of the Craft," the cornerstone of the Confederate monument was set.[5]

Tarboro's Daughters placed a number of commemorative keepsakes, probably enclosed within a metal container, in or near the cornerstone. Items were carefully documented: photographs of Jefferson Davis, Robert E. Lee, and General Pender; "sketch[es] of life" of Pender and Henry T. Clark, North Carolina's early wartime governor (1861–1862) and father-in-law of Judge Bourne; the "Edgecombe Muster Roll CSA"; a Confederate flag; Confederate money; a "North Carolina Greenback"; the constitution of the W. D. Pender Chapter, U.D.C., as well as its first annual report and an "Autograph list" of members; membership rolls of the Lewis-Dowd-Wyatt Camp (United Confederate Veterans), Edgecombe Guards, and Concord Masonic Lodge; two local newspapers; and an "original Poem to Confederate dead by Miss Mary Groome."[6]

Following the ceremony, participants proceeded "in a body to the Town Hall" where Tarboro's remaining Memorial Day activities would be held: an address by the Honorable Claude Kitchen; presentation of U.D.C. Crosses of Honor to Confederate veterans; "The Old North State," sung by the chorus; and "Dixie," played by the band.[7]

Five months later, Edgecombe County's monument was nearly ready. On October 13, the *Southerner* reported "An unusually interesting meeting of the Daughter's of the Confederacy [sic] ... at the residence of Mrs. H. C. Bourne, President of the Chapter." There was "a goodly attendance of members, and some invited guests," to hear "two very interesting well-prepared and admirable sketches" of "distinguished sons of Edgecombe County." In addition, "Plans for the unveiling of the monument on October 29th were perfected."[8]

Perhaps the rapidity and relative ease of raising a monument to the soldiers, not just the Confederate dead, of Edgecombe County should not be surprising. The state's early-wartime governor, assuming power after the sudden death of Governor John Ellis (1859–1861), had been an Edgecombe resident; William Dorsey Pender, one of North Carolina's six Confederate major-generals, was a county native; and Henry Lawson Wyatt, widely considered the Confederacy's first soldier killed in action, had enlisted as a member of the Edgecombe Guards. Tarboro, meanwhile, early in the twentieth century, was a prosperous county seat, located in a rich agricultural region along the Tar River.

Yet the Daughters' efforts could provoke controversy. On October 27, two days before the unveiling, the *Southerner* denounced the anticipated cutting of "magnificent oak[s]" to make room for the monument. Headlined "Spare the Trees," the article related how former commissioners had granted the Daughters "authority to cut down trees, not more than four, if they interfered with the monument." But the newspaper urged Mayor Allsbrook and the new commissioners to rescind permission, "before a single tree is sacrificed," urging instead the removal of "one or two over-hanging limbs" and a "solemn agreement with the U.D.C." that the town would "keep the monument clean of stains which may come from the trees."[9]

Two columns to the left of this plea, the *Southerner* detailed the unveiling itinerary. At 11 A.M. on October 29, a "grand and inspiring procession led by a platoon of police," would "move up Main st. [sic] to the town common." The Tarboro band would follow the police, leading the "Edgecombe Guards, Gov. Aycock and staff, Major-General Julian S. Carr and escort, [and] Distinguished visitors." The mayor, county commissioners, Confederate veterans, the Daughters, and "Schools" came next, followed by "Masons, Odd Fellows, Knights of Pythias, Hook & Ladder Co." and lastly the "Public."[10]

"A gentle rain fell in the early morning [dedication day], laying all dust," the weekly paper reported on November 3. However, "Bright bracing sun shot air" followed, and "All Nature smiled." "Two thousand or more people" attended, and "Every section of the county was well represented," the *Southerner* boasted. Confederate veterans, "120 strong," came as did "about 250 school children dressed in white and red," colors of both the U.D.C. and the former Confederacy.[11]

When the procession reached the veiled monument, the band struck up "Dixie" and the "old Vets gave the Rebel yell." An "eloquent" prayer, delivered with "fervor and impressiveness," opened the formal ceremony. "Nearer My God to Thee," performed by the choir and band, and an "Address of Welcome" followed. Then, in contrast with most dedications, the monument was unveiled prior to the day's featured speeches.[12]

Katherine Wimberly Bourne and William Dorsey Pender, Jr., children from socially prominent Edgecombe County families, had been selected to unshroud the memorial. "Pretty piquant little" Miss Bourne was "a granddaughter of North Carolina's first War Governor, H. T. Clark of this county," the *Southerner* reported, and daughter of Judge Bourne and Maria Toole Bourne, U.D.C. chapter president; Master Pender was "the grandson of Gen. William Dorsey Pender, Lee's right arm, for whom the local Chapter of the U.D.C. is named."[13]

In front of notable attendees including Bishop Cheshire of Raleigh, former Governor T. J. Jarvis (1879–1885) of Greenville, Confederate Brigadier-General William R. Cox of Penelo, and "Mrs. General Pender," the "charming devoted widow of the gallant Pender," the children released the cords, and the "veil in twain." The Edgecombe Guards "fired three salutes, whose salvos could be heard beyond the township"; the band played "Praise God From Whom All Blessings Flow"; while "the stately oaks that have kept guard in the commons for centuries seemed to bow in unison," to the "full notes of the Gregorian chant."[14]

"A Disgraceful Act." Edgecombe County Confederate monument. In 1906, a member of the Edgecombe Guards firing a Memorial Day salute "slipped in a ball cartridge and aimed at the figure of a soldier which surmounts this monument and struck it." A $5 reward was offered by the *Tarborough Southerner* to "ascertain who fired that shot" and make "the scamp ... feel the heavy hand of the law," although it is uncertain if the culprit was ever identified.

Judge Bourne spoke next, "presenting" the monument on behalf of the Daughters. Major-General Julian S. Carr, a wartime Confederate private whose lofty title reflected a leading role in the United Confederate Veterans, delivered the day's featured oration. Governor Aycock, surprisingly, did not speak and, according to both the elaborate hand-bound souvenir program produced by the Daughters and the *Southerner's* printed itinerary, had no scheduled role in the formal ceremony. Yet Aycock's planned participation in the procession marked one of the earliest appearances by a Tarheel chief executive at a county dedication-day event.[15]

After the speeches and benediction, "Dixie" again "stirred the audience to enthusiasm," the *Southerner* reported, "and all dispersed, rejoiced [sic] that Edgecombe, through its good women ... had at last, in enduring granite, and everlasting bronze, told the generations to come that this county is proud of her sons."[16]

Yet Edgecombe's monument was incomplete. Despite the *Southerner's* description of a "stately shaft ... surmounted by a bronze figure of a Confederate soldier, seven feet tall," the statue, manufactured by the American Bronze Foundry of Chicago, Illinois, had not reached Tarboro in time for the dedication. One week later, a single-paragraph notation reported that the statue "has at last arrived and been placed in position." The *Southerner* tendered its approval: "The appearance of the completed monument is much better. The figure of the Confederate soldier adds greatly to the appearance and gives the whole proper proportions."[17]

Thirty years after Appomattox, North Carolina's Ladies' Memorial Associations could look with pride at their commemorative accomplishments. The Confederate dead had been buried and a robust memorial tradition established. Nearly a dozen monuments, most funded by the Ladies, marked massed soldier burials across eastern and central North Carolina. And Confederate commemoration had expanded to the state's civic spaces, most notably with the 1895 unveiling of the towering granite shaft beside the state Capitol in Raleigh.

While monument building had yet to commence across western North Carolina (Chapters 4 and 5), commemorative efforts by the LMAs across the central and eastern regions of the state appeared to be stalling as the nineteenth century drew to a close. Seven Confederate monuments, including at least four primarily funded by the Ladies, had been raised during the 1880s; during the next decade only five would be dedicated, with just one largely funded by women. Men and women of the "sixties"— survivors who had experienced the Civil War as adults — were growing old. One-half of all Confederate veterans had died by 1890, while most commemorative leaders, many of whom had been Southern officers or their wives and widows, were in their sixties or seventies, explaining, in part, the slackening of Tarheel monument building.[18]

The commemorative milieu was also changing. Harsh post-war attitudes — threatening to throw Southern corpses "in the public road," for example, and labeling Confederate burials as "dishonored graves"— were yielding to sectional reconciliation. Led by Union and Confederate veterans as well as businessmen from both sides of the Mason–Dixon Line, a once-severed nation, reunited through force, sought healing, a process exemplified by "Blue-Gray Reunions," two dozen of which were held between 1881 and 1887 with larger extravaganzas to follow.[19]

Demographic and economic changes also marked North Carolina's post-war recovery. Despite remaining overwhelmingly agrarian and one of the nation's poorest states well into the twentieth century, new factories and mills — producing textiles, furniture, and tobacco products — accelerated growth of North Carolina's cash economy as well as its urbanization, trends that laid the foundation for an expanded Confederate commemoration as a new century dawned. In 1870, only Wilmington had a population exceeding 10,000; by 1900, Charlotte, Asheville, Winston, Raleigh, and Greensboro also claimed as many citizens. Six Tarheel towns had between five- and ten-thousand residents, while fifty-two others numbered between one- and five-thousand, resulting in numerous population centers capable of funding Confederate commemorations.[20]

As national attitudes softened and the region's economy improved, new organizations brought tens of thousands of Southerners together in powerful fraternal and social groups. While none of these organizations were chartered exclusively as memorial groups, two would profoundly influence Confederate commemoration.

The United Confederate Veterans (U. C. V.), founded in New Orleans in 1889, led the way. In contrast with earlier Southern veterans' groups, which often limited membership by rank or unit, the U. C. V. was open to all "Confederate veterans, soldiers, and sailors." The men organized with a military hierarchy: a national headquarters; three departments; smaller divisions; and local "Camps." Officials received commissioned titles regardless of wartime rank, leading, in the twentieth century, to former Confederate privates, including North Carolina's Julian Carr, becoming "majors" and "generals."[21]

In addition to being a "general federation" of veterans, the U. C. V., according to founding documents, was to "gather authentic data for an impartial history ... preserve the relics or memories ... cherish the ties of friendship ... care for the disabled ... protect the widow and orphan ... and preserve the record of the services of every member," including those "who have preceded us in eternity." Southern veterans eagerly joined. At its zenith, membership totaled nearly 160,000 men, organized into 1,885 camps.[22]

In North Carolina, the U. C.V. and other veterans played a secondary, although underestimated role in the physical commemoration of the Confederacy. Camps and affiliated veterans sponsored a handful of Tarheel monuments, including those in Bertie (Windsor, 1896) and Macon (Franklin, 1909) Counties. In addition, mixed-gender organizations led by veterans, such as the Tyrrell Monument Association (Columbia, 1902) funded memorials, as did individual soldiers. In all, approximately one dozen of North Carolina's seventy-five Confederate monuments erected between 1896 and 1932 were financed by men.

Tarheel Confederate commemoration, however, would largely remain under the control of women. By side-stepping direct involvement, veterans not only avoided accusations of self-aggrandizement, but enhanced the perception of broad-based commemorative support, furthering a memorial's power to define collective memory. The Ladies' Memorial Associations had effectively forged a Confederate memorial tradition. A new group of younger women would now emerge to revitalize and expand that effort.

Witnessing the popularity and success of the United Confederate Veterans, female commemorative leaders sought a similar women's organization. LMAs had remained independent associations throughout the nineteenth century, and although personal communication among leaders was common, no national organization brought the Ladies together.[23]

Caroline Meriwether Goodlet (1833–1914) and Anna Davenport Raines (1853–1915) were among the women who envisioned a more unified group. Although of different generations and separated by five-hundred miles, the women discussed a potential new organization through a brisk correspondence in the spring of 1894. Both women had significant commemorative experience. Goodlet, of Nashville, Tennessee, was a "woman of the sixties," had a brother slain in battle, and assisted Confederate troops through a wartime soldiers' aid society. After Appomattox, Goodlet helped found Nashville's Monument Association then, following the group's reorganization, served as president in 1890.[24]

Anna Raines, twenty years younger, typified a rising generation of Southern women. Born in 1853, Raines experienced the war as a child, but Reconstruction and post-war devastation likely shaped her generation's attitudes as much or more than the conflict itself. By the age of forty, this Confederate officer's daughter was prominent in Savannah, Georgia's, commemorative community, serving as secretary of the Ladies Auxiliary to the Confederate Veterans' Association.[25]

Chowan County Confederate monument. Edenton, 1904. One of North Carolina's earliest U.D.C.-sponsored monuments, this commemoration was originally in front of the courthouse but later relocated downtown.

On September 10, 1894, Goodlet, Raines, and other invited female leaders met in Nashville at the headquarters of the Frank Cheatham Bivouac, that city's most influential U. C. V. camp. There the women formed the National Association of the Daughters of the Confederacy, an organization "national in its scope," with authority to "charter sub-organizations in all parts of the United States." Membership would be restricted, however, to female descendants of men who had honorably served in the Confederate army or navy. And to maintain an elite status, any woman, regardless of Confederate credentials, could be summarily denied membership through three no votes — "black balls" — cast by local members.[26]

At the meeting, the National Daughters adopted a constitution and organizational structure similar to that of the United Confederate Veterans. Instead of the men's "camps," the Daughters would meet in "chapters." The soldiers' "departments" would be replaced by statewide "divisions," while powerful central leadership would guide each group. The Daugh-

Robeson County Confederate monument. Lumberton. Erected by the Robeson Chapter, United Daughters of the Confederacy. Dedicated May 10, 1907.

ters, like the Veterans, adopted broad-based objectives. Although recognized today as builders of hundreds of civic-space Confederate monuments, the founding women established five primary aims — memorial, historical, benevolent, educational, and social — considering it their duty "to instruct and instill into the descendants of the people of the South a proper respect for ... the deeds of their forefathers."[27]

Caroline Goodlet was elected to lead the new group; Anna Raines was chosen first vice president. Like many organizations, however, internal disputes ensued. Eliza Parsley, of Wilmington, founder of North Carolina's first chapter and the state division's first president, urged increased autonomy for both former LMAs as well as state divisions, reflecting, in part, her belief in states' rights. Parsley, and others, also sought more-inclusive membership criteria, including women who "endured the war themselves" as well as "daughters of men undoubtedly loyal to the Southern Cause but [for] one reason or another were not in active service."[28]

In November 1895, the Daughters met again, adopting a new name—the United Daughters of the Confederacy (U.D.C.)—and amending the group's constitution. Acknowledging that women had shared similarly in the "dangers, sufferings, and privations" of the war years, according to convention minutes, the Daughters elevated the status of "women of the sixties" to that accorded Confederate soldiers and sailors; U.D.C. membership was now based on *either* male or female Confederate ancestry. The organization's historical mandate was similarly expanded to "record the part taken by Southern women," as well as the deeds of Confederate men, themes that would be reflected in Tarheel monument inscriptions.[29]

Formation of the Daughters and the United Confederate Veterans was but one change transforming the Southern commemorative milieu as the nineteenth century drew to a close. Political rapprochement, economic gains, and a widely read regional publication helped accelerate Confederate commemoration as well. As early as 1887, former Confederate General and U. C. V. Commander John B. Gordon longed "to see one more war, that we [Confederate veterans] might march under the stars and stripes, shoulder to shoulder, against a common foe." In 1898, Gordon and his fellow veterans received such an opportunity when the United States declared war on Spain, a conflict widely supported across the South.[30]

Entire U. C. V. camps volunteered to fight for the reunited nation. Former Confederate troops and their sons marched with one-time adversaries, while at least three ex–Confederate generals — including Fitzhugh Lee, nephew of Robert E. Lee, and Joseph Wheeler, Theodore Roosevelt's superior at San Juan Hill — commanded American troops.[31]

A national consensus acknowledging Southern loyalty emerged after the quick military victory. Long-sought political concessions followed. Captured Confederate battle flags were repatriated to Southern states, an idea that generated a political firestorm when proposed by President Grover Cleveland in 1887 yet passed unanimously by Congress in 1905. Federal funds to care for Confederate graves near wartime hospitals and prisons across the North were approved the following year providing, four decades after Appomattox, the respectability for the Confederate dead that Southerners craved.[32]

In January 1893, another key to expanding commemoration began with publication of the *Confederate Veteran*. The *Veteran*, as it was commonly known, would chronicle activities of the U. C. V. and U.D.C., print wartime recollections, list obituaries, serve as a forum for commemorative ideas, and showcase completed Confederate monuments. Owner and proprietor Sumner Archibald Cunningham, a veteran himself, outlined the publication's mission in the initial issue, "an organ of communication between Confederate soldiers and those who are interested in them and their affairs."[33]

7. *The Daughters*

Rutherford County Confederate monument. Rutherfordton. Erected by the Davis-Dickerson-Mills Chapter, United Daughters of the Confederacy. Dedicated November 12, 1910.

Born in 1843, Cunningham served as sergeant in Company B, Forty-first Tennessee Infantry. He was captured at Fort Donelson then exchanged at Vicksburg before fighting at Chickamauga, Atlanta, Franklin, and Nashville. Although "a man of no more than average intellect," according to the Tennessee Division, Sons of Confederate Veterans, Cunningham nevertheless "spoke loudly to thousands of Southern men and women who survived and adapted" to the war and its aftermath.[34]

Yet Cunningham, while loving the South "passionately with every fiber of his being," according to Dr. James I. Vance, was not a Confederate zealot. The *Veteran's* 1893 mission statement included the goal of "be[ing] acceptable to the public, even to those who fought on the other side." The following year, Cunningham expanded that theme, writing that "Confederate veterans have a thoroughly fraternal regard for the men who fought us only to maintain the Union, and we would gladly co-operate with them for the common good of our great country."[35]

Such conciliatory prose must have accurately reflected Southern sentiment. By 1896, three years after commencing publication, the *Veteran* proclaimed on its masthead to be the "Official Organ of the United Confederate Veterans, United Daughters of the Confederacy, Sons of Veterans and other Organizations." Readership soared. Despite an 1894 price doubling to ten cents per issue or one dollar annually, paid "in advance," a cost that remained unchanged for nearly three decades, circulation increased from 79,430 in 1893 to 154,992 in 1895, numbers touted on the cover. The *Veteran* became one of the South's most widely read magazines, and Cunningham, who continued as editor until his death in 1913, was one of the region's most influential commemorative voices.[36]

Forces that would expand Confederate memorialization—powerful veterans' and women's groups, increasing national acceptance, economic gains, and a regional voice to disseminate news and ideas—were in place by the turn of the century. Yet the form that this commemoration would take, or if it would prominently feature monuments, was uncertain as three demographic groups, each with differing perspectives of the war and multiple objectives, advanced varying visions of Confederate memory.

The aging women of the Ladies' Memorial Associations remained a powerful commemorative force. Monument erection, however, had been of secondary importance to these women; properly burying the Confederate dead and establishing a Memorial Day tradition had been their foremost desire. Building on their roles in wartime Soldier Aid Societies, these Ladies also assisted disabled and destitute veterans as well as Confederate widows and orphans, providing charity and lobbying for increased public monies. Efforts by the Wake County LMA and Tarheel veterans, for instance, led in 1891 to the establishment of the state-supported Confederate Soldiers Home in Raleigh.[37]

Memorial activities of the LMAs, reflecting attitudes of most nineteenth-century North Carolinians, honored, even venerated, the Confederate dead, men they had known as fathers, brothers, sons, and neighbors. By the 1890s, however, many Tarheels were too young to have personally known these slain soldiers. Major W. M. Robbins, reminded a crowd of 8,000 people gathered for the 1892 dedication of Cabarrus County's (Concord) monument to the Confederate dead that "a generation has grown up since the war and that the majority of persons now living have no knowledge, derived from memory or experience, of the events of those stirring times."[38]

In this evolving milieu, the United Confederate Veterans and the United Daughters of the Confederacy promoted varied perspectives as each struggled to realize multiple objectives. The veterans focused on historical and collegial aims. Regimental histories, muster rolls, first-person accounts, and defense of actions—personal, state, and regional—were penned as the "thinning gray line" recorded their version of history. Tarheel monuments raised by these men reflect similar themes: honoring Southern survivors as well as the dead; enumerating military units; citing battles; and explaining state and regional acts through some of the most spirited inscriptions on North Carolina Confederate monuments (Chapter 12).[39]

The Daughters, meanwhile, added another perspective. Wartime events and the valor of Southern troops, for this younger generation, were learned largely through oral accounts by surviving veterans and women of the sixties. While honoring the Confederate dead remained a noble act, acknowledging the role of surviving soldiers and war-era women who had shaped these younger people's lives likely had greater personal relevance.

U.D.C. chapters, however, had to set funding priorities. Veterans, widows, and orphans required assistance; future generations needed to learn the "true" history of the conflict; and memorial traditions had to be nurtured as the war generation passed on, leaving the Daughters as the primary Confederate heritage organization. While monument building was a focus of many chapters, it was not a universal priority. Of North Carolina's first sixty-six Daughters' chapters, all chartered by 1904, fewer than half completed a monument by 1917, including units based in the county seats of Martin (Williamston), Duplin (Kenansville), Wayne (Goldsboro) Craven (New Bern), and Guilford (Greensboro) Counties.[40]

Hertford County Confederate monument. Winton. Erected by the Hertford County Chapter, United Daughters of the Confederacy. September 25, 1913.

One hundred eighty-eight North Carolina U.D.C. chapters ultimately formed, and with local control as advocated by Mrs. Parsley, each selected projects to champion. Minutes of the Winnie Davis Chapter of Pittsboro (Chatham County), women who successfully raised a courthouse-lawn monument in 1907, reveal one group's activities and expenditures: "Coming to Soldiers' Home [with] Fruit for Veterans," $10.00; two "prizes," likely awarded for essays, $6.00; "Blankets sent to Robert Burns," $3.00; "Fruit sent to veterans," $3.00; "Arlington [monument]," $5.00; "Crosses [of] Honor," $5.40; "Scholarship," $3.00; and "[General Matthew] Ransom portrait," $1.00. Pittsboro's Daughters also provided a "Box" for two needy brothers, "Gave prizes" in the courthouse on Jefferson Davis' birthday, and ceremoniously presented pictures of the Confederate president, and of General Robert E. Lee, to the local school.[41]

Although the nearly $1,700.00 cost of Chatham's monument dwarfed other outlays, Pittsboro's Daughters appeared especially supportive of the state Soldiers' Home, the facility opened through efforts of the Wake County LMA in 1891. In addition to gifts and visiting "inmates," as the residents were officially termed, the women, one month after unveiling their monument, decided to "make a quilt for our room at Soldiers Home [sic] and stripe it with the red streamers that the monument was unveiled with," the minutes report, a proposal "received joyously for we knew we would have a fine time making that quilt."[42]

Care of elderly and infirm Confederates was a state division priority as well. Beginning in 1908, North Carolina's Daughters, in addition to aiding the veterans' institution, lobbied for a similar women's facility. Seven years later, the Confederate Women's Home opened in Fayetteville, the third such state-supported facility in the former Confederacy. Administered largely through the state U.D.C., the Home housed needy wives, widows, and daughters — aged sixty-five and older — of Confederate veterans until 1981.[43]

The national organization, meanwhile, sought to honor all Confederate soldiers with

Union County Confederate monument. Monroe. A polished sphere tops this memorial, erected by the Monroe Chapter, United Daughters of the Confederacy. Dedicated July 4, 1910.

the Southern Cross of Honor, a military-style decoration awarded for "loyal, honorable service to the South." Introduced in 1898 through the efforts of Mrs. Alexander S. Erwin of Athens, Georgia, the medal, a Maltese cross adapted from a design approved by the Confederate Congress in 1862, features the Southern nation's motto, "Deo Vindice" (God our Vindicator) above "1861–1865." A laurel wreath and "Southern Cross of Honor" complete the obverse, while the Confederate battle flag and "United Daughters Confederacy to the U. C. V." fill the back.[44]

This civilian decoration proved a success with veterans. Twelve thousand five hundred Crosses were awarded within eighteen months, and presentation of these medals became a celebrated part of many early twentieth-century monument dedications. To preserve the award's integrity, the U.D.C. required an arduous application process and maintained meticulous records, administered personally by co-founder Anna Davenport Raines for seven years. Yet by 1913, a total of 78,761 medals, sequentially numbered, had been bestowed.[45]

While honoring and aiding the war generation, Daughters also sought to instill pride of Confederate heritage in future citizens. Monument-building was but one facet of this effort; less-tangible forms of instructing the young—heritage groups, "correct" histories, and educational assistance—might be even more effective. Children could become "living monuments," many Daughters believed, defending the "sacred principles" for which Southerners had fought. To attain these goals, chapters sponsored Confederate-themed essay contests and provided stipends to deserving students while U.D.C. leadership advocated for "correct" textbook histories of the South.[46]

Within two years of their founding, the Daughters formed an affiliate for school-aged boys and girls, the Children of the Confederacy (C. O. C.). Beginning with a single Virginia

To Beaufort County's defenders. Manufactured by the Mutual Machine Company, this white metal plaque was erected in 1905 by the Children of the Confederacy in Washington's Oakdale Cemetery.

A "Children's" monument. Lincolnton. This commemorative drinking fountain in front of the Lincoln County courthouse was sponsored by the Wallace Reinhardt Chapter, Children of the Confederacy, a U.D.C.–sponsored affiliate. Mrs. "Stonewall" Jackson attended the 1911 unveiling.

unit in 1896, the Children received tutelage from sponsoring U.D.C. chapters and often took part in memorial and dedication-day events.

Two Tarheel Children's chapters are credited with raising Confederate monuments of their own. On May 10, 1905, the Washington Gray Chapter, Children of the Confederacy, dedicated a brick-encased cemetery plaque in Beaufort County (Washington) "To the Memory of 17 Soldiers Killed in Defense of Washington, Sept. 6, 1862." The memorial, in the same cemetery as the 1888 monument described in chapter 3, is topped with fourteen stacked cannonballs and credits Margaret Arthur Call with organizing the chapter in 1897.[47]

The Children's most prominent North Carolina memorial is sited in front of Lincoln County's (Lincolnton, 1911) courthouse. A marble water fountain set on a floor of inlaid marble is covered with a flat granite roof supported by four stone pillars. "To the Confederate Soldiers of Lincoln County," is carved in relief across the roof's front; "Erected by Wallace Reinhardt Chapter Children of the Confederacy," adorns the back. The dedication was a grand event, equal to unveilings staged by the Daughters. North Carolina Governor W. W. Kitchin delivered the oration; former Confederate Major-General Robert Hoke was present as was Mrs. "Stonewall" Jackson, in one of the aging widow's last public appearances.[48]

Funding priorities, however, were seldom publicly discussed by the Daughters, and even today chapter records are difficult to access, providing little insight into the shaping of financial decisions. When Confederate veterans proposed a series of monuments honoring Southern women (Chapter 13), sharp retorts provide a glimpse of commemorative tension. Florence Barlow of Kentucky, associate editor of the *Lost Cause*, a periodical published by women, wrote in 1903, "What difference does it [a monument] make?" Noting the large number of Confederate women living in poverty, her response revealed deep frustration,

Rockingham County Confederate monument. Reidsville, 1910. Erected by the Rockingham County Chapter, U.D.C., in a downtown traffic circle, the monument was struck by a car in 2011, toppling and breaking the soldier statue. Controversy ensued with some citizens demanding that the monument be moved.

"In a few years they will all have passed away, but a great monument of stone will be erected recording them as the bravest, most courageous, self-sacrificing women on earth."[49]

Martha Gielow of Alabama pressed the need for education. Citing northern philanthropic efforts to educate African Americans throughout the South, Gielow, advocating "industrial and practical education for white children," asked in a letter to the U.D.C., "What good will monuments to our ancestors be if our Southland is to become the land of educated blacks and uneducated whites?" Readers of the *Confederate Veteran* weighed in as well. An unnamed "Daughter of the Confederacy" urged, in 1897, the "building of a university as a more enduring and useful monument than marble or brass in memory ... of our noble women." Twelve years later, Miss Sallie Hunt of Abington, Virginia, proposed a "Dixie Home" as a "monument to Southern women," wherein "ambitious but poor Southern girls may live."[50]

Cemetery monuments. Although most early-twentieth-century North Carolina Confederate commemorations were civic-space monuments, cemetery memorials were still occasionally erected, including the three pictured on pages 96–98. *Above*: Cemetery arch, Old Town Cemetery. Tarboro, Edgecombe County, 1910.

7. The Daughters

Cemetery arch, Oakwood Cemetery. Raleigh, 1910.

Obelisk inscription, Duke Memorial Baptist Church Cemetery. Justice, Franklin County, 1912.

Even funding of Tarheel soldier monuments could provoke controversy. Five days before unveiling Rockingham County's monument to the Confederate soldier (1910), Reidsville's Daughters publicly defended their efforts. "We strive to aid all living veterans," the women declared in *Webster's Weekly*. "No case of destitution has been neglected; let none think that in our efforts to honor the dead that we have forgotten the living." Yet the Daughters closed with a promise, "After eight years of persistent effort [to erect a monument] we shall in the future devote ourselves to the living."[51]

Just as the Ladies' Memorial Associations had struggled to define early Confederate commemoration, Tarheel Daughters similarly faced competing ideals. The physical aspect of this evolving tradition, however, remained locally inspired and financed, resulting in a plethora of artistic interpretations. No Tarheel Confederate monument, in the century after Appomattox, was sponsored by a national organization, and with the exception of monument companies and statue fabricators (Chapters 10 and 11), little evidence exists of direct outside influence.[52]

Fewer than half of North Carolina's U.D.C. chapters would ultimately complete a monument. The Daughters, however, in North Carolina and throughout the South, would forge a powerful commemorative tradition, and in the process, create a public-space icon that remains among the region's most recognizable, and controversial, symbols.

8. Financing

On September 7, 1904, Mrs. Henry A. London, president of the Winnie Davis Chapter, United Daughters of the Confederacy, deposited $6.50 into Chatham County's Bank of Pittsboro. Eight names, written with impeccable penmanship beside amounts ranging from fifty cents to one dollar, were then inscribed on the first page of a small bankbook. Over the next three years this cardboard-covered record would nearly fill with entries as Pittsboro's Daughters sought to erect a courthouse-square monument honoring Chatham County's Confederate soldiers in one of North Carolina's most well-documented memorial efforts.[1]

Mrs. London, the chapter's founder, president, and monument treasurer, ranked among North Carolina's elite. Granddaughter of Jonathan Worth, the state's first elected post–Civil War governor, Bettie Louise Jackson married attorney Henry A. London, courier to Robert E. Lee at Appomattox, editor of the *Chatham Record*, president pro tem of the state senate, and author of North Carolina's 1904 defense of its "Last at Appomattox" claim.[2]

Bettie London was similarly prominent in women's circles, founding, in 1898, Pittsboro's Winnie Davis Chapter and serving as its president for nearly three decades. From 1906 to 1907 she headed the North Carolina Division, United Daughters of the Confederacy as president then chaired the state UDC's monument committee, playing a leading role in the planning or dedication of nearly a half dozen Tarheel memorials.

When Mrs. London made the Pittsboro chapter's initial bank deposit in 1904, the United Daughters of the Confederacy had yet to emerge as the monument-building juggernaut that it would become by decade's end. In May, the state's first UDC-sponsored civic-space memorial had been unveiled in Chowan County (Edenton); the second, in Edgecombe County (Tarboro), would be dedicated in October. The early Daughters, with a goal of memorializing the Confederacy and its soldiers yet without a well-honed blueprint, were formulating, chapter by chapter, their commemorative strategy.

The minutes of the Winnie Davis Daughters provide insight into the planning, fundraising, and erection of an early twentieth-century Confederate monument. The process was challenging; UDC dues did not cover even a fraction of needed monies, so Pittsboro's fifty-seven Daughters—a mid-sized North Carolina chapter—needed additional funds.[3]

Once committed, however, the women focused tightly on their goal. On October 3, 1904, four weeks after the initial bank deposit, the chapter discussed contributing to "Father Ryan's monument," in Mobile, Alabama. Verses by Ryan, the "poet-priest of the Confederacy," would ultimately be etched into many North Carolina commemorations—including Pittsboro's—

yet the proposed donation "was not seconded, <u>all</u> thinking it best to give to <u>home</u> purposes [words underlined in original]." Instead, "Much interest was shown in regard to the Chatham Monument, each [member] hoping to receive letters with contributions by the next meeting."[4]

More funds would be needed than could be secured through personal donations or direct appeals. The minutes detail the Daughters' attempts over the next three years to raise money as well as maintain community interest in their project. In 1905, the chapter planned a lawn party in the courthouse square "for the Monument"; no results, however, were recorded. That same year Mrs. London suggested a "Bazaar," a commonly used fund-raising technique in which donated items, often including Confederate relics, would be sold or auctioned. The "Daughters concurred in [this] for the Monument — all were interested," according to the minutes. Each member "was expected to bring in articles for the Bazaar at each meeting." Results were summarized in a three-line note, "1905 Had bazaar — cleared $140.00 for monument [sic]."[5]

Other events were less successful. An October 1906 entry related "a letter from a Mr. Williams of Durham wishing to give an entertainment in the Court House on Thanksgiving night, the U.D.C. getting one tenth of the proceeds." Williams' offer was accepted, but a later note in minuscule handwriting reports, "He came and the result was $3.50 as our share for the monument."[6]

The Chapter's August 1906 fund-raising discussion seemed especially contentious. With just fifteen members present — the only meeting with numerical documentation — minutes of the previous gathering were read. Mrs. Eubanks had proposed "that in order to increase our monument fund, each member collect before the next meeting, at least $5.00 for the Chatham monument." Mrs. London, likely aware that "a good many members of the Chapter [were] in arrears with their dues for 1906," a subject the women would later discuss, suggested "that the words 'if possible' be inserted into Mrs. Eubanks proposal," an idea that was "put to the house and carried."[7]

But when Mrs. London suggested that the Chapter sell postcards with "pictures of the Cornwallis House, some of the church's [sic] and views around Pittsboro," the women rebelled. "As we had <u>never used one cent</u> of our <u>monument collections</u>," acting recording secretary Mrs. Bruce Poe wrote, "Every cent of it being put in bank — and being advertised in the Chatham Record. All our money drawing 4 per ct. interest. The ladies doubted our ability to make anything [sic]." A chastened Mrs. London relented only partially, deciding instead "to advance the necessary money and try it herself as there seemed to be no one willing to go ahead with it."[8]

Less controversial requests were launched through the *Chatham Record*, edited by Mrs. London's husband. In a February 15, 1906 letter, Mrs. London appealed "To the Men and Women of Chatham County," for funds "to erect our Confederate Monument, and unveil it at the Soldiers' Reunion in August." The "Local Records" column kept readers abreast of the Daughters' tally: $1,025.89 on January 25 with the admonition, "It ought to be twice that sum"; $1,054.79 on March 8 with "Rally up, men of Chatham, and send your contributions without further delay"; and $1,087.29 by March 29.[9]

As the Daughters' account grew, the women entertained bids from competing monument companies. Carolina Marble Works of Statesville proposed a "24-foot monument costing $2,000.00." C. J. Hulin, a "marble man from Durham," submitted a $1,600.00 bid for a similar memorial. Chatham's Daughters apparently were shrewd negotiators. Mrs. London told the group on June 5 that Hulin "had agreed to give us a bronze instead of a granite statue for our monument — the price to be still 1600."[10]

8. Financing

Chatham County Confederate Monument. Pittsboro. The Winnie Davis Chapter, United Daughters of the Confederacy, worked three years to finance and complete this commemoration. Dedicated August 23, 1907.

At the same meeting, held in Mrs. London's home and where the "required number were present to transact business," the president "asked if the ladies had any choice of inscriptions — Mr. Hulin allowing us 400 letters." The minutes of Mrs. G. R. Pilkington, Recording Secretary, state, "None of us had thought of any. So Mrs. London suggested that the words 'Chatham Confederate Heroes should be on it — Also the list of Chathams Companys [sic]. and some verses of Father Ryans [sic] beautiful poems.'" Acceptance was unanimous, "All agreed that these would be appropriate."[11]

"Mrs. London thanked the ladies," then wavered, saying these "were only suggestions and she would not take the responsibility of making any selections or changes." There would be "time enough," according to the president, "to select the lettering when the dies were polished ... the ladies could do the selecting later."[12]

On July 5, 1906, C. J. Hulin and the Winnie Davis Daughters, represented by Mrs. London, finalized the contract. The full-page signed document, replete with legal terminology, detailed what Hulin would supply "within four months from this date" for a price of $1,600.00. The foundation was "to be of concrete cement, sand and stone, of sufficient depth to prevent any sinking ... and to extend two feet above the surface of the ground and be eleven feet square." The pedestal would be an elegant arrangement of precisely sized granite blocks: the "First Base," "Second Base," "Third Base," "First Die," "First Cap," "Second Die," and "Second Cap"— each defined in all dimensions and all to be of "Mt. Airy Granite." The cost and length of the inscription was specified also: "Four hundred letters without extra cost, exclusive of the lettering on the base, and ten cents a letter in excess of 400 letters."[13]

"A bronze statue of a Confederate soldier of standard government bronze, seven feet in height," a commercially produced rendition, would top the monument. The final design, the contract stipulated, would require the Daughters' approval prior to installation.[14]

Although the women had a signed contract, the monument's location had yet to be finalized. The Daughters' minutes provide no insight as to whether any controversy attended placing the memorial within the traffic circle surrounding the Chatham County courthouse, an elegant building still standing in the center of Pittsboro.[15]

Fully one year after Mr. Hulin and Mrs. London agreed to the four-month delivery deadline, the Chatham County commissioners, on July 8, 1907, "authorized and permitted" the Winnie Davis Chapter "to erect on the court-house square and in front of the courthouse a monument to Chatham's Confederate soldiers, and to cut down the shade tree in front of the court-house near to the place proposed for said monument." The monument, the resolution stated, "may remain in the care and keeping of the said Daughters of the Confederacy and such person or persons as they may hereafter designate."[16]

While the women awaited final commission approval, activity intensified in preparation for an August 1907 unveiling. In April, members unanimously voted to inscribe the Chapter's name — as well as Mrs. London's — on the memorial. The president demurred, however, stating, according to a correction in the June minutes, that "she appreciated the honor done her but did not think she could let it go on."[17]

At that June meeting, Mrs. London shared pictures of the monument "as drawn and corrected by Mr. Hulin." The inscriptions nearly matched those "suggested" by Mrs. London twelve months earlier: "Chatham Companies on one east side Our Confederate Heroes on north front in large letters — on west Father Ryans poem 'we care not [e]tc'— And on South the words Erected by those who honor the memory Confederate soldier." Yet when the president finished, "there was a perfect chorus of dissent and disapproval —'Mrs. London where is your name and that of the Chapter.' We voted to put both on the monument in April."[18]

Chapter minutes, with lines of writing extending perpendicularly across already inscribed horizontal script, record Mrs. London's response: "I did not put them on — because I did not wish my name on it." The document's next two sentences —"Is it too late to change it? She said yes it was."— end the recorded discussion.[19]

One can only surmise the debate that followed. What is known is that when Chatham's Confederate monument was unveiled two months later, the words, "This Monument is the Gift of Those Who Revere the Memory of the Confederate Soldier. Erected Under the Auspices of the Winnie Davis Chapter of the Daughters of the Confederacy, Mrs. H. A. London,

President. Aug. 23, 1907.,'" were inscribed on its south-facing back panel.[20]

Fund-raising, as demonstrated through the tribulations faced by Pittsboro's Daughters, could be challenging. The courthouse Confederate monument, today assumed by many as a ubiquitous feature of Southern cities and towns, was surprisingly difficult to complete; only thirty-three of North Carolina's one hundred counties erected such commemorations between the Daughters' first Tarheel civic-space monument (Chowan County/Edenton) in 1904 and the nation's entry into World War I thirteen years later.[21]

The Daughters' fund-raising methods, with one addition, were similar to those of the Ladies' Memorial Associations and other nineteenth-century commemorative groups. Chapters solicited directly from members, yet even among the socially prominent Daughters, monies raised represented only a fraction of needed amounts. Members were expected to canvass friends for contributions, while sympathetic newspaper editors might assist with public appeals.

Sponsored activities provided additional funds. "Entertainments," including balls, concerts, and lectures; raffles of noteworthy items; food events ranging from bake sales to elegant teas; bazaars featuring sales of donated merchandise; and selling of inexpensive souvenirs all raised commemorative monies for Tarheel Daughters. Such efforts, however, as seen through the minutes of Pittsboro's Winnie Davis Chapter, met with varying success and could spark sharp debate.

"Mrs. London, where is your name and that of the Chapter?" Pittsboro, Chatham County, 1907. **The wording of this dedicatory inscription sparked disagreement among the Winnie Davis Daughters.**

Gifts from wealthy donors as well as governmental appropriations made up a sizable portion of many funds, yet few completed monuments hint at such largess. To retain the perception of broad-based commemorative support, and enhance a memorial's power in shaping collective memory, donors and counties allowed the Daughters wide latitude to claim monuments as their own.

While one-third of the state's counties did erect a Confederate monument during this "golden age" of memorialization — and four other counties had similar civic-space sculptures already in place — numerous commemorative attempts failed. The number of unsuccessful projects, and the commitment behind them, may never be known; failed attempts were neither publicly noted nor officially terminated.[22]

Newspapers and public records can, however, provide insight. In 1905, the *Watauga Democrat*, in a region bitterly divided by wartime loyalties, promoted efforts for a Confederate monument. R. C. Rivers, the *Democrat's* editor, wrote on June 8 that a "number of our sister counties," including neighboring Caldwell, "have erected, or are endeavoring to erect, suitable monuments to the memory of their Confederate dead." This self-described "humble scribe" offered to "give $5 as a starter toward a Confederate monument to be erected in Boone." The following week, Rivers reported that "We are more and more encouraged over the Confederate monument fund" and "most encouraging of all the dear ladies are offering their best efforts to secure funds." In October, at the veterans' annual reunion, a committee was appointed, with Captain Lovill elected chairman and R. C. Rivers secretary. Here, however, documentation ends abruptly. "What became of the committee and monument is unknown," according to Civil War historian Michael Hardy, and to this day, no memorial to Southern soldiers has been raised in Watauga County (Boone).[23]

In Asheville, the United Daughters of the Confederacy received approval from city aldermen in December 1912 "to make alterations to the fountain on the square and erect a monument at an estimated cost of $5,000.00," the *Asheville Citizen* reported. "A plan made by architects," was shown at the meeting, "but the contract has already been let, it is said." The design called for "a monument or pedestal" inscribed "in the form of memorial [sic] to Confederate veterans of Western North Carolina," surrounded with "a basin of white marble." "No request for money was made," the *Citizen* reported, and the memorial apparently was never built.[24]

The Daughters of Guilford County fared little better. This populous and prosperous jurisdiction would have seemed a likely location for a successful commemorative effort. Greensboro and High Point, Guilford's largest cities, were thriving manufacturing centers and each could boast of an ele-

Confederate monument. Weldon. Erected by the Junius Daniel Chapter, U.D.C., "In Memory of the Confederate Soldiers and Sailors of Halifax and Northampton Counties." 1908.

gant Confederate cemetery monument. The amount the Daughters hoped to raise — ten thousand dollars for a monument "in honor of the men and women of the Confederacy"— although high by Tarheel standards seemed reasonable given the county's affluence.[25]

On October 25, 1912, the *Greensboro Daily News* printed much of what is known about this attempt. In a four-paragraph announcement entitled, "Kirmess and a Ball for Raising Funds," the *Daily News* reported an "important entertainment ... in the nature of a Kirmess" [an entertainment and fair usually for raising money], scheduled for "the latter port [sic] of November or the first of December." This gala was expected to attract "approximately 300 people" over "two nights, and one afternoon ... and for the mardi gras [sic] ball."[26]

Guilford's Daughters had big plans and bountiful optimism. Although a final date for the Kirmess had yet to be set, the paper reported that "Another plan for securing funds will be followed through

Scotland County Confederate monument. Laurinburg. Erected in 1912 by the Scotland Chapter, U.D.C., at a cost "between $3,000.00 and $5,000.00." In 1911, the General Assembly authorized Scotland County to appropriate up to $500 to help pay for this monument.

the month of December and possibly longer"—a "Japanese tea room" for "serving dainty lunches all day." Optimism seemed justified. "In the small amount of work already done," the article continues, "$1,000.00 has been raised to go to the [monument] fund.... It is hoped the cornerstone may be laid on January 19, the birthday of Lee, and that the monument may be unveiled on the 10th of May."[27]

Within months, the North Carolina legislature boosted the Daughters' efforts, authorizing Guilford County commissioners to appropriate up to three thousand dollars for the memorial. Yet despite the women's enthusiasm, significant funds already in hand, and governmental backing, the effort failed and Guilford County, would not complete even a modest civic-space Confederate commemoration until the mid–1980s.[28]

Legislative authorizations, like that permitting Guilford monies to help pay for a memorial, were relatively new to Confederate commemorative fund-raising. Nineteenth-century

LMAs rarely enjoyed such benefit; the first public assistance to a Tarheel monument likely was the state's appropriation to help finance the 1895 memorial to North Carolina's Confederate dead (Chapter 4).

Between 1909 and 1917, however, the North Carolina General Assembly, according to Tom Vincent in *The North Carolina Historical Review*, approved thirty-one authorizations, "permitting counties and municipalities to appropriate funds or land for the erection of Confederate monuments." These acts affected twenty-five counties (four appropriations are cited for Burke and two each for Jackson, Macon, and Richmond Counties). Two authorized land donations, two were unspecified, while twenty-seven of thirty-one permitted monetary appropriations ranging from three hundred dollars in Lincoln County to the three thousand dollars allowed Guilford. One thousand dollars was the most common, as well as average, amount, yet not all funds were distributed. Many carried a key stipulation: memorial associations and U.D.C. chapters first had to raise matching amounts.[29]

Stanly County Confederate monument. Albemarle. Erected by the Albemarle Chapter, U.D.C. Soldier statue manufactured by the Mullins Company of Salem, Ohio. Dedicated September 25, 1925.

A surprisingly high failure rate followed. Twelve of twenty-eight authorizations failed to result in a completed monument in the named jurisdiction within five years (three measures allotted funds for already-finished commemorations). While some of these counties eventually built memorials — Stanly fourteen years, Richmond nine-teen years, and Onslow County forty-four years later — four counties receiving authorizations have yet to erect a free-standing, county-seat Confederate memorial.[30]

Governmental support, while not guaranteeing a successful result, would have provided a substantial portion of funding. A second tabulation by Vincent — excluding two expensive commis-sioned bronzes raised in Rowan and Orange Counties — shows that the average cost of an early twentieth-century courthouse memorial was just over two thousand dollars. That a one thousand dollar or greater appropriation, amounts authorized in eight counties not

Left: "Fame." Rowan County Confederate monument. Salisbury. A winged "Fame" supports a dying Confederate soldier in one of North Carolina's most artistically accomplished, and expensive, commemorations. The Rowan Chapter, U.D.C., paid Frederick W. Ruckstahl $15,000 for this sculpture which is nearly identical to his 1905 "Glory," erected in Baltimore, Maryland. Ruckstahl substituted a bent rifle for the furled flag sculpted in "Glory," reduced the price to the Salisbury women by $2,500, and agreed not to produce further copies. Dedicated May 10, 1909. *Right:* Detail Rowan County Confederate monument. Salisbury, 1909.

completing a monument, would fail to result in a finished memorial within five years hints broadly at the challenges faced as well as the failures experienced by Confederate groups.[31]

With even modest sums hard to raise, some memorial groups emulated Raleigh's Ladies by laying a monument's cornerstone before having full funding in hand, hoping that the unfinished structure would spur contributions. But in contrast to Raleigh's women, who unveiled the completed state monument twelve months to the day after placing its cornerstone, at least two counties faced embarrassing delays.

Sometime between 1911 and 1918, a granite pedestal with "OUR CONFEDERATE SOLDIERS" carved across its base was erected on the northwest corner of the Burke County (Morganton) courthouse lawn. A sculpted block, simple yet graceful in design, topped the squat shaft. Whether this minimally adorned piece of granite — resting today near the monument and described as the "original finial"— was to be part of the finished memorial or a temporary element is unclear.[32]

The finial, however, would soon be replaced with a soldier figure. Captain W. J. Kincaid of Griffin, Georgia, according to Blanche Lucas Smith, "gave the bronze statue to complete the monument." Smith does not reveal the motivation for the former Burke County resident's generosity but describes the statue, cast by the American Bronze Foundry of Chicago, as that "of a Confederate private standing on guard. It is nine feet high, and faces North."³³

With great fanfare the revamped memorial was unveiled on Saturday June 22, 1918. "A handsome United States flag was hoisted," according to Smith, while the "Star Spangled Banner" played. Chief Justice Walter Clark, the state's most renowned commemorative speaker, delivered the oration. Captain L. A. Bristol, "the youngest man from the county to be given a captaincy," introduced Clark; shortly thereafter, as the band prepared to play "Dixie," Miss Augusta Bristol, the captain's daughter, pulled the cord to unveil the monument. Captain Kincaid addressed the throng, too, telling "that he counted it a privilege that the Daughters of the Confederacy had granted him the pleasure of giving this statue for the monument."³⁴

Currituck County's monument took longer to complete. In the state's northeasternmost county, Confederate veterans led fund-raising. By September 1912, as the H. M. Shaw Camp of the United Confederate Veterans prepared for their annual reunion, the men appeared poised for success. The old soldiers had "been working long toward the erection of this monument," according to the *Elizabeth City Weekly Advance*. "Wednesday of next week will be Confederate Day at Currituck C. H.," and "when the cornerstone of the monument to the Confederate soldiers of Currituck County will be laid."³⁵

Burke County Confederate monument. Morganton. This soldier statue, cast by the American Bronze Foundry of Chicago, was given by Captain W. J. Kincaid to complete Burke County's memorial. June 22, 1918.

Everything seemed in order. "The contract for the work has been let, the monument is to cost $1,650.00, and will stand on the court house grounds, the site having been donated by the county."³⁶

Festive activities would complement the placement's "appropriate exercises." "The day is not to pass, however, in a tiresome wait for dinner and with an eventless afternoon," the *Advance* promised. "A big basket picnic will be held on the grounds.... There will be music ... and an address by Mr. Herbert Peele," editor of the *Advance*. The local Daughters had received "a special invitation to be present," according to the article, while "doubtless other chapters outside of Currituck County will be represented."³⁷

The Daughters had not played a

major role in the memorial's planning, however, and the women's attendance may have been in question. A second invitation is extended in the article's sixth and final paragraph, a one-sentence stanza. "Major Lee urges especially, through the columns of the *Advance*, the D. H. Hill chapter [sic] of the Daughters of the Confederacy to be present."[38]

That the *Advance* twice appealed to women whose presence would generally be expected at such an event, and that one plea would be personally extended by the leading fundraiser, seems highly unusual. Strains perhaps were developing in the commemorative effort, and these dual invitations may have foreshadowed upcoming difficulties. For despite a contract, a completed design, and a granite base inscribed "TO OUR CONFEDERATE DEAD" in front of the courthouse, the project stalled. A decade after the 1912 cornerstone placement, Currituck's monument remained unfinished.

A philanthropic Northern publishing magnate, Joseph P. Knapp, would eventually bankroll the memorial's completion. A native New Yorker, Knapp enjoyed a life of affluence; his father had been president of the Metropolitan Life Insurance Company, and the young publisher gained further wealth by developing an improved printing press. But hunting, conservation, and philanthropy were Knapp's passions. The publisher owned a large estate on Currituck's Mackay Island, one of the nation's premier waterfowl hunting locales, and his benevolence extended from assisting local schools to founding, with J. P. Morgan and others, the organization that became Ducks Unlimited.[39]

On November 6, 1922, more than a decade after Major Lee and the Confederate veterans placed the cornerstone with "appropriate exercises," Currituck County commissioners formally accepted Knapp's offer "for improving and beautifying the Court House grounds and plans for finishing the Confederate monument." Knapp would "furnish all materials without charge to the County," the resolution continued, "if the people of the County will furnish labor."[40]

Knapp, however, would not underwrite the veterans' design. In addition to requiring local labor, the Northerner demanded creative control, rejecting the monument's original design—a granite

Soldiers' Burying Ground. Weldon. Weldon was a well-known town during the Civil War due to its location beside one of the Confederacy's most important rail lines. The Weldon Wayside Hospital # 9 treated many of the wounded from Richmond-area battlefields and this inscribed tablet marks the graves of 164 Confederate soldiers who died at the hospital. For decades, this small cemetery was privately owned and often uncared for. Later it came "into the hands of a highly respected negro, David Smith," according to the *Confederate Veteran* (March 1928), "who said he had known of these men and learned to love them," eventually "giv[ing] the land to the local Chapter, U.D.C." The cemetery had been previously "cleared of trees and undergrowth by the county," but by 1928, "as the Chapter has no funds for its upkeep, the place [was] gradually growing up again." Today it is mostly cleared although surrounded by dense brush. In 2009, the North Carolina U.D.C. unveiled a large granite monument inscribed with the decedents' names, placed near this much older but undated memorial.

shaft topped with a soldier figure — refusing, according to local lore, "to pay for a damn Rebel soldier." "There was grumbling about a yankee [sic] paying for a Confederate monument," according to Dudley Bagley, a close friend of the Knapps, yet "Knapp did not comprehend the impropriety of it until years later."[41]

W. O. Saunders, editor of the *Independent* in nearby Elizabeth City, wasted little time before railing against this "impropriety," writing on January 12, 1923, that "if the money of Joseph P. Knapp or the money of any other Northern man is required to finish that monument, then it will not be a monument of Currituck's respect for its heroes of the lost cause [sic], so much as a monument of everlasting shame to a county that marks itself as not having enough patriotism and local pride to honor its own."[42]

Yet Saunders, who described himself as "one of those who have never been keen for monuments reminding us of a conflict that we all should forget," offered advice. "If Mr. Knapp is going to finish that monument," the editor opined, "here's hoping it will be completed as a monument to a re-united nation or something like that." Knapp soon proposed a design to Currituck's commissioners that would "commemorate the dead of the World War as well as the Confederate dead," a compromise, according to Bagley, "accepted as a happy solution."[43]

A New York architectural firm, Farrington, Gould, and Hoaglund, drew up plans. The veterans' extant base, would be "further built up" with a bronze cap cast with the years 1861–1865. With "four bronze pillars faced with the traditional acanthus leaves," this cap would support "a solid sphere of highly polished red veined marble three feet in diameter," symbolizing the World War.[44]

A framed watercolor of the proposed monument was hung in the courthouse "without any ceremony," writes Bagley, until "sufficient time" passed "for the people to get used to this unusual and unique design for a Confederate monument." Then, with "no celebration, no fanfare, and no speeches of praise," the red sphere was unloaded from a rail car at Snowden, hauled to the courthouse and "placed on the bronze sub-base one day with the aid of a state highway truck." There "was no story about it in the papers," Bagley said. "When people rode by the next day, it was just there, unadorned with wreaths and without the usual bunting, just as though it had always been complete."[45]

Currituck, in 1923, at last had a

Currituck County Confederate monument. Currituck. The base was dedicated by local veterans on September 18, 1912, but the monument was not completed until 1923 when a northern publisher financed the granite sphere.

finished monument. No celebration or ceremony followed, however. Knapp never revealed the cost of the commemoration or of its centerpiece, a 2,397-pound sphere of polished red granite (not marble). After years of controversy and slow fund-raising, and a decade with a solitary inscribed gray block in front of the courthouse, Currituck's citizens accepted the memorial quietly. "So far as I have heard," Bagley concludes in 1964, "no one to this day has wished it to be different."[46]

9. Dedication Day

Early October 1905 promised to be an exciting time in Winston-Salem, North Carolina. Three "Notable Events"— the "Big Forsyth County Fair," the "Caldwell Memorial Corner Stone Laying by [the] Masonic Grand Lodge," and the "Great Parade and Unveiling of [the] Confederate Monument" at the Forsyth County courthouse — would take place during what the *Winston-Salem Journal* dubbed a "Gala Week."[1]

On Sunday, October 1, the *Journal* outlined the events in a front-page feature then declared that "Every class of our citizenry is interested in one way or another in the events which will take place." The paper also offered assurance that the city "is prepared for the thousands of visitors who will surge through her thoroughfares."[2]

Organizers hoped that three closely timed events would boost attendance. The "laying of the corner stone" of the Robert E. Caldwell Memorial, commemorating "one who was a beloved pastor and an enthusiastic mason [sic]," would commence Monday at 4:30 P.M. On Tuesday morning, a "most elaborate and well-conceived program" was planned "when the noble shaft on the courthouse green will be formally unveiled in the view of thousands to honor the memory of the Confederate dead." "Many hundreds of old soldiers and their friends" were expected for this "occasion [that] has been thoroughly advertised by the Fair authorities as well as by the Southern and Norfolk & Western railroads." Following the dedication, the fairgrounds would open at noon to what the *Journal* reported were "indications" that "pointed to easily the largest crowd that ever assembled in the city."[3]

In contrast with many North Carolina newspapers, the *Journal* does not appear to have published a commemorative edition devoted to the monument's unveiling. The story of Forsyth County's memorial instead was related in small segments which also reveal a community's preparation for the event.

A front-page letter penned by an "Old Soldier" and printed September 30, 1905, outlined the monument's planning, history, and financing. Seven years earlier, on March 30, 1898, according to the missive, twenty-four women organized the James B. Gordon Chapter of the United Daughters of the Confederacy. The women elected seven officers: a president, two vice presidents, a corresponding as well as a recording secretary, an historian, and a treasurer, Mrs. Henry L. Riggins, who was "re-elected every year for the reason that she was indispensable."[4]

Mrs. Riggins spearheaded the Daughters' commemorative efforts. "Those noble women, God bless them," the soldier continued, "without one dollar went to work to erect a mon-

Forsyth County Confederate monument. Winston-Salem. Dedicated October 3, 1905. "Fully 680 Confederate veterans attended, a sight to impress the most indifferent person."

ument to the Confederate soldiers. See what they have done; look at that graceful and most beautiful monument that now stands on our courthouse green." While acknowledging that "many shafts" had been pricier, the veteran emphasized that none are more "elegant in every respect." "We raise our hats, we offer our prayers, and ask God to bless each one of these noble Daughters who have worked so long and so faithfully for the old soldiers."[5]

The veteran's enthusiasm appeared to be widely shared. "Buildings are gay with vari-colored bunting and flags and already there is an air of festivity," the *Journal* reported in its Sunday edition. W. T. Vogler "fitted up an attractive 'Confederate Window'" in his jewelry store, with "many relics of the days of 1861–65." Vogler's "old rifle used ...

throughout the conflict," was on display as were "Confederate flags and Confederate money ... time scarred [sic] coats and blanket that were used by Dr. J. A. Blum [the designer of the soon-to-be-unveiled monument], and ... two calls for volunteers, one signed by Lieutenant H. C. Banner, Ralph Gorrell and Jas. W. Sheppard, all of whom were killed."[6]

Advertisers and fair officials welcomed soldiers. W. L. Hill offered "Veterans and your friends" a "splendid line of all the new dress goods," as well as shoe and carpet close-outs "at such prices that you cannot resist them." G. E. Webb, representing "The Big Fair" which would run from October 3 through 6, urged citizens not to "spend 50 cents to see a circus, when you can see a good one for nothing." Yet while extolling the event's Merry-Go-Round, Ferris Wheel, Fiddler's Contest, and Horse Swapping Convention, Webb's announcement also urged that "Everybody should witness the parade of the veterans on Tuesday the third." The fair's schedule had been arranged as to avoid interfering with the courthouse ceremony. "After the unveiling of the monument the fair will be formally opened at 12 o'clock," the advertisement stated.[7]

The parade preceding the formal dedication would be a complex affair requiring intricate planning. On September 28, the Norfleet Camp, United Confederate Veterans, issued an "official order," published by the *Journal*. "Attention Norfleet Camp. You are ordered to report on the morning of October 3, between the hours of 8 and 9:30 o'clock ... on the Northside of the Court House Square to receive badges and form a line for the procession." Other Southern veterans, the announcement added, "whether members of any camp or not," if at "the court house square at the time appointed would receive the same attention ... accorded to the veterans of Norfleet Camp."[8]

Two days later, a less-demanding request "urged" the local Daughters "to meet at Mrs. Henry L. Riggins' on West Fifth street [sic], Tuesday morning at 9 o'clock." Like the Confederate veterans, Winston-Salem's Daughters also welcomed out-of-towners, "Not only members of the James B. Gordon Chapter, but all others [U.D.C. members]."[9]

"Under the chief marshalship of Mr. P. H. Hanes," and "assisted by scores of marshals," the procession would start "Promptly at 10 o'clock," the *Journal* reported. Three "divisions," organized in different locations, would join together and follow a circuitous route, making eight turns en route to the courthouse. The band, speakers, and Forsyth Riflemen would make up the first division; Confederate veterans the second; while the Daughters, "citizens in carriages," and school children comprised the third. And to assure that "one part of the parade may be able to witness the other," a "countermarch" was arranged, with participants doubling back along Fifth Street.[10]

But on Tuesday October 3, rain poured down. "The big event had to be abandoned," and "a great part of the exercise ... held in the courthouse." Yet "the enthusiasm was superior to the wet weather," according to the *Journal*, and "ceremonies were well received, impressive and brought joy to thousands." The old soldiers, part of "The great gray line [that] is thinning fast," were well represented. "Fully 680 Confederate veterans attended"—twenty-five from Wilkes County, fifteen from Mecklenburg, a dozen from Rowan, and "a number" from each of five neighboring counties—"a sight to impress them ost [sic] indifferent person." The veterans, "the ones whose approbation was most desired," according to the *Journal*, "were thoroughly satisfied," as they "renewed association with one another" then later enjoyed a dinner hosted in their honor by the local Daughters.[11]

Colonel Alfred Moore Waddell was the day's featured orator. One of the state's most popular speakers, Waddell had delivered the keynote address in Raleigh dedicating North

Carolina's monument to the Confederate dead in 1895 (Chapter 4). The Wilmington resident, though a staunch Unionist prior to the War, served as Lieutenant Colonel in the Southern army then became an early champion of Confederate commemoration.[12]

In Winston-Salem, Waddell continued to advocate for such memorialization. As the James B. Gordon Chapter prepared to unveil the Daughters' fifth Tarheel civic-space memorial — all erected within eighteen months — Waddell praised the burgeoning trend. "I thank God that monuments to the Confederate soldiers are rapidly multiplying in the land," he said, yet acknowledged that "There have been people who deprecated the observance of memorial days, or any other public demonstration of respect for our heroic dead, upon the cowardly and hypocritical prentence [sic] that having lost in the war we ought not to provoke further antagonism by such demonstrations."[13]

"Even our former enemies," the speaker countered, "regard such a plea with immeasurable contempt and have proved it by joining in many localities, North and South, in paying respect to the memory of the brave men whom they met in battle." Waddell "rejoice[d]" that rather than "losing interest in this subject, the Southern people have made their increasing prosperity the measure of their contribution to it," and thanked the South's "ever faithful and devoted women" who "will keep alive ... a just sense of the unselfish patriotism and splendid services of the Confederate soldier."[14]

Waddell closed by addressing the Confederate dead, whom he described as those behind "the veil that hides them from our view." "Comrades," the former Confederate officer said, "You are not forgotten by our countrymen and countrywomen, but held in loving remembrance and we who fought and suffered with you in your youth, and have grown gray with years, await the call."[15]

During an era when dedication speeches frequently extended an hour or more, Waddell's 1905 address "lasted scarcely more than 15 minutes," yet the *Journal* reported that the aging veteran had spoken "eloquently on Southern ideals." Three speeches followed the old soldier's oration. North Carolina Lieutenant-Governor Francis D. Winston spoke to the overflow crowd in the packed courthouse, delivering "a splendid address, presenting the monument in behalf of the Daughters"; The Honorable C. P. Watson accepted the memorial "in Behalf of Veterans" with a "powerful, vigorous, and beautiful" oration; and Mrs. Henry A. London of Pittsboro, president of the North Carolina Division, United Daughters of the Confederacy, gave "an appropriate talk about the cherishing of Southern traditions and history."[16]

Following the speeches, and "fine music" from the Salem Boys' Band, the crowd "repaired to the court house lawn." The monument — a twenty-four-foot-high shaft of granite designed by local resident Dr. James Alfred Blum and topped with a six-foot-tall sculpted granite soldier — stood veiled in the inclement weather.[17]

"As the ceremonies reached their climax," the *Journal* reported, the Winston Cornet Band struck up chords of "Dixie." "Miss Mary Barker and Miss Bessie Blum stood ready to pull the cords" and release the cloth covering the monument, but damp weather again interfered. The ropes had swollen and "refused to do their duty." Mr. Frank White had to scale the monument and work to free the cloth. Then as the covering fell away, "Cheers rang out as the beautiful lines of the complete monument were unveiled."[18]

The unveiling of a Confederate monument was more than the removal of a cloth or a series of speeches. Dedications were day-long celebrations featuring parades, veterans'

Randolph County Confederate monument. Asheboro. "A bountiful dinner" was served by the Daughters to Confederate veterans following the unveiling. September 2, 1911.

reunions, orations, banquets and Crosses of Honor for the old soldiers in addition to the ceremonial release of the fabric shrouding the memorial.

"September 30, 1909, was perhaps the greatest day within the history of Franklin, N.C.," the *Confederate Veteran* reported, describing the unveiling of Macon County's Confederate monument. In Catawba County, the dedication brought "Together the County's Largest Crowd and Makes the County's Biggest Day," a *Newton Enterprise* headline declared. And Forsyth County's "Gala Week," with its "events of reverence and commemoration" that attracted thousands, "will remain in the memory of all of us in the years to come," wrote the *Winston-Salem Journal*.[19]

For many Tarheel cities and towns, dedication day was their most memorable early-twentieth-century event. Business and civic leaders joined with commemorative groups in not only memorializing the Confederate dead and honoring Southern veterans but in showcasing the community to state officials and hundreds, perhaps thousands, of out-of-town guests. Mayors and commissioners entertained North Carolina's political elite, while local commemorative leaders, many of whom had worked years for the realization of a monument, received acclaim through highly symbolic and very public roles.

Newspapers assisted organizers by announcing meetings, printing itineraries, and encouraging public participation. Parade routes were detailed; speakers, marshals, clergy, choirs, and bands were publicized; and pleas for last-minute assistance received prominent coverage. Businesses shuttered early on dedication day, or perhaps never opened at all, and railroads, the chief transportation between towns, offered veterans reduced fares.[20]

Granville County Confederate monument. Oxford. When dedicated on October 30, 1909, this monument was located in Oxford's main intersection. Increasing traffic led to its relocation in 1971, beside the public library.

Flowers, greenery, and bunting added to the festive atmosphere. "All the principal business houses and several residences along the line of march were gayly decorated with the Confederate colors, red and white," the *Asheboro Courier* reported in 1911. "In fact the whole town was in holiday array." The speaker's platform and sometimes the monument itself would be adorned as well. The *Newton Enterprise* carried a plea for help, "Let all the men and boys, women and girls come to the courtyard next Wednesday, right after dinner, to decorate." The weekly's same issue printed an additional request beside the event's itinerary. "Friends and relatives of the Confederate soldiers, both living and dead, are earnestly requested to bring their flowers to the Enterprise office on August 15th as the ladies desire the monument mound to be covered with floral tributes to the noble dead."[21]

Although Tarheel dedications included many local variations, the ceremony's basic structure differed little from one early-twentieth-century unveiling to the next. A parade or procession, led by a chief marshal, typically kicked off the day's activities. Dignitaries and Confederate veterans walked near the head of the column, soldiers often arrayed by rank or led by former officers. The local Daughters, especially after spearheading fundraising efforts, also were prominently featured. In Randolph County, "Mr. J. D. Ross led the march, followed by the Winston band and speakers of the day," the *Asheboro Courier* reported. Confederate veterans, "about 100 in number," came next followed by the Randolph Chapter, U.D.C., and the Children of the Confederacy, boys and girls aged three to seventeen who "all bore laurel wreaths and added much to the beauty of the procession." Veterans' wives and widows followed then the "waitresses who had been chosen from the town and county, and last the general public."[22]

Catawba County Confederate monument. Newton. Future North Carolina governor Locke Craig, the state's "orator of orators," delivered the address. Dedicated August 15, 1907.

Marchers moved slowly toward the courthouse where the principal "exercises," the day's formal event, would follow. An invocation by a prominent local clergyman nearly always opened the exercises. Before the formal activities ended, several hours later, seven to ten participants, including a master of ceremonies and two clergy, typically had spoken. In Asheboro, Colonel A. C. McAlister presided over the introduction of the orator; the oration itself, an hour-long presentation; a shorter unveiling speech; three acceptance speeches, one each from the veterans, the county, and the city; and "Eulogies to the Old Soldiers" by the Honorable Robert N. Page "and others."[23]

In Franklin, North Carolina, fourteen individuals spoke during that dedication, including two women, Miss Elizabeth Kelly, delivering the "unveiling address," and Miss Clyde McGuire, reciting "The Conquered Banner." Six people spoke in Alamance County (Graham, 1914) including Mrs. E. C. Murray, local U.D.C. Chapter president, while in Forsyth County, seven individuals including Mrs. Henry A. London, President of the North Carolina Division, United Daughters of the Confederacy, addressed attendees.[24]

Music enlivened exercises; three to four selections typically were performed. "Dixie" was nearly always included, often sung as the cloth fell from the monument — and capped in Newton by a "Rebel Yell" from the veterans. "The Bonnie Blue Flag" and "Maryland, My Maryland," other Southern favorites, were frequently included, while "Tenting on the Old Campground," a tune dear to the old soldiers, was commonly sung. However, one number honoring the reunited nation was also part of many early-twentieth-century Tarheel dedications. "America" was selected most often, but "The Star-Spangled Banner" was played in Burke County (Morganton, 1918), while in Rocky Mount (Nash County, 1917), schoolchildren closed the event by singing "My Country 'tis of Thee."[25]

Despite careful planning, however, problems arose necessitating last-minute changes. Inclement weather forced all but the actual unveiling indoors in both Winston-Salem and Asheville.

Iredell County Confederate monument. Statesville. Veterans gave a "Rebel yell" as the ceremony closed then "formed in line and marched to the opera house, where dinner had been prepared for them." It was dedicated May 10, 1906, although monument is inscribed 1905.

Train schedules created problems, too. In Catawba County (Newton, 1907), a "one-armed Confederate soldier," the Reverend J. D. Arnold, pastor of the Newton Methodist Church, delivered a "touching prayer," substituting for Dr. Gwaltney, a Baptist minister, "who was delayed on the train from the west." North Carolina State Auditor Dr. B. F. Dixon was to have presented Crosses of Honor to Confederate veterans as part of Asheville's Monumental Day but "was left by the train at Raleigh," requiring cancellation of that part of the ceremony.[26]

Welcoming remarks from the mayor, or another well-known local individual, and a musical number would typically follow the invocation. A prominent dignitary would then introduce the featured orator. Presentations varied widely. In Iredell County (Statesville, 1906), former Lieutenant-Governor W. D. Turner introduced Governor Robert B. Glenn. Turner emphasized how "every hamlet should have one [a monument] to teach the unborn generations of the heroic acts of the dead," but also spoke of "macadam roads and evidences ... of industrial progress," introductory remarks that, although "well done," according to the *Statesville Landmark*, "occupied 15 minutes when it should have not exceeded five."²⁷

"A gallant Confederate soldier," Colonel James T. Morehead of Greensboro, former commander of the Fifty-third North Carolina Regiment, did the honors in Randolph County, speaking "in his usual bright, breezy and interesting manner for a short while," according to the *Asheboro Courier*. Morehead told of a valiant "fourteen-year-old boy riding up and down the Confederate lines [during combat] when all the other soldiers were 'hugging the ground.'" The veteran fighters "snatched him to the ground, saying 'You fool, they will shoot your head off.'" Morehead then introduced the "hero of the incident," then-fourteen-year-old Major Walter Clark, the Confederacy's youngest major, now Chief Justice of North Carolina's Supreme Court — and the day's featured speaker.²⁸

Clark was one of the state's most sought-after orators, delivering at least six dedication-day speeches between 1907 and 1918. As the state's pre-eminent Civil War historian, Clark had edited the five-volume *Histories of the Several Regiments and Battalions from North Carolina in the Great War 1861-'65*, a 1901 state publication that remains a standard reference, and chaired the 1904 North Carolina Literary and Historical Association Committee that penned *Five Points in the Record of North Carolina in the Great War of 1861-5*.

Confederate monument. Maplewood Cemetery, Wilson, Wilson County. Dedicated May 10, 1902, atop a mass grave.

The chief justice's speeches, however, were anything but breezy. Three of Clark's dedicatory orations were published in their entirety; all followed a similar pattern and lasted between one and one-and-one-half hours. Defending North Carolina's "Rebel Boast," in addition to explaining Southern defeat, Clark outlined the state's Confederate commitment, "sending more than 125,000 stalwart sons to make her declaration good." But he always praised the commitment of his host county, too, citing in Caldwell County (Lenoir, 1910), for example, how citizens "Quickly ... filled the full measure of devotion to the State and the South. You sent more soldiers to the field than you had voters."²⁹

Clark also detailed handicaps faced by the Confederacy. The region had little manufacturing and few rail lines, and "when our war began," Clark reminded Pender County's (Burgaw, 1914) dedication-day crowd, "the South had no government ... not a soldier and not a dollar." The North, with a vastly larger population, sent nearly three million soldiers into the field yet "engaged ... 45 per cent of their man power," while the South, enlisting "90 per cent of the men between seventeen and forty-five," managed "to put into line 600,000." Yet North Carolina's soldiers, Clark told Caldwell's veterans, though "Half fed and poorly clothed ... marched to eternal fame and proved yourselves in battle worthy comrades of the Tenth Legion of Caesar and of the Old Guard of Napoleon."[30]

The chief justice recounted detailed military records for each of his host's local Confederate units, recitations that comprised most of the address. Nearly all Civil War companies — approximately one hundred men led by a captain — had organized by county, and citizens retained an intense pride in the record of these local men. Nearly a dozen Tarheel Confederate monuments, including those in Caldwell, Chatham, and Randolph Counties in which Clark spoke, prominently identify local companies.

Caldwell County Confederate monument. Lenoir. Six thousand people attended this dedication on June 3, 1910. The orator was state Supreme Court Chief Justice Walter Clark, who, at age fourteen, had been the Confederacy's youngest major.

The former Confederate officer's facts were astounding. At Gettysburg, the Twenty-sixth North Carolina Regiment sustained the most casualties "in any one battle, of any of the 2,500 regiments," North or South, Clark told Caldwell County's throng in Lenoir. But the Twenty-sixth's Company F, the "Hibriten Guards" who had enlisted at Lenoir, was particularly hard hit. Of "3 officers and 88 muskets," that went into the three-day battle, "not one came out untouched. 31 were killed or died of wounds. Of the other 60, all of whom were wounded."[31]

North Carolina governors were popular speakers as well, delivering more than a dozen dedicatory orations. Robert B. Glenn (1905–1909), whose father, a Confederate captain, was killed at the Battle of South Mountain, Maryland, in 1862, was the most prolific, delivering at least four such speeches in addition to joining New Jersey's chief executive in dedicating that state's monument to its Civil War dead in New Bern's National Cemetery (Chapter 14).

Editors, scholars, former Confederate officers, and rising political stars were tapped too. D. H. Hill, Jr., president of the North Carolina College of Agriculture and Mechanic Arts (today North Carolina State University) and son of one of the state's highest-ranking Confederate generals, spoke in Pasquotank County (Elizabeth City, 1911) and in Raleigh

(Confederate Women's Monument, 1914). In Catawba County (Newton, 1907), Locke Craig, a future governor whom the *Newton Enterprise* dubbed the "orator of orators of North Carolina," delivered the keynote address. Josephus Daniels, long-time editor of Raleigh's *News and Observer*, did the honors in Person County (Roxboro, 1922), while Henry A. London, lawyer, editor, author, and courier to Robert E. Lee, spoke in Alamance County (Graham, 1914).[32]

Like Chief Justice Clark and Governor Glenn, orators praised Confederate soldiers— surviving veterans as well as the dead—often directly addressing the ever-thinning gray line. Speakers extolled the men's heroism and courage as they had struggled against insurmountable odds and lauded North Carolinians' efforts for the short-lived Southern nation.

What remained unstated, however, was arguably as significant as the words spoken. Although not all dedication texts are available, and many "secondary" speeches were never published, no Tarheel dedication-day speaker is known to have advocated for renewed sectional independence or expressed regret being part of a reunified nation. The "cause" for which Confederate soldiers had struggled and suffered, although never defined beyond assertions of "rights" and "independence," had indeed been "lost." On this, there was no equivocation.

And although issues surrounding race and racial relations are seldom far from the surface of Southern politics, they remained largely unmentioned during monument dedications. Historian and college president D. H. Hill, Jr., dedicating the 1914 Confederate Women's Monument in Raleigh, acknowledged that "many negroes joined the Federals in the eastern part of the State," yet praised "the faithfulness of the slaves.... Our people ought never to forget the fidelity of the negroes during those defenceless days." But

Pasquotank County Confederate monument. Elizabeth City. College president D.H. Hill, Jr., son of Lieutenant-General D.H. Hill, one of North Carolina's highest-ranking Confederate officers, delivered the keynote address. May 10, 1911.

contemporary racial issues, notably Jim Crow statutes and the increasing disenfranchisement of African Americans, were never broached.[33]

The release of the cloth shroud covering the monument typically followed the featured oration. Many unveilings, however, were purely ceremonial. Since memorials are sited in the most public of spaces, townspeople had not only observed their construction but likely had seen the completed commemoration for weeks, or even months.

In Newton, "several hundred people" watched one Saturday afternoon as the Confederate soldier statue was hoisted atop the granite shaft completing Catawba County's monument. In neighboring Iredell County (Statesville, 1906), that memorial was finished in late December 1905; one week later, the *Statesville Landmark* reported that "May 10th was fixed as the date for the unveiling. Gov. Glenn will be asked to take part in the exercises." As in Pender County, where the Confederate monument was erected five months—and two episodes of vandalism—before its formal dedication, only visitors and rural residents would likely be seeing these commemorations for the first time.[34]

Pender County Confederate monument. Burgaw. The cameo is of General William Dorsey Pender, namesake of Pender County formed in 1875. The monument honors "Confederate Soldiers" and "OUR HEROES." May 27, 1914.

Few photos of veiled monuments survive. An Iredell County image shows a tight wrapping, not a billowy, tent-like covering, shrouding shaft and statue. Forty yards of cloth, "cut up into lengths," covered Chatham County's (Pittsboro, 1907) monument, according to minutes of the Winnie Davis Daughters. Decorative cords, sometimes called streamers or ribbons, held the veil in place. When pulled, these cords released the fabric, allowing it to fall away, as in Macon County (Franklin, 1909), where the cloth "floated gently down right and left of the shaft," revealing the monument "in all its grace and beauty."[35]

Releasing the veil was one of the day's most prominent and cherished roles. Five-year-old Elizabeth Renfroe Cooper, daughter of monument committee president Mrs. S. P. Cooper, performed the function in Vance County (Henderson, 1910). A photo showing Miss Cooper holding a small flag and posed in front of the Stars and Bars illustrates the *Confederate Veteran* article detailing the unveiling. An image of Miss Ella Delight Bernhardt, Maid of Honor who performed the unveiling in Caldwell County, is featured opposite the "Official Programme" in *A Little History of the Monument in honor of the Confederate Veterans from Caldwell County, N.C.*, a 1910 publication. Like the similarly aged Miss Cooper, Miss Bernhardt holds a small Confederate battle flag while standing beside a larger draped banner.[36]

Individuals chosen to unveil monuments were typically socially prominent: children or grandchildren of U.D.C. leaders; benefactors' relatives; or descendents of high-ranking Confederate officers. In Burke County (Morganton, 1918), Miss Augusta Bristol, daughter of Captain L. A. Bristol, "the youngest man from the county to be given a captaincy," pulled the cord. Misses Mae Barber and Bessie Blum, the latter likely a relative of monument designer, Dr. James Alfred Blum, filled the role in Forsyth County (Winston-Salem, 1905). And in Cleveland County (Shelby, 1907), "two young girls," one a Confederate captain's daughter, the other a colonel's child, "pulled the cords that removed the covering."[37]

Men or boys might also perform the unveiling. In Nash County (Rocky Mount, 1917), Robert H. Ricks, Jr., son of the monument's benefactor, and Richard Young Thorpe ceremoniously released the cloth; in Raleigh, Ashley Horne, grandson and namesake of the businessman who financed the memorial, unveiled the monument to Confederate Women; while in Edgecombe County (Tarboro, 1904), W. D. Pender, Jr., son of the Confederate general killed at Gettysburg for whom the local U.D.C. Chapter was named, and Katherine W. Bourne, daughter of that Chapter's president and granddaughter of a former North Carolina governor, performed the ceremony.[38]

Gates County Confederate monument. Gatesville. Erected by the Gates County Confederate Monument Organization. Dedicated July 8, 1915.

Dedication days, however, entailed more than political speeches, symbolic acts, and solemn ceremony. The day was to be festive, and organizers hoped that everyone, especially the veterans, would have a good time.

During an era when agriculture dominated North Carolina's economy and "going to town" might be a multi-day event, unveilings brought together thousands of people and allowed aging veterans to renew old friendships. Reunions were held concurrently with monument dedications in Iredell and Catawba Counties. There were "greetings and handshaking ... being one of the most enjoyable features" in Caldwell County, while in Forsyth, "old comrades," from at least nine counties, "greeted one another [as] they appeared to realize the value of renewed association."[39]

The *Winston-Salem Journal* led its post-event coverage with three paragraphs describing reaction to the day's activities. "I[t] was the day of the old soldier," the *Journal* began, before describing the ceremonies as bringing "joy to thousands." "The old veterans ... whose approbation was most desired," 680 men in all, were treated to dinner after the unveiling. "They had a real good time," the *Journal* concluded, and "went away to their homes last night with hearts overflowing with gratitude."[40]

Dinners honoring Confederate veterans were nearly a universal part of dedication-day activities; most were sponsored by local U.D.C. Chapters. In Randolph County, "a bountiful dinner" was served on the Presbyterian Church grounds. "A table had been

Sampson County Confederate monument. Clinton. The monument is engraved "Ashford-Sillers Chapter U.D.C. May 10, 1916," but the dedication was held on May 12, 1916, according to contemporaneous newspaper accounts.

arranged and tastefully decorated with flowers and red and white bunting," the *Asheboro Courier* reported, and the meal "was served by the Chapter to the veterans, speakers, marshals and members of the Winston band."[41]

Indoor venues were also used. In Pasquotank County (Elizabeth City, 1911), "a bountiful dinner was served by the D. H. H[ill] Chapter in the Masonic Hall and it was a splendid feast." Sixty veterans in Macon County (Franklin, 1909), joined by two state governors, dined at "the Junaluskee Inn through the courtesy of the proprietress." And in Iredell County (Statesville, 1906), after the unveiling and a "Rebel Yell," Confederate veterans "formed in line and marched to the opera house, where dinner had been prepared for them ... served by a number of young ladies." The menu, although "not so very elaborate," according to the *Statesville Landmark*, "was tempting and the veterans enjoyed it very much."[42]

Hints of frivolity appear in some accounts. In Vance County (Henderson, 1910), "A bountiful repast was enjoyed by all, and the impromptu responses to the toasts offered kept the banqueters in good humor and laughter," while after a "sumptious [sic] feast" in

Pender County (Burgaw, 1914), "well-served and hugely enjoyed," according to the *Wilmington Dispatch*, "veterans assembled in the school house and held a sort of jollification session."[43]

Perhaps the most unusual finale, however, occurred in Caldwell County (Lenoir, 1910). Six thousand people attended that dedication, yet the unveiling was met with a "subdued" reaction accompanied with a "feeling of deep solemnity and reverence," perhaps reflecting losses sustained by county troops. Afterwards two hundred veterans, "'Old Boys' as they call themselves," according to Blanche Lucas Smith, were "served a splendid dinner" on the courthouse lawn. However, another official event ended the day on a decidedly modern note — an "AUTOMOBILE RIDE to Veterans." The "Old Boys," men who had walked to war carrying smooth-bore muskets, apparently liked the new technology, since Smith reports that "every one seemed to enjoy [the ride] to the fullest extent."[44]

10. Soldier Statues

On October 20, 1862, "Anne C. Lee, Daughter of Gen. R. E. Lee and Mary Custis Lee.... Died at the White Sulphur Springs, Warren County, N.C." Anne had been a "fragile sufferer," according to J. Randolph Smith, and when Robert E. Lee's family was forced to flee their ancestral home at the beginning of the Civil War, Mrs. Lee and her daughter, "after trying several temporary homes," traveled to White Sulphur Springs, "hoping that here in this quiet place, with the help of the valued waters, Miss Anne Lee might be nursed to health."[1]

Antebellum Warren County — "Old Warren" in Smith's words — "was one of the leading counties of the State," and the resort "was the rallying place of the wealth and beauty of North Carolina and her sister States [sic]." The Springs' proprietor, William Duke Jones, "was an old-time Southern gentleman, and ... in this haven, far from the battles, Mrs. Lee and her daughter made their home." When Anne "sank to sleep" in October 1862, her remains were "laid to rest in this private cemetery of Mr. Jones ... a short distance from the hotel."[2]

Joseph S. Jones, William's son, sought to fund a monument for Anne's grave shortly after her death, but the effort faltered. Soon thereafter, the "Warren women," led by Joseph's wife, "took up the work of love ... collecting funds with which the grave of Anne Lee might be marked by as handsome a stone as they in their own great need could give." "No others were asked to subscribe than the women of Warren County," Smith asserts, thus "this was the first monument ever erected to a woman by women," and "formed the cornerstone" of subsequent commemorative endeavors by women across the South.[3]

The monument — a twelve-foot-high granite shaft topped with an urn, "as symmetrical a monument as one could find"— was not completed until 1866. Robert E. Lee, "by the terms of his parole," could not attend the dedication, a summertime ceremony which included many elements of later soldiers' monument unveilings, but Generals G. W. Custis Lee and W. H. F. Lee were there, "guests of their old West Point comrade, Col. Wharton J. Green."[4]

Captain James Barron Hope, the "Poet of the Confederacy," was the day's orator. Hope recited a lengthy "Elegiac Ode" that spoke more of a defeated nation's unrequited grief than sentiments for a single individual,

> He chastens us as nations and as men;
> He smites us sore until our pride doth yield;
> And hence our heroes, each with hearts for ten,
> Were vanquished in the field;
> And stand to-day beneath our Southern sun
> O'erthrown in battle and despoiled of hope,
> Their drums all silent and their cause undone,
> And they all left to grope.[5]

While not a true soldiers' monument, Anne Lee's memorial is considered by many, including Blanche Lucas Smith and Ralph Widener, as North Carolina's earliest Confederate commemoration. Certainly this effort by Warren's women launched a robust memorial tradition; nearly a dozen commemorations in Warren and neighboring counties honor individuals or Confederate troops.[6]

In 1903, Mrs. Lucy Polk headed an effort that raised a monument "To the Confederate Dead of Warren County" in Warrenton's Fairview Cemetery. A bare-headed marble soldier, arms crossed and eyes cast pensively, stands atop a seven-layer base of rough-hewn granite blocks. At the infantryman's feet, an inscription reads,

> Brave and fearless,
> Proud and peerless,
> Were Warren's Sons who wore the gray.

"Coopers Raleigh," etched into the marble base, denotes the memorial's fabricator, Cooper Brothers, while a smooth granite slab on a lower step reads, "Erected by the efforts of Mrs. Lucy E. Polk."

Despite Warren's rich commemorative heritage, the county had yet to raise a civic-space Confederate commemoration as the Civil War's fiftieth anniversary neared. The Warren Chapter, United Daughters of the Confederacy, and the "Sons of Warren" jointly worked for such a monument. Little is known about fund-raising except that, in 1913, the North Carolina General Assembly authorized county commissioners to appropriate up to $1,500.00 for the memorial.[7]

Cooper Brothers again was selected to build this monument. The well-established Raleigh firm specializing in cemetery statuary and memorial carving crafted a skillfully executed commemoration to "OUR HEROES," carved in relief across the monument's base. A partially furled Confederate flag nearly fills the tapering shaft's front face, and a stylized "CSA" is enclosed within a carved shield below the banner. Inscriptions, including words by Rudyard Kipling and Father Joseph Ryan adorn the sides, while a cast Confederate seal and "Erected to the Confederate Soldiers of Warren County 1861–1865" complete the front panel.

A carved soldier, however, would not top this monument; an infantryman of stamped sheet copper, with an applied bronze patina, would stand near the courthouse. It is doubtful that Warren's Sons and Daughters asked any well-known sculptors for proposals, and none were likely submitted. Committee members, probably assisted by a Cooper's representative, instead reviewed catalogs and advertisements illustrating available statues, standardized figures manufactured domestically or carved overseas by low-wage laborers in factory-like workshops.

The committee had many options. More than a dozen firms produced statues for Civil War commemorations, and the Sons and Daughters selected an effigy from a Salem, Ohio, manufacturer that specialized in low-cost, stamped-metal figures. W. H. Mullins Company was already well-known in North Carolina. C. J. Hulin and the Durham Marble Works, who promised Mrs. London and the Pittsboro Daughters a "bronze statue of a Confederate soldier ... seven feet in height," used a "7 ft. statue, No. 8678 ... in sheet copper, antique bronze finish," according to a 1913 Mullins' catalog.[8]

Randolph County's Confederate monument (Asheboro, 1911) was also topped with a Mullins' figure, a six-foot-high Confederate infantryman, "No. 5608 ... made in sheet bronze," while four of the company's statues, three of individuals and one of a "Minute Man" adorned monuments on the "Guilford Revolutionary Battle Ground" in Greensboro (today's Guilford National Battlefield).[9]

Warren's committee selected a "Confederate infantryman at Parade Rest," an aging veteran, model 8678-A, available "in sheet copper, antique bronze finish; also in sheet bronze." This infantryman, however, appears largely identical to Pittsboro's youthful Confederate, available in the same materials. The soldiers, models 8678 and 8678-A, are featured side-by-side in Mullins' 1913 catalog, with identical poses, accoutrements, and uniforms. The men differ only in facial features, hat, and perhaps hair; both were likely stamped from the same set of body molds then had different heads and hats attached.[10]

Warren County Confederate monument. Warrenton. Dedicated October 29, 1913.

As dedication-day approached, the (Warren) *Record* did not detail the soldier's features — or announce that it was manufactured in a Northern factory. "A beautiful Monument 'TO OUR HEROES' is ready for unveiling," the paper proclaimed. "The Warren Chapter Daughters of the Confederacy, and the sons of this good county, have cause for rejoicing," for a monument "stands majestically upon the Court House square, surmounted by a Confederate Infantryman, in bronze, a loving and enduring tribute of love for the men who laid down their lives upon the field of battle and to the men who returned to their homes and evolved order from chaos — Confederate Soldiers, all."[11]

Nearly fifty years after Appomattox, Warren County's unveiling highlights the ongoing resolution of societal grief that had been expressed so poignantly through James Barron

Hope's lamentation delivered at Anne Lee's memorial in 1866. Portions of Hope's "Elegiac Ode," nevertheless were reprinted in the *Record*, perhaps to demonstrate healing, as well as proclaim Warren's commemorative legacy, that "Miss Annie Carter Lee, whose Dust mingling with Warren County's soil is a precious heritage."[12]

The October 29, 1913, dedication had the airs of a celebration, not a wake, "proclaim[ing] to all the world," according to the *Record*, "that Warren County loved the living and honored the dead Confederate soldier." The parade featured "guests" and Southern veterans riding "in decorated automobiles," as well as "the Brass Band; the Military; the Boy Scouts," and schoolchildren from across the county. Former governor Robert Glenn was the orator, his speech "the best ever delivered here by any speaker," the *Record* declared. The band played "America" and "The Star-Spangled Banner," as well as "Carolina" and "Dixie."[13]

Stamped-metal soldier. Warren County Confederate monument. This stamped, sheet-copper infantryman with an antique bronze finish was manufactured by the W. H. Mullins Company of Salem, Ohio. Warrenton, 1913.

Commissioner Charles G. Moore, accepting the memorial on behalf of the county, spoke of the Confederate soldier and his legacy. "They were only plain American Citizens," Moore said, "who, of their own accord, left all the endearments of Home at the call of duty." "They are dear friends," he continued, "as palpable to us now as when luminous with the glory of Chancellorsville or sublime in their failure at Gettysburg.... But let no man dream they died in vain." Instead, the commissioner declared, "we are richer today than if the demon of strife had never wasted on high places.... Providence will never permit such seas of blood to have been shed in vain."[14]

"You have wrought nobly in marble and bronze," Moore told the Daughters in closing, "and coming generations will rise up and call your memory blessed."[15]

The selection by Warren's Daughters and Sons of the monument's soldier of "bronze," however, may have been a late decision. Two engravings depict the monument prior to its unveiling; one, in the 1913 Mullins' catalog, features the monument beside a curving rural road, the commemoration topped with the aging Confederate veteran ultimately used. The other, published in the *Record* five days before the unveiling shows an identically carved shaft but is topped with a youthful soldier, probably the aging veteran's near-twin, model 8678.[16]

For most North Carolinians, the courthouse-lawn Civil War monument was their first exposure to public art. Confederate monuments, many reflecting classical influences and erected under the leadership of elite, often well-educated women, had, for three decades, been placed in some of the state's largest urban cemeteries. As the nineteenth century closed, however, Tarheel Confederate commemoration shifted to the state's civic spaces and spread beyond its most populous cities.

Monument committee members planning these new memorials, although well-intentioned, often had little artistic knowledge. Illustrations, cemetery statuary, advice of stone carvers and salesmen, as well as visits to nearby cities, shaped design decisions. In addition, creativity had to be tempered with commemorative aims and financial realities. As the twentieth century dawned, one form, the solitary soldier atop a granite shaft, came to the fore.

These soldier statues — cast from bronze, stamped from sheet metal, or hewn from granite or marble — serve as the focal

Model 8678-A. From W. H. Mullins' 1913 catalog.

point for most civic-space Confederate monuments as well as similar commemorations raised across the victorious North. Effigies are life-size or slightly larger; a ten-foot-tall infantryman atop the state monument in Raleigh and a nine-foot-high soldier in Burke County (Morganton, 1918) are likely North Carolina's tallest.

Committees, however, seemed to pay scant attention to the sculptural qualities of most cast and carved images. Accomplished artists were rarely available to local groups, and funding constraints often trumped aesthetics, especially for a figure which on average stood nearly twenty feet above the ground and whose finer details could only be appreciated through binoculars.

Critics wasted little time assailing these armies of stone and bronze deployed across

Anson County Confederate monument and courthouse. Former Confederate sergeant John Richardson, a local veteran, served as the model for this Confederate soldier, produced by Scoggins Memorial Art. Wadesboro, 1906.

North and South. In 1898, American sculptor Karl Bitter wrote of "the customary column with its customary soldier ... the same man with the same meaningless features." French art critic William Jean Beauley, touring the northern United States in 1904, spoke even more harshly. "Everywhere I am shown the same soldier, same overcoat, same rifle, same position.... I have often heard of the horrors of war, but never before have mine eyes beheld them."[17]

Across North Carolina, except for a handful of commissioned bronzes placed upon short pedestals, there seemed a similar lack of creativity. A closer study of these soldier figures, however, reveals that many were not unique renditions at all but mass-produced ornaments manufactured in northern factories or carved by overseas laborers and sold through traveling salesmen. The commemorative Confederate soldier, like his Union counterpart, was seldom intended to be a sculptural masterpiece. Indeed, he was often little more than a commodity.

North Carolina's soldier figures may loosely be categorized into five groups: the commissioned, well-executed sculpture signed by a renowned artist; a lower-cost, widely distributed bronze cast, one of many copies; the frequently unsigned rendition crafted by a local stonecarver; a marble or granite figure produced in factory-like foreign shops; and hollow, sheet-metal soldiers assembled by welding stamped-metal pieces into a finished form.

In 1948, Lewis W. Williams, II, in an MFA thesis entitled *Commercially Produced Forms of American Civil War Monuments*, analyzed the artistic tradition and commercial production of soldier statues. Although Williams focused on Northern commemorations, his analysis is applicable to Tarheel memorials since stone and metal firms supplied Confederate as well as Union figures.

The solitary soldier — with gaze straight ahead, left knee sometimes bent with foot slightly forward, and hands gripping a vertical rifle whose butt rests on the ground — quickly became the standard depiction. Randolph Rogers, an American living in Rome, likely sculpted the earliest iteration of this motif, a bronze commissioned in 1863 for the Spring Grove Cemetery in Cincinnati, Ohio. Cast by Frederick von Muller in Munich, Germany, and erected "by public subscription" the following year, this statue on a granite pedestal represents, according to an 1869 handbook, "a Union soldier standing upon guard."[18]

While Rogers may have pioneered the form, Irish-born Martin Milmore popularized it, developing, according to art historian Chandler Post, "this kind of monument to its culmination." Milmore's first monument was an "immediate success," writes Williams. Erected in Roxbury, Massachusetts' Forest Hills Cemetery in 1867, the figure was described by contemporary critic Henry Tuckerman as "represent[ing] the American volunteer, the private soldier equipped with his overcoat, resting on his gun and contemplating the graves of his comrades."[19]

North Carolina's first "Skirmisher." Fayetteville. This Cumberland County monument is topped with a "skirmisher," a soldier holding his rifle as if ready for action, the earliest use of this form in the Tarheel State. 1902.

Milmore's work was pricey. Roxbury's "simple granite pedestal" and cast bronze soldier reportedly cost $13,000.00, forty-three times the amount of North Carolina's first Civil War memorial. Yet "orders for this kind of commemorative sculpture soon began to pour in on Milmore in such number," according to Post, "that it became his custom to supply ... replicas of already executed figures." Within two years, Roxbury's soldier "was repeated" three times, twice in New Hampshire and once in Massachusetts.[20]

Representations of other service branches followed. Rogers cast an artilleryman, a cavalryman, and a sailor in addition to an infantryman for Detroit, Michigan's, monument, commissioned in 1867 and completed six years later for $75,000.00. The flag-bearer, the fifth and final troop motif commonly used in Civil War sculptural commemoration, debuted in 1872, executed independently by Milmore in Erie, Pennsylvania, and by Launt Thompson in Pittsfield, Massachusetts.[21]

In North Carolina meanwhile, monuments were smaller and much less expensive. Prior to 1883, only one Tarheel commemoration (Wilmington, 1872) was topped with a soldier figure. This bronze, however, was an original, sculpted by William Rudolph O'Donovan and cast by Maurice J. Power at the National Fine Art Foundry in New York City. And like Milmore's creations, copies were made; two Northern commemorations reportedly feature O'Donovan's depiction.[22]

Nash County Confederate monument. Rocky Mount. This seventy-five-foot-tall monument, funded by Confederate veteran Robert Ricks and given by him to the U.D.C., originally featured five carved figures, one on each of the lower pedestals plus the flag-bearer, which remains atop the column. Two of the lower figures were stolen in the 1970s and have not been recovered; the others were removed for safekeeping. Dedicated May 14, 1917.

Four Tarheel monuments featuring solitary soldier figures were raised between 1883 and the unveiling of North Carolina's capitol-grounds monument twelve years later. Two statues were of stone: Craven County's (New Bern, 1885) marble cavalier, reportedly carved by the "finest workman" in Carrara, Italy, "after a design expressly for this monument"; and Beaufort County's (Washington, 1888) granite soldier, probably a local creation since a county veteran served as the model.[23]

Less is known about the metal renditions. Neither is signed, and attribution of Greensboro's stamped sheet-copper infantryman remains uncertain. What is known—that Wayne County's (Goldsboro, 1883) monument was fabricated by the Baltimore, Maryland, firm of Gaddess Brothers Steam Marble Works and topped with a sand-blasted zinc figure from the Philadelphia White Bronze Monument Company for a total price of $992.00, and that Guilford County's (Greensboro, 1888) commemoration was "thought" by an early U.D.C. historian to have cost $400.00—means that both soldier figures almost certainly are less-expensive reproductions.[24]

The increasing popularity of this sculptural design in North Carolina mirrors national trends. Foundries and factories produced scores of nearly identical soldiers as commemorative fervor spread. "This form of monument [is] so popular," one critic complained, "that it has been reproduced in varying degrees of incompleteness and ineffectiveness over the whole United States." Yet as the nation industrialized and mass production surged, similar or even identical works were cherished as "modern." A common appearance often took precedence over creativity.[25]

North Carolina's monument to the Confederate dead, dedicated in 1895, was the state's most elaborate and expensive memorial of its era. Featuring three well-executed bronze figures by Ferdinand von Miller, II, "the finest sculptor in bronze living," according to the (Raleigh) *News and Observer*, this complex commemoration would prove a stylistic aberration. As with other contemporaneous civic-space memorials, the solitary soldier retains his place of prominence atop the seventy-five-foot-tall memorial. This infantryman, however, is complemented by a sword-wielding cavalryman to the south, while to the north, a bronze artilleryman brandishes a ramrod as if preparing for battle. These two

Soldiers. Nash County Confederate monument. Rocky Mount. These marble soldiers, an officer and an infantryman, were removed from Nash County's Confederate monument following the theft of two other figures, a cavalryman and a sailor, in the 1970s. They are stored in a city-owned warehouse where this photograph was taken in 2011.

figures—the earliest Tarheel commemorative representations of these services—flank the base of the granite shaft, their lower height allowing ready appreciation of von Miller's sculptural details.[26]

More than two decades would pass, however, before multiple figures or other military services again appeared on a Tarheel monument. Whether due to artistic taste, or cost, the solitary soldier depiction remained the state's dominant commemorative form for another generation.

In 1902, the "Women of Cumberland" (Cumberland County/Fayetteville) introduced a variation of the standard infantryman to the Tarheel state. Fayetteville's bronze soldier, sculpted by I. W. Durham, does not rest his rifle on the ground. Instead the seven-foot-high figure holds the weapon with both hands near his chest, the gun's nearly horizontal barrel raised slightly and pointed left. Striding forward as if ready for action, this "Skirmisher" is posed more aggressively than previous North Carolina infantrymen, all of which had been sculpted as though standing guard.[27]

The new motif ultimately would top ten Tarheel memorials — eight to the Confederate dead and one each to Confederate soldiers and Confederate heroes — yet never achieve the popularity of the "Parade Rest" infantryman. By necessity these skirmishers were of metal; a slender exposed gun barrel of marble or granite would have been technically difficult to carve and prone to breakage, especially from vandalism.

As the United Daughters of the Confederacy assumed commemorative leadership from the Ladies' Memorial Associations early in the twentieth century, solitary soldier monuments near courthouses and in other prominent civic locations quickly became the state's dominant memorial style. During the Daughters' monument-building heyday, from 1904 to 1917, twenty-six of thirty-three Tarheel civic-space commemorations depicted lone infantrymen at parade rest or as skirmishers. Yet few of these figures were original works of art. Manufactured copies or less-expensive reproductions — much like today's more affordable limited edition prints — topped most monuments.[28]

Pitt County Confederate monument. Greenville. The soldier is a Mullins' figure. Governor Locke Craig delivered the dedication-day oration. November 13, 1914.

"Each metal company and every granite firm, although probably attempting exact copies, produced figures slightly differently," Williams states. Sculptural excellence, however, was difficult to discern from twenty feet below the statue, and creativity seemed limited to accoutrements, posture, and facial features.[29]

Union as well as Confederate troops were manufactured, with allegiances differentiated by a blanket roll, hat, or backpack (Chapter 3) and by uniform insignia, some of which were kept in stock and could be "welded upon the figure for a specific patron." Troops made of copper, zinc, or antique bronze might have youthful faces, or a buyer could opt for a grizzled veteran in any of these metals. Most figures sported a mustache, although clean-shaven or fully bearded soldiers were also available.³⁰

New technology and plunging prices undoubtedly accelerated adoption of this motif. In the late 1890s, the W. H. Mullins Company of Salem, Ohio, developed a "new method of making statuary," using "stamped sheets of metal which were soldered together to form statues." These depictions — at least six of which top North Carolina monuments — "looked exactly like cast bronze figures," according to company literature.³¹

Founded in 1872, Mullins gained prominence by manufacturing decorative cornices, metal roofing, and embossed ceiling panels before expanding into the stamping of fenders and body parts for the nascent automobile industry. The firm also fabricated art: Saint-Gaudens' "Diana"; statues for the Naval Academy; sculpture exhibited at Chicago's 1893 World's Fair; and a thirty-two-foot-high stamped metal effigy of the god Herman for New Ulm, Minnesota, the largest statue ever created by this method.³²

Sheet-metal military figures of Civil War, Spanish-American, and later World War I soldiers became one of the firm's leading products, a line of statuary that would be produced until 1928. Stamped

Assembly detail. Sampson County Confederate monument. This aging statue clearly shows where stamped-metal pieces have been joined. Clinton, 1916.

from sheets of copper or bronze then bent under high pressure between cast-iron molds, the pieces of pressed metal were soldered together and braced internally with copper or iron supports forming lightweight, low-cost effigies.³³

In 1913, the company published an advertising catalog illustrating dozens of its stock figures. *The Blue and Gray* opens with "an effusive and sentimental forward," as described by Williams, "concerned with the sacredness of the task of erecting monuments and the appropriateness of Mullins [sic] statuary." Full-page illustrations of forty-two monuments from across the nation incorporating the company's sheet metal figures follow, each with "the location, contractor, and code number of the statue used."³⁴

"Cuts and brief descriptions" of twenty-three soldier statues are also showcased, providing an overview of the firm's offerings. "The Skirmisher," perhaps symbolically, is illustrated first, followed by an "Artilleryman"; two parade rest infantrymen, one of which is wearing a great coat; and two sailors, one holding a spyglass, the other an oar. All are succinctly identified—Sailor, Artilleryman, Infantryman at Parade Rest—and most are the same height, "Six feet high" above the base, "Made in sheet copper, antique bronze finish; also in sheet bronze." Basal dimensions and specifications are standardized as well and cited to a fraction of an inch, "One-eighth-inch plate base."[35]

Spanish-American War soldiers and "two specifically made statues of Generals Morehead and Lee," are shown next followed by four Confederates: "two Confederate Parade Rest infantrymen, one with a beard; Confederate Cavalryman; another Confederate Infantryman, here the musket has a bayonet." Williams illustrates only one of these Southern troops, however, the "Confederate Infantryman at Parade Rest," model number 8678-A. This aging veteran, wearing a slouch hat instead of a kepi and with a blanket roll looped around his torso, was available in the same metals as the other troops, yet this bearded soldier, partly due to a higher hat, stands a full foot taller than Mullins' other figures.[36]

Soldier detail. Caswell County Confederate monument. This bronze soldier, produced by the American Bronze Foundry, is a "skirmisher." Caswell County's antebellum courthouse is in the background. Yanceyville, 1921.

Mullins "advertised heavily in all trade magazines," according to Williams, and "maintained a staff of salesmen on the road." Price and selection, however, more than artistic excellence, may have provided the firm's competitive edge. For although the soldier figure is the focal point of most monuments, the granite shaft and base cost far more, exceeding the price of all but the costliest metal figures.[37]

The Blue and Gray did not list prices, but at least one Mullins' competitor advertised theirs. The J. L. Mott Iron Works, with offices in New York and Chicago, offered a "U.S. Infantry Soldier Resting Arms" for $150.00, "Painted one coat." This six-foot-three-inch figure, in great coat and kepi with a bayonet by his side, was also available in bronze—price $165.00.[38]

T. F. McGann and Sons Company in Boston, the Philadelphia White Bronze Monument Company, Jonathan Williams, Inc., of New York, and Chicago's American Bronze Foundry also ranked among well-known suppliers of Civil War statuary. All showcased products through catalogs and advertisements; four McGann figures—two infantrymen, a cavalryman, and a sailor—are illustrated by Williams as well as a six-image page of Jonathan Williams' work, including both a Union and a Confederate soldier.[39]

American Bronze Foundry crafted numerous Confederate figures, including at least four topping North Carolina memorials. "We furnish Statues for ALL KINDS of Monuments," the company boasted in a February 1909 advertisement. The image of a mustachioed, unarmed Confederate soldier, entitled "In Memoriam," with eyes downcast and slouch hat in hand, filled much of the quarter-page ad, a graphic that would appear six times that year in the *Confederate Veteran*.[40]

The majority of North Carolina's Confederate soldier figures, however, are unsigned. Only eighteen of the state's fifty-one commemorative troops can be reliably attributed. Six are Mullins' products, all parade rest models erected between 1911 and 1925. Four American Bronze Foundry castings—two skirmishers and two parade-rest infantrymen with deeply etched corporate signatures—topped Tarheel memorials between 1904 and 1921.[41]

Jackson County Confederate monument. Sylva. This soldier figure is a Mullins' statue, nearly identical to Asheboro's Mullins' infantryman except for placement of the backpack. Dedicated September 18, 1915.

Seven additional signed or otherwise attributed works are part of the state's commemorative landscape; each piece, however, is a different sculptor's creation. Other Tarheel figures were cut by unidentified "local carvers," while at least four marble soldiers, including New Bern's 1885 creation by the "finest workman" in Carrara, were crafted by unnamed artisans in Italy, known for lower-priced statuary.[42]

Future research will likely increase these numbers. Some may be Mullins' statues; several unidentified North Carolina Confederates are welded sheet-metal figures, yet the firm "signed" their work with a nameplate that could easily be pried off. Other statues may be signed less conspicuously or marked internally. Cleanings and restorations might uncover identification that even the most meticulous ground-level examination would fail to discern.

That barely one-third of North Carolina's Confederate soldier statues have known attribution is perhaps revealing. Like Pittsboro's Daughters who contracted for "a bronze statue of a Confederate soldier of standard government bronze, seven feet in height," yet recorded no further discussion as to design selection, memorial groups often treated the soldier figure as little more than an ornament.[43]

This seeming lack of concern as to provenance or artistic merit is frequently blamed on committee members possessing little knowledge of fine art. Although this undoubtedly played a role, commercial realities, cost, and even commemorative goals contributed as well. Most aspects of production — granite procurement, decorative carving, inscriptions, assembly — could be accomplished locally or obtained regionally, facts often cited proudly. But the monument's visual focus, frequently selected from a catalog and determined by affordability, was nearly always purchased from Northern manufacturers or mass-produced overseas, sources widely disdained across the South.[44]

"Silent Sam." University of North Carolina, Chapel Hill, Orange County. Sculpted by John Wilson and produced by the Gorham Company, this soldier is "silent" because he does not wear a cartridge box. Three hundred twenty-one university students, alumni, and faculty died fighting for the Confederacy. Co-funded by the North Carolina U.D.C. and university alumni. Dedicated June 2, 1913.

The anonymity and similarities of the sculpted infantrymen — Karl Bitter's "same man with the same meaningless features" — may reflect a deeper commemorative yearning as well. North Carolina's civic-space memorial consensus, although delayed by economic hardship and the need to forge a collective memory in the wake of defeat, was strongly egalitarian, honoring *all* the dead, *all* soldiers, *all* "heroes." The hewn and stamped figures atop the state's Confederate monuments celebrate neither sculptor nor individual soldier. The generic infantryman represents no *one*, yet honors *all*.[45]

Although the popularity of the public-space soldier figure waned rapidly following World War I, the theme of an anonymous representation honoring all military personnel endured. In 1921, this symbolism assumed a physical expression in Arlington National Cemetery when a thirty-two-ton block of marble inscribed, "Here Rests in Honored Glory an American Soldier Known but to God," marked a single grave — the Tomb of the Unknown Soldier — and became the nation's most hallowed military shrine.[46]

11. Monument Companies

Eight-hundred-eighty-nine Macon County men enlisted to fight for Southern independence. Company H, Sixteenth North Carolina Regiment, organized at the county seat of Franklin on May 14, 1861, less than five weeks after the shelling of Fort Sumter. The Nantahala Rangers, a cavalry unit, formed next. In all, seven companies — four infantry and three cavalry — would be raised in one of North Carolina's westernmost counties, "enough [men] for a full regiment," W.A. Curtis reminded the crowd gathered on September 30, 1909.[1]

In a region where men dominated early-twentieth century commemoration, Macon's veterans maintained strong ties through reunions of the Charles L. Robinson Camp #947 of the United Confederate Veterans. At their first gathering, in 1889, the men listened as Miss Maggie Moore, "standing under the tattered and battle-scarred flag of the 39th North Carolina Regiment," recited "The Conquered Banner," Father Abram Ryan's despairing ode acknowledging Southern defeat. "Furl that banner softly, slowly.... Let it droop there, furled forever, For its people's hopes are dead."[2]

Fourteen years later, spirits seemed higher. At the September 1903 reunion, a two-day event, "The ladies were in charge of the dinner, hence it was a feast," the *Confederate Veteran* reported, and "Major N. P. Rankin drilled and marched the old boys as when they were in their teens." Rankin, the Camp Commander, also suggested to the 130 veterans "that a memorial association be formed for Macon County, and that an effort be made to erect a monument on the public square of Franklin."[3]

Less than three months later, "at the Major's call," veterans met and organized the Macon County Monument Association. Rankin was elected president and W. A. Curtis, U. C. V. Adjutant, chosen as secretary-treasurer, "positions held ever since by them," according to Curtis' dedication-day remarks. Seven vice presidents, one from each of the seven companies, rounded out the Association's officers.[4]

"The idea of erecting a monument to the memory of Macon County veterans was first conceived by Maj. N. P. Rankin," Curtis told the dedication-day throng in 1909. "He has labored with persistency and zeal ... and he deserves all the credit and honor for what has been accomplished."[5]

There is little documentation, however, of the men's fund-raising efforts. In 1907, the Association was incorporated; two years later, the North Carolina General Assembly authorized Macon County commissioners to "donate a plat of land in the Public Square," measuring 68 by 83 feet, "to the Association on which to erect the monument."[6]

The veterans selected McNeel Marble Company of Marietta, Georgia, to construct the memorial. Headquartered one-hundred miles from Franklin and touting seventeen years' stoneworking experience, McNeel was becoming the pre-eminent supplier of Confederate commemoration. The contract was likely signed in spring 1909; within six months the monument was complete.[7]

There is no record of the men's deliberations as to design or inscriptions or if advice was tendered by McNeel. Curtis, however, cited the monument's specifications and cost on dedication day. "The monument consists of twenty-seven stones, is twenty-five feet high above the concrete foundation, and built of fine Georgia marble." "The entire weight ... is about 35,000 pounds," the adjutant said, crediting "the McNeel Marble Co. of Marietta, Ga.," with raising the monument "at a cost of $1650." A six-foot-tall soldier statue topped the memorial, a sculpture the veteran described as "made in Italy of fine Italian marble" and "beautiful as a work of art in its simplicity, its symmetry of form, and its magnificent pose," before adding, "It alone cost $600."[8]

"September 30, 1909, was perhaps the greatest day within the history of Franklin, N.C.," the *Confederate Veteran* trumpeted. "The country people began to arrive early, and it was estimated that over fifteen hundred people were present." Sixty veterans and two state governors attended as well.[9]

Major Rankin called the assembly to order. W. A. Curtis served as master of ceremonies; the Rev. J. A. Deal "invoked the divine blessing," then the Franklin Choir sang "The Old North State Forever!" Three brief speeches, an "address of welcome," a response, and an "unveiling address," followed. Then seven ladies, "descendants of the commanding officers of the seven companies that went from Macon County to the war ... marched to the front of the monument and pulled the cord." The veil "fell gracefully from the statue and floated gently down right and left ... the monument stood unveiled in all its grace and majestic beauty, while the assembly applauded."[10]

The choir sang "Dixie" then later "America." North Carolina

Macon County Confederate Monument. Franklin. Funded by the Charles L. Robinson Camp, United Confederate Veterans; constructed by McNeel Marble Company of Marietta, Georgia. Dedicated September 30, 1909.

Governor W. W. Kitchin delivered a "magnificent oration" that "held his audience spellbound for an hour or more," according to the *Veteran*. An "intermission for dinner" followed. "The sixty old veterans present ... dined at the Junaluskee Inn through the courtesy of the proprietress, Mrs. Laura Bryson, with the Governors of the two States, North and South Carolina, at each end of the long table."[11]

A sumptuous meal for veterans was a typical dedication-day event, but this unusual scheduling necessitated dividing the public activities. Miss Clyde McGuire, daughter of Maggie Moore McGuire, began the afternoon program by reciting "The Conquered Banner," the same poem her mother delivered twenty years earlier at the veterans' first reunion. Both presentations were made under the "tattered and battle-scarred flag," upheld each time by "J. W. Shelton, the last color bearer of the regiment."[12]

An address by South Carolina's governor was followed with the reading of "Sketches of the seven companies ... written by Maj. N. P. Rankin." Each unit had received enduring recognition on the just-unveiled memorial. Company H, Sixteenth North Carolina Regiment, the county's first Confederate military force, received premier placement, directly above the monument's primary inscription. The remaining sides featured paired inscriptions, the upper honoring an infantry unit, the lower a cavalry company.[13]

Macon's veterans dedicated North Carolina's westernmost Confederate monument "In Memory of the Sons of Macon County Who Served in the Confederate Army." Yet when the old soldiers sought to complete the inscription by naming the conflict in which they had fought, they encountered the same difficulties faced by other commemorative groups. The men chose to describe their time of service with a phrase that remains unique in the state, "War Period," engraved with the largest font of the inscription's three closing lines, "During the WAR PERIOD 1861–1865."

In April 1909, the McNeel Marble Company of Marietta, Georgia, directed a full-page advertisement in the *Confederate Veteran* to the "Daughters of the Confederacy." This "Word From McNeel," addressed two sources of commemorative angst, fund-raising and a desire to honor aging veterans before the men passed on. "Why wait and worry about raising funds?" McNeel asked. "Why not buy it [a monument] now and have it erected before all the old veterans have answered the final roll call?"[14]

The company offered its solution. "Our terms to U.D.C. Chapters are so liberal and our plans for raising funds are so effective as to obviate the necessity of either waiting or worrying." During the "last three or four years," McNeel claimed, "we have sold Confederate monuments to thirty-seven of your sister Chapters." These memorials, erected across five states including one in Lumberton, North Carolina, ranged in price from $1,250.00 to $22,500.00, yet "None of these Chapters have experienced any difficulty in raising sufficient funds to meet their payments." "In each and every case," McNeel asserted, chapters found "that it is much easier to raise funds after you have bought the monument than before."[15]

This self-proclaimed "largest builders of monuments in the Southern States," made the process of erecting a memorial seem easy, even when chapters "had but small amounts in hand at the time they placed their order." "We cover the entire Southern States, and can ship the most massive monuments to any point in this territory," McNeel boasted, although the firm thus far had erected monuments only in Georgia and four neighboring states. "What your sister Chapters have done, you can do," McNeel promised. "The information will only cost you the price of a postal, and it may be worth a monument to you."[16]

McNeel was neither the first regional monument company nor the first of these firms to advertise widely. Six years earlier, the Muldoon Monument Company of Louisville, Kentucky, claiming to be the "Oldest and Most Reliable House in America," boasted in a half-page *Veteran* advertisement of "hav[ing] erected nine-tenths of the Confederate Monuments in the United States." A "partial list" of twenty-one installations followed, flanked by an engraved image of a parade-rest soldier statue. The company's monuments were pricey, ranging "from five to thirty thousand dollars." Yet among Muldoon's expanding list of Confederate memorials, documented through at least seven years of *Veteran* advertisements, were commemorations in prominent cities across seven Southern states, including North Carolina's state monument in Raleigh (1895). "To see these monuments is to appreciate them," the firm repeatedly declared.[17]

Northern firms also sought Confederate commemorative commissions. The Monumental Bronze Company of Bridgeport, Connecticut, manufacturers of "Soldiers' Monuments in White Bronze," claimed to have erected "Over a Hundred" such memorials in "recent years, including many Confederate monuments." The company and its seven affiliates, firms located from Philadelphia to New Orleans and Des Moines, specialized in zinc and white bronze statuary, lower-cost materials that peaked in popularity during the 1880s.[18]

A monument of zinc. This commemoration beside the Tyrrell County courthouse in Columbia features the most extensive use of zinc in a North Carolina monument. An easily worked metal, zinc allows a range of low-cost inscriptions; sixteen panels are included on this monument. Monumental Bronze Company, Bridgeport, Connecticut. 1902.

Advertisements in the 1907 *Confederate Veteran* extolled the virtues of "white bronze," a sandblasted zinc with a long-lasting, stone-like finish. This proprietary treatment, the firm claimed, resulted in statues "more enduring than the best of granite and much handsomer as well as cheaper." The surface's weather resistance was also touted. A Massachusetts testimonial praised one of the firm's monuments that "looks more noble, more beautiful and more grand ... than the day it was erected," despite twelve years' exposure to "the salt sea air."[19]

"Every community should have a monument in memory of the brave men who went out to defend what they considered a just cause," the Connecticut firm declared in the May 1907 *Veteran*. Three months earlier, the company had cited eight of its installations across five Southern states, including one in Tyrrell County (Columbia,

1902), North Carolina. Yet the advertisement requested "communication with every [U.C.V.] Camp raising funds or contemplating the erection of a monument, large or small," ignoring the United Daughters of the Confederacy and its Chapters. Monumental Bronze had likely dealt extensively with Union veterans, a primary funding source for nineteenth-century Northern memorials, yet slighting the Daughters may have proved costly. For although the company claimed that "Every community can afford such a monument," and praised its "easy plan to raise funds," there is no record of further sales in the Tarheel State.[20]

Smaller firms advertised as well. Virgil L. Fuller of Quincy, Massachusetts, ran a small ad in the February 1912 *Veteran* offering "Granite — Marble & Bronze Memorials" with "quality unsurpassed" as well as monuments, fountains, tablets, and markers. Readers were urged to "write — for designs & estimates." However there is no evidence that Fuller erected any commemorations in North Carolina.[21]

Fairview Cemetery, Warrenton. 1903. "To the Confederate Dead of Warren County, N.C.," and "Erected by the efforts of Mrs. Lucy E. Polk," are engraved on this monument constructed and signed by Cooper Brothers of Raleigh.

Many North Carolina Civil War monuments were instead erected by local stonecutting firms whose primary business was family cemetery memorials. Cooper Brothers of Raleigh installed two Warren County monuments. The first, erected in 1903, features a carved marble soldier atop a base of stone and marble in Warrenton's Fairview Cemetery, a monument to the Confederate dead funded by the Memorial Association of Warren County.

Ten years later, the United Daughters of the Confederacy and "Sons of Warren" again tapped the firm, this time for a courthouse-lawn granite shaft honoring "Confederate Heroes," topped with a Mullins' soldier figure. Coopers signed the cemetery memorial but, like most contractors of early twentieth-century Tarheel Confederate commemorations, did not sign the courthouse shaft. And while Mullins showcased — and credited — Coopers' "Heroes" monument in its 1913 catalog, an undated though probably contemporaneous Coopers' publication did not illustrate any of its Confederate monuments.[22]

The Durham Marble Works of Durham, North Carolina, was another Tarheel contractor. C. J. Hulin, the "marble man from Durham" who dealt directly with the Pittsboro Daughters (Chapter 8), likely owned the firm. His Pittsboro installation was apparently well-received, for within two years Durham Marble raised a virtually identical monument, differing only by a handful of decorative cuts and topped with the same stamped-metal soldier figure, in Pearisburg, Virginia, less than 150 miles away. Both commemorations garnered full-page photos in Mullins' 1913 catalog and were credited to "the Durham Marble Works, Durham, N.C. Surmounted by 7 ft. [Mullins] statue, No. 8678."[23]

In October 1909, six months after McNeel's "Word" to the Daughters, the firm next advertised in the *Veteran*. In the interim, thirteen orders from seven states had been booked, including one from Macon County, North Carolina. With total monument sales at fifty, McNeel reiterated its twin themes of "liberal terms, and reasonable prices," that would allow U.D.C. Chapters "to secure handsome monuments ... *now*, before the Confederate Veterans and good women of the sixties have passed away."[24]

This advertisement, however, singularly addressed U.D.C. Chapters, as if the Daughters were the South's only commemorative organization. Even Macon County's monument, funded by Confederate veterans, was included on the firm's "list of [U.D.C.] Chapters sold," a tally repeated two months later when total sales had increased to fifty-three.[25]

The following February, McNeel extolled its "Phenomenal Record" across the *Veteran's* back cover. "More Confederate Monuments have been erected throughout the South by the United Daughters of the Confederacy during the past year than during any previous *ten* years since the War" [italics in original document], the company claimed, and "records will show that THE McNEEL MARBLE CO. has been entrusted with the execution of more than 95% of all orders for Confederate

Gaston County Confederate monument. Gastonia. Funded by the Gastonia Chapter, U.D.C., and the J. D. Moore Chapter, Children of the Confederacy. Constructed by the Southern Marble and Granite Company. Dedicated November 21, 1912.

Monuments that have been given in the South during the year 1909." McNeel again offered a "solution [that] is yours for the asking," one that "puts a Confederate monument within the reach of every Chapter."[26]

The sales tactics were wildly successful. In August 1910, proclaiming itself "The Largest Monumental Mill South," McNeel reported four additional contracts "this month," including two from North Carolina: a soldier-topped memorial to Confederate Heroes in Pasquotank County (Elizabeth City, 1911) and a courthouse-lawn obelisk — the last use of this form in Tarheel civic-space Civil War commemoration — in nearby Perquimans County (Hertford, 1912).[27]

By February 1911, with "Twenty years experience in the manufacture of monuments" and "a state of perfection in material, design and workmanship," the firm's tally had soared to "Over one hundred." The full-page, back-cover announcement trumpeting this achievement, however, contained a verbal miscue. "We Have Erected Over One Hundred Monuments to the Confederate Dead for U.D.C. Chapters," the banner headline read. Six McNeel monuments were in North Carolina. Yet at least one of these commemorations had been chiefly funded by a group other than the U.D.C., and only two of the firm's six Tarheel installations primarily honored the dead, with the most recent contracts, Caldwell County (Lenoir, 1910) and Rutherford County (Rutherfordton, 1910) honoring "The Men Who Wore the Gray" and the "Men and Women of the Confederacy," respectively.[28]

Perquimans County Confederate monument. Hertford. North Carolina's last civic-space Confederate obelisk. Dedicated June 12, 1912; constructed by McNeel Marble Company.

There is no evidence of protest against the use of "Confederate Dead" or "U.D.C. Chapters"— nor would *Veteran* editor S. A. Cunningham likely have printed such grievances — but when McNeel next advertised three months later, the firm's tone changed. Beneath a doubly underlined banner of "Honoring the Brave," McNeel addressed "Chapters and [U. C. V.] Camps throughout all the Southland." The firm repeated its claim of "more than one hundred monuments" but followed these words with "to the **Soldiers and Women of the Confederacy**," emphasis added through bold type, a stylistic rarity for the firm's ads. Three times in four paragraphs McNeel referred to "Chapters and [or]

Camps" before concluding with a plea to "Let us help you in erecting a memorial to **those who wore the Gray**, or to those equally deserving of honor, the **loyal women of the Confederacy**."²⁹

The adoption of inclusive terminology was long-lasting. McNeel described the design and manufacture of "Confederate monuments" in June; addressed the "Soldiers and Women of the Confederacy" beneath the headline "A Lasting Tribute" in August; and always included "Camps" as well as "Chapters."³⁰

By October, the company seemed back on track, with "twenty-one orders for Confederate monuments, most of which are to be unveiled next Memorial Day." "Now is the time to place order [sic] if monument is to be unveiled next spring," McNeel stressed, resuming its high-pressure style. Further inducements followed. In December, the firm offered "A Valuable Present Absolutely Free"—a "Five-Dollar Marble Breadboard" that would "make very appropriate and acceptable Christmas presents"—to "two officers or members of any Chapter or Camp" that would "furnish us the names of one or more Chapters or Camps that propose to erect a monument next year."³¹

Two months later, a company advertisement provided insight into the acquisition of soldier statues. "We have decided to carry in stock a number of statues of Confederate soldiers, and now have on hand twelve of our most popular statues," McNeel declared. "It requires from five to six months to import these statues from Italy," the firm continued, and "a monument complete [sic] could not be furnished short of that time." But as the "only company carrying statues of Confederate soldiers in stock.... We can furnish monument complete within sixty to ninety days," thereby permitting a springtime dedication.³²

By April 1912, the Daughters of Alamance County (Graham, 1914), North Carolina, had placed their order. So too had commemorative groups from Florida and Arkansas, purchasing monuments to "Honor Their Women." Yet by August, McNeel reported that due to "Camps and Chapters tak[ing] vacations during the summer months ... our department having in charge

Alamance County Confederate monument. Graham. Funded by the Graham Chapter, U.D.C.; constructed by McNeel Marble Company. Dedicated May 16, 1914.

all Confederate monuments is not so busy." "Special inducements," including a "liberal discount," were offered for orders placed by September 15.³³

Fewer orders, however, likely reflected more than a seasonal slowdown. Confederate commemoration was evolving. The Alamance monument, ordered from McNeel in 1912 and dedicated May 16, 1914, was the state's twenty-eighth civic-space Confederate memorial erected within ten years. Combined with six earlier monuments, fully one-third of North Carolina's counties now had such commemorations; less than half that number would complete similar memorials over the next dozen years. And two tiny advertisements on opposite corners of page 492 in the October 1912 *Veteran*—one by Jonathan Williams, Incorporated, "casters" of fine statues, the other by the renowned Gorham Company—advertising "Bronze Memorial Tablets," foreshadowed a new, less-expensive commemorative form.³⁴

Behind the hype of monument retailing was a complex, demanding, and dangerous industry. Granite had to be quarried, transported, and inscribed. Once on site, blocks were lifted with ropes and pulleys then muscled into position to form a level and stable commemorative shaft. Finally the soldier statue, weighing hundreds of pounds if of stone or cast bronze, was lifted and attached atop the pillar. Assembly took weeks and often attracted intense interest.

Even a monument's arrival could prove a memorable event. In 1926, a train stopped in front of Beaufort Town Hall (Carteret County), a location where "we had never seen it stop," recalls Neal Willis. "A large wooden crate was unloaded and placed on the curb." After the train departed, a curious Willis and fellow elementary schoolboys "rushed over ... peeked inside and saw the biggest man we have ever seen. He was a giant and greenish in color. We didn't linger long to further investigate."³⁵

At times the drama was more intense. On March 9, 1898, "several hundred people" in Asheville's Pack Square watched as a "100 foot boom" attempted to place a capstone "weighing little less than a ton," atop the Vance obelisk. "Suddenly there was a sound of cracking of timbers that struck terror to those who watched," the *Asheville Weekly Citizen* reported. A wooden splice had broken as the stone was lifted, and the "boom groaned and strained." People fled in "a wild rush," for many "expected part of it [the boom] to crash down into the street."³⁶

One man "tripped over an apple vendor's baskets and the stock in trade was scattered to the winds," the *Citizen* reported. But the damaged boom held. "The windlass men paid out the rope until the strain was relieved," and two days later, with a repaired and strengthened boom, workers successfully placed the capstone atop the seventy-five-foot-high shaft.³⁷

George E. Coulter of Newton and C. B. Webb of Statesville were in charge of erecting Catawba County's (Newton, 1907) Confederate monument. The contract, awarded in January 1907, called for a shaft "of the Barre Vermont granite [sic], 26 feet tall, with a figure of a Confederate soldier at the top," to be "ready for the unveiling at the next annual reunion of the old soldiers in August."³⁸

As the reunion neared, the *Newton Enterprise* monitored progress. "The monument was at Hagerstown, Md. Saturday, and is expected to reach here any day," the paper reported on August 1, two weeks prior to the scheduled unveiling. "It will certainly be up before reunion," the *Enterprise* added with optimistic bravado. One week later, with a "great relief to all," the "monument arrived at the depot." "Tell the news to everybody that the monument is here and will be unveiled next Thursday.... The bare possibility of its not reaching here was very straining on many nerves."³⁹

Webb and his associates set to work. "The monument is in eight pieces," the *Enterprise* reported on August 8. "The heaviest is the base which weighs 17000 pounds…. It was brought down on rollers, like a house." Another block weighed four tons. It, and six lighter pieces, were "hauled on wagons, but it was heavy work."⁴⁰

"All the heavy pieces were put in position by hand," under Webb's "personal supervision," the *Enterprise* reported one week later, adding that it "was a heavy, tedious job." Mr. Flanagan of Statesville, who "says he has put monuments all over the country," "did the cement work." Then "several hundred people were on the streets Saturday afternoon to see the last piece of the monument, the statue of a Confederate soldier, placed in position." "Mr. Webb understands his business," the *Enterprise* concluded, for "every piece was put to its place without an accident or a hitch."⁴¹

Lenoir County Confederate monument. Constructed by McNeel Marble Company, this commemoration was originally placed mid-street in downtown Kinston. This 2004 photograph shows the monument at its third location, the CSS Neuse State Historic Site; it has since been relocated beside Kinston's visitor center. Dedicated May 10, 1924, the same day as the similar Durham monument.

In Randolph County (Asheboro, 1911), the Blue Pearl Granite Company of Winston-Salem oversaw that monument's construction. The base and shaft of Mt. Airy Granite and a sheet-bronze soldier figure, manufactured by Mullins Company of Salem, Ohio, were shipped by rail. Zell Brown, a twenty-four-year-old horse trader—"the only man in town with a wagon long enough for the job"—hauled the pieces from the train depot, his four-horse team pulling loads three blocks to the courthouse. The massive blocks were assembled and scaffolding built. Then a youthful-faced infantryman of bronze, left foot resting upon a knapsack and hands gripping a vertical, bayonet-tipped rifle, was hoisted with ropes and bolted atop the twenty-foot-high shaft.⁴²

Weather could play havoc, however. In Iredell County (Statesville, 1906), locally based Carolina Marble and Granite Company purchased stone from two sources: the monument's shaft and statue from Barre, Vermont, the base from neighboring Rowan County. When the nearly 15,000-pound base arrived at the depot in August, the block was "loaded on a wagon and a traction engine hitched to it," the *Statesville Landmark* reported. The engine, however, "got stuck in the mud ... and though the engine tore up the mud in a frantic effort, and broke some cogs ... never an inch could it budge the load."[43]

No details are available as to how the block eventually arrived at the courthouse, but three months later, on November 3, 1905, the *Landmark* reported that the rest of the monument "was shipped from Barre, Vt., October 27," and "if there is no delay ... will probably be put up by the 20th [November]." On November 24, the *Landmark* announced the monument's arrival at the depot. "Upon the base put down in the court house yard some time ago," the paper explained, "two more bases will be placed today and tomorrow, and about one week's time will be necessary to put inscriptions on the monument. After that is done it will take only three days to get the monument in place."[44]

This timetable proved wildly optimistic. "The Confederate monument was completed Saturday," the paper reported on December 29,

Durham County Confederate monument. Durham. This monument, built by McNeel, was dedicated May 10, 1924, the same day as the similarly styled Lenoir County commemoration, constructed by the same company.

"and now stands in the court house yard as a monument also to the patience and determined efforts of the daughters of Confederacy [sic]," as well as "do[ing] credit to the Carolina Marble and Granite Company which erected it."[45]

By 1924, monument companies had ceased advertising in the *Confederate Veteran*, and the popularity of the parade-rest soldier figure was rapidly waning. McNeel, however, remained active. An undated postcard illustrates a "Proposed Confederate Memorial, Kinston, N.C. Designed and Manufactured by the McNeel Marble Company." Whether an advertising ploy or fund-raising item, this card accurately depicts Kinston's (Lenoir County) completed monument, dedicated May 10, 1924.[46]

That same day, one-hundred miles away, a remarkably similar monument — a modest shaft flanked with symmetrical elements and fronted with four cannonballs stacked atop a short pedestal — was unveiled in Durham, North Carolina. An unsigned, probably identical, parade-rest metal infantryman topped each memorial. Neither monument is signed, but the 1924 McNeel catalog confirms that both are company products.[47]

Behind McNeel's hucksterish promotion, however, stood a reputable company that built quality monuments and erected more Confederate memorials in North Carolina than any other firm. Founded in 1892, McNeel dominated the region's commemorative stonecraft industry through much of the early twentieth century and remained in business until 1960, exclusively crafting stone monuments. "The company was the finest creator of quality artistic memorials," Burton Fletcher, president of the Georgia Monument Builders Association, wrote in 2005. "Although no longer in existence, this influential company left a legacy that will live forever."[48]

12. Poetry and Prose

"The Confederate Monument Will Be Unveiled Wednesday, May 13th. Come and Bring Your Friends," the *Franklin Times* announced with a banner headline *above* the newspaper's masthead on May 8, 1914. The Louisburg weekly included a front-page photograph of the just-completed memorial, images of Governor Locke Craig and North Carolina Attorney General Thomas W. Bickett, the event's orator and master of ceremonies, respectively, and the itinerary, "Exercises" to be conducted in three "Parts."[1]

For more than a month, the *Times* detailed preparation and stoked interest in the upcoming ceremony. On April 3, as part of a front-page article entitled "Monument Fund Completed," the paper reprinted a letter from Mr. J. M. Allen to U.D.C. chapter president Mrs. J. P. Winston. "I understand that the funds necessary," Allen wrote, "have all been subscribed except the sum of five hundred dollars," an amount that likely represented one-quarter of the monument's total cost. Allen, however, continued, "I desire in memory of my deceased wife, Mamie Helen Allen, who was a daughter of the gallant soldier in whose honor your chapter was named, to subscribe this remaining amount."[2]

Shortly after this contribution, the Joseph J. Davis Chapter, United Daughters of the Confederacy, announced dedication-day plans. "As May 10th [Confederate Memorial Day] is Sunday," the women noted, and in deference to the Sabbath, "it was decided to change the date" to later that week. The chapter also selected "four little girls," all members' daughters, to "pull the ribbons" for the unveiling and opted to include historically themed floats in the parade. In addition, "to raise money to defray the expense of the unveiling," a dinner was scheduled. "All those who will contribute toward this dinner are requested to communicate with Mrs. C. K. Cooke stating what their contribution will consist of," the *Times* announced.[3]

"The Greatest Day In Franklin County Since 1861," the *Times* declared on April 24, in a front-page announcement, typeset to resemble an advertisement. "Wednesday May 13.... The Governor of the State will deliver the address. A Military band of the Third Regiment will play Dixie. Three Military Companies in full Uniform[.] Great Horseback Parade[.] Let Everybody Come." In the same issue, the weekly reported that "with the exception of a little lettering," the monument was complete and assured readers that the Suffolk Marble Works of Suffolk, Virginia, had erected "a fine piece of work [that] presents a most beautiful appearance in the position it occupies on the college hill."[4]

The following week, editor and manager A. F. Johnson, encouraged attendance through two items heading the editorial page, "See your friends in Louisburg at the unveiling on May 13th," followed by "Everybody is coming to the unveiling on Wednesday, May 13th. We presume that includes you."[5]

"Fully Five Thousand Devoted Sons and Daughters" attended the unveiling, with "throngs from ... far and near crowding into our little city," the *Times* reported. "Providence smil[ed] upon the occasion in a most beautiful day." The procession formed at 11 A.M. under the stewardship of J. M. Allen, chief marshal and the monument's primary benefactor. The Third Regiment Band led the way, followed by two automobiles, carrying the Governor, Attorney General, Mayor, and six other dignitaries.[6]

Five floats showcasing Tarheel Confederate history were part of the procession, with "Mounted Guards" from local townships riding between displays. "The spirit of 1861" came first, the *Times* reported, representing "the life of the South just before the call to arm." "Tenting" was next, with "a tent and ... such equipment as was the Confederate soldiers lot [sic]." A "Confederate hospital" followed, then a float "picturing the home guard"— the women and children left behind — complete with "the old spinning wheel," a symbol of wartime scarcity and domestic resourcefulness. "Return home" was the final scene, a "masterful" display featuring a one-armed soldier, sweethearts, and young children as well as "Mrs. W. H. Macon [who] did well the role of the old black mammy."[7]

Franklin County Confederate monument. Five thousand "devoted sons and daughters" attended this commemoration's unveiling in Louisburg on May 13, 1914.

On a gentle hill overlooking Louisburg, an invocation opened the ceremony's second portion. Attorney General Bickett, master of ceremonies, related "the history of the first money contributed which was by a widow of a Confederate soldier over thirty years ago," a story detailed by the *Times* through a letter from one of the principals, and a reminiscence that directly linked the day's ceremony with losses endured by an earlier generation of Tarheel women. Then with the crowd gathered around the monument, Mrs. Winston, U.D.C. chapter president, in "a most beautiful and well prepared address," presented the veiled memorial to North Carolina Division President Mrs. Marshall Williams.[8]

"The veil ... was drawn away by the aid of cords in the hands" of the four little girls, revealing, according to the

Times, "a most handsome piece of architecture." Mrs. Williams then presented the commemoration to the chairman of the county commission, delivering a "well prepared and masterly" address that detailed national U.D.C. accomplishments, including awarding "annually 250 scholarships valued at $31,000," decorating "70,000 veterans with crosses of honor," and erecting "over 700 monuments to Confederate causes."[9]

After a "chior [sic] of young ladies" sang a "decoration hymn" and "the little boys and girls of the first and second grades scattered flowers around the base of the monument," the military companies fired a "regulation salute," concluding the day's second event. The crowd then moved to the "grove" beside the "graded school," assembling around a stand prepared for North Carolina Governor Locke Craig.[10]

Craig, whom the *Newton Enterprise* had earlier dubbed the "orator of orators of North Carolina," apparently did not disappoint, with applause frequently interrupting his speech. "I will not stand here and argue about who was right or wrong, but leave that to the erudite historian," the governor said, but "we remember that there were 40,000 soldiers from North Carolina ... [now] with the immortals of the earth."[11]

"We do not rear this monument to victories [sic] soldiers," Craig acknowledged, but instead to heroism, which, he asserted, is never lost. "Was it lost? Was heroism like that every lost [sic]," the governor asked, before immediately answering, "If we had never won a victory, it still was not lost."[12]

The governor then expanded this argument, seeming even to question who had ultimately been victorious following the Civil War, a theme on which he would elaborate the next month while dedicating the North Carolina monument to Confederate women in Raleigh (Chapter 13). "Who was triumphant?" Craig asked the Louisburg crowd, "Pontius Pilate or Jesus? Socrates or the judges?" "Southern ideals were driven like an exile dynasty from place and power and it looked like they were gone forever." "But they have come back," Craig said, declaring, "The men and women who triumph are those who see their duty and dare to do it."[13]

Like the governor's themes, which would be used on other occasions, inscriptions on Franklin County's just-unveiled monument drew from other venues as well. Three lines from Alfred, Lord Tennyson's, "Charge of the Light Brigade," a poem detailing the deadly outcome of a mistakenly ordered British assault, are etched into the memorial's main face. A passage by Salisbury resident Mrs. Frances Fisher Tiernan — widely known as author Christian Reid — is inscribed on the shaft's right panel. Words of Thomas W. Bickett, dedication-day master of ceremonies and a future North Carolina governor, adorn the back panel, while the left face features prose of another Salisbury resident, the Honorable John Steele Henderson.[14]

Mrs. C. D. Malone, acting president of the Louisburg Daughters, explained the inscriptions' meanings in the December 1914 *Confederate Veteran*: Tennyson's words describe "how they [Confederate soldiers] fought"; Mrs. Tiernan's prose details "why they fought"; Bickett's words are a "tribute to those who survived"; while no elaboration is provided for Henderson's straightforward prose.[15]

Mrs. Malone acknowledges that the Salisbury prose — also inscribed on Rowan County's (Salisbury) 1909 Confederate monument — was "borrowed by permission of the Salisbury [U.D.C.] Chapter" and that Bickett's words were "from an address" by the Franklin County native. She did not, however, mention Tennyson's name.[16]

Such omission was likely not mere oversight, for Tarheel memorial prose rarely credits authorship. The *Franklin Times*, on May 15, quotes the monument inscriptions but includes no attribution. And, most significantly, none of the authors are credited on the monument itself, and only Tennyson's lines are enclosed within quotation marks.[17]

In the decades after Appomattox, North Carolinians designing the state's Confederate monuments needed words and symbols to publicly express a people's grief and despair. With the exception of fund-raising, perhaps no task was as challenging as choosing the combination of poetry, prose, and symbols that would not only convert a shaft of stone into a vibrant commemoration but convey both grief and honor.

Defeat and devastation was the state's post-war reality. The men and women of monument committees, as nearly all North Carolinians, likely experienced personal trauma or familial loss during the conflict and undoubtedly suffered similar psychological reactions that survivors of horrific events endure today. In an era when such emotions were held tightly in check and seldom discussed, words and symbols for public commemoration provide rare insight into a people's psyche.

Turn-of-the-century inscriptions and images needed to address three Tarheel groups: "aging survivors" who had experienced the war as adults; middle-aged and younger citizens with little or no personal recollection of the conflict, yet deeply impacted by the economic and human devastation; and future generations, for whom prose and chiseled images might convey the valor with which their forebears had struggled. In addition, a monument might also provide a degree of "closure" to a people scarred by a military defeat that left one-quarter of a generation of men dead.

North Carolinians found expression from a variety of sources: American and British writers, the classics, and contemporary political thought. Prior to modern copyright laws, however, citizens freely inscribed verse and prose without attribution and often without quotation marks. Authors' words were altered, perhaps giving an aura of local originality, and making provenance determination challenging.

Company K, Third North Carolina Infantry. Burgaw. Pender County was not formed until 1875 (from New Hanover County), but area men organized Company K on June 10, 1861. Little is known about this commemoration except that in 1978 it was relocated from the Six Forks community to Pender County's courthouse grounds.

Few details survive as to how committees selected words and images. In Chatham County (Pittsboro, 1907), minutes of the Winnie Davis Chapter, United Daughters of the Confederacy, report the president offering "suggestions" as the contract was finalized, ideas that were accepted unanimously. Chapter president Mrs. London, had spearheaded fund-raising efforts for three years and served as state U.D.C. president. Her proposal likely was well-thought out: "Chatham's Heroes should be on it — Also the list of Chatham's Companys [sic] and some verses of Father Ryans [sic] poems."[18]

Poetry and prose selected by North Carolinians for the state's Civil War monuments, like dedication-day orations, rarely express defiance, instead acknowledging Southern defeat while honoring soldiers who had fought and died. In 1868, Fayetteville's Ladies excerpted Theodore O'Hara's "Bivouac of the Dead" for the state's first Confederate monument. Two of these selected lines,

> On Fame's eternal camping ground
> Their silent tents are spread,

are part of a four-line quotation widely used on subsequent Tarheel memorials — and later inscribed on Arlington National Cemetery's main gate.

Latin inscriptions of death and honor are cited, too. "Dulce et decorum est pro patria mori" (It is sweet and fitting to die for one's country), from Horace's *Odes* (23 B.C.), was inscribed on monuments in Averasboro (1872) and New Bern (1885). A few years later, sponsoring Bertie County (Windsor, 1896) veterans, offered a spirited, likely self-penned, explanation of wartime actions, words filling most of the monument's front panel:

> We fought an/honest fight
> We kept the/Southron's faith
> We fell at the/post of duty
> We died for the/land we loved.[19]

Words of Father Joseph Abram Ryan (c. 1839–1886), the "Poet-Priest of the Confederacy," were used on North Carolina monuments perhaps more than any other author's. Described as "mystical and spiritual" by a biographer, Ryan, a staunch proponent of Southern independence, joined the Confederate army in 1862 following his ordination as a Roman Catholic priest, serving as chaplain for the duration of the conflict. Like many Southerners, Ryan suffered a devastating loss when his brother was killed in action. In response, the priest turned to poetry.[20]

"We died for the land we loved." A brief explanation of actions, perhaps penned by local veterans, fills most of the front panel of Bertie County's monument in Windsor, dedicated 1896.

Thirteen months after Appomattox, Ryan achieved renown with publication of "The Conquered Banner," a seven-stanza lamentation of Southern defeat, set, in the poet's words, "to the exquisite measure ... from one of the Gregorian hymns." The poem was an instant success, "read or sung in every Southern household," making Ryan the most popular poet "within the limits of the Southern Confederacy," according to the 1913 *Catholic Encyclopedia*.[21]

"The Conquered Banner" unequivocally describes defeat and despair. There is no denial or naïve hope. Ryan wrote bitterly:

> Take that banner down, 'tis tattered;
> Broken is its staff and shattered;
> And the valiant host are scattered,
> Over whom it floated high...
> Hard that those who once unrolled it,
> Now must furl it with a sigh.

Such sentiments, penned months after Appomattox, were perhaps too hopeless, especially decades later, when most Tarheel monuments were raised. Although lines from "The Conquered Banner" may not have been used, Ryan's poetic imagery was incorporated into nearly all depictions of Southern flags carved into North Carolina Confederate commemorations for the next half-century.

"The Conquered Banner." Gastonia, Gaston County, 1912. A carved Confederate flag furled around a broken staff leaves little doubt as to the war's outcome.

Across the state, Confederate banners, some combining elements of both battle and national flags, while not "tattered," are depicted tightly furled. "Broken is its staff," describes at least four additional large-scale, front-panel renditions. In Robeson County (Lumberton, 1907), a fully carved battle flag hangs limply from a broken pole, while in Scotland (Laurinburg, 1912), Gaston (Gastonia, 1912), and Burke (Morganton, 1918) Counties, stylized banners not only dangle from, but are furled around, shattered staffs.[22]

A decade after Appomattox, however, Ryan's tone softened. Two of the poet's later works, published in 1879, gave voice to North Carolinians' commemorative emotions. "The March of the Deathless Dead" is excerpted on at least six Tarheel monuments, while lines from "The Sword of Robert E. Lee" are inscribed on two others. These evolving sentiments likely reflect the poet's, as well as the South's, resolving grief and express North Carolina's twin, turn-of-the-century commemorative themes: honoring the Confederate dead, and praising the valor of its soldiers — and sometimes its women as well — who had struggled for a worthy, though undefined, "cause."

Chatham's Daughters selected the fourth stanza of "The March of the Deathless Dead" as the "verses of Father Ryans" for their 1907 monument:

> We care not whence they came,
> Dear in their lifeless clay!
> Whether unknown, or known to fame,
> Their cause and country still the same,
> They died — and wore the gray.

These sentiments must truly have expressed the women's feelings, for they required nearly one-third of the contractually allotted four hundred characters to inscribe the entire stanza. Ryan's name, however, was omitted, as were quotation marks.

The Daughters and citizens of Scotland County (Laurinburg) chose the same passage for their 1912 courthouse-lawn memorial. So too did Stanly County's Daughters (Albemarle, 1925) and the Frank M. Parker Chapter in Enfield (Halifax County) who, in 1928, cast Ryan's words into a bronze plaque to adorn a memorial water fountain. Quotation marks were included on all three commemorations, but the poet's name was not.

Earlier Tarheel monuments excerpted other passages from the "Deathless Dead." "The Women of Cumberland" inscribed "For them should fall the tears of a nation's grief" on Fayetteville's 1902 civic-space memorial, while in Iredell County (Statesville, 1906) lines modified from the poem's first stanza about death, "trust," and a "cause" were used:

> They bore the flag of a
> Nation's trust,
> And fell in a cause
> Though lost, still just,
> And died for me and you.[23]

Lines from another Ryan poem, "The Sword of Robert E. Lee," extolling the South, its soldiers, and a "cause," were contextually modified for use in Catawba County (Newton, 1907):

> No braver bled/for brighter land
> Nor brighter land/had a cause so grand.

Six years later, Warren County (Warrenton, 1913) citizens further modified Ryan's words:

> No braver bled/for better land
> Nor better land/had cause so grand.[24]

North Carolinians also excerpted multiple passages from Theodore O'Hara's ode, "Bivouac of the Dead," including this well-known quatrain:

> On Fame's eternal camping ground
> Their silent tents are spread,
> And Glory guards with solemn round,
> The bivouac of the dead.

Fayetteville's Ladies paired the first two of these lines with a couplet from the work's next-to-last stanza in 1868; in 1883 the Goldsboro Rifles inscribed all four lines, the state's first commemorative use of the complete quotation. Alamance County Daughters (Graham,

1914) chose the same words, while in Forsyth County (Winston-Salem, 1905), O'Hara's sentiments were modified to, "In camp on Fame's eternal camping ground."

The Daughters of Robeson County (Lumberton, 1907) also inscribed these popular lines but prefaced them with words from "Bivouac's" final stanza to describe a monument's enduring role:

> This marble minstrel's voiceless stone
> In deathless song shall tell,
> When many a vanished age hath flown,
> The story how ye fell.

Another quatrain, also first used by Fayetteville's Ladies (1868), then by the Goldsboro Rifles (Bentonville/Johnston County, 1895) and Caldwell's Daughters (Lenoir, 1910), memorialized the dead through powerful imagery:

> Nor shall your glory be forgot
> While Fame her record keeps
> Or honor points the hallowed spot
> Where valor proudly sleeps.

Although widely inscribed, O'Hara's words, like Father Ryan's, were never attributed. Such slights were all but universal. From 1870, when eight lines penned by George M. Whiting were inscribed above the author's name in Raleigh's Oakwood Cemetery, until 1934, when John Dimitry received similar recognition in Anson County (Wadesboro, Women's Monument), only one attributed quotation was carved into a Tarheel Confederate monument.

"God Bless North Carolina," four of the state's most cherished words, was etched by the Daughters of Rockingham County into their 1910 Reidsville commemoration. "R. E. Lee" is chiseled below the quotation, citing the Confederate commander's praise of Tarheel soldiers as they marched proudly, despite retreating with the rest of Lee's army, toward Appomattox.

Expanding commemoration necessitated altering other quotations. "Ode Sung on the Occasion of Decorat-

Davidson County Confederate monument and antebellum courthouse in Lexington, 1905.

ing the Graves of the Confederate Dead" had been accurate when South Carolinian Henry Timrod (1829–1867), the unofficial "Poet-Laureate of the Confederacy," recited the five stanzas during an 1866 Charleston memorial service. Timrod despaired of the lack of Confederate memorialization, writing,

> Though yet no marble column craves,
> The pilgrim here to pause,

a couplet hopelessly outdated in the midst of a monument-building boom in the early twentieth century. Lexington's Daughters—although erecting a granite shaft topped with a bronze soldier statue—updated Timrod's stanza for Davidson County's 1905 monument:

> Sleep softly in your humble graves
> Sleep martyrs of a fallen cause
> *For lo a* marble column craves
> The pilgrim here to pause [emphasis added].

Less well-known authors were quoted as well. Eight lines from "The Cadets at New Market," by James Barron Hope, delivered at the Virginia Military Institute in 1870, were inscribed in Forsyth County (1905). Reverend James Preston Burke of Reidsville penned a "deeply thoughtful and inspiring inscription" used by the Caswell County Daughters on Yanceyville's 1921 monument, while in Vance County (Henderson, 1910), local author Orren Randolph Smith—widely credited with designing the first Confederate national flag—memorialized the Confederate dead:

> Peace to their ashes
> Honor to their memory
> Glory to their cause.[25]

British poets were cited as well, although, like their American counterparts, without recognition. Two North Carolina monuments feature passages from Alfred, Lord Tennyson's, "Charge of the Light Brigade" (1854). Pitt County Daughters (Greenville, 1914) summarized the soldiers' duty:

> Theirs not to make reply
> Theirs not to reason why
> Theirs but to do and die.

Franklin County's (Louisburg, 1914) excerpt, meanwhile, showcased enduring fame despite defeat:

> When can their glory fade?
> O the wild charge they made
> All the world wondered.

"Peace to Their Ashes." Vance County Confederate monument. Inscription penned by Orren Randolph Smith, a county resident widely credited with designing the first Confederate national flag. Henderson, 1910.

Similar sentiments of a heroic death echo in the final stanza of "The Battle of Alexandria," by James Montgomery (1771–1854), etched into Chowan County's (Edenton, 1904) monument:

> Gashed with honorable scars,
> Low in Glory's lap they lie,
> Though they fell, they fell like stars,
> Streaming splendour through the sky.

Rudyard Kipling, however, would become the state's most-quoted British author. Five years after publication of Kipling's "Recessional" (1897), Cumberland's Women inscribed a two-line plea from the work on Fayetteville's civic-space memorial:

> Lord God of Hosts, be with us yet
> Lest We Forget—Lest We Forget.

Five years later, "Lest We Forget" stood alone, carved in massive raised letters—without attribution or quotation marks—across the base of Cleveland County's (Shelby) 1907 commemoration. And although the couplet was cited in Stanly County (Albemarle, 1925), Tarheel inscriptions generally consist of Kipling's three key words, "Lest We Forget," featured on memorials in Randolph (Asheboro, 1911), Warren (Warrenton, 1913), Richmond (Rockingham, 1930), and Onslow (Jacksonville, 1957) Counties, among others.

Philosophical prose was also selected. "They Died in Defence of Their RIGHTS" [sic], reads one panel of Cumberland County's 1902 memorial. "Defenders of State Sovereignty," is inscribed across the front of Edgecombe County's (Tarboro, 1904) monument, words repeated two years later on the back of Iredell County's (Statesville, 1906) commemoration. The Daughters of Greene County (Snow Hill, 1929), on the other hand, addressed the future with a single line from

"Lest We Forget." Rudyard Kipling's words, penned in 1897, are featured on Cleveland County's (Shelby) 1907 Confederate monument—without attribution or quotation marks.

Thomas Gray's "Elegy Written in a Country Churchyard" (1751): "And read their history in a nation's eyes."

Words from the masthead of the *Confederate Veteran*, a widely read Southern periodical, mark another Tarheel monument. In front of the Mount Zion Methodist Church in Cornelius, North Carolina, a tall shaft topped with a soldier statue reads:

> Though men deserve,
> They may not win success,
> The brave will honor the brave,
> Vanquished none the less.[26]

More lengthy passages eloquently defend Southern troops and their actions. The Daughters and citizens of Franklin County (Louisburg, 1914), inscribed words of "our gifted townsman and attorney, Gen. T. W. Beckett [sic]," (who also served as master of ceremonies during the dedication event), praising the Confederate soldier while intimating that defeat may have been divinely ordered:

> At Appomattox God said to the Confederate soldier,
> "About Face."
> In obedience to the celestial order
>   there was a change of front,
> and the gray line faced the future
>   unashamed and unafraid.[27]

"Though Men Deserve..." Words from the *Confederate Veteran* masthead are inscribed on the front panel of this monument in Cornelius, Mecklenburg County, 1910.

In Rowan County (Salisbury, 1909) — and on a panel adjoining the previous quotation in Franklin County — identical inscriptions penned by Mrs. Frances Fisher Tiernan (Christian Reid) emphasize fealty to the nation's founding principles:

> They gave their lives and fortunes for constitutional liberty
> and state sovereignty in obedience to the teachings of the
> fathers who framed the constitution of the United States.[28]

Adjoining this lengthy passage, Rowan's monument features the state's shortest inscription. The Daughters boldly carved the Confederate motto, "Deo Vindice" (God will vindicate), across the upper back panel, the surface's focal point. As if in reply, three letters are carved well-beneath this inscription — "R. I. P." (rest in peace) — exemplifying early-twentieth-century North Carolinians' acknowledgement of the permanent loss of Southern independence.[29]

North Carolina's veterans forged a different commemorative style from that of the Ladies or Daughters. Nearly a dozen Tarheel memorials were funded largely by Confederate veterans' organizations or individual soldiers, and while all groups unequivocally acknowledged defeat, sponsoring veterans rarely included poetry or borrowed prose, opting instead for often lengthy inscriptions explaining wartime actions, citing units or former officers, listing military engagements, or enumerating local troops.

Bertie County's (Windsor, 1896) former soldiers led the way in 1896, penning a previously cited eight-line summary of their wartime actions. Six years later in nearby Tyrrell County (Columbia, 1902), the Tyrrell Monument Association, headed by veterans, erected one of the state's few zinc monuments, an easily worked metal permitting low-cost inscriptions. Across sixteen panels, the monument cites the War's major battles; includes a bust of Robert E. Lee and a tribute "in appreciation of our faithful slaves"; lists Tyrrell County's Confederate officers and surviving veterans; and includes a tribute in "memory of Mary Alexander Beasley," a woman devoted "to nursing our soldiers,"—and mother of Lieutenant-Colonel William F. Beasley, "the youngest officer of his rank in the Confederate Army" and the Monument Association's president.[30]

"In Appreciation of Our Faithful Slaves." This inscription, one of sixteen stamped-zinc panels on Tyrrell County's Confederate monument, is one of the state's few memorial references to slavery—and its most direct. Columbia, 1902.

In western North Carolina, Candler's (Buncombe County, 1903) cemetery monument, funded by Captain A. B. Thrash, lists officers and men of Thrash's Company I, Twenty-fifth North Carolina Regiment and the unit's "noted battles." Asheville's (Buncombe County, 1905) courthouse memorial (Chapter 6), funded largely by members of the Sixtieth North Carolina Regiment, lists Buncombe's generals and colonels, documents the unit's war record, and supports its claim of "Farthest at Chickamauga," while in Macon County (Franklin), sponsoring veterans etched designations of seven local companies into their 1909 marble memorial.

Two hundred miles east, meanwhile, in Anson County (Wadesboro, 1906), the Daughters and their chief benefactor, William Alexander Smith, a veteran of the Anson Guards who had been severely wounded at Malvern Hill, inscribed the state's most defiant defense of Southern actions. Above the name Anson, carved in raised, block letters, the monument pays "homage for the soldiers of Anson County who served in the War between the government and the Confederate States." An adjoining inscription, penned by Colonel R. T. Bennett, a member of the Anson Guards who had risen to command the Fourteenth North Carolina Regiment and would be the dedication-day's featured speaker, furthers the rationale:

These men embraced the principles of their leaders.
They believed our social institutions and our right of
local self-government imperiled by the avowed
hostility of a large section of the union.
They resisted with every device of honorable warfare.
"The glory and grief of battle won and lost sold[i]ered them."[31]

No other Tarheel monument so vociferously defends Confederate actions. Even as the monument-building boom waned, other North Carolina veterans held fast to earlier themes; the Gates County Monument Organization (Gatesville, 1915) saluted county native William P. Roberts, "the youngest general officer in the Confederate States Army ... commissioned Brigadier General at the age of 23"; Robert Ricks, financier of Rocky Mount's 1917 memorial praised veterans' "exalted and unselfish patriotism" as an "unfailing inspiration to all future generations of Americans"; while in Burke County (Morganton, 1918), Holly Springs (Wake County, 1923), and Faison (Duplin County, 1932) benefactors enumerated soldiers' names into stone and bronze.

Not all sponsoring veterans, however, recited military action or lauded Southern valor. In Salisbury, John Buis, an "expert monument man," carved a tombstone-shaped memorial honoring four unknown Southern dead. The soldiers had been part of a group of "10 or 20 men," according to a later *Salisbury Post* report, who, while returning from furlough, "met a detail of Stokes Pickets" near Salisbury. "A brief engagement" left the four dead and drove their comrades off. The soldiers' remains had to be interred "nameless and unidentified."[32]

Sometime late in the nineteenth century, Buis, "himself a Confederate soldier," carved a marble slab honoring these men. Little else is known about the memorial, located in Salisbury's prestigious Old English Cemetery just yards from the grave of John W. Ellis, North Carolina's first wartime governor. The troops' remains may not even be under the slab, since the *Post* headline described it as a "Tombstone Without a Grave." This memorial, however, although a fraction of the height of most Tarheel commemorations, features one of the state's simplest yet most poignant tributes:

"God Bless Them." Not all monuments were raised by heritage organizations or wealthy benefactors. This marble slab in Salisbury's Old English Cemetery was carved by John Buis, a Confederate veteran and local stonecarver, to honor four unknown Confederate dead. Rowan County, c. late–nineteenth century.

> Four Unknown Confederate Soldiers
> For us they fought
> For us they died
> God bless them.[33]

13. Women of the Confederacy

"My Dear Colonel:—I have been thinking for a long time that the State would never build a Woman's Confederate Monument," wrote Ashley Horne to North Carolina Secretary of State J. Bryan Grimes on December 12, 1911. A successful North Carolina farmer and businessman, Horne was clearly frustrated, doubting such a memorial would ever be erected.[1]

Concern seemed justified. For eight years the United Confederate Veterans had considered raising such a memorial. Seventy-six designs, most submitted by prominent sculptors, had been rejected by the national organization. The most recent proposal—an elaborate group of three figures, identical castings of which were to be erected near each state capitol—languished amid bickering and slow fund-raising.

North Carolina's commemorative effort had been similarly unsuccessful. Months earlier, legislation introduced by Representative Julian S. Carr authorizing state funds for a women's memorial had been rejected. Horne, a fellow representative, had participated in that debate and remained keenly disappointed by its outcome. Now seventy, the businessman from Clayton would wait no longer.

Horne's missive got right to the point, its first sentence ending with the declaration, "I have decided to build this monument myself." Offering "about ten thousand dollars" to cover the cost of the project, Horne, who had unsuccessfully sought the 1908 Democratic gubernatorial nomination, told Grimes that "the time has come in my life when I think no citizen of the State could think that I have any ulterior motive." He then requested the Secretary to "ascertain" if the Committee on Public Building and Grounds "will agree to let this monument be erected on the ground which I have selected with your assistance." "If they will do so," Horne continued, "I will be pleased for you to see what you can do in the way of designs from some studio in America and make such selections as you think would be attractive to the eye and to the women of our country."[2]

This aging Confederate veteran, an orderly sergeant with the Fifty-third North Carolina Regiment, who, according to R. D. W. Connor, had been sent from Appomattox "to bear to General Johnston at Greensboro and General Sherman, near Durham's Station, the official news of Lee's surrender," closed his letter to Grimes with a reminder of past relationships. Recalling the Secretary of State's father, a celebrated Confederate major-general, he reminded the younger man that "you will remember that I bent my gun around a black-jack tree at Appomattox Court House under Grimes' command."[3]

Seven months later, on July 24, 1912, a committee of five men and one woman—

including Secretary of State J. Bryan Grimes — selected noted sculptor Augustus Lukeman to create North Carolina's "Memorial to the Women of the Confederacy."[4]

Lukeman's bronze was unveiled with typical commemorative fanfare on June 10, 1914. The old veterans were there; even the day's prayers were offered by clergymen who had served in two of North Carolina's most celebrated regiments: the Rev. E. A. Osborne, colonel of the Fourth, and the Rev. R. H. Marsh, D. D., chaplain of the Twenty-sixth. Daniel Harvey Hill, Jr., historian and president of North Carolina College of Agriculture and Mechanic Arts (later North Carolina State University) and son of the late Confederate Lieutenant-General D. H. Hill, delivered the keynote address, extolling "the spirit, the character, and the deeds of the North Carolina women of the Confederacy."[5]

Despite beginning with a dry defense of the state's political actions, Hill's words grew more animated as he related how the state's Confederate women met difficulties

North Carolina monument to the women of the Confederacy. Sculpted by Augustus Lukeman; designed by architect Henry Bacon. Dedicated on the state Capitol grounds, June 10, 1914.

"not with mere passive fortitude, but with aggressive spirit." "She was a woman of steel," Hill said, who "meted out encouragement and help" to a "husband promptly volunteering." Yet to "the husband who faltered," delaying enlistment, "she said 'I know how to live as the widow of a brave man, but I do not know how to live as the wife of a coward.'"[6]

Hill spoke too of deprivation and hardship — and the resourcefulness of Tarheel Confederate women. "Home spun cloth as durable as it was ugly was made in almost every home," while "women of wealth" joined "their poorer friends in manual toil." Yet even as the Southern nation crumbled and its armies surrendered, when "negroes quit the fields" and "want 'stalked like an armed man,'" Tarheel women "found spirit to jest at poverty." "In honor of the returned soldiers," Hill said, "'Starvation parties' and 'Tacky sociables,'" were held, "'where each came hungry and each left empty.'"[7]

After the war, such resiliency facilitated the South's recovery. "Under the inspiration of these Confederate women," the college president said, "homes once more became homes indeed, industries were revived, fields again returned their yields, order and system and law once more reigned" in "a glorious part of our history." Seeking to "preserve the memories of that momentous struggle," Hill added, "they denied themselves rest and comfort that public monuments might be reared." Then ending with a nearly evangelical flourish, Hill said of the Confederate woman, "she ate not the bread of idleness. Her children rose up and called her blessed; her husband also."[8]

Governor Locke Craig, formally accepting the monument on behalf of the state of North Carolina, was even more grandiloquent, calling the statue "epic," then comparing North Carolina's Confederate women with the biblical Abraham. Like the patriarch who prepared to sacrifice his son Isaac, "The Women of the Confederacy, in supreme consecration, did lay upon the altar of Dixie their first born, the fairest and the bravest of the world," Craig said, "And because they did this thing, we too are the children of the Covenant."[9]

The governor continued mixing religious, secular, and classical themes as he spoke of a once-defeated South. "The immediate result is not the final judgment," the governor declared, using another evangelical term, and "Disaster does not always destroy." "Who was victorious at the Alamo, Santa Ana or Travis?" Craig asked rhetorically, "Who triumphed, Socrates or his judges, Jesus or Pontius Pilate?" "The heroic past is our priceless heritage," the governor asserted, "the legacy of the war is our richest possession."[10]

Yet the governor acknowledged the cost of this legacy. Like the woman of ancient Sparta who "delivered the shield to her son with the command: 'Return with it or upon it,'" the "mothers of the South" exhorted their sons to bravery. As losses mounted, these women "wept in silent desolation, but in their grief there was exhalation," Craig said, for their sons "had fought and fallen beneath the advancing flag ... had suffered without complaint ... had died, as a conqueror without a murmur."[11]

Returning to biblical themes, Craig closed his salute proclaiming "Hail to you Women of the Confederacy, that bore them and nurtured them, and offered them for sacrifice! In you and in your descendants is vouchsafed the promise to Abraham: Henceforth all generations shall call you blessed."[12]

Ashley Horne, however, was not present as Craig spoke nor when the benefactor's

East panel detail. North Carolina Confederate women's monument, Raleigh.

grandson stepped forward to unveil the sculpture. The man who, two-and-one-half years earlier, had despaired that a monument would never be raised to North Carolina's Women of the Confederacy did not live to see his gift dedicated. Veteran, farmer, politician, and businessman, Ashley Horne died October 22, 1913.[13]

Southern "women of the sixties" had cared for sick and wounded soldiers through four years of war then reburied the Confederate dead with dignified ceremonies in "proper" graves following the conflict's end. These ladies had aided infirm veterans, raised monuments of stone and bronze to honor the "men who wore the gray"—and passed these values to their daughters and granddaughters, women born into a New South who had no personal memories of the war or Reconstruction.

As monument building intensified early in the twentieth century, aging Confederate veterans and their sons sought to honor these women. The idea was not new. E. P. Morrisett, speaking in Montgomery, Alabama, in April 1866, proposed "a lofty Corinthian monument whose summit shall pierce the skies" to commemorate the "glorious deeds of the women of our own dear Southern land." But twelve months after Appomattox, in a defeated and impoverished region, such a proposal was little more than flowery rhetoric.[14]

By the turn of the century, however, improving economic conditions coupled with powerful heritage organizations made such an undertaking feasible. James Mann, a veteran from Norfolk, Virginia, chaired the Woman's Memorial Committee, a group representing both the United Confederate Veterans and the Sons of Confederate Veterans. In the November 1905 *Confederate Veteran*, Mann wrote that "a memorial in the form of a school or hospital or something of the kind would be preferable," ideas floated earlier by women's representatives. Mann, however, was "convinced that this committee will never be able to raise sufficient funds to endow an institution of that kind." The chair instead endorsed a plan by C. Irvine Walker a committee member from Charleston.[15]

Walker not only doubted the feasibility of a benevolent institution but also rejected a proposal favored by many veterans of "one grand monument," tactfully sidestepping the divisive issue of its ultimate location by declaring that, with a single memorial, "only one place can be so graced." Instead the South Carolinian proposed "giving each State the highest and most brilliant design of fine art," by inviting "artists of the world to compete and submit magnificent and artistic designs." By offering "enough," perhaps twenty-five thousand dollars, a "truly great design" could be realized. Understanding that "the cost of such work is in the value of the artistic conception," rather than the "comparatively trifling cost" of the actual bronze, Walker proposed that each participating state receive a cast— "all would be from the same model and all be equal in artistic value and originality"— to be placed "upon a pedestal in the State capital or other such city."[16]

A 1907 design competition drew seventy-five entries. All, however, were rejected. Two years later, a proposal by Louis Amateis, a well-known Italian-born sculptor, met with the committee's approval. But when a sketch of the design — a classically robed woman holding an unsheathed sword (by the blade) in her right hand and a furled Confederate flag with her left, standing upon a platform inscribed with "UPHOLD OUR STATE RIGHTS"— appeared in the *Confederate Veteran*, a storm of protest followed. S. A. Cunningham, editor and proprietor of the *Veteran* and one of the most influential commemorative voices in the South, wrote of favoring "from the first" a monument to Southern women but that the proposed sculpture "is too grievous a representation ... to go on without emphatic protest."

The "clenched hand around the sword instantly pains," the editorialist wrote, before adding, "The war is certainly over and our women are not in politics; so the demand, 'Uphold Our State Rights [sic],' the conspicuous line at the feet of the figure, is another objectionable feature."[17]

In the same issue of the *Veteran*, Dr. H. M. Hamill of Nashville, Tennessee, railed against the "defiant pose" of this "brawny Southern Amazon ... brandishing an antique sword which she grips by the blade and not by the hilt!" Admitting though not an artist but thinking, "I know a work of art when I see it," Hamill decried that "not a line of womanly grace or modesty or tenderness," was etched in the design and that he was "tolerably sure that the Confederate woman does not care to be reincarnated in bronze as a composite of the classic Amazon, the Wagnerian Brunehilda, and Carrie Nation!"[18]

Not surprisingly, two months later at the U.C.V.'s 1909 annual meeting, Amateis' proposal was rejected while the chastened committee was enlarged and ordered to find a less assertive design. In December of that year, a submission by Belle Kinney, a twenty-three-year-old veteran's daughter from Nashville, Tennessee, received the committee's nod.

The three-figure grouping proposed by Kinney, trained at the Art Institute of Chicago, was thematically and symbolically reminiscent of Frederick Ruckstahl's earlier *Glory* (Baltimore, Maryland, 1905) and his related *Fame* (Salisbury, North Carolina, 1909). In the young artist's depiction — which garnered what was widely considered the largest sculptural commission yet awarded a woman — an allegorical winged Fame stands behind a dying Confederate soldier and a seated Southern woman. The soldier, clutching a furled flag, slumps against a disabled cannon. Fame supports the wounded man with her left arm while reaching with her right to place a wreath of laurels upon the woman's head. The kneeling woman, meanwhile, seemingly oblivious to the gesture, extends a "palm of glory" to the soldier, an emblem, according to historian Cynthia Mills, of the woman's "belief that he [the soldier] is triumphant even in death."[19]

In a region that championed individualism and states' rights, however, artistic agreement would prove elusive. Consensus for Kinney's design, a nine-foot-high grouping to be cast by Tiffany Companies, faded, and only Mississippi (1917) and the sculptor's home state of Tennessee (1926) ultimately erected bronzes of her work.

Five other states, including North Carolina, opted instead for individually designed Confederate women's monuments. Ashley Horne, the successful businessman and Confederate veteran from Clayton, singlehandedly funded Tarheel efforts. The Johnston County native's financial acumen had led to presidencies of the Clayton Banking Company (1899), the Clayton Cotton Mill (1900), and the Capudine Chemical Company (1904). But the businessman had no plans to become an art critic; the design would be decided by committee, members of which Horne personally selected and in "whom he entrusted entirely [with] the execution of his plans."[20]

The august body of five men and one woman selected by Horne boasted inscrutable Confederate and state credentials: newspaper editor Henry London, a 1904 defender of the Tarheel Rebel Boast and a courier at Appomattox; Secretary of State J. Bryan Grimes, chairman of the North Carolina Historical Commission and son of a Confederate general; historian R. D. W. Connor, Historical Commission secretary and first state archivist; and W. H. S. Burgwyn, a lawyer, doctor, author, and banker — "The most versatile person ever to have lived in Vance County," according to William Powell — who served as assistant adjutant to Confederate General Thomas Clingman. James A. Long chaired the Monument Commission, and Mrs. F. M. Williams — Fannie Ransom Williams of Newton, president of the North Carolina Division of the United Daughters of the Confederacy from 1910 to 1913 — was its sole female member.[21]

The committee rejected Kinney's design, turning instead to Augustus Lukeman, a Paris-trained sculptor born in Richmond, Virginia. With studio and workshop in New York, Lukeman specialized in historical monuments, crafting, during a four-decade-long career, memorials to Union and Confederate heroes, American presidents, biblical figures, as well as designing and carving much of the South's largest sculptural commemoration, the massive figures at Stone Mountain, Georgia.[22]

Lukeman's bronze honoring North Carolina's Confederate-era women, completed in less than two years, features a plainly dressed older woman seated with a large book opened across her lap. With her right hand, she turns several pages as she gazes toward a well-dressed boy kneeling beside her. The young man, in a double-breasted suit, necktie, knee-length pants, and leather shoes, grasps a sheathed sword with both hands, staring slightly to his left.

The differences are stark. The aged woman appears weary and sad; the eager youth, resting on one knee intently looks forward. The Old South beside the New. The war generation, worn down by grief and hardship, and their descendents, imbued with proud memories of a difficult past, seeking a brighter future.

In contrast to Kinney's design, however, Lukeman's casting does not include an adult male. Artists frequently arrange three objects in a balanced, stylistic triangle. Two figures, especially side-by-side and similarly sized, often create tension. Lukeman, a talented sculptor, likely sought this unease, a feeling intensified by depicting the figures gazing, not directly at each other or toward a common point, but in crossed directions, each perhaps contemplating the war and its legacy differently.

Where — and who — is the missing man? Was he the child's father? The woman's husband or son? Or might the absent figure that would provide balance and harmony symbolize the 40,000 North Carolina soldiers who perished during four years of conflict?

Governor Locke Craig, in accepting the memorial on behalf of the state, tendered one explanation. Opening his remarks by declaring the monument's theme as "heroism and devotion; the inheritance of the children of the South," Craig, in his second paragraph, spoke of that legacy's tragic side. "The bronze represents the grandmother unrolling to the eager youth, grasping the sword of his father, the scroll of his father's deeds," actions which the soldier is not there to relate, while the "etchings on the faces of the pedestal suggest the outline of her story."

These "etchings," actually two bronze plaques, adorn the lateral sides of the granite pedestal. To the woman's left, facing east and the rising sun, an allegorical female figure encourages eight well-attired soldiers marching off to war. One carries a flag, a second beats a drum. A mounted man, the plaque's central figure, brandishes a sword as his spirited steed rears up on its hind legs. The enthusiasm of a newly formed nation and its young men girding for battle are vividly depicted, but the energetic horse is an ominous omen; soldiers sculpted astride rearing mounts traditionally represent men killed in battle.[23]

To the youth's right, on a plaque illuminated by the setting sun, five men clad in worn garments return from war, flanked by an emaciated, riderless horse. The grand banner has been replaced with a scrap of cloth; one man's arm rests in a sling; even the drum's covering appears thin and loose. Two women meet the survivors; one embraces a returning soldier, the other reaches for a withered corpse cradled in the arms of a comrade.

The site selected by Horne is on the south side of Capitol Square placing the sculpted individuals with backs literally and figuratively turned to the North. Architect Henry Bacon completed the installation with a plain granite bench on each side of the pedestal, allowing passersby to pause and reflect upon Lukeman's symbolically laden work. Even Governor Craig, in his dedicatory remarks, noted the monument's complexity. "To the earnest beholder the statue is illumed with unfolding meaning. His vision will determine its revelation."[24]

North Carolina's memorial to the Women of the Confederacy was erected near the end of the state's most prolific monument-building period. Only one other commemoration primarily dedicated to Confederate women would be raised, yet the role of these women would be celebrated with inscriptions on civic-space soldier memorials across the state.

As Confederate commemoration widened early in the twentieth century, Tyrrell County (Columbia, 1902) led the way, dedicating two of its monument's sixteen panels to women: one to Mary Alexander Beasley, who "devoted the four years of our war to nursing our soldiers"; a second "to the noble women of Tyrrell County, whose devotion to our cause and sacrifices in its behalf, and for their loved ones in the field, entitle them to rank with the heroines of all ages."

In 1910, the Davis Dickerson Mills Chapter of the United Daughters of the Confederacy inscribed its Rutherford County (Rutherfordton) soldier memorial "To the Men and Women of the Confederacy"; five years later, a bronze plaque on Jackson County's (Sylva, 1915) monument praised "our valiant fathers" and "heroic mothers," the latter described as "Spartan in devotion, Teuton in sacrifice, in patience superior to either, and in modesty and grace matchless among womankind." Even the widely used "Confederate Heroes" inscription, discussed previously (Chapter 5), likely encompassed both men and women.

Following World War I, as Tarheel commemorations began to include veterans of more

Anson County Confederate women's monument. Funded by Confederate veteran William Alexander Smith and dedicated September 22, 1934, on the courthouse grounds in Wadesboro. The vase is inscribed "To Our Mothers from Anson Chapter United Daughters of the Confederacy 1934."

recent conflicts, women continued as part of this expanded legacy. In Montgomery County (Troy, c. 1926), the courthouse-lawn granite pedestal supporting a grenade-wielding marble Doughboy featured three faces dedicated to county soldiers — one each for those who had fought in the "World War," in the "Spanish-American War," and "for the Confederacy"— while the fourth was "in memory of Montgomery County women who did their part in all wars."

The state's second and final monument honoring Confederate women was unveiled in Wadesboro on September 22, 1934. Located beside the courthouse, not far from Anson County's 1906 Confederate soldier statue, this granite triptych, while effusive in praise, was more than a singular celebration of Civil-War era white women. Through image and inscription, these three panels, although simple in design and execution, broached some of the era's most contentious themes and pushed the boundaries of Tarheel commemoration.

One hundred and one words "To the Women of the Confederacy" fill nearly two-thirds of the central panel. The prose is direct and concise, clearly articulating contemporary beliefs: with "Utter Devotion to the Cause [these women] Helped to Send to the Front More Than Six Hundred Thousand Soldiers in One of the Greatest and Most Unequal Conflicts Recorded in History"; their "Hope and Courage.... Never Faltered"; and "By Their Faith in God, By Their Magic Influence and Immeasurable Good Works" inspired "Our Citizen Soldiery."

Right panel detail. The Anson Guards receive the company's flag, an 1861 gift from the women of Anson County. William Alexander Smith, the monument's benefactor, was a member of the Guards and later penned a history of the unit.

By 1934, however, most of the women of the '60s were dead. Yet this inscription continues, extending commemorative praise to Southern women of a younger generation, the "Fair Daughters [who] With Unshaken Fidelity, Have Preserved the Fame of our Glorious Dead."

In contrast to Lukeman's 1914 bronze plaques in Raleigh, symmetrical granite carvings on each side of Wadesboro's memorial exclusively highlight the antebellum South. The right panel, dated 1861, depicts in recessed sculpted relief an elegantly attired woman presenting a flag inscribed "Anson G" (presumably Anson Guards, the unit of monument benefactor William Alexander Smith) and "Anson Honor" to a saluting soldier at the head of a column of troops.[25]

The left panel depicts a scene dated two decades earlier: a female with African features handing a swaddled infant to a woman comfortably seated in a rocking chair. The setting is genteel; slave and owner are well-fed and nicely dressed. Dated 1840, the infant might represent the soldier — or one of his charges — receiving the banner in the right panel, preparing to lead the Anson Guards to war.

This image, however, subtly features an idealized "faithful slave," in this case a "Black Mammy," one of the most esteemed positions held by enslaved people. Only one Tarheel memorial explicitly addresses slavery — Tyrrell County's (Columbia, 1902) Confederate soldier monument, with a single panel "In Appreciation of our Faithful Slaves"— while just a handful of small monuments across the South honor this demographic.

By the 1920s, the central tenets of Confederate memory — often termed the Lost Cause ideology — had been widely embraced nationally. Slavery, however, despite isolated sculptural attempts such as in Tyrrell County to portray free and bonded persons of color as loyal and content participants in the antebellum South, remained a nearly universally unmentioned facet of an otherwise celebrated past.

In 1931, the United Daughters of the Confederacy broached this subject with a notable commemoration in Harpers Ferry, West Virginia. Dedicated to Heyward Shepherd, the memorial praised this "industrious and respected colored freeman [who] was mortally wounded by John Brown's raiders" and "became the first victim of this attempted insurrection." The inscription not only lauded Shepherd, a free black, but also "the character and faithfulness of thousands of negroes who ... so conducted themselves that no stain was left upon a record which is the peculiar heritage of the American people."[26]

The Black Mammy, however, was the most powerful, and became the most controversial, of the "faithful slave" icons. African Americans, working as paid servants and nannies, were a common feature of middle- and upper-income Southern households throughout the first half of the twentieth century. Drawing on these cherished relationships as well as memories of elders raised by caring yet enslaved women three-quarters of a century earlier, commemorative groups sought to erect a memorial to these women that might somehow soften the perception of slavery.

A decade-long campaign was launched in the 1920s to erect a monument in Washington, D. C., honoring the Black Mammy, an attempt doomed by determined opposition and economic depression. The designers of Wadesboro's monument were undoubtedly aware of this highly publicized effort, and the "1840" image of a faithful yet enslaved mammy reflects this contentious theme. Like the three Confederate national flags carved atop the monument's center panel (discussed in an earlier chapter) and the defiant words "The Men of the South will ever be EQUAL TO VICTORY SUPERIOR TO DEFEAT" chiseled below the salute to Confederate women, Wadesboro's rendition of the faithful slave tested the limits of Tarheel commemoration.

That such commemoration, although nuanced and highly symbolic, would be part of a monument honoring women may seem surprising. Perhaps it should not be. The measured determination of the Ladies caring for the Confederate dead launched the state's memorial tradition; efforts by their daughters and granddaughters extended it into civic spaces. Wadesboro's monument, like the women it honors, took North Carolina's Confederate tradition to new levels with what might be the state's most encompassing and assertive memorial.

14. Across the Chasm

Wednesday, May 17, 1905. A train filled with aging veterans steamed into Goldsboro, North Carolina. The Raleigh Rifles, "acting as [North Carolina] Governor Glenn's escort," and a company of the "local Boy's Brigade in spotless white uniforms," were drawn up at "present arms." A seventeen-gun salute greeted the arriving soldiers who were then led to the nearby Hotel Kennon, where "a royal Southern reception was given them by Governor Glenn and Staff."[1]

Joseph E. Robinson, fiery editor of the *Goldsboro Argus*, who, a decade earlier, had led efforts in erecting a monument to the Confederate dead at nearby Bentonville battlefield, welcomed the guests. The old men were passing through Goldsboro on what the newspaperman termed a "mission," to unveil a monument in New Bern honoring their comrades "who gave up their lives for their country." Robinson reminded those gathered that "monuments have been erected from time immemorial, by all peoples in honor of their dead soldiers, not alone gratefully to commemorate their patriotism and valor, but also to inculcate these virtues into the hearts and souls of the youth of passing generations." The editor spoke too of the need in "teaching our children the truths of history, and glorifying in our common country ... the grandest government under the sun."[2]

The soldiers stayed in Goldsboro but a short while, re-boarding the train for New Bern within an hour, now with Governor Glenn's private rail car attached. Preparing to depart, the veterans thanked those assembled, giving "three rousing cheers for 'the good people of Goldsboro.'"[3]

Arriving in New Bern two hours later, the men received a similarly hearty welcome. A salute was fired in their honor, and citizens "exert[ed] themselves to their utmost to extend a proverbial Southern welcome." They were to be "comfortably quartered" during their two-night stay at the local military academy, where Miss Ruth Watson welcomed the vets. "We are proud and glad to offer you the comforts and cheer of our homes, our schoolrooms, and the warm greetings of our hearts," she told the men.[4]

That evening, a public reception was "tendered" by the "people of New Berne in their beautiful Court House." The Honorable M. De W. Stevenson, a Confederate veteran and member of New Bern's Camp # 1162 of the United Confederate Veterans (U. C. V.), "warmly welcomed" the visiting troops. In front of a "large audience" that included North Carolina's governor and the New Bern Camp of Confederate Veterans, Stevenson spoke of "the long period since the war," and how feelings "had changed and softened." The former Confederate still "gloried in the record of the Confederate officers and soldiers," yet he "loved his country and was proud to be a citizen of the United States of America."[5]

As examples of Southern loyalty to the now reunited nation, Stevenson pointed to the recent war with Spain, citing the service of former Confederates. "President [Theodore] Roosevelt and General [former Confederate Major General and now-retired U.S. Army General] Joe Wheeler were together at San Juan," he reminded the group, and the "gallant Fitzhugh Lee," former Confederate General and nephew of Robert E. Lee, commanded a brigade in the Spanish-American War, providing "great services to his reunited country." Stevenson spoke also of commitment by Southerners too young to remember the sectional hostilities, citing Ensign Bagley, "a North Carolina boy" who had given "his life for his country" in 1898, the first American Naval officer killed in the Spanish-American War.[6]

The next speaker, John Boyd Avis, also praised Wheeler and Lee, but spoke too of a time when "the North and South differed in their construction of our Constitution ... the South declaring that each state was sovereign and an independent unit; the North maintaining that we were a union of States, one and inseparable." Acknowledging that "these opinions were honest ones on both sides," Avis, referring to the armies of former sectional foes, urged that "may we hereafter speak of the heroism and courage of American soldiers, fighting for ideas, each believing themselves to be right, as their training and surroundings gave them the power to see and distinguish."[7]

The United Daughters of the Confederacy and the U. C. V. jointly hosted the evening's next, and final, event, a "delightful reception" that had "the rooms being filled to overflowing." "Your mission here is a noble one," declared U. C. V. Camp Commander J. J. Wolfenden, speaking on behalf of the Daughters, the Confederate veterans, and the citizens of New Bern. "We beg to assure you," the Commander continued, "a desire on our part to render such services as in our power rests, to make the occasion which brought you in our midst, a success."[8]

The following day, "under delightful weather conditions," marchers assembled. The visiting soldiers would lead the column through the streets of New Bern; on their right, local Confederate veterans would serve as escort. Behind the aging soldiers the Raleigh Rifles took their place, followed in turn by the Goldsboro Rifles, the Goldsboro Guards, New Bern's Naval Reserves, two state governors, the "State Commissioners for erecting the monument," and "invited guests and ladies." En route to the unveiling, participants would pay homage to the Southern dead, pausing to decorate "the Confederate monument and graves of the Confederate heroes in the New Berne Cemetery."[9]

Yet as these men who had been so warmly welcomed by a prominent Democratic newspaper editor, local Confederate veterans, Daughters of the Confederacy, and citizens of two eastern North Carolina cities paraded through New Bern, thoughts must have drifted back four decades. For these out-of-state guests now leading a procession that included North Carolina's governor were not Virginians, Mississippians, or other former Confederates here to raise yet another monument to the Southern dead. They were men who had worn the blue of the Federal army, members of the Ninth New Jersey Regiment of Volunteer Infantry, a Northern force that seized New Bern on March 14, 1862.

Over the next three years, the unit fought bloody battles across eastern North Carolina and southern Virginia — Kinston, Whitehall, Goldsboro, Drewry's Bluff, Cold Harbor, Petersburg — before being reassigned to New Bern, just months before the war ended. Now marching to the National Cemetery flanked by former adversaries, the

Ninth's survivors were returning to North Carolina's colonial capital to dedicate a "beautiful and substantial memorial" of the "best dark Barre granite," honoring their fallen comrades.[10]

After decorating the Confederate monument and surrounding graves in Cedar Grove Cemetery, the procession continued on to the National Cemetery with "not an unpleasant incident occurring to mar the day's proceedings in any manner." At the federal facility, "the monument of the Fifteenth Connecticut Regiment was also decorated, and the graves of the Ninth New Jersey Volunteers strewn with flowers."[11]

A "beautiful invocation" opened the formal proceedings, the prayer delivered by Reverend G. T. Adams of New Bern. Then, in an order that differed from many Confederate dedications, the memorial was uncovered prior to the day's orations. Mrs. James Stewart, Jr., Matron of Honor and wife of the commission's president, "pulled the cord holding the drapery, and the beautiful monument was unveiled." In acts symbolizing reconciliation, a "handsome wreath of flowers, presented for that purpose by Mrs. Emma Henderson Powell of New Berne," was placed by Mrs. Stewart upon the monument, then the Matron of Honor with "her four aides"—two New Bern women and two from New Jersey—"took seats on the speaker's platform."[12]

"Patriotic airs by the band" followed then General James Stewart, Jr., commission president and Civil War-era colonel of the Ninth New Jersey, spoke of the state's soldiers who had been "sent into the field to uphold the integrity of our National Government," and of the "between eighty and ninety of our comrades buried in this cemetery." In a recitation of regimental history hauntingly reminiscent of Tarheel commemorations, Stewart spoke of the Ninth's "three years and nine months of active service in the field." The regiment had been organized as "riflemen"—"sharpshooters," Stewart explained—and "drew to its ranks a very intelligent body of men," with thirty-three of its original thirty-five officers promoted during the conflict. The regiment had been part of the Burnside Expedition, participating in the Battles of Roanoke Island and New Bern, as well as the siege of Ft. Macon, actions that resulted in

New Jersey monument. New Bern National Cemetery, 1905. Funded by the state of New Jersey to honor its Ninth Regiment, this monument's unveiling included participation by North Carolina's governor.

Federal control of the Pamlico Sound and domination of northeastern North Carolina for the rest of the war.[13]

As Southern resistance crumbled in the spring of 1865, Federal authorities again ordered the Ninth New Jersey from New Bern, eventually assigning the regiment to Greensboro following the Confederate surrender, there to "establish patrol in the town and protect public property." Receiving word that General Joseph Johnston's defeated army "was without commissary supplies," Stewart and his men "carried with them in the same train 60,000 rations, which were turned over to the Confederate soldiers." Speaking to his hosts, the former Colonel concluded his regimental history, "So you see, citizens of North Carolina, that the Union soldier, as soon as the smoke of battle had cleared away, extended the hand of friendship and hospitality to the brave soldiers, who, for near [sic] four years had so gallantly confronted them."[14]

The monument that General Stewart then formally turned over to New Jersey Governor Edward C. Stokes — a carved soldier at parade rest atop an inscribed and decorated granite shaft — differed little in overall appearance from contemporaneous courthouse memorials honoring North Carolina's Confederates. Funded by the State of New Jersey at a cost of five thousand dollars, this commemoration was not, as had originally been intended, "a shaft of any great height." The cemetery's topography and its "foliage and shrubbery being so dense," had necessitated a more modest structure, one designed by "a draughtsman" and chosen by the state-appointed commissioners — three former officers of the Ninth Regiment, including Stewart.[15]

The new memorial, located near the middle of the National Cemetery beside rows of headstones marking New Jersey's dead, stood just over sixteen feet in height. "Proposals and designs" for the structure had been "solicited from prominent stone and marble establishments in New Jersey, Pennsylvania, New York, and New England," according to official records. Cost and bureaucracy, however, may have trumped aesthetics, as the contract was "finally awarded to the lowest bidder — M. C. Lyons' Son, Camden, N. J."[16]

Governor Stokes, thanking the commissioners for their "splendid" efforts, described the just-unveiled monument as "a magnificent work of the sculptor, artistic in its design, beautiful in its contour and pleasing in its proportions." But the governor's address to the "vast assemblage" focused on sectional reconciliation. "I can scarcely realize," Stokes told the crowd, "that those you are now honoring were one time your foes." "This morning," the governor continued, "I beheld a great spectacle — the men in gray and men in blue marching side by side under the folds of the emblem of the Confederacy and the flag of the United States ... drop[ping] garlands of flowers upon the graves of those who wore the gray and those who wore the blue." Concluding, New Jersey's chief executive echoed sentiments spoken the previous evening when he said "the time has come when Grant and Lee, Meade and Jackson and all the leaders and men of both armies shall be regarded as American soldiers only, and belonging to the Nation."[17]

The monument was formally accepted on behalf "of the War Department of the United States Government," by Major Gardner P. Thornton, superintendent of New Bern's National Cemetery, then, to "a roar of cheers," North Carolina Governor Robert B. Glenn rose to deliver the event's closing oration, an "admirable address," according to New Jersey state documents, and one "rapturously received by the thousands assembled."[18]

In remarks similar to other speeches Glenn gave that year, North Carolina's governor spoke of the two states' common American heritage then defended North Carolina's record, citing how the "'Old North State' was very reluctant to enter the war," how, after the firing on Fort Sumter "there was no other honorable course [than secession] for North Carolina to adopt," and how the state's "choicest sons" had "advanced farthest at Gettysburg, and fought last at Appomattox." "We of the South," the governor continued, "have no apology to make for the course that we took in the late war. We did what we thought was right."[19]

After vigorously defending state actions, the governor returned to themes of reconciliation, expressing "delight that the Union soldiers present cheered at the name of Lee, and the Confederates at the name of Grant," then "thanked God that he lived to see the day when such evidences were given of complete reconciliation." Glenn spoke too of the monument's symbolism and prose. "The color of the stone is neither blue or gray," the governor noted, "but the sculptor ... by accident or design, has so fixed its unfading tint, as to show a mingling of the blue and gray into the one solid color."[20]

Perhaps most tellingly of the trust that had developed between the former adversaries was Glenn's allowance that New Jersey could "place any inscription upon it [the monument] that was desired." When aides worried that "something offensive" might be inscribed, the governor assured them "that brave men never strike below the belt." "My prediction has proven true," the governor exclaimed, "the monument is beautiful in its design, chaste in its every feature, and in its inscription descriptive of its object."[21]

North Carolina's eight Union monuments — like the state's more numerous Confederate counterparts — reflect evolving emotions, contemporaneous public opinion, influences of multiple constituencies, as well as gradual sectional reconciliation. While seven were funded by out-of-state sources, these Northern memorials provide powerful insight into how, over time, the victorious federal government, six Northern states, and African Americans chose to remember the conflict that violently reunited the nation.

A federally funded memorial on federal land in Salisbury's National Cemetery is the Tarheel State's earliest Union commemoration. Authorized by Congress March 3, 1873, to be completed within four years, this towering obelisk honors the 11,700 Union soldiers who died in that city's Confederate prison. Designed during the waning days of Reconstruction, this massive totem highlights death as well as honor yet speaks undeniably of federal power — and of victory.

At the base of the tapering shaft, a carved sword, chain, and Spartan helmet rest on a narrow ledge in front of an oval shield engraved with the stars and stripes of the United States. Above this tilted emblem, an elegantly carved drapery nearly surrounds the number 11,700, numerals deeply incised on a raised tablet, while higher still, the wreath-encircled words "PRO PATRIA" (for country) are enclosed within the laurels of victory. Beneath the helmet and supporting ledge, filling the large front panel, the memorial's primary inscription is surprisingly matter-of-fact, citing the monument's erection through an "Act of Congress" and its dedication to the "Memory of the Unknown Union Soldiers Who Died in the Confederate Prison at Salisbury, N.C."

To the right, an identically sized panel contains just seven words: "They Died That Their Country Might Live." The back panel details the history and significance of the site: "In 18 Trenches, Just South of this Spot, Rest the Bodies of 11,700 Soldiers of the United States Army, Who Perished During the Years 1864 and 1865 While Held by the Confederate Military Authorities as Prisoners of War in a Stockade Near this Place." The fourth and final panel contains another concise quote: "For Our Country Tis a Bliss to Die."

In 1873, just eight years after Appomattox, Congress authorized national monies to fund this massive memorial dedicated to the dead of an army that many Tarheels still considered a conquering force. Reconstruction and federal military occupation remained firmly entrenched across the former Confederacy; the Ladies' Memorial Associations were just completing their task of reburying the Southern dead, a job which the federal government had refused to fund; and a financial panic was sweeping the globe, ushering in an economic depression that would last six years.

Just five monuments had been raised to North Carolina's Confederate dead by 1873. None of these memorials stood more than twenty feet high. Now, in a regional transportation hub that was one of the state's most prominent cities, the national government would erect a five-story-tall obelisk that could be seen for miles and serve as the focal point of the well-maintained, fortress-like Salisbury National Cemetery. Alexander McDonald, a well-known stone carver from Mt. Auburn, Massachusetts, was selected to create this "Federal Monument to the Unknown Dead."[22]

McDonald operated a thriving "stone yard"—complete with a railroad spur for the delivery of granite and marble — near Cambridge's Mt. Auburn Cemetery, a famed graveyard widely considered the nation's first modern burial ground. The federal contract called for the sculptor to complete his work "by December 31, 1876," at a total cost of ten thousand dollars. No known records detail design considerations, artistic symbolism, selection of prose, or dedication event; even the exact completion date remains uncertain.[23]

The Federal dead. Salisbury National Cemetery, c. 1876. A massive granite obelisk—topped with a sculpted laurel wreath symbolizing victory—marks the graves of 11,700 Union soldiers who died at the Salisbury Confederate prison.

What is known is that McDonald's completed obelisk was, and would remain for nearly two decades, North Carolina's largest Civil War memorial, measuring fifty feet in height with a width of eighteen feet at the base. And if height and heft and artistic grandeur wasn't statement enough, McDonald carved a sculpted wreath atop the shaft — the laurel wreath of victory.[24]

The national mood was beginning to mellow when the state's next Union monument — a sculpted granite block honoring the dead of the Fifteenth Regiment, Connecticut Volunteers — was dedicated November 14, 1894, in New Bern's National Cemetery. A modified obelisk with upwardly sloping sides and a pyramidal top, the memorial's width was nearly half its height giving the short sculpture a squat appearance, markedly different from the narrow, and arguably more elegant, profile typical of the commemorative form.

A star-studded drape symbolizing the national flag, carved atop the structure, nearly covers the pyramidal apex. "To the Men who Died of Yellow Fever in 1864, and Those Who Fell in Action Before Kinston March 8, 1865," protrude in bold relief from the obelisk's front surface. Connecticut's motto and state shield, the latter surrounded by laurel branches of victory, are sculpted above the primary inscription and face the cemetery's main entrance. The monument's sides are unadorned, but the back features a pair of crossed rifles, a kepi, a canteen, and a knapsack carved in high relief above the words "15th CONN. VOLS." cut in raised letters across the memorial's base.

Although the monument's form may be uninspiring, its design is tastefully simple and skillfully executed. The fabric folds atop the memorial are deep and graceful, the accoutrements well-sculpted. All prose is in raised letters, while all objects and symbols are similarly carved above the obelisk's primary surface, making this one of North Carolina's few monuments that relies exclusively on this beautiful, but challenging, sculpting style.

Connecticut monument. New Bern National Cemetery, 1894. A modified draped obelisk honors soldiers of the Fifteenth Connecticut Volunteers who "Died of Yellow Fever," as well as those who "Fell in Action."

Senator Orville H. Platt of Meriden, Connecticut, delivered the keynote oration, addressing gathered survivors of the Fifteenth. "Thirty years of peace have smoothed over the deep furrows of war," Platt declared, "and to the praise of the God of all Peace be it said, have smoothed over the passions of the conflict."[25]

That smoothing, however, at least judging from the Senator's remarks, seemed limited. Claiming "not to exult over the victory won," Connecticut's long-serving Republican Senator spoke singularly of the Northern soldier, men "who stood by the flag, the Union, our country and its destiny." Speaking in New Bern, North Carolina, although in a National Cemetery and to a group of Union veterans, the Senator never mentioned the Confederacy, Southern troops, or gave any hint that the men the Fifteenth had engaged in battle had once been — and again were — fellow American citizens. The regiment had helped "put down the rebellion," yet those who had fought for an independent Southern nation remained as nameless and faceless this November day as Congress had hoped the Confederate dead would stay when, just months after Appomattox, care for the region's fallen had been denied.[26]

Union veterans—like their former foes—undoubtedly still suffered psychological trauma and stresses. Platt addressed an apparent angst among the survivors. "The personal aspects of the war have in a large measure given way to the historical," he told the men, explaining how public memory was melding individual soldiers' experiences into a collective whole.[27]

Comparing Civil War veterans—most of whom would have been in their 50s or early 60s at the time—with the "venerable men" who had fought in the American Revolution, Platt explained that "the personal experience of the soldier ... will be blended with the deeds of all who faced danger" in a collective forgetting of individual experience that, "as years take us farther and farther from the scenes of conflict," result in "the army rather than the individual soldier which will be remembered."[28]

"We erect monuments, not to the living, but to the dead," the Senator told the men, addressing another aspect of societal memory. "The great significance of this day and occasion is that the living patriotism of our State honors the dead patriots who rest here forever, and honors not only them but their comrades and brothers who in this sacred presence, in this still resting place of the dead, mourn them as fallen companions." A patriot's grave, Platt reminded his listeners, "has a power which no other grave can equal. It is akin to the power of an endless life."[29]

By 1905, when the next Northern monument was raised on North Carolina soil, national attitudes had softened and the commemorative milieu had changed. Southern support of the Spanish-American War, including the enlistment by five former Confederate generals to lead American troops in battle, had demonstrated the region's commitment to the reunited nation as well as acceptance by their former adversaries. The Foraker Bill, appropriating federal monies to care for Confederate graves across the North—a tacit recognition of the Southern dead as worthy soldiers—was working its way through Congress, destined to become law the following year. And in highly symbolic actions, captured Confederate battle flags, emotionally charged emblems of the Southern army, were being returned by the federal government and Northern states to organizations throughout the former Confederacy.

Detail, Massachusetts monument. New Bern National Cemetery, 1908. "In Grateful Memory" of Massachusetts' "Soldiers and Sailors who Died in the Department of North Carolina 1861–1865."

Between 1905 and 1910, five

Northern states dedicated memorials to their Civil War soldiers who had fought or died on North Carolina soil. All of these commemorations, however, were sited on federal lands: New Jersey (1905), Massachusetts (1908), and Rhode Island (1909) in New Bern's National Cemetery; Maine (1908) and Pennsylvania (1910) in Salisbury's federal graveyard.

While artistically varied, these monuments share many similarities. All were sponsored by state governments and exclusively honor one state's dead or a single military unit; all were generously funded and skillfully crafted; and all, while unequivocally honoring and praising the Union soldier, nevertheless exhibit a reserved sensitivity toward a defeated region.

At least four of these states—New Jersey, Maine, Massachusetts, and Pennsylvania—published official book-length reports following dedication events. While only passing mention is made of design and artistic considerations, planning and detail of dedications, including full-length texts of most speeches, are carefully documented. These sources reveal a consistent commemorative pattern. Ceremonies were elaborate

Rhode Island monument. New Bern National Cemetery. To "Rhode Island Volunteers who gave up their lives in North Carolina during the Civil War 1861–1865." Dedicated October 6, 1909.

and inclusive, with joint participation by Union and Confederate veterans. Governors and prominent officials of both North Carolina and sponsoring states had featured roles, while Tarheel citizens by the thousands lined parade routes and attended unveilings. Multiple orations were typical; ten men spoke at the dedication of Pennsylvania's monument in Salisbury on November 16, 1910. And while orators briefly defended actions taken nearly half a century earlier, speeches inevitably emphasized reconciliation, a common American history and heritage, shared national values, and loyalty to a permanently reunified country.[30]

Reconciliation and sectional goodwill, however, were more than dedication day facades. New Bern's United Confederate Veterans Camp #1162 assisted New Jersey's efforts throughout planning and construction of that state's memorial. General Stewart, speaking on the eve of the monument's dedication, publicly thanked the Southern vets for "the great help ... rendered our Commission during the past six months, in looking after the details of our work at this end of the line." Salisbury officials were similarly supportive. When two Maine representatives — including Colonel Joseph L. Small, a former prisoner-of-war at the city's Confederate prison — made a planning visit to Salisbury in May 1907, the men "were delighted" at their reception, according to a local newspaper account, expressing "appreciation at the courtesies extended by Mayor Boyden and Alderman Parker."[31]

Federal bureaucrats could be more difficult to deal with than Tarheel officials. When Pennsylvania commissioners sought the United States Army Quartermaster General's approval for their state's Salisbury memorial — permission required even for state-sponsored commemorations in National Cemeteries — a "long and vexatious delay" ensued. While the monument's proposed location was readily granted, all inscriptions, including those penned by committee members, were rejected. "Weeks of correspondence and numerous visits to the War Department" were followed "with revisions of the original inscriptions and presentations of new ones."[32] Even the Quartermaster General's later "unequivocal approval" was fleeting; within days the official, for unstated reasons, ordered "all work upon the memorial" stopped until the phrase "Death Before Dishonor" — "objectionable words" according to the Quartermaster — be effaced. Frustrated Pennsylvania commissioners, to avert additional delay, "gracefully submit[ted]" to the demands without further appeal.[33]

The monument's ultimate design and prose seemed to mirror changing attitudes. Constructed of "celebrated" Mt. Airy Granite paired with marble from Georgia and Italy, the thirty-two-foot-high arcade is located barely one hundred yards from the cemetery's two earlier Northern commemorations. While the 1876 federal obelisk is capped with a laurel wreath of victory and Maine's 1908 commemoration features a rifle-bearing soldier standing guard at parade rest, Pennsylvanians placed an unarmed man, a prisoner of war according to official documents, atop their memorial.[34]

The eight-foot-high bronze, however, has been cast with muscular features more typical of a victorious warrior than a starving prisoner. The soldier's head is bent forward and the eyes, nearly obscured by a modified kepi, look down, giving the figure a contemplative rather than either a dispirited or martial pose. Soldier and memorial are non-threatening; open

"One Country — One Flag." Maine monument, Salisbury National Cemetery. Dedicated June 8, 1908.

arches invite the viewer into a covered space, there to view a pair of inscribed bronze tablets and a cast illustration of the prison camp.

The monument's prose is similarly firm yet conciliatory. While referring to the conflict as the "War of the Rebellion"—a widely used Northern term reviled by Southerners—and stating that Pennsylvania soldiers "used the sword only to preserve the peace and unity of their country," a conciliatory explanation follows: "Respecting the example of the Romans, who never raised emblems of triumph over a foe, the Commonwealth of Pennsylvania erects this monument to perpetuate the memory of the dead, and not as a commemoration of victory."[35]

While Northern attitudes may be judged by a monument's design and prose as well as by official reports, Tarheel sentiment toward their former foes can be surmised by words and actions on many levels. Two of the well-documented Northern monument dedications were attended by sitting North Carolina governors. Robert Glenn, as noted previously, hosted survivors of New Jersey's Ninth Regiment in New Bern in 1905, while five years later, his successor, Governor W. W. Kitchin, speaking to Pennsylvanians in Salisbury, welcomed their "peaceful invasion" to dedicate a "monument [that] stands in no enemy's country."[36]

Unarmed prisoner of bronze. Salisbury National Cemetery, 1910. "Death Before Dishonor" was briefly inscribed on this elaborate Pennsylvania monument but removed by order of the Army quartermaster general who deemed the phrase "objectionable."

Local officials extended similar greetings. Salisbury Mayor A. H. Boyden, himself a Confederate veteran, assured Northern attendees at Maine's 1908 monument unveiling that "the season of heated blood, I rejoice, has passed," offering visitors "a certainty that my comrades and myself give you earnest, hearty welcome." The city's Confederate veterans, like their counterparts in New Bern, led in assisting guests. "Nothing was left undone by the members of the Confederate Camp," according to Pennsylvania's official report, "to make the stay of the Yanks in Salisbury, one of the most enjoyable occasions of their lives, and ever to be remembered by them."[37]

Thousands of North Carolinians joined in the day's celebration. A company of North Carolina National Guards, the Salisbury brass band, and a unit of coastal artillery all marched with the Pennsylvanians, helping create a column "fully a mile long." Arriving at the National Cemetery an hour later, the formal event commenced in front of "an immense concourse of the citizens of Salisbury, Durham, Raleigh and the surrounding country," Tarheels who paid "close and respectful attention ... during the entire proceedings."[38]

Goodwill and promotion of sectional reconciliation were reciprocated by Northerners. The Foraker Bill, signed by President Theodore Roosevelt in 1906, funded care for thousands of Confederate graves near Northern hospitals and former prison camps; the Southern dead, once denounced as "disgraced Rebels," would finally be accorded the respect given all fallen American soldiers.

Praising the valor of Southern troops and affirming these men as worthy citizens of a reunited nation was also a common theme during the era's Northern monument unveilings. In 1905 New Jersey Governor Edward C. Stokes declared in New Bern that "men of both armies shall be regarded as American soldiers only, and belonging to the nation." Leroy F. Pike of Maine, "speaking for his Excellency Governor Cobb," during the 1908 unveiling ceremonies in Salisbury, told how "the leaders and the soldiers of that war have not been surpassed in valor for then American met American." Two years later in the same National Cemetery, Robert S. Murphy, Pennsylvania's Lieutenant Governor spoke of "our high esteem for the unflinching devotion of those soldiers who gave to the army [sic] of Northern Virginia the laurel of imperishable renown."[39]

New Jersey officials, as part of the 1905 ceremonies dedicating its monument to the Ninth Volunteer Regiment in New Bern's National Cemetery, brought with them the "bullet-ridden flag" of the Beaufort Plow Boys. Forty-three years earlier, the banner had been seized by the Ninth "in a desperate struggle on the outskirts of New Berne." In a highly symbolic act of respect and reconciliation, John Boyd Avis, Speaker of the New Jersey House of Assembly, presented the flag in the "name of the State of New Jersey" to North Carolina Governor Robert B. Glenn, returning the banner to "the people of North Carolina to whom it belongs."[40]

"The joy of the sons and daughters of the Confederacy knew no bounds," according to New Jersey's official report, and for "several minutes the scene was one of indescribable enthusiasm" as the governor and speaker "stood clasping hands with the flag gently swaying on the arm of the Governor."[41]

The return of the Plow Boys' tattered

United States Colored Troops. Perquimans County. Located on Academy Green near one of Hertford's oldest black churches, this monument, funded by the United Daughters of Veterans — likely a group of African American church women — honors African American volunteers who fought for the Union army and navy. Few details are known about this obelisk, believed to have been erected about 1910. The crossed flags are the Stars and Stripes and a Navy banner. Two monuments honoring Colored Troops — the official designation of African American soldiers — were erected across the states of the former Confederacy prior to the late twentieth century. The other, in Norfolk, Virginia, was begun in 1906 but not completed until 1920, making this Hertford commemoration the oldest completed memorial to African American troops in the South.

battle emblem was followed by yet another symbolically laden event, the presentation by the Ninth New Jersey Veterans Association of a silk United States flag to the local Confederate Encampment. Colonel David L. Ward, representing Governor Glenn, accepted the banner on behalf of Southern veterans. Wearing a blue uniform, "the uniform of a united country" explained the Colonel, Ward thanked the Northern veterans for this "silken emblem of loyalty," assuring the visitors that "it shall float in our Southern breezes and under our clear skies, over a nation of brothers." If threatened, the Colonel continued, "the old veterans who followed the Stars and Bars ... would rally around it," as would their descendants, and "defend it with their lives."[42]

Ward's concluding sentence, however, perhaps best expresses Tarheel hopes as part of a reunited nation at the dawn of the twentieth century: "May your stay among us," the former Confederate officer told the New Jersey veterans, "be long remembered as the meeting of brave men, now united, who once stood in hostile array."[43]

Section III
Expanding Commemoration, 1919–1961

15. New Expressions

On January 6, 1915, Wilmington businessman Gabriel James Boney, a former city alderman and ex–Confederate corporal, died at age sixty-nine. Described by the *Wilmington Morning Star* as "a brave Confederate soldier," Boney's wartime service record was not unlike that of many fellow Tarheel troops.[1]

At age eighteen, the Duplin County native, on March 10, 1864, enlisted as a private in Company H, Fortieth North Carolina Regiment. At Fort Anderson the young soldier fought Federal gunboats then, after promotion to corporal, commanded twenty men during a clash at Town Creek. But at Bentonville, in 1865, the largest land battle waged in North Carolina, Boney was captured and spent the war's final weeks as a prisoner at Point Lookout, Maryland.[2]

After swearing an oath of allegiance, Boney returned to Duplin County, working at "mercantile pursuits" for eight years, before moving to Wilmington in 1873, where he established the Boney and Harper Milling Company and attained "much prominence and gratifying success." The ex-soldier never married but was active in Wilmington's political, civic, and commemorative efforts and, at his death, was described by the *Morning Star* as "always close to every work for the perpetuation of Confederate memories."[3]

When Boney's will was filed on January 21, 1915, his estate totaled nearly $43,000.00 (equivalent to approximately $1,000,000.00 today). Two siblings each received $5,000.00; the First Presbyterian Church and its pastor were given $1,500.00; friends and distant relatives were bequeathed smaller amounts; while the Cape Fear Camp #254, United Confederate Veterans, was allotted $50.00, and "Five hundred dollars is to be deposited in the Bank of Duplin, Wallace, for benefit of Millie Murphy, colored, of Duplin ... to be paid in weekly installments of $1.25." The remaining funds, approximately $20,000.00, were to be used "to have erected in the City of Wilmington, North Carolina, a monument to the Confederate soldiers who fought in the Civil War."[4]

Boney included precise instructions how this was to be accomplished. "I desire my executor and trustee to request the Cape Fear Camp, No. 254, United Confederate Veterans of Wilmington, N.C., to appoint one of their number, and the Cape Fear Chapter of the Daughters of the Confederacy of Wilmington, N.C., to appoint one of their number, who, together with the president of the Wilmington Savings & Trust Co. shall be ... a committee to pass upon and approve the plans, designs, specifications and point of erection of said monument."[5]

Surprisingly, Wilmington had yet to erect a civic-space memorial honoring Confederate troops at the time of Boney's death, fifty years after Appomattox. Through much of the nineteenth century, this commercial hub along the banks of the Cape Fear River had been North Carolina's most populous city, and one of its most prosperous. During the Civil War, protected by Fort Fisher, Wilmington was the Confederacy's last open port, a base for blockade-runners and a critical supply depot for Robert E. Lee's Army of Northern Virginia.

After Appomattox, Wilmington's Ladies' Memorial Association, organized in 1866, led one of North Carolina's earliest commemorative efforts, raising nearly eight thousand dollars and placing a commissioned bronze statue, the state's first soldier figure, atop the massed remains of 367 soldiers in Oakdale Cemetery. The city's women were also instrumental in launching the United Daughters of the Confederacy. Wilmingtonian Mrs. Eliza Parsley helped forge the organization's founding principles, and the city's Cape Fear Chapter #3, the third unit organized in the nation, was founded by Parsley who also served as the North Carolina Division's first president.[6]

A gift of Gabriel James Boney. In New Hanover County, Wilmington's Confederate soldiers' monument was sculpted by Francis H. Packer of New York, designed by architect Henry Bacon and unveiled in 1924.

Wilmington's men promoted memorialization as well. Alfred Moore Waddell, former Confederate colonel, U.S. Congressman, and civic leader, in an 1885 Memorial Day address to Raleigh's Ladies' Memorial Association, declared that the period of mourning after the war should be over and that the Confederate dead, in addition to cemetery memorials already raised, deserved civic-space monuments. Ten years later, Waddell addressed another Raleigh crowd, as keynote speaker for the unveiling of North Carolina's monument to the Confederate dead, the state's most prominent Confederate commemoration.[7]

Yet Wilmington's commemorative direction differed from much of the Tarheel State. This may have been due, in part, to the legacy of the 1898 race riot, considered by some historians a "coup d'état," in which elected black officials were driven from office and fled for their lives. Perhaps it was the city's affluence and famous citizens that delayed a more egalitarian monument. Wilmington's commemorations are nearly all pricey commissioned works, while the city claims as its own three Confederate generals buried in Oakdale Cemetery and Confederate Attorney General George Davis (1864–1865), the highest-ranking

Southern official from North Carolina who was honored with a larger-than-life downtown statue erected in 1913.

Despite Gabriel Boney's generous bequest, plans for Wilmington's Confederate soldiers' monument progressed slowly. On May 24, 1922, seven years and a World War after the soldier's death, the *Wilmington Dispatch* reported that the "committee in charge" — "H. C. McQueen of the United Confederate Veterans, Mrs. L. W. Berry [sic-should read Beery] of the Daughters of the Confederacy, and C. E. Taylor, one of the executors [and president of Wilmington Savings and Trust]" — had requested city commission approval to place the monument at one of two prominent locations, both on Market Street and each within three blocks of the George Davis memorial. The request, however, was "referred to the city plannig [sic] board for its investigation and recommendation," with a meeting, the *Dispatch* opined, to "be held at an early date."[8]

Nearly five months later, on October 6, the *Dispatch* reported that the committee had "appeared before the city commission this morning" and received permission to erect the memorial at "the southern end of the plaza at Dock and Third Streets." This location, however, was not one of the requested sites along Market Street, the city's main thoroughfare, yet the *Dispatch* offered assurances that the memorial would be "a bronze figure upon a pedestal that will be a fitting tribute to the men who wore the gray," and that "The work will be done by an artist of note," although "who will be selected ... is not yet decided."[9]

By January 1923, not only had an "artist of note" been selected — Francis H. Packer of New York who had executed the Davis monument — but a model of the proposed commemoration was available to "be seen [locally] by Daughters of the Confederacy and others interested." Although the *Morning Star* announced eight months later that the monument was "Nearing Completion," it was not until May 1924 that the *News-Dispatch* could report that "All plans and specifications by the sculptor ... have been approved by the Confederate monument committee." However, there would be a delay of "several months" before the work started, "as trouble has been experienced in securing some of the materials."[10]

Packer would be assisted by architect Henry Bacon, designer of the Lincoln Memorial in Washington, D. C., who briefly "collaborated" with the

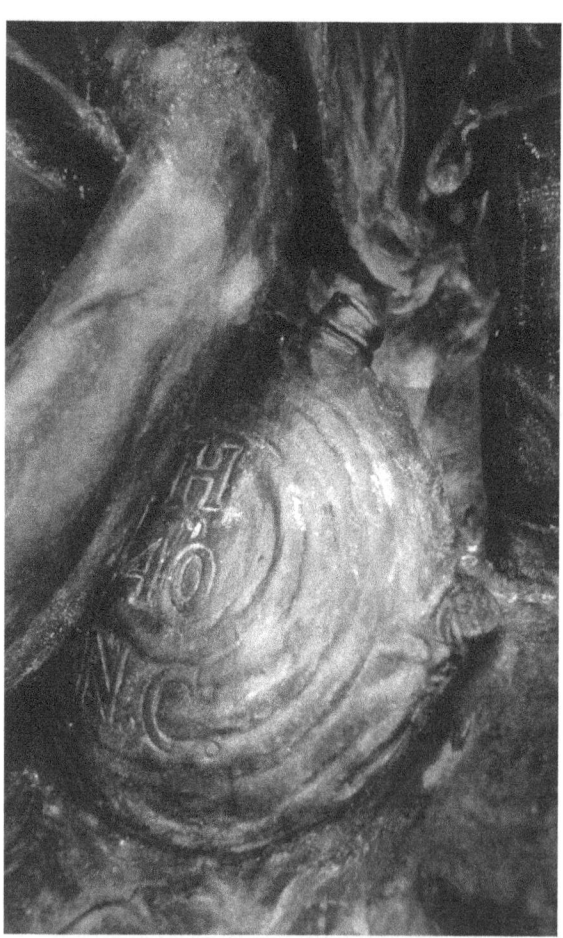

Canteen detail. Packer sculpted "H 40 N.C.," denoting benefactor Gabriel Boney's military company, on both soldiers' canteens.

sculptor shortly before the architect's death, although "all of the work was done by Mr. Packer," according to the *News-Dispatch*. The bronze would be impressive, with the taller figure standing nearly nine feet high. A semi-circular pedestal, inscribed, in part, "Pro Aris Et Focis" (for alter and home), elevated the sculpture nearly five feet off the ground, while a granite slab reading, "1861–1865 To The Soldiers of the Confederacy," provided a sixteen-foot-high backdrop.[11]

The *Morning Star* described the sculpture as that of "a Confederate soldier standing erect over a wounded comrade," while the *News-Dispatch* added that one man's face "denot[ed] courage, the other self-sacrifice and suffering." Packer included personalizing details as well; "[Co.] H. 40th NC," Gabriel Boney's unit, is inscribed on both soldiers' canteens.[12]

Leslie Boney, an architect and great-nephew of the benefactor, provided additional insight into the memorial's creation. "The granite was quarried in Salisbury, North Carolina and a Mr. Ramsey was the salesman for the company," Boney wrote in a 1976 letter to the North Carolina Museum of Art. "Mr. Packer liked the strong facial features of this young man and used his face as the model for the Confederate soldier."[13]

On September 14, 1924, the finished monument was formally accepted by the three-person committee. The process, however, had not been without protest. A "CITIZEN," writing two weeks earlier under the headline, "Seeks Information," asked if, before "a man from New York" had been awarded the commission, "our local monument people had an opportunity of submitting designs, models or prices." "If not, why not?" the short missive concluded, although no evidence exists of any response.[14]

Progress accelerated and three weeks later the Cape Fear Chapter, United Daughters of the Confederacy, who had, one year earlier, been given "charge of the unveiling of the monument," finalized the dedication itinerary. A "mammoth crowd" was expected, according to the *Morning Star*, with the *News-Dispatch* adding, "Traffic will be diverted from the streets affected during the hour of the ceremony," slated to begin at 4:00 P.M. The Daughters were "especially desirous of having every veteran in New Hanover County present," offering "arrangements whereby the veterans may be brought to the monument in automobiles."[15]

The unveiling went flawlessly. "No more beautiful setting could have been found for the exercises," the *Morning Star* effused. Although shorter and less elaborate than some earlier Tarheel dedications, this event highlights the state's evolving commemorative milieu. The parade formed at the Wilmington Light Infantry armory, with the band of Company A leading the procession. A Light Infantry detachment came next followed by Confederate veterans, the U.D.C., Children of the Confederacy, and Sons of Confederate Veterans. The Reverend A. D. P. Gilmour, pastor of the First Presbyterian Church which had also received funds from Gabriel Boney's estate, delivered the invocation, then General A. H. Boyden was introduced by Dr. A. M. Baldwin, local U. C. V. camp commander.[16]

In typical commemorative style, Boyden told of the Confederate army's deeds, "Recalling the battles of Manassas, Sharpsburg, Gettysburg, and the second battle of Cold Harbor," according to the *Morning Star*. But the general spoke too of soldiers' pensions, a contentious state issue, advocating for less stringent restrictions and declaring "that every Confederate veteran is entitled to a pension."[17]

The orator echoed another traditional dedication-day theme as he "paid tribute to the Cape Fear section," and "a number of old Cape Fear families." Boyden then related a personal incident from shortly after the fall of Fort Fisher during the waning days of the Confederacy. "Hoke sent me back to see if there were any stragglers left behind," Boyden said, referring to his role as General Robert Hoke's courier. "As I was riding through Wilmington ... a woman opened the blind and asked me if Fort Fisher had been evacuated and I told her 'yes.' She then asked me to come in, and she filled my haversack to overflowing with food." Six decades later, a still-grateful Boyden added, "I have always wanted to find out the name of this kind woman."[18]

The unveiling combined traditional elements with new features as well. A young child, "Little Miss Virginia Boney," would unveil the monument which had been covered with Confederate battle flags instead of a white shroud. Yet the accompanying music would not be a Confederate standard. The Wilmington Light Infantry "presented arms," according to the *Morning Star*, as the grandniece of the benefactor released the flags, uncovering the monument. Then, perhaps reflecting pride in a reunited nation recently victorious in a World War, the "band of the headquarters company" struck up the "Star-Spangled Banner."[19]

Monument building slowed by 1915 as the nation prepared for another war, one that would again necessitate Tarheel sacrifice and alter the state's commemorative course. Some of the Civil War's deadliest tactics — frontal assaults like Pickett's Charge (1863) and the equally disastrous Union attack at Cold Harbor (1864), and trench warfare as demonstrated at Petersburg — reached greater intensity during this World War as armies fought in a years-long conflict that claimed ten million lives.

This "war to end all wars" was not the United States' first post–Civil War conflict. In 1898, the re-united nation achieved a lopsided victory against Spain, a fight in which former Confederate states proved their loyalty and Southern troops showed their valor. Casualties were light, however, with "just two North Carolinians in regular service" losing their lives, according to William Powell, and the state's commemorative response was muted.[20]

The World War was a much bloodier affair with 126,000 Americans, including 2,375 North Carolinians, among the dead. Following the armistice on November 11, 1918, commemorative planners faced a conundrum. Within living memory, Tarheel troops had engaged in three wars, and like the situations faced by the LMAs shortly after Appomattox, and the Daughters at the turn of the century, no commemorative blueprint existed as how best to honor these men.[21]

Monument building ceased as North Carolinians pondered a commemorative response. For fifty years, the state had almost exclusively honored the "men who wore the gray." Now, the sons and grandsons of these soldiers had also fought and died in large numbers, and new commemorative questions emerged. Should men of three generations — including those who sought independence *from* the United States as well as those fought *for* the reunited nation — be honored with a common monument? Should earlier wars, such as the American Revolution, be included on these memorials? Might this situation offer counties internally divided about the Civil War a commemorative alternative? And could memorial planners fuse the causes, celebrating the state's Confederate heritage while emphasizing its commitment to a reunited nation?

Following the armistice, three years passed before another Tarheel Confederate soldiers' monument was unveiled, and when commemoration resumed, new styles and expanded themes heralded a wider and more complex memorialization. During the "Golden Age" of U.D.C.-sponsored monuments (1904–1915), three-fourths of the state's Confederate monuments featured a solitary private atop a granite pillar sited in a prominent civic location.

Twenty-nine of these commemorations had been raised during this period, but only one such memorialization would be dedicated in each of the next three years.

After the World War, the single-soldier motif would never regain dominance. Seven of these once-standard Confederate designs were raised between the World Wars, all between 1921 and 1926. The expanding commemorative fluorescence, however, added wider themes, additional honorees, new commemorative partners, and novel sculptural iterations. While some of these works are not soldiers' monuments, as defined in this book, and are not included in statistical analyses, an overview provides needed insight into the state's commemorative environment as North Carolinians forged a "multi-war" collective memory.

Civil War battles and notable events were marked as part of this effort, often in locations easily accessible to the burgeoning number of motorists. Roadside plaques commemorating Civil War–era individuals and events were co-sponsored by the state U.D.C. and the North Carolina Historical Commission during the 1920s. (These bronze tablets differ from current black-on-silver historical signs, an ongoing state program begun in 1935.) The Daughters also raised a rock pyramid in Haywood County (Waynesville, 1923), site of the "Last Shot" of the Civil War east of the Mississippi River, while the Samuel Tate Morgan family funded the "Unity Gate" at Bennett Place near Durham (November 8, 1923), a memorialization marking Southern surrender — and erected by the state despite protests from the Daughters who considered the twin-columned structure a "monument of defeat."[22]

Two memorial highways crossed the state as well. The Jefferson Davis Highway, a coast-to-coast route honoring the Confederate president, roughly followed current U.S. Highway 15 through the Tarheel State. Along this route, North Carolina's Daughters placed identical bronze plaques, inscribed "Jefferson Davis Highway," approximately every ten miles, with larger tablets marking the state's borders. In addition, the women landscaped the roadway with crepe myrtles of red and white, the Confederate colors.

In western North Carolina, Tarheel Daughters, led by Mrs. James Madison Gudger, Jr., of Asheville, marked the Dixie-Lee Highway, a route honoring Robert E. Lee and tracking modern U.S. 25. Identical bronze plaques, designed by Mrs. Gudger and featuring Lee astride his horse, Traveller, denoted the route. These "highway markers," according to the September 1924 (Asheville) *Souvenir Magazine*, "will meet the eyes of more people in a week than will many other monuments in a year."[23]

On Sunday May 2, 1926, the first two plaques, one at the base of the Vance obelisk in downtown Asheville, the other beside the Calvary Episcopal Church in Fletcher, were dedicated. "The governors of Virginia and North Carolina participat[ed]" in the Fletcher unveiling, according to the *Confederate Veteran*, which included an image of the plaque on its May cover. A handwritten note, penned on the 1924 *Souvenir* in Asheville's Pack Library, claims that "Ten markers [were] placed" in all. At least four of these prominently sited plaques remain, the two noted above and one each beside courthouses in Henderson and Madison Counties.[24]

In addition to this expanded Confederate commemoration, other organizations funded monuments honoring "Doughboys," as soldiers of the World War were colloquially named, filling another commemorative niche. While no comprehensive list of these monuments, comparable to Smith's (1941) or Widener's (1982) compilation of Tarheel Confederate monuments, has been published, most of these approximately one-dozen courthouse-grounds commemorations singularly honoring veterans of the World War were erected in jurisdictions that had yet to raise a civic-space Confederate memorial.

Confederate soldier commemorations, meanwhile, took on new forms as well. While

An early multi-war memorial. Wilson, 1926. This commemoration beside the Wilson County courthouse was erected through joint efforts of the U.D.C. and the D. A. R. The plaque reads, "To the Valor of Wilson County Soldiers."

a majority of North Carolina's newly unveiled Confederate monuments still exclusively honored Southern troops, four memorials honored Confederate soldiers as well as later veterans.

In Wilson County (Wilson), site of a 1902 Confederate monument in Maplewood Cemetery, the United Daughters of the Confederacy joined the Daughters of the American Revolution (D. A. R.) in sponsoring a 1926 courthouse-grounds memorial. The center panel of this modified granite triptych features a pair of unfurled flags, the Stars and Stripes crossed with the Confederate battle flag, both sculpted as though waving in the wind. Below, a bronze plaque reads, "To the Valor of Wilson County Soldiers." A pyramidal cap tops each end of this symmetrical work, while the reverse is inscribed, "Erected by the John W. Dunham Chapter U.D.C. and the Thomas Hadley Chapter D. A. R. November 11, 1926."

Eighteen months later, in nearby Halifax County (Enfield), the Frank M. Parker Chapter, United Daughters of the Confederacy, probably in partnership with the American Legion, unveiled a white marble drinking fountain. This commemoration is shaped and sized nearly identically with Wilson's memorial, except that fountains replace the decorative caps at each end.

The front is Confederate-themed. The battle flag, depicted as if in a breeze, is carved high on the central panel. Beneath the banner, a bronze plaque with the U.D.C. logo reads, "1861–1865 To the Memory of the Veterans of the War Between the States," followed with five frequently quoted, but unattributed lines of Father Joseph Ryan's poem, "The March of the Deathless Dead" (Chapter 12). "Erected by the Frank M. Parker Chapter," is inscribed on the left marble panel, while the right reads, "United Daughters of the Confederacy May 30, 1928."

Marble Drinking Fountain. This 1928 monument in Enfield, Halifax County, with paired fountains and bowls, honors Confederate soldiers as well as World War I veterans. While providing classic symmetry, the dual structures, according to Smith, were racially designated, one for whites, the other for African Americans.

The memorial's reverse, of nearly identical design, features a similarly sculpted 48-star American flag. The plaque, with an American Legion emblem, reads, "1917–1918 In Honor of our Veterans of the World War," above three [attributed] lines by poet Joyce Kilmer.

Since dedication on *national* Memorial Day, 1928, inscriptions have been added, expanding this sculpture's commemorative role. "World War II 1941–1945" and "Persian Gulf War" are inscribed to the right of the plaque; "Korean Conflict 1950–1953" and "Vietnam War 1961–1975" are incised on the left. "Relocated by Claude N. Kimball, Jr. V. F. W. Post No. 6813" is carved below the front bronze, denoting the fountain's move to a small park beside Enfield's Elmwood Cemetery.

More-inclusive monuments, celebrating soldiers of all three wars within living memory, were raised in Holly Springs (Wake County, 1923) and in Montgomery County (Troy, c. 1926). Captain G. B. Alford, the Confederate officer praised by Raleigh's *News and Observer* in 1895 for delivering a thirty-six pound ham to help feed veterans attending the state monument dedication, funded a multi-war, yet predominantly Confederate-themed memorial at the Holly Springs United Methodist Church. In raised letters, the front base reads, "Confederate Soldiers 1861–1865." "Their Sons Who Were in the Spanish-American War," is cut into the left base, while the back is inscribed "Their Sons Who Were in the World War."[25]

A youthful-appearing soldier of stone, outfitted as a Confederate infantryman, tops the granite pillar, giving the monument the aura of a typical Confederate commemoration. Two massive bronze tablets — the front featuring a roster of local Confederate soldiers, the back citing commemorative and heritage groups — complete the memorial.

A similarly inclusive monument was erected three years later in front of Montgomery County's courthouse (Troy, c. 1926). Here, veterans of the World War, not Confederate soldiers, were accorded commemorative dominance. A Doughboy of white stone tops this monument. The unsigned figure, likely a commercially produced statue — although such manufactured forms never achieved the popularity of Civil War soldiers — depicts a uniformed infantryman striding forward, carrying a rifle with his left hand. The right arm is upraised, grenade in hand, as if preparing to hurl the explosive.

"In Memory of Montgomery County Sons Who Served in the World War," is inscribed on the front panel. In identical font, and with nearly identical prose, the left panel reads, "In Memory of Montgomery County Sons Who Served in the Spanish-American War," while the back reads "In Memory of Montgomery County Sons Who Served in the Confederate States Army." The final panel reflects a concurrent commemorative theme, "In Memory of Montgomery County Women Who Did Their Part in all Wars."

As some North Carolinians sought tributes to soldiers of multiple wars, others opted for more traditional Confederate monuments or skillfully executed commissioned works, such as Wilmington's two-figure sculpture described above. Although the solitary soldier form was declining in popularity across the nation — and commercial production of the soldier figures would largely cease by the late 1920s — seven such statues, all but one in prominent public spaces, were raised in North Carolina between 1921 and 1926.

The process through which these memorials were raised differed little from that of previous decades. In Caswell (Yanceyville, 1921), Person (Roxboro, 1922), Lenoir (Kinston, 1924), Stanly (Albemarle, 1925), and Carteret (Beaufort, 1926) Counties, the U.D.C. led fund-raising. Public monies aided the women's efforts in Stanly County, while in Durham County (Durham, 1924) the monument was erected, according to its inscription, "By the People of Durham County."[26]

Soldier statues were still commercially purchased. Caswell's Daughters selected a rugged-appearing skirmisher manufactured by the American Bronze Foundry; in

Holly Springs, Wake County, 1923. Funded by Confederate veteran Captain G. B. Alford, this commemoration features two bronze tablets listing local Confederate veterans but also includes prominent inscriptions to "Their Sons" who fought in the Spanish-American War and the First World War.

Stanly County, a Mullins' stamped-metal figure was chosen. McNeel Marble Company remained active as well. Two similarly styled McNeel memorials, topped with identical but unsigned metal infantrymen, were dedicated in Durham and Lenoir Counties on Confederate Memorial Day, May 10, 1924.[27]

Dedication events similarly remained little changed. Josephus Daniels, former editor of Raleigh's *News and Observer*, and Navy Secretary under President Woodrow Wilson, spoke in Person County; Governor Cameron Morrison spoke in Lenoir County; while Judge Henry A Grady, addressed the crowd in Carteret, delivering an oration entitled "In God's Acre."[28]

One noticeable difference, however, was the ever-thinning gray line, reflected in the selection of speakers as well as veteran attendance. In 1924, General Albert Cox gave the featured oration in Durham. Although "of distinguished Confederate heritage," according to the *Durham Morning Herald*, Cox was neither a Confederate general nor a U. C. V. official but an American commander of World War fame. And in contrast with the one thousand veterans Julian Carr led from Durham to the capitol in 1895 for the state monument unveiling, "Approximately 60 heroes of gray" attended Cox's oration.[29]

Montgomery County Doughboy. Troy, c. 1926. Topped by a World War I soldier statue, this multi-purpose commemoration includes panels honoring veterans of the "World War," the Spanish-American War, and Confederate soldiers—as well as "In Memory of Montgomery County Women Who Did Their Part in all Wars."

"Some [were] now bent with age," the paper reported of Durham's aging soldiers, "and walking with faltering step, others still able to stand and walk erect, with clear vision and strong brain." These men, however, were accorded a reverence few troops have ever known. "Wherever they went during the day they were marked men in whom the people made it known that their sacrifices were not in vain and that their service was appreciated."[30]

While some dedications, as in Wilmington and Durham, celebrated a Confederate heritage fused with pride in the reunited nation, at least one soldier statue, perhaps inadvertently, may have done likewise. "Mr. T. O. Sharpe has the contract for the monument and he is enthusiastic over the job," the *Roxboro Courier* reported on May 3, 1922, days before the planned unveiling of Person County's Confederate monument. "The monument has arrived and is being erected," the *Courier* added, without naming sculptor or source of either statue or shaft, both of which are unsigned.³¹

Termed a "handsome tribute to the Old Confederate" by the *Courier*, this soldier statue is one of the state's most unusual depictions. Partially backed by a sculpted tree trunk, the infantryman stands erect, supporting a rifle resting between his feet. Outfitted with a tall, almost pointed hat — neither military issue nor typical Confederate slouch hat — this soldier does not carry the standard blanket roll across his torso. Instead he is sculpted with an oval bedroll, in the shape and size of a Doughboy's rucksack, on his back and wearing a high-collared, tight-fitting shirt with large buttons, appearing as much a World War I soldier as a Civil War veteran.

The demise of the standard Confederate monument form coincided with the aging and death of all but the last Southern soldiers. The state's final unveiling of this typical form to be witnessed by Confederate veterans, a monument topped with a bronze infantryman and inscribed in part, "Not Even Time Can Destroy Heroism," took place in Carteret County in 1926. Just ten veterans, all cited by name in the *Beaufort News*, attended, yet "a crowd that packed the building [courthouse] to the doors" turned out for the event. "A nice dinner was served the veterans," then "a procession was formed ... composed of the veterans, the orator and selected others, the Fort Macon [U.D.C.] chapter, the Emmeline J. Piggott [U.D.C.] chapter and the Children of the Confederacy [sic]."³²

Funding woes, however, plagued Carteret's Daughters. The monument cost three thousand dollars, the *News* reported, "and there is still something due on it." On dedication day, "Some $200 or more was realized by the sale of tags, refreshments and the collection which was taken up in the court room." In addition, Mr. F. S. Dickinson, "a prominent business man of Rutherford, New Jersey, but a native of Carteret County ... delighted the ladies with a check for $500," allowing the Daughters to "hope to pay the rest of the debt on the monument before the close of the year."³³

Person County soldier statue. Dedicated in Roxboro on May 20, 1922, this sculpted soldier figure features accoutrements and uniform details from both the Confederacy and World War I.

"How Firm a Foundation," led off the day's program, followed by the invocation and an "appropriate recitation" by Mrs. Ida Eaton of Morehead City. Judge Grady, of Clinton, "described by those who knew him as having the wisdom of Solomon," "spoke about an hour," describing how the perception of Confederate veterans had changed. "Confederate soldiers were no longer referred to as rebels and traitors to their country," the jurist declared. "That sectionalism had passed away.... Lee, Grant and other leaders on both sides should be regarded as great Americans." The judge also "paid fine tribute to the Confederate soldiers of Carteret County, both the living and the dead," receiving hearty applause and "many congratulations" for his remarks.[34]

A "tremendous crowd" then assembled on the courthouse lawn for the unveiling. "Rosa Lee Chadwick, granddaughter of Mr. W. S. Chadwick and David Poole Clawson grandson of the late Captain James Pool [sic] of Co. H, 10th regiment of N.C.," did the unveiling, followed by a quartet singing "Tenting Tonight" with the Children of the Confederacy joining in the chorus. Then in an act reflecting the foundation of Confederate commemoration, and one little changed from deeds carried out by the LMAs in the 1860s, the event concluded with "a part of the crowd [going] to Live Oak cemetery [sic] where the graves of the soldiers were decorated."[35]

Carteret County Confederate monument. Dedicated in Beaufort on May 10, 1926, it would be the last North Carolina unveiling of this iconic monument form to be witnessed by Confederate veterans.

16. Hard Times

The Confederate Memorial Forest would be a commemoration like no other. This novel venture, funded by the United Daughters of the Confederacy, North Carolina Division, and undertaken in partnership with the federal Forest Service, would create the Tarheel State's largest and loftiest Confederate soldiers' memorial, nearly one-quarter square mile in size and one mile above sea level.

The concept was approved by the Daughters at their 1939 convention in Asheville. On August 2, 1940, represented by Division President Ethel Harris (Mrs. L. E.) Fisher, the Daughters and the Forest Service signed a "cooperative agreement," a summary of which, according to the *Asheville Citizen-Times*, was "engraved," with a framed copy "presented to the Hall of History in Raleigh for future reference."[1]

With precise legal terminology, this document outlines the plan and its terms. "The Forest Service desires to cooperate with the United Daughters of the Confederacy" in establishing "on National Forest lands," a planting "to be known as the North Carolina Memorial Forest," and the Daughters will "honor the 125,000 soldiers that North Carolina gave to the Confederate Armies," while assisting "in reforestation and the restoration of the natural resources of the Southern Region."[2]

In addition, the agreement set a 99-year lease with the following stipulations: One acre of trees would be planted by the Forest Service for each $5 contribution; "the same protection from fire, disease, and trespass as is given other National Forest land in the vicinity" would be provided; and the Service agreed to "erect and maintain an appropriate marker," denoting the site. The U.D.C., meanwhile, was given a choice of location, from the Croatan National Forest on the coast to the Nantahala in the state's southwestern tip.[3]

The women opted for a rugged area in the Pisgah National Forest near the headwaters of the Pigeon River. This Haywood County site, along a ridgeline thirty miles southwest of Asheville, had been logged earlier in the century, leaving a barren, flood-prone mountainside. But this remote, denuded location had been carefully chosen by the Daughters. A new scenic byway was being cut through the mountains connecting the Shenandoah and Great Smoky Mountains National Parks, and soon this road, the Blue Ridge Parkway, would be the nation's most-visited Park Service unit. Mrs. Fisher, of Asheville, project committee chair and now past–U.D.C. president, recognized the site's potential, exclaiming in 1942, "The vistas at the forest entrance are gorgeous and the traveler will naturally stop there…. Literally millions of tourists from every corner of the world."[4]

The Forest Service could not keep pace with the women's fund-raising. By the summer of 1942, the Daughters had collected sufficient monies to achieve their goal, funding one tree for each of the 125,000 Tarheel soldiers who had fought for the Confederacy. Yet just 55,000 trees — red spruce and balsam set every six feet — had been planted, a delay, according to the *Citizen Times*, "occasioned by a decision to use larger and hardier four-year seedlings."[5]

Despite unfinished planting, the Daughters scheduled the dedication for Sunday, July 12, 1942. Although this memorial was a new commemorative form, the itinerary was similar to prior monument unveilings. A luncheon would be held at Asheville's George Vanderbilt Hotel followed by an outdoor ceremony at the forest. Wartime rationing, "the rubber and gasoline situation," as the *Times* termed it, necessitated that "the main program will be at the luncheon here," although "a number of cars have been secured to make the trip to the forest" for "brief exercises."[6]

"Approximately 100 persons" attended the luncheon, the *Citizen* reported, "including many prominent state and national U.D.C. officers." Women assumed more prominent roles in this event than in most previous dedications. Mrs. R. O. Everett, of Durham, state U.D.C. president, conducted the lunchtime proceedings. Addressing the gathering, Mrs. Everett

Confederate Veterans Memorial Forest. Between 1941 and 1943, a total of 125,000 red spruce trees — one for each North Carolinian who fought for the Confederacy — were planted beside the Blue Ridge Parkway in Haywood County. The large evergreens behind the sign are from the original planting.

praised the forest's setting, "where the mists gather around the brow of these tall mountains," and described how the seedlings would grow into a "silent grove" honoring the "heroic lives of the 125,000 dead whose memories are there perpetuated."[7]

"The luncheon was opened with the singing of a verse of the 'Star Spangled Banner,' and closed with the singing of two verses from 'America,'" the *Citizen* reported. Josephus Daniels, former editor of Raleigh's *News and Observer* and Navy Secretary under Woodrow Wilson, was the featured speaker, introduced by Citizen-Times Company president, Charles A. Webb, a last-minute substitution for Mrs. E. L. McKee, of Sylva, who had been scheduled to introduce the orator.[8]

Daniels, who had, a half-century earlier while seeking funds for the state Confederate monument, railed against a North Carolina legislature that "endorsed" miscegenation, (Chapter 4), told the Asheville gathering of "the wrongs inflicted upon a brave and helpless people" by those "who from greed and political ambition brought the horrors of reconstruction on the heads of the prostrate South." Admitting that this "mistreatment ... is nothing compared to the treatment now being given" German-occupied European nations, the former editor claimed that the "memory of the denials of self-government and freedom during reconstruction [sic] had inspired the South to lead the nation in voluntary military enlistments both before and after Pearl Harbor."[9]

Following the mid-day luncheon, seventy-five people traveled to the forest site for the unveiling, a ceremony in which women filled nearly all roles. Mrs. L. E. Fisher, who had guided the project and signed the 1940 agreement, presided. Mrs. Paul Borden, of Goldsboro, gave the invocation; Mrs. Walter Woodard, a past division president from Wilson, provided "Readings from the U.D.C."; and Mrs. Glenn Long, another past-president, sang "Trees." Mrs. Everett, current U.D.C. president, gave the "dedicatory address" then "presented" the forest to H. B. Bosworth, Pisgah National Forest supervisor, the only adult male on the program.[10]

Two Confederate descendants, "Mary Caroline Simmons, of High Point, granddaughter of Mrs. Fisher and Robinson Oscar Everett, son of Mrs. Everett," unveiled the "temporary marker" denoting the forest. An "imposing permanent U.D.C. bronze tablet set up in a huge mountain boulder" would "eventually" take its place, the *Citizen-Times* told readers, citing Mrs. Fisher. However, the replacement would have to wait until "after the war when bronze can be secured."[11]

Fourteen years after this dedication closed with an accordion solo of "Dixie," and eleven years after the Second World War ended, the State Literary and Historical Association and the Western North Carolina Historical Association joined the U.D.C. on August 11, 1956, in unveiling the long-awaited plaque. A member of the original forest committee, Mrs. R. N. Barber, Sr., of Waynesville, "presided," the *Asheville Citizen-Times* reported, with Mary Barber and Sarah Thomas unveiling the marker.[12]

Even this plaque, however, would not endure. In 1979, the bronze was pried from the boulder and stolen. A wooden placard replaced the metal commemoration, and today, a painted sign, little different from the "temporary marker" unveiled in 1942, denotes the North Carolina Confederate Veterans Memorial Forest.[13]

The pace of Tarheel Confederate memorialization changed little as the state endured a decade-long economic depression. Thirteen commemorations — twelve of stone or metal plus the memorial forest — were dedicated between 1929 and 1942. New and less costly forms, however, replaced the granite shaft and soldier statue of previous decades.[14]

Bronze plaques and inscribed stone slabs became the state's dominant physical commemorative expression, a style that would persist through much of the twentieth century. Cast inscriptions, however, were not a recent innovation. In 1905, the Washington (N.C.) Gray Chapter, Children of the Confederacy, placed a brick-encased, white-metal tablet in Washington's Oakdale Cemetery (Beaufort County), honoring the "17 Soldiers Killed in Defense of Washington, Sept. 6, 1862."

By 1912, competition between bronze foundries was intense. The Murdock-Reed Company of Boston, advertising in the May 1912 *Confederate Veteran*, offered "Distinctive

Tablets in Bronze," boasting of "Our experience ... cover[ing] a period of many years," and "careful attention ... to the artistic arrangement of the inscription." Two months later, another Massachusetts firm, Woodland Bronze Works, touted "Bronze Memorial and Inscription Tablets," with "Estimates and Designs Furnished Upon Request," and in October, two New York foundries, Jonathan Williams and the Gorham Company, each advertised "Bronze Memorial Tablets"— on opposite corners of the same *Veteran* page.[15]

North Carolina's Daughters adopted this motif as part of the widening Southern commemorative response following World War I, denoting the Jefferson Davis and Dixie-Lee Highways with such markers and teaming with the North Carolina Historical Commission to erect a series of distinctive plaques interpreting historical events (Chapter 15). Captain Alford, in Holly Springs (Wake County), also used cast metal, adding two massive bronze inscriptions to his 1923 monument, while in Wilson, the Daughters and the D. A. R. included a plaque "To the Valor of Wilson County Soldiers" on their jointly sponsored 1926 memorial.

The Greene County Chapter (Snow Hill), United Daughters of the Confederacy, took the next stylistic step in 1929, erecting a courthouse-lawn memorial consisting solely of a bronze plaque set into a roughly shaped granite block. Dedicated "In Memory of the Greene County Soldiers of the Confederate States Army," this plaque includes the date 1861–1865, credits the Greene County Chapter with erecting the memorial, includes the U.D.C. logo, and features an enigmatic but unattributed quotation—"And Read Their History in a Nation's Eyes"—a single line from Englishman Thomas Gray's poem, "Elegy Written in a Country Churchyard" (1751).

Bishop Thomas C. Darst delivered the dedicatory address. The Snow Hill Choral Club sang a "Group of Negro Spirituals," and the "honor of unveiling" the small memorial, according to Blanche Lucas Smith, was "given to twenty-five children of the Confederacy, many of them too small to realize the significance of the occasion, but all deeply concerned with upholding the dignity of the occasion."[16]

Four similar civic-space commemorations, all funded by the Daughters, were added across the state prior to World War II. In 1932, the Lee-Eaves-McDaniel Chapter of Forest City (Rutherford County) erected a bronze plaque bolted to a rectangular granite slab in the median of Forest City's Main Street, a busy thoroughfare later denoted as U.S. Highway 74, the "Main Street of North Carolina," according to Smith.[17]

The Chapter's namesakes and their units are cited: "Capt. H. D. Lee and Company D 16th Regiment ... the first to leave from Rutherford County for the War Between the States"; "Capt. J. B. Eaves and

A lower-cost form. This 1929 plaque on the Greene County courthouse grounds in Snow Hill is the first county Confederate commemoration consisting solely of a bronze plaque bolted to a granite slab.

Company I 50th Regiment," men who left the next year, who also "departed from this sacred spot"; and "A. H. McDaniel Co. I 50th Regiment, Commander of the Davis-Dickerson-Mills Camp of Rutherford County Confederate Veterans." The inscription closes, "This site was the muster ground of the Burnt Chimney Volunteers now Forest City."

The monument, with its thin metal plaque, cost just $150.00, but its dedication, during the depth of the Great Depression, nevertheless showcased pomp and symbolism that rivaled earlier Tarheel unveilings. The weekly *Forest City Courier* ran five articles over four weeks, beginning with a May 19 announcement that "Mrs. Glenn Long, of Newton, N.C., U.D.C. division president, will be present for the occasion." The itinerary was detailed on May 26 then repeated, with the monument's description, one week later.[18]

In addition, the June 2 *Courier* detailed the units' history, declaring that "These companies represented the flower of the community's young manhood." A "good deal of friendly rivalry" had occurred "between the Burnt Chimney Volunteers [Company D, Sixteenth North Carolina Regiment] and Davis' Volunteers of Rutherfordton as to which company would ... enter service first," the *Courier* continued, with the Burnt Chimney soldiers filling their ranks days before the men from the county seat filled theirs. On June 3, 1861, the company held "a final drill at the muster ground," where the Reverend Butler Justice, "a noted divine of the county," delivered a "farewell sermon and invoked the blessing of Providence on the company."[19]

"Practically every resident of Forest City and Cool Springs township are related [sic] in some manner to these men of 1861," the *Courier* declared, explaining its printing of Company D's roster, a recitation covering nearly half a page. Forty of the unit's 146 soldiers had been killed in action or died from wounds or disease. Seven more had been "discharged for disability," five had lost a limb or been "injured or handicapped for life," while "Practically every member of this company suffered minor wounds."[20]

Seventy-one years to the day after these men marched to war, Forest City's dedication event revealed a community's acceptance of loss and eventual pride as part of a reunified nation. The Stars and Stripes flew at half-mast as Mrs. Charles Z. Flack, president of the Lee-Eaves-McDaniel Chapter, U.D.C., chaired activities. "America," performed by the high school band, opened the ceremony; "Dixie" followed an "Historical Address" by attorney

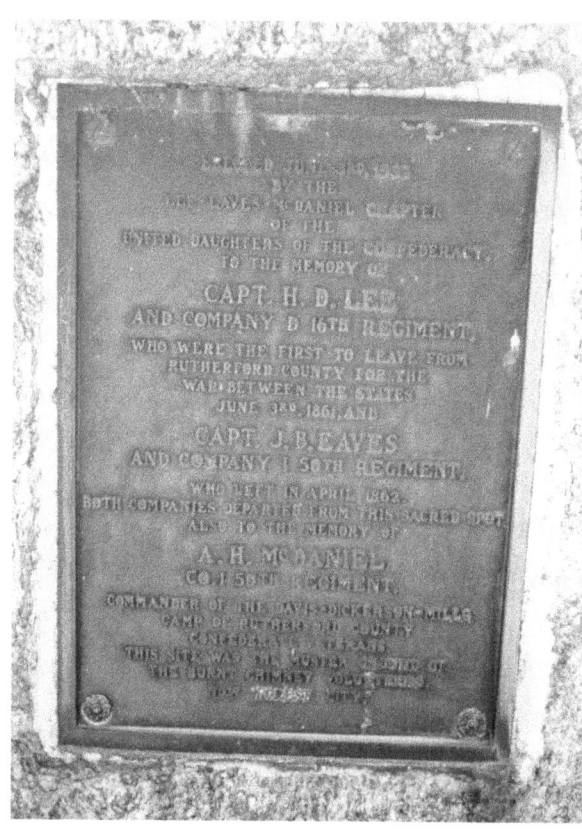

Forest City, Rutherford County, 1932. This plaque and granite slab cost just $150 but was dedicated at the depth of the Great Depression. Located in the median of Main Street, the memorial honors local Confederate units and their commanders.

Robert S. Eaves. A. H. McDaniel, one of two Confederate veterans present, "placed a wreath on the monument," according to the *Courier*, and as the band played the "Star Spangled Banner," "little Miss Caroline Flack and Master Grover McDaniel drew aside the large Confederate flag which draped the monument."[21]

Professor Charles C. Erwin accepted the memorial "on behalf of the Mayor and the town of Forest City." "What we say here today, we shall not long remember but what we place here shall stand," Erwin stated, thanking the Daughters for the monument.[22]

The professor also emphasized dual themes that were becoming common aspects of Tarheel dedicatory orations, praising Confederate soldiers' valor and honor while tempering regional pride with loyalty to the reunited nation. "We owe a debt to those who gathered here ... who offered themselves as a gift to their State," Erwin said, referring to the Confederate soldier, before adding, "May no citizen, looking upon this monument,

"Our Confederate Dead." Bayboro. The Neuse Chapter, United Daughters of the Confederacy, placed this 1940 plaque in front of the Pamlico County courthouse.

be incited to a militant patriotism unless in defense of his own beloved country." The monument should instead serve "as a grim reminder of the futility of settling disputations by bloody wars." And as if to emphasize that grim reminder, "Taps" closed the day's event.[23]

U.D.C. chapters erected similarly styled monuments in front of two courthouses, in Pamlico (Bayboro, 1940) and Haywood (Waynesville, 1940) counties and beside the Cherokee Indian Council House (1935). The courthouse commemorations, at opposite ends of the state, reflect the regional commemorative divergence that began in 1903 (Chapter 5). Haywood's Daughters erected their memorial "To Honor and Commemorate the Confederate Veterans of Haywood County," an inclusive, and widely used, western North Carolina theme. In Pamlico County, the Neuse Chapter, U.D.C., dedicated their plaque "In Memory of Our Confederate Dead," a common inscription across the state's coastal plain.

In addition to bronze plaques, inscribed granite slabs became another common commemorative form. Richmond County's (Rockingham) Pee Dee Guards Chapter, U.D.C., on November 14, 1930, dedicated a polished granite tablet inscribed "In Loving Memory of Our Confederate Soldiers." The American Legion and Boy Scouts led the "March to Old Courthouse Square." The singing of "America" opened the event; former Governor Cameron

Morrison, a Richmond County native, delivered the oration; and a "Quartette" of "Negro boys from Morrison Training School" sang an unidentified selection prior to the keynote speaker's introduction.[24]

In Faison (Duplin County), the "Sons of Co E CSA," aided by a committee of four including at least one woman, erected a ten-foot-high slab inscribed with the "Original Roster" of the Confederate Grays, Company E, Twentieth North Carolina Regiment, "Organized at Faison, N.C., April 16, 1861." During this dedication, May 20, 1932, the same Confederate flag which had ceremoniously covered North Carolina's Gettysburg monument at its 1929 unveiling, was again used.[25]

Three granite panels form a commemorative triptych on Anson County's courthouse grounds in Wadesboro. William Alexander Smith, a 90-year-old Confederate veteran of the Anson Guards — the "First Company in the State to Offer its Services," according to the memorial's inscription — funded this monument to Confederate women "as a gift of love to his mother." A long-serving commander of North Carolina's United Confederate Veterans, Smith, however, did not witness the unveiling, dying months before the September 22, 1934 dedication.

Depression-era Tarheel Confederate memorialization also featured a widening of commemorative venues. Following an eighteen-year hiatus, cemetery memorialization resumed in 1930 with the placement of a metal arch over the entrance of Littleton's Sunset Hill Cemetery. Designed and erected by Campbell Brothers of Raleigh at a cost of four hundred dollars, this arch, featuring the words "Sunset Hill," was unveiled at sunset on June 3, Jefferson Davis' birthday. Paired pillars of rough-cut granite brick support the arch with each column containing an inscribed, smoothly finished stone tablet. The left reads, "The Roanoke Minute Men Chapter Daughters of the Confederacy," while the right is "In Memory of Our Beloved Confederate Soldiers 1861–1865."[26]

Top: Confederate monument. Haywood County. This 1940 plaque, on the courthouse grounds in Waynesville, is "To Honor and Commemorate the Confederate Veterans of Haywood County." *Above:* Richmond County Confederate Monument. Located on the town square in downtown Rockingham, this granite slab was dedicated on November 14, 1930. Reverse is inscribed, "1861–1865 'Lest We Forget.'"

16. Hard Times

Raleigh's women added decorative elements to their city's Oakwood Cemetery, site of the 1870 marble monument (Chapter 1) and a 1910 gate. On September 27, 1931, "just as the shadows lengthened and the sun went down," according to Wake County LMA's history, the James Johnston Pettigrew Chapter, United Daughters of the Confederacy, dedicated a 365-foot-long wall of 52,000 bricks which provided "protection and beauty" to the Confederate graves. An attached plaque reads in part, "To Commemorate the Heroism of the soldiers and sailors of the Confederate States Army and Navy who rest buried in this cemetery."[27]

Four years later, the Pettigrew Chapter placed the cornerstone for the House of Memory, a well-known, multi-war commemoration at Oakwood. Although not singularly a Confederate memorial, as defined in this book, six of twelve plaques highlight contemporary Tarheel Confederate themes: the North Carolina Rebel Boast is featured on one; an enumeration of Oakwood's Confederate dead fills another; while a tribute "To the Confederate Women of North Carolina," erected by the Children of the Confederacy, comprises a third. The "Private Soldiers of the Confederacy" are honored on

Top: "Confederate Grays." Faison, Duplin County. Inscription lists the roster of Company E, Twentieth North Carolina Regiment. The Confederate flag that ceremoniously covered North Carolina's Gettysburg monument at its 1929 dedication was used for this 1932 unveiling. *Above:* 16-H: Sunset Hill Cemetery. Littleton, Warren County, 1930. Inscribed granite pillars credit the Roanoke Minute Men Chapter, U.D.C., with erecting this arch: "In Memory of Our Beloved Confederate Soldiers."

another, a tablet closing with six unattributed lines from Father Ryan's despairing 1866 ode, "The Conquered Banner."[28]

Other U.D.C. chapters extended Confederate commemoration to western North Carolina cemeteries. In 1941, the Battle of Bentonville Chapter erected a tall granite slab in Mooresville's Willow Valley Cemetery (Iredell County) inscribed, "In Memory of the Soldiers of the Confederacy 1861–1865 Who Lie Buried Here," listing eighty-nine names.[29]

That same year, McDowell County (Marion) Daughters began the process of erecting dual plaques — each engraved with a pair of crossed, furled Confederate flags — on columns flanking the entrance to Oak Grove Cemetery. Marion's women honored both the War's dead and surviving veterans, with the left bronze in "Memory of the Confederate Veterans of McDowell County 1861–1865," and the right inscribed "Erected 1941 by United Daughters of the Confederacy of Marion in Honor of the Men of McDowell County who Died in the Cause of the Confederate States."

Western North Carolina's Daughters also extended Confederate commemoration into the Cherokee nation , erecting, in 1935, a plaque engraved with the profile of Will West Long, "a living descendant of a Cherokee Indian Confederate veteran," according to the *Asheville Citizen-Times*, and inscribed "In Honor of those brave Cherokee Indians loyal to the Confederacy 1861–1865 commanded by Col. Wm. H. Thomas."[30]

Like much of the Tarheel State, the Eastern Band of Cherokee Indians was "divided in sentiment" at the start of the War, according to Smith. Encouraged, however, by William Holland Thomas, the only white man ever to serve as principal chief, "about every able-bodied man in the tribe" eventually enlisted, filling Companies A and B of the Sixty-ninth North Carolina Regiment. Serving predominantly as "scouts and homeguards along the Tennessee–North Carolina border," the Cherokee rendered "good service to the South," reported one high-ranking officer, and, under Thomas' command, were the last Confederate units to surrender in North Carolina (May 10).[31]

The first district of the North Carolina Daughters — thirteen southwestern chapters from Hendersonville and Black Mountain west to Murphy — sponsored this memorial. In addition to celebrating

Willow Valley Cemetery. Mooresville, Iredell County. This 1941 memorial is "In Memory of the Soldiers of the Confederacy Who Lie Buried Here"; eighty-nine names are listed.

Cherokee loyalty, the monument acknowledges Colonel Thomas, the tribal chief, who, beginning in 1862, commanded Thomas' Legion of Indians and Highlanders, a Confederate military force numbering up to 2,500 men that included cavalry and light artillery. The Colonel, however, did not fare well after the war, suffering financial setbacks and spiraling into insanity by 1867.[32]

On June 21, 1935, the district's Daughters, at their annual convention in Asheville, listened to a "Report of Indian Marker," presented by Mrs. W. A. Hyatt then, during the luncheon, raised toasts to "The Boys of the Sixties," the "Girls of the Sixties," and "The Loyal Cherokees." Three months later, "in front of the tribal house," the Daughters unveiled the memorial, a plaque encased by "native stone ... six feet high, two feet thick and 36 inches wide," the *Citizen-Times* reported.

A "Boy Scout Bugler" opened the September 29 ceremony with an "Assembly Call" at 3:00 P.M. "America," sung by a male "Cherokee Indian Quartette," followed the invocation then three western North Carolina U.D.C. officials spoke briefly. "Master John F. Hodges, Jr., grandson of Colonel Thomas, and ... Master John Tatum Ellis, Jr.," performed the unveiling. Dr. Harold Fought, reservation "superintendent" and a "Government Agent," according to Smith, accepted the monument on behalf of the Cherokee, while the *Citizen-Times* added that tribal chief Jarrett Blythe also had a role in the acceptance.[33]

One of two plaques paired at the entrance to Oak Grove Cemetery in Marion. This 1943 bronze honors the "Confederate Veterans of McDowell County," the other, local men "Who Died in the Cause of the Confederate States."

Like Thomas' decline and the Cherokee's post-war struggles which included a deadly smallpox epidemic in 1865, this monument has had a troubled existence. The Council House was destroyed, and the monument was subsequently removed for highway expansion. Little is known about its subsequent locations except that an early-twenty-first century photograph shows the rock-encased tablet beside two similar World War I commemorations alongside a little-used parking lot. The memorial would be moved yet again, however, and when photographed by the author in 2011, was at the edge of a field, out of the ground and facing a poison ivy-filled thicket.[34]

Not all Depression-era Confederate commemorations were lower-cost, however. In New Hanover County, the North Carolina Division, United Daughters of the Confederacy, erected a towering granite shaft south of Wilmington to mark the site of Fort Fisher and honor the defenders of this "Gibraltar of the South."

Tarheel Daughters hoped to raise $35,000.00 by "popular subscription" to fund the memorial. In May 1930, however, Senator Furnifold Simmons introduced an appropriation request that "came as a complete surprise" to the Daughters, according to the *Wilmington Star*. Simmons, in the midst of a tough re-election battle, proposed a *federal* outlay of $25,000.00, urging, since Fort Fisher was among "the approved sites recommended by the War department for suitable commemoration," that the national government finance the memorial.[35]

If approved, this appropriation, championed by Simmons and U.S. Representative J. Bayard Clark, would have created North Carolina's first federally funded Confederate memorial—and the state's first nationally financed Civil War commemoration since the Salisbury National Cemetery obelisk, authorized in 1873 to honor the Union dead. The proposal, however, like Simmons' re-election bid, ultimately failed.[36]

Seventeen months later, North Carolina's Daughters, the *Wilmington News* reported, "approved the architect's design for the memorial," a "Grecian column of granite surmounted by a bronze eagle," standing twenty-four feet high. Funded by the state U.D.C. and designed by a "Greensboro architectural firm," the monument would cost between nine and ten thousand dollars and would be erected by Charles C. Johnson of Greensboro, who had "gained national fame a few months ago following the erection of the North Carolina memorial at Gettysburg, which he built."[37]

Johnson began setting the foundation on December 16, 1931, under the watch of U.D.C. monument committee chair Mrs. L. B. Newell of Charlotte and Louis T. Moore, executive secretary of the Wilmington Chamber of Commerce. The chamber head lobbied hard for maximum economic benefit for the region, even recalling former sectional strife. On December 7, the *Star* reported that Moore, writing to

Loyal Cherokees. Swain County, 1935. This plaque depicts Will West Long wearing the "typical one-feather headdress of the Cherokees." Sponsored by thirteen western North Carolina U.D.C. chapters, this is the state's only Confederate memorialization honoring a single ethnic group.

Mrs. Newell, had related "the apparent inconsistency of the Fort Fisher memorial ... being built of granite from a northern state," and advancing "The suggestion ... that the granite come from some southern state if not from North Carolina." The following week, Moore "requested," as reported in the *News*, that Johnson also "use local labor whenever possible."[38]

By May 27, 1932, construction was complete, with Moore reporting that "grass [had been] planted and a circular road built by the state highway department." The unveiling would be June 2, one day before Jefferson Davis' birthday, but timed, according to the *News*, with the "Rail-Water Coordination program" and "the opening of the inland waterway," events expected "to draw persons of prominence from throughout the state and South Atlantic seaboard." To encourage the Daughters' acceptance of this date, from the originally planned May 18, the "city board ... agreed to the diversion of $250" from the waterway funds to underwrite the monument unveiling.[39]

On June 1, the *Star* requested that "All Wilmington citizens who are descendants of men who fought at Fort Fisher ... place flags in front of their homes Thursday to lend a spirit to the town." The same article also reported the availability of "Printed programs detailing the exercises," four-page booklets featuring a cover sketch of the monument. Members' names of the "Memorial Committee," details of the 11:00 A.M. public program, and the announcement of a "1:00 P.M. Luncheon, by Card" at the St. James Parish House, "Tendered by the City of Wilmington," fill the other pages.[40]

Fort Fisher, New Hanover County. Sponsored by the North Carolina U.D.C., this 1932 granite pillar topped with a bronze eagle commemorates the defenders of Fort Fisher, the "Gibraltar of the South."

The dedicatory exercises "were brief but impressive," the *News* reported. "America" opened the ceremony followed by the invocation, delivered by the Right Reverend Thomas C. Darst, "Episcopal bishop of East Carolina." Governor O. Max Gardner, the principal orator, stressed the military importance of Fort Fisher—"The very meat and bread of the Confederacy" passed by its guns en route to Wilmington, the South's last open port—and described the "terrific bombardments to which it [the fort] was repeatedly subjected." But the governor "rose to forensic heights" the *News* reported, by declaring, in closing, "that man can have no higher heritage than the knowledge that he is a descendant of such gallant men as comprised the Confederate army."[41]

Mrs. Glenn Long, U.D.C. state president, followed, delivering a "Stirring" speech, printed in full by two Wilmington newspapers. "More monuments to Southern valor have been erected upon Southern soil than have been set up in any other land to any other people," Mrs. Long told the crowd. "By erecting a monument on this historic and hallowed spot, the Daughters ... hope to voice and perpetuate the heroism, the valor and the sacred memories of those native sons who here displayed courage unsurpassed ... and to know that here a grateful people have taken pride in inscribing their history on imperishable stone."[42]

Yet even dignified ceremonies can have lighthearted moments. "It tickled our sense of humor no little bit yesterday at the Fort Fisher monument unveiling," the *Wilmington Star* noted, "when several good staunch rebel cows appeared on the scene and bawled with unabashed enthusiasm." One was likely the "unruly Bossie," the *Star* asserted, a bovine that "some months ago ... took a gustatorial liking" to the flagpole rope "and started munching away," jerking Old Glory down in "ignominous [sic] shame." A "timely spectator put her to rout," the *Star* added, but not before "a lone-handed cow had done something that the whole Confederacy couldn't do — lower the American flag."[43]

17. The Centennial Nears

The soldier was just eighteen. But on a hot afternoon in July 1863, this young man, flanked by thousands of battle-hardened veterans, stepped from a wooded Pennsylvania ridge and started across one thousands yards of open ground. The teenager's doubts and fears may have been lessened by the resolve of the men around him, soldiers who, for two years, had successfully waged war under the commands of Lee and Jackson, scoring decisive victories against numerically superior foes.

This afternoon these proud soldiers were advancing toward the center of the Union army, a force well-positioned on high ground. Breastworks, earthen mounds, and rock walls protected Northern troops, but the open field offered Southerners no cover, the fences and shallow ditches across this exposed terrain only slowing the attack.

With each Federal volley, Confederates fell by the score. Yet the gray wave of humanity surged forward. Smoke from black gunpowder filled the air. Over the din of constant rifle fire and the roar of cannon, the young soldier could hear the screams of the injured and perhaps the groans of the dying. Horses whinnied in terror, while commanders, including North Carolinian James Johnston Pettigrew, urged men on.

Some Confederates reached Union lines, but only a handful of men breached them and soon they too were driven back. By evening, the Southern assault had been repulsed; an army had been shattered; and thousands lay dead and dying across that open field.

And the young man? He too had been shot. "Oh fate of the just," he may have murmured that afternoon, "thou gavest me this bitter cup, and I bow to thy behest and drink it up." Then days before his nineteenth birthday, the soldier breathed these final words exemplifying "How bravely her [Southern] sons can say farewell."[1]

Ninety-five years later, a likeness of this "Lad of 'The Old South'" was chiseled in Italy from a block of nearly translucent white marble. The depiction would stand atop a Confederate monument in front of Alexander County's courthouse; plaques on the pedestal would relate the soldier's story as outlined above.[2]

No commemorative soldier figure had been raised in the Tarheel State for more than three decades when Virgil Gustavius "Gus" Beckham, a long-time Taylorsville attorney, launched a fund-raising effort in the late 1950s. But monies were slow to come in from this western Piedmont county, and Beckham soon decided to finance the monument himself.[3]

Little fighting took place in this rural region during the Civil War, but county troops paid a terrible human toll. Beckham wished the marble lad, "whose name is known but to me," to represent all Alexander County Confederate soldiers. The young man's fate was not atypical: eight hundred seventy-six county men voted in the 1860 election; three hundred eighty died during the Civil War, possibly the highest fatality rate of any Southern county.[4]

Beckham's effort also highlights the changed commemorative environment following World War II. The attorney began building the monument on June 5, 1958, according to the *Taylorsville Times*. The seventy-one-year-old World War I veteran not only financed the monument but did much of the work.[5]

"The base ... is composed of equal parts of sand and cement, and reinforced with steel," the *Times* reported, while "The pedestal is of Tennessee granite which is said to be the hardest of all granite, and was laid by an expert, Belt Campbell." Beckham, however, "hauled every pound of material that went into the monument," "around two-and-one-half tons," in his 1953 Chevrolet truck. On June 1, 1959, the statue was transported by "a truck from [supplied by] Carson Hardware" to the courthouse and "mounted chiefly by the Duke Power Company of Taylorsville, without which we would have been unable to place it on its mooring as it weighs 1345 pounds."[6]

Beckham installed three plaques, two of granite and one of bronze, as part of the monument. At the pedestal's base an inclined slab tells of Lee, Jackson, and Grant, including their views about slavery. As part of the shaft's front face, a second stone tablet lauds "The Heroic Sons and Daughters of the Old South" while claiming that "Our Greatest Heritage States Rights," not slavery, motivated Southern resistance. Higher still, a sixty-three-word bronze plaque describes the "Lad of 'The Old South,'" killed at Gettysburg during Pickett's Charge, on which the figure and Beckham's apocryphal story are based.

North Carolina's last Confederate soldier statue. This marble figure, financed by a local attorney and carved in Italy, stands atop a rock pillar beside the Alexander County courthouse in Taylorsville, completed in 1959.

There are no reports of any dedication ceremony following completion of the monument in June 1959. Six months earlier, however, Alexander County commissioners had appropriated $1175.00 for a "Jones six-pounder" cannon that had "belch[ed] and roar[ed]" at Gettysburg on July 3, 1863, to be placed beside the soldier statue. An accompanying granite plaque tells of "the bravest body of infantry that ever careered the fields of battle" and "hurled itself against the Union batteries ... only to be annihilated in a blaze of glory that will glow undimmed throughout the rolling flood of endless ages."[7]

Beckham never revealed the carved soldier's identity. Time, however, and perhaps the death of the benefactor, allowed details to emerge. The sculpted image is widely believed modeled from a photograph of Jacob Lentz, father-in-law of Beckham's sister. Lentz, however, was not killed at Gettysburg; he did not even join the Confederate army until four months after the battle and then only following conscription.[8]

Private Lentz was assigned to Company D, Mallett's North Carolina Brigade (Camp Guard) before enlisting "for the war" with the Twenty-ninth North Carolina Regiment on June 22, 1864. Twelve days later, he was captured near Smyrna, Georgia, defending a bridge leading to Atlanta.[9]

Following brief confinements in Nashville and Louisville, Lentz was transferred to Camp Douglas, a prison near Chicago. The North Carolinian, however, survived the war and "the dreaded diarrhea that killed so many in Yankee prisons," according to military records and family history. After taking the Oath of Allegiance, Lentz was released on January 31, 1865, and

Alexander County Confederate monument, Taylorsville. Monument and cannon placed in 1959. The tablet at right, a later addition, lists the names of Confederate "Alexander County Boys" who "Gave Their All."

"nursed back to health" in Anna, Illinois, by his brother who had been "instrumental" in the release. By September 1865, the war was over and Jacob Lentz was again residing in Alexander County.[10]

Monument construction across North Carolina ceased during World War II, and even after the conflict ended in 1945, Confederate commemoration never regained its former dominance. The decline that began following the First World War accelerated with only one Confederate monument — a granite slab in Mt. Airy's Oakdale Cemetery dedicated by the Surry County U.D.C. in 1950 — erected during the decade immediately after the Second World War.

Little documentation explains this commemorative decline, but a glance at the nation's post–World War II social milieu can provide insight. In 1945, the United States was the world's sole superpower, with atomic weapons and overwhelming military superiority as well as a robust economy. The reunified nation had waged three declared wars since Confederate surrender, achieving unequivocal victories in all. And after a decade of economic depression, and four years of wartime rationing, Americans faced a future of great potential, perhaps dampening enthusiasm for honoring the dead of a failed cause eight decades earlier.

Demographics likely contributed as well. "True" daughters and sons — not heritage group members claiming *any* Confederate ancestry but men and women who were *biological* children of Confederate veterans — were aging and passing from positions of power and influence. Half of all Confederate veterans had died by 1890, and with shorter life expectancies, relatively few mid-twentieth-century North Carolinians under the age of sixty-five would have been raised by Civil War soldiers or "women of the '60s."

The new leaders, men and women who could lead fund-raising campaigns or effect large business contributions, had scant experience listening to first-hand accounts of the Civil War or Reconstruction, at least on a regular basis. The immediacy of loss, and depth of anger and grief, felt by previous generations wasn't as intense in these emerging leaders, whose beliefs were almost certainly shaped more by the Second World War.

Waning enthusiasm for physical Confederate commemoration may also have reflected psychological healing. The first four stages of grief—denial, anger, rationalization/bargaining, and depression—were expressed through monument inscriptions, dedicatory speeches,

Left: Confederate Monument. Oakdale Cemetery, Mt. Airy. Little is known about this granite slab erected in 1950 by the Surry County U.D.C. Reverse reads, "1861–1865." *Right:* A second Rockingham County commemoration. Greenview Cemetery, Reidsville. This 1956 granite slab was Rockingham County's second Confederate monument. Forty-six years earlier, the same U.D.C. chapter unveiled a soldier statue in downtown Reidsville.

and memorial events from the months immediately after Appomattox through the early twentieth century. Grief's fifth stage, acceptance, a recognition that the changed situation requires adaptation and the new reality will be permanent, is increasingly evident in post–World War I Confederate commemoration.

These later dedications featured veterans of subsequent wars as well as Confederate soldiers. The Stars and Stripes was showcased along with Confederate banners, and "America" or "The Star-Spangled Banner"—and sometimes both—joined "Dixie," as standard musical fare. Speakers extolled the virtues of, and stressed loyalty to, a reunified nation, while Confederate soldiers and generals were lauded, not just as regional icons, but as American heroes.

Perhaps the region's commemorative work was nearly done. Southern women, and to a lesser extent men, had for decades memorialized the dead and honored soldiers who had fought unsuccessfully to establish an independent nation. The Ladies' Memorial Associations accomplished what the state couldn't do, and the federal government wouldn't do, respectfully rebury the Confederate fallen in decent graves.

These women raised monuments to the dead then, joined by their daughters, erected commemorations honoring all

An unfinished monument in Jacksonville, Onslow County? This inscribed base, dated December 1957, reportedly was placed to support a Conederate soldier statue. The statue was never purchased, however, and stacked miniature cannonballs were later added.

Confederate soldiers. In the process, these women helped forge a region's collective memory, establishing a physical commemorative presence in the most prominent of public spaces, and helped a society channel anger and grief and despair into a near reverence for the fallen and admiration for surviving veterans. By the mid-twentieth century, civic-space Confederate monuments, although panned by art critics, were a regional icon, and Southerners pointed with pride to their Confederate heritage.

Monument building ticked up slightly as the Civil War centennial (1961–1965) neared. In 1956, the Rockingham County Chapter, United Daughters of the Confederacy, added to that county's commemorative landscape. Forty-six years earlier, this chapter had erected a tall granite shaft topped with a soldier statue in a downtown Reidsville intersection. The women now raised a granite slab "Dedicated to the Honor and Sacrifice of the Men of the Confederacy 1861–1865" in Reidsville's Greenview Cemetery.

The "Onslow Guards Chapter" and the "Young Onslow Confederates of the United Daughters of the Confederacy" unveiled an inscribed urn in front of the Onslow County courthouse (Jacksonville) in December 1957. Today this solid granite structure supports a stack of miniature cannonballs; local lore states that the base was intended to showcase a soldier statue, which was never purchased, but for years held a flagpole that was repeatedly vandalized.[11]

In 1959, Virgil Beckham completed his self-financed Confederate monument on the courthouse grounds in Alexander County (Taylorsville), while that same year, the Jefferson Davis Chapter, United Daughters of the Confederacy, installed an inscribed marble plaque inside the Columbus County courthouse (Whiteville) "To the Gallant and Heroic Men of Columbus County Who Served in the War Between the States."

North Carolina's last pre-centennial Civil War monument was erected in 1960 beside the Jones County courthouse in Trenton. Sponsored by Trenton's Daughters, the granite slab reads, "In Memoriam to Our Beloved Confederate Dead of Jones County."

Dedications of these monuments, however, were likely low-key events. Conversations with librarians, local historians, and newspapers editors, many with personal recollection of that era, failed not only to unearth descriptions of dedicatory activities but were often unsuccessful even in determining unveiling dates.

As North Carolina and the nation prepared to observe the Civil War centennial, nearly a century of memorial effort, primarily by the Ladies and Daughters, had resulted in one of the most successful commemorative campaigns in history. In large measure these women had defined Southern collective memory and claimed the most prestigious civic-space locations for monuments. They had channeled grief and despair into reburying the dead then, as summarized by North Carolina U.D.C. president Mrs. Glenn Long, erected "More monuments to Southern valor ... than have been set up in any other land to any other people."[12]

The Civil War, however, while militarily reuniting the nation and ending slavery, did not achieve lasting equality. As white Southerners acknowledged defeat and worked through decades of grief, African Americans chafed under economic hardship and an erosion of rights under Jim Crow segregation.

The Civil War centennial years, envisioned as a celebration of a common heritage honoring the valor of soldiers — North and South — that forged a *United* States of America, witnessed instead a second internal struggle for human equality, an issue as divisive as any since Reconstruction. Physical Confederate commemoration across North Carolina largely ceased for more than a quarter-century as societal

Indoor commemoration. This marble plaque was installed inside the Columbus County courthouse in Whiteville by the Jefferson Davis Chapter, U.D.C. 1959.

norms were challenged, and a collective memory honed by four generations of white Southerners was questioned.

Few art critics would maintain that North Carolina's Civil War monuments, especially mass-produced soldier statues and commemorations designed by committee, represent "high art." Yet these 109 memorials, like great art, continue to raise questions, prompt debate, challenge assumptions, and are open to multiple interpretations. Few of the Ladies or Daughters who sponsored most of these memorials had formal art training, yet these commemorations remain the most controversial — and perhaps the most challenging — widespread American public art.

These monuments, 101 Confederate commemorations and eight Union memorials, represent a body of work — artistically, culturally, and psychologically — a century-long retrospective documenting changing sculptural styles and technology, the resolution of societal grief, the importance of public space and design, and the forging, at least among the state's white citizens, of consensus and collective memory. These monuments also document a unique American experience; only the states of the former Confederacy have endured military defeat and subsequent occupation.

Commemoration proceeded step-by-step, filling local physical and emotional needs before ultimately meeting many of

Jones County Confederate monument. Trenton, 1960. North Carolina's last pre–Civil War centennial monument echoes sentiments inscribed on the state's first Confederate memorial, "In Memoriam to our beloved Confederate Dead."

society's cultural and psychological demands. Through this process, Tarheels shaped a collective memory that helped them accept defeat and join as full partners in a reunified nation. And as efforts advanced, North Carolinians, through stone and metal, preserved a record of evolving emotions and beliefs as well, leaving an enduring heritage detailing a people's response to overwhelming military defeat and a nearly incomprehensible loss of human life.

Appendix A: North Carolina Confederate Monuments

See ABBREVIATIONS on pages 227–228.

County	City	Date	Chapter	Location	Mon.Type	Honor	Sponsor	Statue/Shaft	Cost	Sculptor/Co.	Speaker
Alamance	Graham	5/16/1914	C-11	CH-cur	Soldier PR	Soldiers	UDC/Co.	Marble/Granite	2,100	Ital-uns/McNeel	H. A. London/Pittsboro
Alexander	Taylorsville	6/1/1959	C-17 (2)	CH-cur	Soldier PR	Soldiers	Ind.-Virgil Beckham	Marble/Rock		Ital-uns/B. Campbell	No dedication
Anson	Wadesboro	1/19/1906	C-10	CH-cur-R	Soldier ATT	Soldiers	UDC/ men/ WA Smith	Bronze/Granite		Scoggins/Wadesboro Marble & Granite	Col. R. T. Bennett
Anson	Wadesboro	9/22/1934	C-13 (2)	CH-cur	Tablet	Women	Ind. William A. Smith	Granite		Scoggins Mem. Art/ Charlotte	Mrs. John H. Anderson/UDC
Beaufort	Washington	5/10/1888	C-3 (2)	Cem.-pub-R	Soldier ATT	Dead	LMA	Granite/Granite	2,250		Future Gov. Daniel Fowle
Beaufort	Washington	5/10/1905	C-7	Cem.-pub	Plaque/Brick	Dead	Children	Metal/Brick		Mutual Machine Co.	
Bertie	Windsor	8/13/1896	C-12	CH-cur	Soldier PR	Dead	Veterans	Wh. Br./Granite		Philadelphia Wh. Br. Mon. Co	Democratic nominee for Lt. Gov. Thomas W. Mason
Buncombe	Asheville	1903	C-5	Cem.-pub	Obelisk	Dead	Public Subscription	Granite			
Buncombe	Candler	1/1/1903	C-5	Cem-church	Obelisk	Co. I 25th NC Reg.	Ind.-Cap. A. B. Thrash	Marble		GW Sellers & Son New Port, TN	
Buncombe	Asheville	11/8/1905	C-8 (3)	CH-R	Minie Ball	Soldiers	60th NC Reg.	Marble/Marble		Cherokee Marble Works/CMW	Gov. R. B. Glenn
Burke	Morganton	6/22/1918	C-8	CH-old	Soldier ATT	Soldiers	UDC/Ind.-Cap. Kincaid	Bronze/Granite		A.B.F.	Chief Justice Walter Clark
Cabarrus	Concord	5/5/1892	C-3	CH-old	Shaft/Sphere	Soldiers	Mem. Assoc.	Marble			Maj. W. M. Robbins
Caldwell	Lenoir	6/3/1910	C-9	CH-R	Obelisk	Soldiers	UDC	Granite	2,100	McNeel	Chief Justice Walter Clark
Carteret	Beaufort	5/10/1926	C-15	CH-cur	Soldier PR	Dead	UDC	Bronze/Granite	3,500		Judge H. A. Grady/Clinton
Caswell	Yanceyville	9/10/1921	C-10	CH-old	Soldier SK	Soldiers	UDC	Bronze/Granite	3,500	A.B.F./J. F. Manning Co.	Mrs. W. O. Spencer, substituting for governor
Catawba	Newton	8/15/1907	C-9	CH-old	Soldier PR	Soldiers	People	Granite/Granite	2,150	Purchased/GE Coulter/CB Webb	Future Gov. Locke Craig
Chatham	Pittsboro	8/23/1907	C-8 (2)	CH-cur	Soldier PR	Soldiers	UDC	Copper/Granite	1,600	Mullins/Durham Marble Works	Chief Justice Walter Clark
Chowan	Edenton	6/3/1904*	C-7	Square-R	Soldier SK	Dead	UDC	Bronze/Granite	1,000		
Cleveland	Shelby	5/10/1907	C-12	CH-old	Soldier SK	Heroes	UDC	Bronze/Granite	2,500	A.B.F./CM Walsh Marble, Co., VA.	Future Gov. Locke Craig
Columbus	Whiteville	1959	C-17	CH-cur	Plaque-In CH-Cur	Soldiers	UDC	Marble			
Craven	New Bern	5/11/1885	C-2 (2)	Cem-pub	Soldier PR	Dead	LMA	Marble/Marble		Italian/unk	Rev. L. C. Vass

County	City	Date	Chapter	Location	Mon.Type	Honor	Sponsor	Statue/Shaft	Cost	Sculptor/Co.	Speaker
Cumberland	Fayetteville	12/30/1868	C-1 (2)	Cem-pub	Shaft	Dead	LMA	Marble	300	George Lauder/Fayetteville, NC	Rev. Joseph C. Huske
Cumberland	Fayetteville	5/10/1902	C-10	Roadside-R	Soldier SK	Dead	Women	Bronze/Granite		UNS/I. W. Durham	Major E.J. Hale
Currituck	Currituck	1923	C-8	CH-cur	Sphere	Dead	Vets/Ind. Knapp	Granite/Granite		Farrington, Gould, and Hoaglund	No dedication
Davidson	Lexington	9/14/1905	C-12	Square	Soldier SK	Dead	JDC	Bronze/Granite			C. B. Watson of Winston-Salem
Duplin	Faison	5/20/1932	C-16	Street	Tablet	Co. E 20th NC Reg.	Sons of local veterans	Granite			J. O. Carr of Wilmington
Durham	Durham	5/10/1924	C-11	CH-cur	Soldier PR	Soldiers	People	Bronze/Granite	5,000	Metal/McNeel	Gen. Albert L. Cox
Edgecombe	Tarboro	10/29/1904	C-7 (2)	Commons	Soldier PR	Soldiers	UDC	Bronze/Granite	2,250	A.B.F./Cockade Marble Works	Julian S. Carr
Edgecombe	Tarboro	10/1910	C-7	Cem-pub	Gate	Dead	UDC	Marble/Stone			
Forsyth	Winston-Salem	10/3/1905	C-9	CH-old	Soldier PR	Dead	UDC	Granite/Granite			Alfred M. Waddell
Franklin	Justice	5/10/1912	C-7	Cem-ch	Obelisk	Dead	Community	Marble	475		Gov. Locke Craig
Franklin	Louisburg	5/13/1914	C-12	Mid- Street	Soldier SK	Dead	UDC/Co.	Bronze/Granite		Suffolk Marble Works/Suffolk, VA	
Gaston	Gastonia	11/21/1912	C-11/C-12	CH-new-R	Soldier PR	Heroes	UDC/Children	Stone/Granite	3,000	UNS/Southern Mar. and Gran. Co.	A. E. Woltz/Gastonia
Gates	Gatesville	7/8/1915	C-9	CH-cur	Soldier PR	Dead	Co./Conf. Mon. Assoc.	Marble/Granite			John J. Gatling
Granville	Oxford	10/30/1909	C-9	Library-R	Soldier SK	Dead	UDC/Co.	Bronze/Granite			Gov. W. W. Kitchin
Greene	Snow Hill	5/10/1929	C-16	CH-cur	Plaque	Soldiers	UDC	Bronze Plaque			Bishop Thomas C. Darst
Guilford	Greensboro	6/3/1888	C-2	Cem-pub	Soldier PR	Dead	LMA	Copper/Granite			F. C. Robbins/Julian S. Carr
Guilford	High Point	7/4/1899	C-3	Cem-pub	Shaft	Dead	J.O.U.A.M.	Marble			Col. R. E. Lee
Halifax	Weldon	9/17/1908	C-8	Side street-R	Soldier PR	Soldiers/Sailors	UDC	Granite/Granite			
Halifax	Enfield	5/30/1928	C-15	Park-R	Drinking Fountain	Vets/Multi-War	UDC	Marble	1,300		O. P. Dickinson/Wilson, NC
Halifax	Weldon	UNK	C-8	Cem-Confed	Tablet/Gravestone	Dead	UNK	Granite			
Harnett	Averasboro	5/10/1872	C-1	Cem-battlefield	Shaft	Dead	LMA	Sandstone			Hon. Thomas C. Fuller
Haywood	Waynesville	7/12/1940	C-16	CH-old	Plaque	Soldiers	UDC	Bronze Plaque			J. Harden Howell of Waynesville
Haywood	Beech Gap	7/12/1942	C-16	Blue Ridge Parkway	Forest	Soldiers	UDC	Wood/Trees			Josephus Daniels

County	City	Date	Chapter	Location	Mon. Type	Honor	Sponsor	Statue/Shaft	Cost	Sculptor/Co.	Speaker
Henderson	Hendersonville	8/25/1903	C-5	CH-old-R	Obelisk	Soldiers	Public Subsc.	Marble	432.45		Col. S. V. Pickens
Hertford	Winton	9/25/1913	C-7	CH-cur	Soldier SK	Dead	Co./UDC	Bronze/Granite	2,500	Suffolk Marble Works, Suffolk, VA	Attorny General T.W. Bickett
Hoke	Ft. Bragg	c. 1870	C-1	Cem-ch	Obelisk	Dead	Public Subsc./Church	Marble			
Iredell	Statesville	5/10/1906*	C-9	CH-old	Soldier PR	Soldiers/Dead	UDC	Granite/Granite	1,850	Carolina Marble and Granite	Gov. R. B. Glenn
Iredell	Mooresville	5/9/1941	C-16	Cem-pub	Tablet	Dead	UDC	Granite			Dr. R. A. White
Jackson	Sylva	9/18/1915	C-10	CH-old	Soldier PR	Heroes	Citizens/Co.	Bronze/Granite	1,400	Mullins/UNS	Gen. Theodore F. Davidson
Johnston	Smithfield	5/10/1887	C-2	Cem-pub	Obelisk	Dead	Fellow Citizens	Marble			Alfred M. Waddell
Johnston	Bentonville	3/20/1895*	C-3	Battlefield	Shaft	Dead	Goldsboro Rifles	Marble	800	David Grantham/Goldsboro	Wade Hampton/South Carolina
Jones	Trenton	1960	C-17	CH-cur	Tablet	Dead	UDC	Granite			
Lenoir	Kinston	c. 1892	C-2	Cem-pub	Obelisk	Dead	People/City of Kinston	Marble			
Lenoir	Kinston	5/10/1924	C-11	Visitor Center-R	Soldier PR	Soldiers	UDC	Bronze/Granite		Metal/McNeel	Gov. Cameron Morrison
Lincoln	Lincolnton	5/11/1911	C-7	CH-cur	Drinking Fountain	Soldiers	Children/Co.	Granite/Marble	1,250		Gov. W. W. Kitchin
Macon	Franklin	9/30/1909	C-11	CH-cur	Soldier PR	Veterans	Veterans/Co.	Marble/Marble	1,650	Ital (UNS)/McNeel	Gov. W. W. Kitchin
McDowell	Marion	5/9/1943*	C-16	Cem-pub	Plaque-dual	Soldiers/Dead	UDC	Bronze Plaque		James H. Matthews & Co.	Former Gov. Clyde Hoey
Mecklenburg	Charlotte	6/10/1887	C-2	Cem-pub	Obelisk	Soldiers	LMA	Granite			
Mecklenburg	Cornelius	8/4/1910	C-12	Church	Soldier SK	Dead	UNK	Granite/Granite			Judge Armistead Burwell
Montgomery	Troy	c. 1926	C-15	CH-cur	WW1 Soldier	Soldiers	UNK	Marble/Granite			
Nash	Rocky Mount	5/14/1917	C-10 (2)	Roadside Park	Five Figures	Soldiers	Ind. Robert Ricks	Marble/Marble	15,000	Roberts Marble/Roberts Marble	Gov. T. W. Bickett
New Hanover	Wilmington	5/10/1872	C-1	Cem-pub	Soldier PR	Dead	LMA	Bronze/Granite	7,000-8,000		Maj. Charles W. McClammy
New Hanover	Wilmington	11/6/1924	C-15 (2)	Street	Sculpture	Soldiers	Ind. Gabriel James Boney	Bronze/Granite	20,000	Frank H. Packer/Carolina Granite	A. H. Boyden
New Hanover	Kure Beach/Fort Fisher	6/2/1932	C-16	Battlefield	Eagle/Column	Soldiers	UDC	Bronze/Granite	9000-10,000	UNS/Charles C. Johnson	Gov. O. M. Gardner
Onslow	Jacksonville	12/1/1957	C-17	CH-cur	Urn	Soldiers	UDC	Granite			
Orange	Chapel Hill	6/2/1913	C-10	University	Soldier SK	Dead	UDC/Alumni	Bronze/Granite	7,500	John Wilson/Gorham	Julian S. Carr
Pamlico	Bayboro	4/26/1940*	C-16	CH-cur	Plaque	Dead	UDC	Bronze Plaque			Rev. Charles E. Williams
Pasquotank	Elizabeth City	5/10/1911	C-9	CH-cur	Soldier-PR	Heroes	UDC	Granite/Granite		UNS/McNeel	D. H. Hill, Jr.
Pender	Burgaw	5/27/1914	C-9	CH-cur-R	Soldier PR	Heroes	UDC/Co.	Granite/Granite	1,500	UNS/Cooper	Chief Justice Walter Clark

County	City	Date	Chapter	Location	Mon. Type	Honor	Sponsor	Statue/Shaft	Cost	Sculptor/Co.	Speaker
Pender	Burgaw	UNK	C-12	CH-cur-R	Tablet	Co. K 3rd NC Reg.	UNK	Granite			
Perquimans	Hertford	6/12/1912	C-11	CH-cur	Obelisk	Soldiers	UDC	Granite	2,000	UNS/McNeel	Chief Justice Walter Clark
Person	Roxboro	5/20/1922	C-15	CH-cur	Soldier PR	Soldiers	UDC	Stone/Granite	3,000	UNS/T. O. Sharpe	Josephus Daniels
Pitt	Greenville	11/13/1914	C-10	CH-cur	Soldier PR	Dead	Co./People	Bronze/Granite		Mullins/UNS	Gov. Locke Craig
Randolph	Asheboro	9/2/1911	C-9	CH-old	Soldier PR	Heroes	UDC	Bronze/Granite	1,700	Mullins/Blue Pearl Granite Co.	Chief Justice Walter Clark
Richmond	Rockingham	11/14/1930	C-16	Town Square	Tablet	Soldiers	UDC/Co.	Granite			Ex-Gov. C. Morrison
Robeson	Lumberton	5/10/1907	C-7	CH-cur-R	Soldier PR	Dead	UDC	Stone/Granite	4,000	UNS/McNeel	Gov. R. B. Glenn
Rockingham	Reidsville	6/29/1910	C-7	Traffic Circle	Soldier PR	Soldiers	UDC	Granite/Granite			C. B. Watson
Rockingham	Reidsville	1956	C-17	Cem-pub	Tablet	Men	UDC	Granite			
Rowan	Salisbury	5/10/1909	C-8 (2)	Mid-street	Sculpture	Soldiers	UDC	Bronze/Granite	15,000	F. W. Ruckstahl/W. A. Eason Co.	Bennett H. Young/Kentucky
Rowan	Salisbury	UNK	C-12	Cem-pub	Tablet/Gravestone	Dead	Ind.-John Buis	Marble		John Buis	
Rutherford	Rutherfordton	11/12/1910	C-7	CH-cur	Soldier PR	Men/Women	UDC/Co.	? Stone/Granite	2,500	UNS/McNeel	Future Gov. Locke Craig
Rutherford	Forest City	6/3/1932	C-16	Mid-street	Plaque	Local Cos	UDC	Metal/Granite	150		Robert Eaves/Charles Erwin
Sampson	Clinton	5/12/1916*	C-9/C-10	CH-cur	Soldier PR	Soldiers	UDC/Co.	Bronze/Granite	1,950	UNS/Cooper Bros.	Gov. T. W. Bickett
Scotland	Laurinburg	11/14/1912	C-8	CH-cur-R	Soldier SK	Heroes	UDC	? Stone/Granite	3,000–5,000		Gen. W. R. Cox
Stanly	Albemarle	9/25/1925	C-8	CH-old-R	Soldier PR	Soldiers	UDC/Co.	Bronze/Granite		Mullins/Palmer StoneWorks	Mr. R. L. Brown/Albemarle
Surry	Mt. Airy	1/30/1950	C-17	Cem-pub	Tablet	Dead	UDC/City	Granite			
Swain	Cherokee	9/29/1935	C-16	Field-R	Plaque	Loyal Cherokees	UDC	Bronze Plaque			Mrs. E. L. McKee
Tyrrell	Columbia	8/7/1902	C-11/C-12	CH-cur	Soldier PR	Dead	Tyrrell Mon. Assoc.	Zinc/Zinc		Monumental Bronze/Mon. Br.	
Union	Monroe	7/4/1910	C-7	CH-old	Shaft/Sphere	Soldiers	UDC	Granite/Granite	2,150	Jacob Efird/Efird Marble Works	Gov. T. W. Bickett
Vance	Henderson	11/10/1910	C-12	CH-cur	Soldier SK	Dead	UDC/Co.	Bronze/Granite	3630.10	UNS/Suffolk Marble Works	Gov. W. W. Kitchin/Julian Carr
Wake	Raleigh	1870	C-1	Cem-pub	Obelisk	Dead	LMA	Marble		King & Whitelaw	
Wake	Raleigh	5/20/1895	C-4 (4)	Capitol	Three figures	Dead	LMA/State	Bronze/Granite	25,000	F. von Miller/Muldoon	A. M. Waddell
Wake	Raleigh	6/10/1914	C-13 (2)	Capitol	Sculpture	Women	Ind.-Ashley Horne	Bronze/Granite	10,000	A. Lukeman	D. H. Hill, Jr.

County	City	Date	Chapter	Location	Mon. Type	Honor	Sponsor	Statue/Shaft	Cost	Sculptor/Co.	Speaker
Wake	Holly Springs	10/25/1923	C-15	Church	Soldier PR	Soldiers	Ind.-Cap. G. B. Alford	Marble/Granite/ Bronze		UNS/McNeel	Gen. Albert L. Cox
Warren	Warrenton	8/27/1903	C-11	Cem-pub	Soldier PR	Dead	LMA	Marble/Stone		Cooper Bros./Cooper Bros.	Hon. W.A. Montgomery
Warren	Warrenton	10/29/1913	C-10 (2)	CH-cur	Soldier PR	Heroes	UDC/Sons/Co.	Bronze/Granite	3,000	Mullins/Cooper Bros.	Gov. R.B. Glenn
Warren	Littleton	6/3/1930	C-16	Cem-pub	Gate	Soldiers	UDC	Metal/Granite	400	Campbell Brothers/ Raleigh	Hon. Jno. M. Picot
Wayne	Goldsboro	5/10/1883	C-2 (2)	Cem-pub	Soldier PR	Dead	Goldsboro Rifles	Wh. Br./ Granite	992	Philadelphia Wh. Br. Mon. Co./Gaddess	Gen. M.W. Ransom
Wilson	Wilson	5/10/1902	C-9	Cem-pub	Soldier PR	Dead	Confederate Veterans	Granite/Granite	1,000	Yves St. Laurent	
Wilson	Wilson	11/11/1926	C-15	CH-cur	Plaque/ Tablet	Soldiers	UDC/DAR	Marble	1,500		Hon. H.G. Conner

Notes

Six dates are marked with an asterisk:

(1) Chowan County/Edenton is very uncertain with some sources giving a date as late as 1909.
(2) Iredell County/Statesville. Dedication May 10, 1906; monument boldly inscribed 1905.
(3) Johnston County/Bentonville. Dedication March 20, 1895; monument inscribed October 10, 1894.
(4) McDowell County/Marion. Dedication of cemetery gate columns May 9, 1943; bronze plaques, although dated 1941, were added following World War II.
(5) Pamlico County/Bayboro. Dedication April 26, 1940; plaque inscribed 1939.
(6) Sampson County/Clinton. Dedication May 12, 1916; monument inscribed May 10, 1916.

Abbreviations

Chapter

If marked with second number (x) multiple images in same chapter.

Location

CH — courthouse
cur — current
old — former courthouse (may still be used as county offices but not primary courthouse)
Cem-pub — public cemetery
Cem-ch — church cemetery
Cem-Confederate — Confederate cemetery
R — monument relocated

Mon. Type

Soldier PR — parade rest
Soldier ATT — attention
Soldier SK — skirmisher

Honor

Vets — veterans
Co. NC Reg. — Company and Regiment (North Carolina)

Sponsor

UDC — United Daughters of the Confederacy
DAR — Daughters of the American Revolution
LMA — Ladies' Memorial Association
UCV — United Confederate Veterans
Co. — partial county funding or permission to partially fund monument granted by NC legislature
Ind. — individual
Children — Children of the Confederacy
Mem. Assoc. — Memorial Association
Mon. Assoc. — Monument Association
J.O.U.A.M.: Junior Order United American Mechanics
Public Subsc. — public subscription (donations)

Statue/Shaft

Wh. Br. — white bronze (a sand-blasted zinc)
? — very uncertain, cannot determine if soldier statue is of treated metal (to look like stone) or carved stone

Sculptor/Company

UNS — unsigned
UNK — unknown
Ital. — Italian

Appendix A

A.B.F. — American Bronze Foundry Company, Chicago, Illinois
Mullins — W. H. Mullins Company, Salem, Ohio
McNeel — The McNeel Marble Company, Marietta, Georgia
Muldoon — The Muldoon Monument Company, Louisville, Kentucky
Gaddess — Gaddess Brothers Steam Marble Works, Baltimore, Maryland
Monumental Bronze (Mon. Br.) — The Monumental Bronze Company, Bridgeport, Connecticut
Philadelphia Wh. Br. Mon. Co. — Philadelphia White Bronze Monument Company
Southern Mar. and Gran. Co. — Southern Marble and Granite Company

*Appendix B:
North Carolina
Union Monuments*

County	City	Date	Location	Monument	Honor	Sponsor	Statue/Shaft	Speaker	Cost	Sculptor/Manufacturer
Craven	New Bern	11/14/1894	National Cemetery	Draped, modified obelisk	Dead/15th Connecticut Regiment	Connecticut	Granite	Sen. O. H. Platt		
Craven	New Bern	5/18/1905	National Cemetery	Soldier	Soldiers/9th New Jersey Regiment	New Jersey	Granite/Granite	Col. James Stewart/ NJ Gov. Edward C. Stokes, NC Gov. Robert B. Glenn	5,000 Mon. 1,500 Ded.	M. C. Lyons' Son Camden, NJ
Craven	New Bern	11/11/1908	National Cemetery	Allegory	Dead/Massachusetts	Massachusetts	Bronze/Granite	Cap. A. A. Putnam	5,000 Mon. 4,000 Ded.	Melzar H. Mosman
Craven	New Bern	10/6/1909	National Cemetery	Allegory	Dead/Rhode Island	Rhode Island	Bronze/Granite	William W. Douglas Gov. Aram Pothier	3,000 Mon. 1,578.73 Ded. 399.20 Misc.	Cap. William W. Manatt, Providence, RI
Perquimans	Hertford	c. 1910	Private Land	Modified obelisk	U.S. Colored Troops	United Daughters of Veterans—likely a group of local African American church women	Granite			
Rowan	Salisbury	c. 1876	National Cemetery	Obelisk	Dead	U.S. Government	Granite		10,000	
Rowan	Salisbury	6/8/1908	National Cemetery	Soldier	Dead/Maine	Maine	Granite/Granite	Hon. Charles D. Newell	4755.56	Bodwell Granite Co. Vinalhaven, ME
Rowan	Salisbury	11/16/1910	National Cemetery	Soldier/Prisoner	Dead/Pennsylvania	Pennsylvania	Bronze/Granite/Marble	Harry White/ PA Gov. Edwin S. Stuart, NC Gov. W. W. Kitchin	15,000	Clark's Monumental Works, Americus, GA

ABBREVIATIONS

Mon.—Monument cost
Ded.—Dedication-day expenses
Misc.—Miscellaneous expenses

Notes

Introduction

1. William S. Powell, *North Carolina Through Four Centuries* (Chapel Hill: University of North Carolina Press, 1989), pp. 355–356.
2. John C. Inscoe and Gordon B. McKinney, *The Heart of Confederate Appalachia: Western North Carolina in the Civil War* (Chapel Hill: University of North Carolina Press, 2000), p. 244.
3. Powell, pp. 343–348.
4. Ibid., p. 356. The number of North Carolina's Civil War dead has long been cited as 40,275 based on a tally conducted shortly after hostilities ended. This total gives the Tarheel State the dubious distinction of having the highest death toll among the former Confederate states but has also become a source of considerable pride, part of North Carolina's "Rebel Boast." Josh Howard, with the North Carolina Office of Archives and History, is re-evaluating Tarheel soldier fatalities, deleting duplications from multiple sources and verifying reported deaths with troop rosters, hospital records, subsequent census data, etc. The survey is nearly complete, and Mr. Howard estimates that the final fatality figure will be about twenty percent lower. Even with this reduced number, however, North Carolina will remain as the Confederate state that paid the highest human toll. Personal communication, May 20, 2011.
5. Inscoe, p. 164.

Chapter 1

1. Tom Vincent, "'Evidence of Womans Loyalty, Perseverance, and Fidelity': Confederate Soldiers' Monuments in North Carolina, 1865–1914," *The North Carolina Historical Review* 83:1 (January 2006), p. 64.
2. John A. McGeachy, "History 546: May 2003," North Carolina State University, http://www4.ncsu.edu/~jam3/Sherman.htm. (accessed April 20, 2011).
3. Vincent, pp. 64–67.
4. Ibid., pp. 67–68.
5. Ibid., pp. 68–70.
6. Ibid., p. 70.
7. "North Carolina Civil War Monuments," http://www.ncmonuments.ncdcr.gov/ (accessed June 4, 2011); Vincent, p. 70.
8. Vincent, p. 71.
9. Caroline E. Janney, *Burying the Dead but Not the Past: Ladies' Memorial Associations and the Lost Cause* (Chapel Hill: University of North Carolina Press, 2008), pp. 44–46; Catherine W. Zipf, "Marking Union Victory in the South," *Monuments to the Lost Cause: Women, Art, and the Landscape of Southern Memory,* ed. Cynthia Mills and Pamela Simpson (Knoxville: University of Tennessee Press, 2003), p. 29.
10. Janney, p. 44.
11. Zipf, pp. 30–41; North Carolina's National Cemeteries are located in Raleigh, Wilmington, New Bern, and Salisbury.
12. William A. Blair, *Contesting the Memory of the Civil War South, 1865–1914* (Chapel Hill: University of North Carolina Press, 2004), p. 53.
13. Ibid., p. 53.
14. Janney, pp. 21–22.
15. Ibid., pp. 8, 88.
16. Mrs. William J. Behan, *History of the Confederated Memorial Associations of the South* (New Orleans: Graham, 1904).
17. Catherine W. Bishir, "'A Strong Force of Ladies': Women, Politics, and Confederate Memorial Associations in Nineteenth-Century Raleigh," *The North Carolina Historical Review* 77:4 (October 2000), p. 457.
18. L. C. Vass, *Ladies' Memorial Association: Confederate Memorial Addresses, Monday May 11, 1885, New Bern, North Carolina* (Richmond: Whittet and Shepperson, 1886), p. 5; SIRIS-Smithsonian Institution Research Information System, http://www.siris-artinventories.si.edu/ipac20/ipac.jsp?session (accessed October 14, 2008).

A plaque in front of the New Bern Confederate monument—installed at a later date—lists 68 names. The tablet reads: "In memory of the Confederate soldiers killed during the battle of New Bern North Carolina 1862 interred in vault beneath this monument." Under this inscription, names are listed by state: North Carolina—35 names; South Carolina—27; Alabama—2; Georgia—1; Florida—1; "state unknown"—2.

19. "Historic Old Hotel and Heroine's Grave Remind High Point of Civil War Days" *Greensboro Daily News*, April 15, 1951 (no page number on library copy).
20. Ethel Stephens Arnett, *Greensboro North Carolina: The County Seat of Guilford* (Chapel Hill: University of North Carolina Press, 1955). Reportedly only four of the 234 Bentonville casualties identified themselves before dying.
21. Bishir, p. 458.

22. Behan, p. 229; Bishir, p. 461.
23. LMA quoted by Bishir, p.462; Behan, p. 230; Pescud quoted by Bishir, p. 465. Numerous accounts of this episode have been published. Following Pescud's 1882 history in which he relates the order's revocation and subsequent rebuke of its issuer, most accounts prior to Bishir's 2000 article mention only the Federal threats.
24. Gaines Foster, *Ghosts of the Confederacy: Defeat, the Lost Cause, and the Emergence of the New South, 1865–1913* (New York: Oxford University Press, 1987).
25. The date of (Confederate) Memorial Day varied across the South, timed with historical anniversaries as well as the local blooming of spring flowers needed for decoration. April 26 remained the preferred date for Georgia and much of the Deep South; May 10, the anniversary of General "Stonewall" Jackson's death, was chosen in both North and South Carolina, while Virginia opted for later dates, including June 3, Jefferson Davis' birthday.
26. (Raleigh) *Sentinel*, May 3, 1867, quoted in Bishir, p. 467.
27. Behan, p. 232.
28. *Sentinel* pp. 25–26, as quoted in Bishir, pp. 467–469.
29. Bishir, p. 469.
30. Blanche Lucas Smith, *North Carolina's Confederate Monuments and Memorials* (Raleigh: NC Division, United Daughters of the Confederacy, 1941), pp. 21–22. Averasboro Battlefield and the Chicora Cemetery are located just north of today's Harnett County/Cumberland County line. Harnett was formed in 1855 from Cumberland. In 1911, according to David Lee Corbitt in *The Formation of North Carolina Counties 1663–1943*, an additional portion of Cumberland was transferred to Harnett County, perhaps explaining why a Cumberland County-based association led memorial efforts at Averasboro. In addition, Smith*ville* is not to be confused with Smith*field*, the Johnston County seat.
31. Ibid.
32. Ibid.
33. Ibid., p. 23.
34. *Wikipedia*, "Dulce et decorum est pro patria mori," http://en.wikipedia.org/wiki/Dulce_et_decorum_est_pro_patria_mori (accessed May 23, 2011).
35. Bishir, p. 470.
36. Bishir, p. 470; http://www.petersburgbreakthrough.org "47th NC Companies."
37. Bishir, p. 470.
38. Lewis Waldron Williams, II, *Commercially Produced Forms of American Civil War Monuments* (unpublished master's thesis, University of Illinois, 1948).
39. *SIRIS-Smithsonian Institution Research Information System*, http://www.siris-artinventories.si.edu/ipac20/ipac.jsp?session, (accessed October 14, 2008).
40. Charles Washington McClammy (1839–1896) served in the Confederate Army throughout the Civil War, rising to the rank of major in the Third North Carolina Cavalry Regiment. After the War, he served in a number of elected positions including the United States Congress (1887–1891). William Powell, *Dictionary of North Carolina Biography*, vol. 4 (Chapel Hill: University of North Carolina Press, 1991), p. 125; Vincent, pp. 72–75. The number of dead in the mass grave at Oakwood Cemetery is variously cited as 367, 467, or 550. The plaque at the base of the memorial places the number at 550, but Ann Huttleman states, "There are 366 unknown casualties [plus one identified] on the lot, who are buried with their heads toward the railing and their feet toward the monument.... That number [550] refers to the Confederates who died at Fort Fisher, not all of whom are buried in Oakdale." Ann Hewlett Huttleman, "Confederate Mound," unpublished document from Oakdale Cemetery.

Chapter 2

1. L. C. Vass, *Ladies' Memorial Association: Confederate Memorial Addresses, Monday May 11, 1885, New Bern, North Carolina* (Richmond, VA: Whittet and Shepperson, 1886). All quotes and details of the dedication are from this source.
2. William S. Powell, *North Carolina Through Four Centuries* (Chapel Hill: University of North Carolina Press, 1989), pp. 380–406.
3. William A. Blair, *Cities of the Dead: Contesting the Memory of the Civil War in the South, 1865–1914* (Chapel Hill: University of North Carolina Press, 2004), pp. 85, 154–156. Robert E. Lee did not attend memorial events and refused to publicly support the erection of monuments, fearing such actions might inflame Northern feelings.
4. W. Fitzhugh Brundage, ed., *Where These Memories Grow: History, Memory, and the Southern Identity* (Chapel Hill: University of North Carolina Press, 2000) provides an in-depth study of the creation of memory.
5. During the past few decades in the United States, for example, Columbus Day has been relegated to a barely noticed federal day off while Confederate Memorial Day, the premier civic holiday across the South for nearly a century after Appomattox, has been largely forgotten, celebrated in the twenty-first century by only a few heritage groups. Veterans' Day meanwhile has become a robust celebration, and a new commemoration, Dr. Martin Luther King Day, has been created.
6. Ralph W. Widener, *Confederate Monuments: Enduring Symbols of the South and the War Between the States* (Dallas: R. W. Widener, 1982).
7. Ibid., p. 177.
8. Caroline E. Janney, *Burying the Dead but Not the Past: Ladies' Memorial Associations and the Lost Cause* (Chapel Hill: University of North Carolina Press, 2008), pp. 88–93.
9. Brundage, pp. 3–6.
10. Information and quotes about the Eclectic Club are from original handwritten documents and letters on file in the Greensboro, North Carolina, Public Library.
11. Ethel Stephens Arnett, *Greensboro North Carolina: The County Seat of Guilford* (Chapel Hill: University of North Carolina Press, 1955), p. 317.
12. Amy Crow, "'Memory of the Confederate Dead' Masculinity and the Politics of Memorial Work in Goldsboro, North Carolina, 1894–1895" *North Carolina Historical Review* 83:1 (January 2006) 36–37; Blanche Lucas Smith, *North Carolina's Confederate Monuments and Memorials* (Raleigh: NC Division, United Daughters of the Confederacy, 1941), pp. 70–71; *SIRIS-Smithsonian Institution Research Information System*, http://www.siris-artinventories.si.edu/ (accessed October 14, 2008).
13. *SIRIS-Smithsonian Institution Research Information System*, http://www.siris-artinventories.si.edu/ (accessed October 14, 2008).

Chapter 3

1. North Carolina Civil War Trails sign, Oakdale Cemetery, Washington, NC; "North Carolina's First

Confederate Memorial" http://www.pamlico.com/washington/attractions/local-attractions.shtml (accessed February 8, 2011).
   2. Mrs. William J. Behan, *History of the Confederated Memorial Associations of the South* (New Orleans: Graham, 1904), p. 239; United Daughters of the Confederacy, North Carolina Division, George B. Singletary Chapter 313, Greenville, North Carolina, "Confederate Ancestor Biographies and Histories," http://www.gbsudc.org (accessed March 2, 2011).
   3. Fritz Fuzzlebug, *Prison Life During the Rebellion: The Miseries and Sufferings of Six Hundred Confederate Prisoners* (Singer's Glen, VA: Joseph Funk's Sons, 1869), p. 27.
   4. Ibid., pp. 33–37.
   5. Ibid., p. 36; National Park Service Ft. Pulaski National Monument "Immortal 600 Living History Event," http://www.nps.gov/fopu/parknews/immortal-600-living-history-event-.htm (accessed March 2, 2011). In addition to a description of rations, this official website uses the term human shields: "in front of Union artillery positions, to literally use these prisoners as human shields."
   6. United Daughters of the Confederacy, North Carolina Division, George B. Singletary Chapter 313, Greenville, North Carolina, "Confederate Ancestor Biographies and Histories," http://www.gbsudc.org (accessed March 2, 2011).
   7. Fuzzlebug, pp. 10–12.
   8. Behan, pp. 237–240.
   9. Tony Horwitz, *Confederates in the Attic: Dispatches from the Unfinished Civil War* (New York: Pantheon, 1998), p. 225.
   10. Ralph W. Widener, *Confederate Monuments: Enduring Symbols of the South and the War Between the States* (Dallas: R. W. Widener, 1982).
   11. William S. Powell, *North Carolina Through Four Centuries* (Chapel Hill: University of North Carolina Press, 1989), pp. 351–356, 364–365, 380–403; John C. Inscoe, *The Heart of Confederate Appalachia: Western North Carolina in the Civil War* (Chapel Hill: University of North Carolina Press, 2000).
   12. "North Carolina's First Confederate Memorial," http://www.pamlico.com/washington/attractions/local-attractions.shtml (accessed February 8, 2011).
   13. United Daughters of the Confederacy, North Carolina Division, George B. Singletary Chapter 313, Greenville, North Carolina, "Confederate Ancestor Biographies and Histories," http://www.gbsudc.org (accessed March 2, 2011).
   14. Letter from D. Ray McEachern, Clerk of Court Cabarrus County, to D. L. Corbitt, September 5, 1957. *D. L. Corbitt Papers* (NC State Archives); monument inscription (Bertie County); *The* (Raleigh) *News and Observer*, May 20, 1895; Catherine Bishir (ed. Brundage) in *Where These Memories Grow: History, Memory, and Southern Identity* (Chapel Hill: University of North Carolina Press, 2000), pp. 143–144, estimates the crowd at "about thirty thousand."

Chapter 4

   1. Catherine Bishir cites the crowd as "an estimated thirty thousand people," while the *News and Observer* puts the figure at 15,000 to 20,000. Catherine Bishir, "'A Strong Force of Ladies': Women, Politics, and Confederate Memorial Associations in Nineteenth-Century Raleigh," *The North Carolina Historical Review* 77:4 (October 2000), p. 482; "It Is Finished," (Raleigh) *News and Observer*, May 20, 1895, p. 1.
   2. "It Is Finished," (Raleigh) *News and Observer*, May 20, 1895, p. 1; Catherine Bishir, "'A Strong Force of Ladies': Women, Politics, and Confederate Memorial Associations in Nineteenth-Century Raleigh," *The North Carolina Historical Review* 77:4 (October 2000), p. 455.
   3. "It Is Finished," (Raleigh) *News and Observer*, May 20, 1895, p. 1.
   4. William Powell, *Dictionary of North Carolina Biography*, vol. 6 (Chapel Hill: University of North Press, 1996), pp. 102–103.
   5. Catherine Bishir, "'A Strong Force of Ladies': Women, Politics, and Confederate Memorial Associations in Nineteenth-Century Raleigh," *The North Carolina Historical Review* 77: 4 (October 2000), pp. 472–475.
   6. Alfred Moore Waddell, *Address at the Unveiling of the Confederate Monument, at Raleigh, N.C., May 20th, 1895* (Wilmington: LeGwin Brothers, 1895), p. 3; fifty-three items are listed by the *News-Observer-Chronicle* as having been "received to go in the corner stone box." Some were prosaic: "Sketches" of seven North Carolina Confederate generals, addresses by "Gen. Scales on the Battle of Fredericksburg," "Col. Waddell on The Confederate Soldier, delivered in New York," "Senator Vance ... on the Social Conditions of the South during the war," a "roster of the North Carolina Troops in the war, published in four volumes by the state," a "Confederate song book," and a "North Carolina Almanac for 1894." Confederate relics were also included, many given by Mrs. R. B. Peebles (nee Miss Margaret Cameron): "a lock of General Lee's hair cut in the tent of Gen. Pettigrew, with his autograph card," "a strand plucked from the tail of Gen. Lee's horse, Traveler, by Walker Anderson," "The bullet that killed the horse ridden by Gen. Pettigrew," a "Piece of the apple tree at Appomattox," and a "manuscript copy" of Lee's Farewell Order at Appomattox. "A Historic Day," (Raleigh) *News-Observer-Chronicle*, May 22, 1894, p. 1.
   7. "It Is Finished," (Raleigh) *News and Observer*, May 20, 1895, p. 1. The purported Mecklenburg Declaration of Independence was signed on May 20, 1775, however, there is no public record of this document until 1819. William Powell, *North Carolina Through Four Centuries* (Chapel Hill: University of North Press, 1989), p. 177.
   8. Waddell, p. 5.
   9. As quoted by Catherine Bishir, "Landmarks of Power: Building a Southern Past in Raleigh and Wilmington, North Carolina, 1885–1915," in W. Fitzhugh Brundage, *Where These Memories Grow: History, Memory, and Southern Identity* (Chapel Hill: University of North Carolina Press, 2000), pp. 144–145.
   10. William Powell, *Dictionary of North Carolina Biography*, vol. 6 (Chapel Hill: University of North Press, 1996), pp. 102–103.
   11. Waddell, p. 16.
   12. Ibid., p. 17.
   13. Ibid., p. 18.
   14. Ibid., p. 20.
   15. Ibid., p. 21.
   16. Ralph W. Widener, *Confederate Monuments: Enduring Symbols of the South and the War Between the States* (Dallas: R. W. Widener, 1982).
   17. William Powell, *Dictionary of North Carolina Biography*, vol. 4 (Chapel Hill: University of North Carolina Press, 1991), pp. 234–235.
   18. *Address of Hon. T. W. Mason, before the Ladies' Me-*

morial Association, at the laying of the Corner-Stone of the Confederate Monument, Raleigh, N.C. May 20, 1895 (Raleigh: E. M. Uzzell, 1898), pp. 8–10. The title's date and year are both incorrect. The cornerstone placement occurred on May 22, 1894, although some commemorative items cite the date as May 20, 1894, to coincide with the Declaration and the state's secession.

19. Mason, p. 12.
20. Ibid.
21. Mason, p. 13.
22. As quoted by Catherine Bishir, "'A Strong Force of Ladies': Women, Politics, and Confederate Memorial Associations in Nineteenth-Century Raleigh," *The North Carolina Historical Review* 77: 4 (October 2000), p. 477.
23. Ibid.
24. Nancy Branch Jones' father was the late Confederate Brigadier-General Lawrence O'Bryan Branch, a Princeton-educated attorney and former president of the Raleigh and Gaston Railroad, whose life was ended by a sniper's bullet at Sharpsburg (Antietam) in 1862. As quoted by Catherine Bishir, "'A Strong Force of Ladies': Women, Politics, and Confederate Memorial Associations in Nineteenth-Century Raleigh," *The North Carolina Historical Review* 77:4 (October 2000), p. 472; "It Is Finished," (Raleigh) *News and Observer*, May 20, 1895, p. 1.
25. "A Historic Day," (Raleigh) *News-Observer-Chronicle*, May 22, 1894, p. 1.
26. Catherine Bishir, "'A Strong Force of Ladies': Women, Politics, and Confederate Memorial Associations in Nineteenth-Century Raleigh," *The North Carolina Historical Review* 77: 4 (October 2000), p. 476.
27. "28 to 8!" (Raleigh) *News and Observer*, February 24, 1895, p. 2.
28. Ibid.
29. Ibid.
30. Ibid.
31. "Shame, Shame, Shame!" (Raleigh) *News and Observer*, February 24, 1895, p. 1.
32. "Miscegenation Endorsed," (Raleigh) *News and Observer*, February 22, 1895, p. 4.
33. "The Climax of Infamy," (Raleigh) *News and Observer*, February 23, 1895, p. 4.
34. (Raleigh) *News and Observer*, February 24, 1895, p. 1.
35. (Raleigh) *News and Observer*, March 1, 2, 1895; (Raleigh) *News and Observer*, March 8, 1895; as quoted by Catherine Bishir, "'A Strong Force of Ladies': Women, Politics, and Confederate Memorial Associations in Nineteenth-Century Raleigh," *The North Carolina Historical Review* 77:4 (October 2000), p. 479.
36. "A Historic Day," (Raleigh) *News-Observer-Chronicle*, May 22, 1894, p. 1.
37. "It is Finished," (Raleigh) *News and Observer*, May 20, 1895, p. 1.
38. Catherine Bishir, "'A Strong Force of Ladies': Women, Politics, and Confederate Memorial Associations in Nineteenth-Century Raleigh," *The North Carolina Historical Review* 77:4 (October 2000), p. 482.
39. "Unveiling Confederate Monument at Raleigh, N.C., May 20th, 1895," (Raleigh) *News and Observer*, May 19, 1895, p. 8; "A Welcome to All," (Raleigh) *News and Observer*, May 19, 1895, p. 5.
40. "The Guests of Honor," (Raleigh) *News and Observer*, May 22, 1895, p. 3.
41. www.findagrave.com/cgi-bin/fg.cgi?page=gr&GRid=7723941 (accessed August 2, 2012); "It is Finished," (Raleigh) *News and Observer*, May 21, 1895, p. 3; "Proud of Durham's Showing," (Raleigh) *News and Observer*, May 22, 1895, p. 6; "Echoes of the Unveiling," (Raleigh) *News and Observer*, May 22, 1895, p. 1.
42. "There Must Be Food for an Immense Crowd," (Raleigh) *News and Observer*, May 19, 1895, p. 5; "Where the Veterans Will Meet," (Raleigh) *News and Observer*, May 19, 1895, p. 5; "Echoes of the Unveiling," (Raleigh) *News and Observer*, May 22, 1895, p. 1.
43. "The Official Badge," (Raleigh) *News and Observer*, May 18, 1895, p. 5; "J. D. Riggan," advertisement (Raleigh) *News and Observer*, May 22, 1895, p. 8.
44. "To-Day," (advertisement) (Raleigh) *News and Observer*, May 19, 1895, p. 2; "Echoes of the Unveiling," (Raleigh) *News and Observer*, May 22, 1895, p. 1.
45. "Some Visitors of the Day," (Raleigh) *News and Observer*, May 22, 1895, p. 5.
46. "Mrs. Jackson Honored," (Raleigh) *News and Observer*, May 22, 1895, p. 5.
47. "To Raleigh and the Ladies," (Raleigh) *News and Observer*, May 22, 1895, p. 5; "Unveiling German," (Raleigh) *News and Observer*, May 22, 1895, p. 5.
48. As quoted by Catherine Bishir, "'A Strong Force of Ladies': Women, Politics, and Confederate Memorial Associations in Nineteenth-Century Raleigh," *The North Carolina Historical Review* 77:4 (October 2000), p. 455; "It is Finished," (Raleigh) *News and Observer*, May 20, 1895, p. 1.
49. Waddell, p. 21.
50. As quoted by Catherine Bishir, "'A Strong Force of Ladies': Women, Politics, and Confederate Memorial Associations in Nineteenth-Century Raleigh," *The North Carolina Historical Review* 77:4 (October 2000), p. 482; Catherine Bishir, "Landmarks of Power: Building a Southern Past in Raleigh and Wilmington, North Carolina, 1885–1915," in W. Fitzhugh Brundage, *Where These Memories Grow: History, Memory, and Southern Identity* (Chapel Hill: University of North Carolina Press, 2000), pp. 144–145.

Chapter 5

1. "Monument Funds," *The Western North Carolina Times*, June 12, 1903 (no page cited, clipping file, Henderson County Genealogical and Historical Society, Inc.).
2. Memminger's summer home, Connemara, near Flat Rock, North Carolina, would be acquired decades later by Carl Sandburg, poet and biographer of Abraham Lincoln. Today the house and grounds are a National Park site open to the public.
3. John C. Inscoe and Gordon B. McKinney, *The Heart of Confederate Appalachia: Western North Carolina in the Civil War* (Chapel Hill: University of North Carolina Press, 2000), p. 6.
4. "Monument Funds," *The Western North Carolina Times*, July 10, 1903 (no page cited, clipping file, Henderson County Genealogical and Historical Society, Inc.).
5. "Monument Funds," *The Western North Carolina Times*, July 31, 1903 (no page cited, clipping file, Henderson County Genealogical and Historical Society, Inc.).
6. "Monument Funds," *The Western North Carolina Times*, August 7, 1903 (no page cited, clipping file, Henderson County Genealogical and Historical Society, Inc.); "Monument Funds," *The Western North Carolina Times*, August 21, 1903 (no page cited, clipping file, Henderson County Genealogical and Historical Society, Inc.).
7. "Monument to be Unveiled," *The Western North Carolina Times*, August 21, 1903 (no page cited, clipping

file, Henderson County Genealogical and Historical Society, Inc.).

8. "The Monument Unveiled," *The Western North Carolina Times*, August 28, 1903 (no page cited, clipping file, Henderson County Genealogical and Historical Society, Inc.).

9. Ibid.

10. "Buncombe Landmarks: Vance Monument," *Asheville Citizen-Times* (undated with no page cited, clipping file, Pack Library, Asheville, North Carolina).

11. "The Monument is Dedicated," *Asheville Citizen*, May 10 1898, no page cited (Clipping file, Pack Library, Asheville, North Carolina).

12. For a detailed description of the Civil War in western North Carolina, see John C. Inscoe and Gordon B. McKinney, *The Heart of Confederate Appalachia: Western North Carolina in the Civil War* (Chapel Hill: University of North Carolina Press, 2000).

13. Ibid., pp. 118–119; North Carolina Governor Zebulon Vance was especially outraged by the Shelton Laurel killings, terming the executions "an atrocity." The next month, upon hearing rumors that Lt. Col. James A. Keith of the Sixty-fourth North Carolina Regiment, the officer who had ordered the killings, might be allowed to resign from the army rather than face court-martial, Vance threatened to "follow [Keith] to the gates of hell or hang him." Keith, however, avoided prosecution although later relinquishing his command. According to Weymouth Jordan, "it appears that no member of the 64th North Carolina was ever punished for this episode." Weymouth T. Jordan, *North Carolina Troops 1861–1865 A Roster* vol. XV (Raleigh: Office of Archives and History, 2003), pp. 142 144.

14. Martin Crawford, *Ashe County's Civil War: Community and Society in the Appalachian South* (Charlottesville: University Press of Virginia, 2001), pp. 142–143.

15. The 1985 monument, in front of the (now-former) Etowah Public Library, reads, "In Honor of Union Veterans of the Civil War 1861–1865 Henderson and Transylvania Counties North Carolina in Great Respect for the Women who Carried on at Home While Husbands and Brothers were Fighting to Preserve the Union Funded and Erected in 1985 by the Descendents and Friends of the Union Veterans." Henderson County's Confederate monument was recently relocated from its 1925 placement on the courthouse lawn (see note 29) to a much less prominent site in a small alcove to the right of the building's main entrance. Now one of a series of veterans' memorials located along the (now-former) courthouse's walls, the 1903 obelisk is flanked by a 2008 memorial which reads: "In Honor of the Citizens of Henderson County who Served in the Union Army During the Civil War for the Preservation of the United States of America and in Gratitude to their Families Erected in 2008."

16. John C. Inscoe and Gordon B. McKinney, *The Heart of Confederate Appalachia: Western North Carolina in the Civil War* (Chapel Hill: University of North Carolina Press, 2000), p. 121.

17. North Carolina's "mountain counties" are defined slightly differently by various sources, resulting in numbers generally ranging from 20 to 25. In this book "mountain counties" will include the state's twenty-one present-day counties wholly or partly in the mountains and/or foothills of western North Carolina. These include, from north to south: Ashe, Alleghany, Watauga, Wilkes, Avery, Caldwell, Mitchell, Yancey, Burke, McDowell, Madison, Buncombe, Swain, Haywood, Graham, Cherokee, Clay, Macon, Jackson, Transylvania, and Henderson. "Western Piedmont" counties will include the thirteen counties east of the foothills but west of U.S. Highway 29, a roadway paralleling present-day Interstate 85 for much of its length, and include (from north to south): Surry, Stokes, Yadkin, Forsyth, Alexander, Catawba, Iredell, Davie, Polk, Rutherford, Lincoln, Cleveland, and Gaston.

18. A bronze plaque featuring an image of General Robert E. Lee astride his horse "Traveller" marks the Dixie Highway in front of the Madison County courthouse in Marshall. Placed by the Asheville Chapter, United Daughters of the Confederacy, in 1926, and one of four identical bronzes attached to free-standing boulders along this roadway through western North Carolina, these markers—and similar tablets denoting the Jefferson Davis Highway through the state's eastern Piedmont—are, in the broadest sense, part of Confederate commemoration. However, their placement required much less money, effort, and local support than typical courthouse "soldier" monuments. Therefore these plaques, and similar contemporaneous bronzes erected by the North Carolina Historical Commission in partnership with the U.D.C., are not included among this book's statistical analysis of North Carolina's monuments and memorials. However, they will be discussed in chapter 15.

19. Davie County (Mocksville) lies both to the west and south of Forsyth County (Winston-Salem) but is closely affiliated economically with Forsyth and Yadkin Counties. Davie County did not erect a Confederate monument until 1987. In addition, Stokes County Daughters erected a cemetery, not a civic-space, memorial in 1950.

20. John C. Inscoe and Gordon B. McKinney, *The Heart of Confederate Appalachia: Western North Carolina in the Civil War* (Chapel Hill: University of North Carolina Press, 2000), pp. 211–212.

21. "Wolfe Trophy to Be Awarded, Marker to Be Unveiled Saturday," *Asheville Citizen*, October 18, 1959 (no page cited, clipping file, Pack Library, Asheville, North Carolina).

22. Ibid.

23. "The History of America's Largest Home," http://www.biltmore.com/our_story/our_history/default.asp (accessed October 14, 2011); "Biltmore's Lasting Legacy of Forestry," http://www.biltmore.com/our_story/forestry.asp (accessed October 14, 2011); "Biltmore Estate."

24. W. T. Rogers, "Monument at Candler, N.C.," *Confederate Veteran* September 1909, 473; "Captain Thrash and His Monument," *Confederate Veteran* May 1907, pp. 210–211.

25. "Captain Thrash and His Monument," *Confederate Veteran*, May 1907, pp. 210–211.

26. W. T. Rogers, "Monument at Candler, N.C.," *Confederate Veteran*, September 1909, p. 473.

27. Blanche Lucas Smith, *North Carolina's Confederate Monuments and Memorials* (Raleigh: NC Division, United Daughters of the Confederacy, 1941); Ralph W. Widener, *Confederate Monuments: Enduring Symbols of the South and the War Between the States* (Dallas: R. W. Widener, 1982).

28. North Carolina's Civil War–era banner differed just slightly from the state's present-day flag. The colors of the vertical bar and two horizontal stripes were rearranged after the war, but the single five-pointed star surrounded by two dates remains. May 20, 1775, the signing of the purported Mecklenburg Declaration of Independence, and May 20, 1861, the day of secession, were used during

the war. Afterwards, with the rearrangement of colors, the latter date was replaced with April 12, 1776, in recognition of the Halifax Resolves.

29. "Monument Being Moved to Lawn of Courthouse," *Hendersonville Times-News*, April 15, 1925 (no page cited, clipping file, Henderson County Genealogical and Historical Society, Inc.); similar relocations were done in a number of North Carolina cities to improve traffic safety.

30. Iredell County's (Statesville, 1906) and Forsyth County's (Winston-Salem, 1905) monuments, both funded by the U.D.C., arguably represents transitional forms. "To the Soldiers of Iredell County 1861–1865" is inscribed on the main front panel, placing this monument in the "soldiers" category. "Our Confederate Dead," however, is also prominently carved across the front in raised letters, extending nearly the width of the monument's step-like base.

31. Eastern North Carolina, also referred to as the coastal plain, is generally defined as the land from the "fall line"—where river rapids block further upstream navigation by large vessels and the rolling terrain of the Piedmont ends—eastward to the coast. This line approximates the route of present day Interstate 95. In this book eastern North Carolina will be defined as including the following present-day counties (north to south): Northampton, Hertford, Gates, Pasquotank, Camden, Currituck, Halifax, Bertie, Chowan, Perquimans, Edgecombe, Wilson, Martin, Washington, Tyrrell, Dare, Wayne, Greene, Pitt, Beaufort, Hyde, Sampson, Duplin, Lenoir, Jones, Craven, Pamlico, Bladen, Pender, Onslow, Carteret, Columbus, New Hanover, and Brunswick.

Chapter 6

1. "Unveil Today the Monuments to Soldiers of Confederacy," *Asheville Citizen*, Wednesday November 8, 1905, p. 6; "Monument to Volunteers Is Unveiled," *Asheville Citizen*, November 9, 1905, p. 1.

2. Little is known about this recently "'rediscovered" monument, not even its dedication date. It is not listed in Smith's 1941 book nor in Widener's 1982 photo compilation. The date inscribed on the front panel—1903—would, if accurate, make this obelisk the oldest UDC-sponsored memorial in North Carolina. In light of the uncertainty, however, this monument will not be considered in this work as the state's oldest UDC memorial.

3. I have seen photocopies of two of these ribbons. In addition to the illustrated example, a second variety, found in the Creasman family Bible, reads "Unveiling—Girls for Creasman Monument Grandchildren of 29TH N.C. Regiment," instead of "Asheville Chapter Daughters of the Confederacy," in a style and ink appearing otherwise identical to the illustrated ribbon's lettering. (Photocopy dated February 2000 in Pack Library, Asheville, NC).

4. The monument cites six companies from Buncombe County. However, Jordan lists only five of the regiment's ten companies as having been recruited from Buncombe; Weymouth T. Jordan, Jr., *North Carolina Troops 1861–1865 A Roster*, vol. XIV (Raleigh: North Carolina Division of Archives and History, 1998), pp. 504–592.

5. James Mitchel Ray is identified by different sources as general, colonel, and lieutenant colonel. The monument he helped dedicate lists him as one of Buncombe County's 18 colonels. However Weymouth T. Jordan, Jr., in *North Carolina Troops 1861–1865 A Roster* (p. 502), lists Ray as a lieutenant colonel. According to Jordan, Ray suffered a compound fracture to his right arm at Chickamauga on September 20 and resigned from the service due to "disability from wounds on November 28, 1863." The appellation "General" as used by the *Asheville Citizen* on November 9, 1905, may refer to an honorary postwar title or to a rank in the United Confederate Veterans.

6. The two articles from the *Asheville Citizen* disagree as to the persons unveiling the Creasman monument. On November 8, the paper lists under its "program" the "Unveiling of the monument–To Col. Creasman, by grandchildren of members of the regiment." The following day the paper reported, "The unveiling of the monuments [*sic*] to Col. W. B. Creasman was by his descendants." The ribbon cited above, states "Grandchildren of 29TH N.C. Regiment."

7. For a more detailed discussion of the Mecklenburg Declaration see Chapter 4, Note 7.

8. "Monument to Volunteers Is Unveiled," *Asheville Citizen*, November 9, 1905, p. 1.

9. Ibid.
10. Ibid.
11. Ibid.
12. Ibid.
13. Ibid.
14. Ibid.
15. Ibid.
16. Ibid.
17. Ibid.
18. Ibid.
19. Ibid.

20. Weymouth T. Jordan, Jr., *North Carolina Troops: 1861–1865, A Roster*, vol. VII (Raleigh: North Carolina Division of Archives and History, 1979), p. 466; Weymouth T. Jordan, Jr., *North Carolina Troops: 1861–1865, A Roster*, vol. V (Raleigh: North Carolina Division of Archives and History, 1975), p. 413; Weymouth T. Jordan, Jr., *North Carolina Troops: 1861–1865, A Roster*, vol. XIV (Raleigh: North Carolina Division of Archives and History, 1998) p. 662.

21. Martha Wren Briggs, *The Compass Windows of Old Blandford* Church (Sedley, VA: Dory, 1992), pp. 4–5.

22. John C. Inscoe and Gordon B. McKinney, *The Heart of Confederate Appalachia: Western North Carolina in the Civil War* (Chapel Hill: University of North Carolina Press, 2000), pp. 32–34.

23. Ibid., pp. 40–42.

24. William S. Powell, *North Carolina Through Four Centuries* (Chapel Hill: the University of North Carolina Press, 1989), p. 345.

25. Inscoe, pp. 44–52.

26. Ibid., p. 56.

27. Powell, *North Carolina Through Four Centuries*, p. 369; William S. Powell, *Dictionary of North Carolina Biography*, vol. 6 (Chapel Hill: University of North Carolina Press, 1996), pp. 85–87.

28. Powell, *North Carolina Through Four Centuries*, p. 368

29. Ibid., pp. 369–370.

30. Ibid., pp. 368–370.

31. Pender County's Confederate monument, dedicated in 1917 and inscribed, "In Honor of the Confederate Soldiers of Pender County," includes a cameo bust of Major-General William Dorsey Pender, a North Carolinian killed at Gettysburg. Though Pender is prominently featured on the front panel, and is mentioned as the

county's namesake on the back panel, this memorial is primarily a soldier monument, not unlike the courthouse memorials in Gates (1915) and Tyrrell (1902) counties on which side panels cite local notables. Secondary images are also included on at least two monuments. Robert E. Lee is depicted on one of the sixteen panels of the Tyrrell County monument as well as on the front of Oakdale Cemetery's memorial (Wilmington, 1872) while General Thomas J. "Stonewall" Jackson's visage adorns the back of Oakdale's structure. In recent years, a possible exception to this egalitarian tradition has been installed outside Lee County's new courthouse in Sanford. The county, formed in 1907 and named for the Confederate general, has recently installed two bronze plaques, a timeline of Lee's life and a bust relief of the general outside of the new courthouse.

32. *The Sun*, December 12, 1892, as quoted in "Wake County, NC — North Carolina's Confederate Monument," http://files.usgwarchives.org/nc/wake/military/statue01.txt (accessed January 16, 2009).

33. Ibid.

34. Ibid. This book does not seek to validate (or refute) North Carolina's Confederate claims. These assertions, coupled with explanatory support, serve to highlight the contemporary commemorative milieu faced by North Carolinians at the beginning of the twentieth century.

35. Virginians and North Carolinians not only debated the role of each others' troops, they argued also over the name of this disastrous assault. Originally known as "Longstreet's Assault," since the troops involved were under his overall command, or the "Assault on Cemetery Ridge," in reference to the contested ground, Virginians soon promoted the moniker "Pickett's Charge." North Carolinians countered with "Pettigrew's Charge," citing both the "farthest" claim and the fact that the Tarheel general Pettigrew personally led his men across the field, being wounded and having his horse killed from under him, while neither General George Pickett nor his superior, General James Longstreet, participated in combat. That people would vie to name a devastating military defeat for one of their own speaks to the near-reverence that the post-war South held for its former soldiers.

36. *Five Points in the Record of North Carolina in the Great War of 1861–5* (North Carolina Literary and Historical Association, 1904), pp. 73–79.

37. Ibid., p. 3.

38. "Clark," William S. Powell, *Dictionary of North Carolina Biography*, vol. 1 (Chapel Hill: University of North Carolina Press, 1979), pp. 378–379; "Ashe," William S. Powell, *Dictionary of North Carolina Biography*, vol. 1 (Chapel Hill: University of North Carolina Press, 1979), pp. 54–55; "Montgomery," William S. Powell, *Dictionary of North Carolina Biography*, vol. 4 (Chapel Hill: University of North Carolina Press, 1988), p. 291; "Bond," William S. Powell, *Dictionary of North Carolina Biography*, vol. 1 (Chapel Hill: University of North Carolina Press, 1979), p. 189; "Hale," William S. Powell, *Dictionary of North Carolina Biography*, vol. 3 (Chapel Hill: University of North Carolina Press, 1988), pp. 4–5; "Avery," William S. Powell, *Dictionary of North Carolina Biography*, vol. 1 (Chapel Hill: University of North Carolina Press, 1979), pp. 66–67; "London," William S. Powell, *Dictionary of North Carolina Biography*, vol. 4 (Chapel Hill: University of North Carolina Press, 1991), pp. 85–86. Ashe was later commemorated with a tablet dedicated September 13, 1940, on the state Capitol grounds in Raleigh.

39. *Five Points in the Record of North Carolina in the Great War of 1861–5* (North Carolina Literary and Historical Association, 1904), p. 5.

40. Ibid., pp. 11–12. Part of this expanded commemorative effort included North Carolina erecting out-of-state memorials, notably the North Carolina monument at Appomattox, marking the site of the final charge, and two nearby plaques citing the final skirmish and the last seizure of federal artillery.

Chapter 7

1. "Monument Unveiling," *Tarborough Southerner*, November 3, 1904, p. 1; William Powell, *Dictionary of North Carolina Biography*, vol. 1 (Chapel Hill: University of North Carolina Press, 1979), p. 197.

2. October 27, 1904, p. 4.

3. Letter, Tarboro Library files.

4. *Southerner*, undated article, Edgecombe County Memorial Library files.

5. Ibid.

6. "Articles deposited in the Receptacle of the Cornerstone of the Confederate Monument at the time of the laying of the cornerstone," undated typed document, Edgecombe County Memorial Library files. Similar items were placed in Oxford, North Carolina's, monument. A cornerstone box, "covered with what appeared to be a white marble cover bearing date May 10, 1909," was recovered when that monument was moved in 1971, *Oxford Public Ledger*, June 18, 1971 (no page listed) vertical file, Granville County Public Library.

7. Edgecombe County Memorial Library files.

8. "The Daughters of the Confederacy," *Tarborough Southerner*, October 13, 1904, p. 3.

9. "Spare the Trees," *Tarborough Southerner*, October 27, 1904, p. 3.

10. "Monument Unveiling Programme," *Tarborough Southerner*, October 27, 1904, p. 3.

11. "Monument Unveiling," *Tarborough Southerner*, November 3, 1904, p. 1.

12. Ibid.

13. Ibid.

14. "Monument Unveiling," *Tarborough Southerner*, November 3, 1904, p. 1; "Personal Intelligence," *Tarborough Southerner*, November 3, 1904, p. 2; Penelo was the name of General Cox's plantation, located in Edgecombe County. William Powell, *Dictionary of North Carolina Biography*, vol. 1 (Chapel Hill: University of North Carolina Press, 1979), pp. 450–451.

15. Ibid.; "Monument Unveiling Programme," *Tarborough Southerner*, October 27, 1904, p. 3.

16. "Monument Unveiling," *Tarborough Southerner*, November 3, 1904, p. 1.

17. "Monument Unveiling," *Tarborough Southerner*, November 3, 1904, p. 1; "Now Complete," *Tarborough Southerner*, November 10, 1904, p. 4.

18. Richard Kolb, "Thin Gray Line: Confederate Veterans in the New South," Veterans of Foreign Wars of the United States (2000), http://vaudc.org/confed_vets.html (accessed October 13, 2008).

19. Mrs. William J. Behan, *History of the Confederate Memorial Associations of the* South (New Orleans: Graham, 1904), p. 230; William A. Blair, *Contesting the Memory of the Civil War South, 1865–1914* (Chapel Hill: University of North Carolina Press, 2004), p. 53; Richard Kolb, "Thin Gray Line: Confederate Veterans in the New South," Veterans of Foreign Wars of the United States (2000), http://vaudc.org/confed_vets.html (accessed October 13, 2008).

20. William S. Powell, *North Carolina Through Four Centuries* (University of North Carolina Press: Chapel Hill, 1989) pp. 414–415.
21. "United Confederate Veterans Association Records (Mss.1357)," Special Collections LSU Libraries, http://www.lib.lsu.edu/special/findaid/u1357.html (accessed May 22, 2012).
22. Ibid.; S. A. Cunningham, "The United Confederate Veterans," http://www.civilwarhome.com/confederate veterans.htm, accessed December 10, 2008.
23. In 1900, a number of Ladies' Memorial Associations formed the Confederate Southern Memorial Association (CSMA). This group, although working closely with the U.D.C., did not primarily fund any North Carolina monuments.
24. "Founder and Co-Founder," United Daughters of the Confederacy, http://www.hqudc.org/about/founder.html (accessed May 22, 2012); Karen L. Cox, *Dixie's Daughters: The United Daughters of the Confederacy and the Preservation of Confederate Culture* (University Press of Florida: Gainesville, 2003), p. 17.
25. "Founder and Co-Founder," United Daughters of the Confederacy, http://www.hqudc.org/about/founder.html (accessed May 22, 2012); pp. Cox, 16–17.
26. As quoted by Cox, pp. 18–19, 22.
27. *Minutes of the First Annual Convention,* pp. 1–3, as quoted by Cox, p. 20.
28. E. H. Parsley to Mrs. L. H. Raines, October 1 and 29, 1894, as quoted by Cox, pp. 21–22.
29. *Minutes of the First Annual Convention,* pp. 1–3, as quoted by Cox, p. 24.
30. Richard Kolb, "Thin Gray Line: Confederate Veterans in the New South," Veterans of Foreign Wars of the United States (2000), http://vaudc.org/confed_vets.html (accessed October 13, 2008).
31. Ibid.; "Joseph Wheeler," Encyclopedia of Alabama, http://www.encyclopediaofalabama.org/face/Article.jsp?id=h-2140 (accessed May 26, 2012).
32. "Grover Cleveland and the Great Confederate Battle Flags Furor," The American Catholic, http://the-american-catholic.com/2011/05/19/grover-cleveland-and-the-great-confederate-battle-flags"-furor (accessed May 26, 2012); "History and Development of the National Cemetery Administration," Department of Veterans Affairs National Cemetery Administration, http://www.cem.va.gov/cem/docs/factsheets/history.pdf (accessed May 26, 2012).
33. *Confederate Veteran* vol. I, January 1893, p. 1.
34. "Sumner Archibald Cunningham-Tennessee State Museum," Tennessee Portrait Project, http://www.tnportraits.org/210-cunningham-sumner-archibald.htm (accessed May 22, 2012); "Sumner A. Cunningham," Tennessee Division, Sons of Confederate Veterans, http://www.tennessee-scv.org/sac.htm (accessed May 22, 2012).
35. "Sumner A. Cunningham," Tennessee Division, Sons of Confederate Veterans, http://www.tennessee-scv.org/sac.htm (accessed May 22, 2012); *Confederate Veteran* vol. I, January 1893, p. 1; *Confederate Veteran* vol. II January 1894, p. 1.
36. *Confederate Veteran* vol. IV, January 1896, p. 1.
37. R. B. Rosenberg, *Living Monuments: Confederate Soldiers' Homes in the New South* (Chapel Hill: University of North Carolina Press, 1993), pp. 35–37.
38. "Major Robbins' Speech," *The [Concord] Times,* May 12, 1892, p. 2; William McKendree Robbins, a Statesville lawyer and former U.S. congressman served with the Fourth Alabama Regiment, rising to the rank of major. In 1894, President Grover Cleveland appointed Robbins Confederate commissioner of the Gettysburg Battlefield Commission, a post he held until his death in 1905. Powell, *Dictionary of North Carolina Biography,* vol. 5 (Chapel Hill: University of North Carolina Press, 1994), pp. 225–226.
39. The Sons of Confederate Veterans, organized in Richmond, Virginia, in 1896, did not play a major commemorative or monument-building role until the latter half of the twentieth century.
40. "Active Chapters by Location," North Carolina Division United Daughters of the Confederacy, http://www.ncudc.org/NCUDCChapters.html (accessed June 9, 2012); "Defunct Chapters," North Carolina Division United Daughters of the Confederacy, http://www.ncudc.org/Chapters-defunct.html (accessed June 9, 2012).
41. "United Daughters of the Confederacy — Winnie Davis Chapter Records," North Carolina State Archives (ORG. 121), minutes.
42. Ibid.
43. "Marker: I-64 — Confederate Women's Home," North Carolina Department of Cultural Resources, http://www.ncmarkers.com/Markers.aspx?ct=ddl&sp=search&k=Markers&sv=I-64 (accessed May 28, 2012).
44. "Southern Cross of Honor," United Daughters of the Confederacy, http://www.hqudc.org (accessed December 10, 2008).
45. Ibid.
46. Cox, p. 111.
47. At least two additional memorials were sponsored by the Children of the Confederacy — an ornate fountain on Tarboro's (Edgecombe County) town common erected by the Dixie Lee Chapter and dedicated on August 3, 1910, in honor of Henry Lawson Wyatt and the Buncombe County monument to General Thomas C. Clingman (Chapter 6). Both, however, honor individual soldiers and therefore are not included in this discussion.
48. Blanche Lucas Smith, *North Carolina's Confederate Monuments and Memorials* (Raleigh: North Carolina Division, United Daughters of the Confederacy, 1941) p. 109.
49. Cox, pp. 77–78.
50. Cox, p. 87; "Living Monument to Southern Women," *Confederate Veteran* vol. V, August 1897, p. 420; "Women Want Building for Monument," *Confederate Veteran* vol. XVII, April 1909, p. 181.
51. "Daughters of the Confederacy," (Reidsville) *Webster's Weekly,* June 24, 1910.
52. Monuments in Burke and Currituck Counties were partially funded by out-of-state individuals. In Burke, the statue was donated by a county native; in Currituck, the memorial was completed with a granite sphere given by a northern businessman who was a part-time county resident and large local landowner.

Chapter 8

1. "United Daughters of the Confederacy — Winnie Davis Chapter Records," North Carolina State Archives (ORG. 121), bank book.
2. William S. Powell, *Dictionary of North Carolina Biography,* vol. 4 (Chapel Hill: University of North Carolina Press, 1991), pp. 85–86.
3. *Minutes of the Eleventh Annual Meeting of the United Daughters of the Confederacy, Held in St. Louis, Mo., October 4–8, 1904* (Nashville, TN: Foster and Webb, 1905), p. 44; The membership of the Winnie Davis Daughters varied little over three years: fifty-eight members in 1902; fifty-five in 1903; and fifty-seven in

1904. In 1903, North Carolina UDC Chapters ranged in size from 144 members in Wilmington's Cape Fear Chapter #3 to 11 members in the Faison, N.C., Chapter. *Minutes of the Tenth Annual Meeting of the United Daughters of the Confederacy, Held in Charleston, S.C., November 11–14, 1903* (Nashville, TN: Foster and Webb, 1904).

4. "United Daughters of the Confederacy — Winnie Davis Chapter Records," North Carolina State Archives (ORG. 121), minutes; Father Ryan and his poetry is discussed in chapter 12.

5. Ibid.
6. Ibid.
7. Ibid.
8. Ibid.

9. *Chatham Record* as quoted by the Chatham Rabbit website http://chathamrabbit.blogspot.com/2007/07/reads-record-11-1906-jan-mar.html (accessed January 14, 2012).

10. *Chatham Record*, as quoted by the Chatham Rabbit website; Winnie Davis Daughters, minutes.

11. "United Daughters of the Confederacy — Winnie Davis Chapter Records," North Carolina State Archives (ORG. 121), minutes.

12. Ibid.

13. "United Daughters of the Confederacy — Winnie Davis Chapter Records," North Carolina State Archives (ORG. 121), signed contract.

14. Ibid.

15. In March 2010, a fire extensively damaged this courthouse. Court sessions and other official functions were relocated to the judicial center across the street while the old courthouse was reconstructed. The Confederate soldier statue was undamaged by the fire and remains in its original location. Personal communication. Debra Henzey, Chatham County director of community relations, December 19, 2012.

16. "United Daughters of the Confederacy — Winnie Davis Chapter Records," North Carolina State Archives (ORG. 121), legal document, "Office of the Board of the County Commissioners of Chatham County, N.C."

17. "United Daughters of the Confederacy — Winnie Davis Chapter Records," North Carolina State Archives (ORG. 121), minutes.

18. Ibid.
19. Ibid.

20. With the phrase, "Erected by those who honor the memory of the Confederate soldier," as suggested by Mrs. London — and assuming all other inscriptions were accepted as proposed — Pittsboro's monument would have had 427 inscribed letters, just over the 400-letter allotment specified by contract. The additional words, however, pushed the final count to 552. (Both figures exclude eleven large raised characters, C. S. A. 1861–1865, high on the granite shaft.)

21. These counties are: Chowan (Edenton, 1904); Edgecombe (Tarboro, 1904); Iredell (Statesville, 1905); Davidson (Lexington, 1905); Forsyth (Winston-Salem, 1905); Buncombe (Asheville, 1905); Anson (Wadesboro, 1906); Cleveland (Shelby, 1907); Robeson (Lumberton, 1907); Catawba (Newton, 1907); Chatham (Pittsboro, 1907); Rowan (Salisbury, 1909); Macon (Franklin, 1909); Granville (Oxford, 1909); Caldwell (Lenoir, 1910); Rockingham (Reidsville, 1910); Union (Monroe, 1910); Rutherford (Rutherfordton, 1910); Scotland (Laurinburg, 1912); Vance (Henderson, 1910); Pasquotank (Elizabeth City, 1911); Lincoln (Lincolnton, 1911); Randolph (Asheboro, 1911); Perquimans (Hertford, 1912); Gaston (Gastonia, 1912); Hertford (Winton, 1913); Warren (Warrenton, 1913); Alamance (Graham, 1914); Franklin (Louisburg, 1914); Pitt (Greenville, 1914); Gates (Gatesville, 1915); Jackson (Sylva, 1915); Sampson (Clinton, 1916). All of these monuments except for Rockingham County's were erected at the county courthouse or a nearby prominent public space. Rockingham County's memorial was placed prominently in Reidsville, the county's commercial center, not the county seat of Wentworth, a much smaller community. The Confederate monument on the University of North Carolina, Chapel Hill, campus (1913), a mid-intersection monument in Weldon (1908), and a churchyard monument in Cornelius (1910) have been excluded from this discussion of county monuments.

22. The four counties erecting civic-space monuments prior to 1904 were Cabarrus (Concord, 1892), Bertie (Windsor, 1896), Cumberland (Fayetteville, 1902), and Tyrrell (Columbia, 1902).

23. "A Confederate Monument," *Watauga Democrat*, June 8, 1905, p. 3; untitled editorial, *Watauga Democrat*, June 15, 1905, p. 3; Michael C. Hardy, *A Short History of Watauga County* (Boone, NC: Parkway, 2005), pp. 123–124.

24. "Will Erect Monument to Replace Fountain," *The Asheville Citizen*, December 7, 1912 (no page cited, clipping file, Pack Library, Asheville Public Library).

25. "Kirmess and a Ball for Raising Funds," *Greensboro Daily News*, October 25, 1912 (no page cited, clipping file, Greensboro Public Library).

26. Ibid.
27. Ibid.

28. Tom Vincent, "'Evidence of Womans Loyalty, Perseverance, and Fidelity': Confederate Soldiers' Monuments in North Carolina, 1865–1914," *The North Carolina Historical Review*, 83: 1 (January 2006), p. 69. The *Gastonia Gazette* reported an "interesting situation" from Greensboro in November 1912. Greensboro Daughters, represented by twelve committee members, signed a contract for a $9,000.00 Confederate monument. When the news was reported, "the 99 or more other members of the chapter" called a meeting, and the "twelve who had made the contract were raked over the coals good and proper," with fellow Daughters "tell[ing] them that they could get the same monument for a good deal less money." Untitled article, *Gastonia Gazette*, November 22, 1912, p. 4.

29. Ibid.

30. These counties are Brunswick, Nash, Northampton, and Polk. Robert Ricks personally financed a large Nash County monument in Rocky Mount's Battle Park — not in the county seat of Nashville — dedicated in 1917.

31. Vincent, p. 83; According to the U.S. Bureau of Labor Statistics, the Consumer Price Index, a widely used inflation measure, increased approximately 23-fold since record-keeping began in 1913. A $2,000.00 early twentieth-century monument, therefore, would today cost between $45,000.00 and $50,000.00. "Consumer Price Index," ftp://ftp.bls.gov/pub/special.requests/cpi/cpiai.txt (accessed February 4, 2012).

32. In 1911, thirty-seven people petitioned Burke County commissioners to "pay over to the Daughters of the Confederacy" $500 annually for three years, according to text quoted in 2004 from a document then owned by Joy Shivar of JustaJoy Historical Treasures. The signatories apparently also promised to match the appropriation. The quoted text reads: "NORTH CAROLINA —

BURKE COUNTY—A.D. 1911 To The board [sic] of County Commissioners: The undersigned qualified voters of Burke County respectfully petition the Board of County Commissioners of Burke County in accordance with the provisions of Chap. 512 of the Public Laws of 1911 to subscribe and pay over to the Daughters of the Confederacy of Burke County, the sum of five hundred ($500.00 dollars[)] each and every year for three years to be expended in part payment for the building of the Confederate Monument in the Public Square in the Town of Morganton upon the terms prescribed in said act." Ms. Shivar further states, "Below this paragraph are 37 signatures of people who promised the $500.00 for 3 years to build the monument." http://genforum.genealogy.com/propst/messages/439.html (accessed January 16, 2009).

33. Blanche Lucas Smith, *North Carolina's Confederate Monuments and Memorials* (Raleigh: NC Division, United Daughters of the Confederacy, 1941), p. 91; "The Confederate Monument at Morganton, N.C., *Confederate Veteran*, vol. XXVI (November 1918): pp. 477–480.

34. Blanche Lucas Smith, *North Carolina's Confederate Monuments and Memorials* (Raleigh: NC Division, United Daughters of the Confederacy, 1941), p. 91.

35. *Elizabeth City Weekly Advance*, September 13, 1912. http://ncmonuments.ncdcr.gov/Photos.aspx?searchterm=27 (accessed January 20, 2012).

36. Ibid.
37. Ibid.
38. Ibid.

39. "Joseph P. Knapp," *Wikipedia*, http://en.wikipedia.org/wiki/Joseph_P._Knapp (accessed January 20, 2012).

40. Dudley Bagley, *The Joseph P. Knapp I Knew* (unpublished manuscript, 1964), from Currituck County Library—inscribed "This copy for Currituck County Library at my death. D. B. B. 2/11/69," chapter III, p. 2–3 (no page numbers on manuscript).

41. Ibid., p. 4.

42. "Editorial," *Elizabeth City Independent*, January 12, 1923, as quoted in Bagley, p. 4.

43. Ibid., pp. 3–4.
44. Bagley, chapter III, p. 5.
45. Ibid., pp. 5–6.
46. Ibid., p. 6.

Chapter 9

1. "A Gala Week Now," *Winston-Salem Journal*, October 1, 1905, p. 1.

2. "A Week of Many Events," *Winston-Salem Journal*, October 1, 1905, p. 4; "A Gala Week Now," *Winston-Salem Journal*, October 1, 1905, p. 1.

3. Ibid.

4. "Praise for Daughters," *Winston-Salem Journal*, September 30, 1905, p. 1.

5. Ibid.

6. "A Gala Week Now," *Winston-Salem Journal*, October 1, 1905, p. 1; "Novel Confederate Window," *Winston-Salem Journal*, October 1, 1905, p. 4.

7. *Winston-Salem Journal*, October 1, 1905, pp. 4, 7.

8. "Getting Ready for October 3," *Winston-Salem Journal*, September 28, 1905, p. 1.

9. "Notice, United Daughters of the Confederacy," *Winston-Salem Journal*, October 1, 1905, p. 4.

10. "A Gala Week Now," *Winston-Salem Journal*, October 1, 1905, p. 1.

11. "Confederate Monument Unveiled," *Winston-Salem Journal*, October 4, 1905, p. 1.

12. William Powell, *Dictionary of North Carolina Biography*, vol. 6 (Chapel Hill: University of North Carolina Press, 1996) pp. 102–103.

13. "Confederate Monument Unveiled," *Winston-Salem Journal*, October 4, 1905, p. 1.

14. Ibid.
15. Ibid.
16. Ibid.

17. Ibid.; "Confederate Soldier (sculpture)," SIRIS-Smithsonian Institution Research Information System, http://siris-artinventories.si.edu/ipac20.jsp?session=12YN921221772.72828&profile (accessed October 13, 2008).

18. "Confederate Monument Unveiled," *Winston-Salem Journal*, October 4, 1905, p. 1.

19. "Confederate Monument at Franklin, N.C.," *Confederate Veteran*, vol. XVII (November 1909): pp. 540–541; "The Confederate Monument," *Newton Enterprise*, August 22, 1907 (no page cited); "A Week of Many Events," *Winston-Salem Journal*, October 1, 1905, p. 4.

20. "Unveiling Confederate Monument at Raleigh, N.C., May 20th, 1895," (Raleigh) *News and Observer*, May 19, 1895, p. 8; "A Welcome to All," (Raleigh) *News and Observer*, May 19, 1895, p. 5.

21. "Randolph County's Unveiling Day," *Asheboro Courier*, September 7, 1911, p. 1; "Locals," *Newton Enterprise*, August 8, 1907 (no page cited).

22. "Randolph County's Unveiling Day," *Asheboro Courier*, September 7, 1911, p. 1.

23. "Programme," *Asheboro Courier*, September 7, 1911, p. 1.

24. "Confederate Monument at Franklin, N.C.," *Confederate Veteran*, vol. XVII (November 1909): pp. 540–541; "Programme for Unveiling Confederate Monument, May 16th," *The Alamance Gleaner*, May 7, 1914 (no page cited); "Confederate Monument Unveiled," *Winston-Salem Journal*, October 4, 1905, p. 1.

25. "Locals," *Newton Enterprise*, August 8, 1907 (no page cited); "Tenting on the Old Campground," a favorite of Union veterans as well, was included in several Tarheel dedications including Pender County (Burgaw, 1914), "Pender Unveils Confederate Shaft," *Wilmington Dispatch*, May 27, 1914, p. 7 (from Reaves Collection, Burgaw volume, Wilmington Public Library); Blanche Lucas Smith, *North Carolina's Confederate Monuments and Memorials* (Raleigh: N.C. Division, United Daughters of the Confederacy, 1941), p. 91; "Program," *Rocky Mount Evening* Telegram, May 12, 1917, p. 5.

26. "The Confederate Monument," *Newton Enterprise*, August 22, 1907 (no page cited); "Monument to Volunteers Is Unveiled," *The Asheville Citizen*, November 9, 1905, p. 4.

27. "The Unveiling Yesterday," *Statesville Landmark*, May 11, 1906 (no page cited).

28. "Randolph County's Unveiling Day," *Asheboro Courier*, September 7, 1911, p. 1.

29. "Pender Unveils Confederate Shaft," *Wilmington Dispatch*, May 27, 1914, p. 7 (from Reaves Collection, Burgaw, Wilmington Public Library); *Address on the Occasion of the Unveiling of the Monument to the Confederate Soldiers from Caldwell County at Lenoir, June 3rd, 1910* (Hickory: Clay, 1910), pp. 5–7.

30. "Pender Unveils Confederate Shaft," *Wilmington Dispatch*, May 27, 1914, p. 7 (from Reaves Collection, Burgaw, Wilmington Public Library); *Address on the Occasion of the Unveiling of the Monument to the Confederate Soldiers from Caldwell County at Lenoir, June 3rd, 1910* (Hickory: Clay, 1910), pp. 7–8.

31. *Address on the Occasion of the Unveiling of the Mon-*

ument to the Confederate Soldiers from Caldwell County at Lenoir, June 3rd, 1910 (Hickory: Clay, 1910), p. 18.

32. "The Confederate Monument," *Newton Enterprise*, August 15, 1907 (no page cited); "Confederate Monument Unveiled Saturday," *The Alamance Gleaner*, May 21, 1914 (no page cited).

33. R. D. W. Connor, *Addresses at the Unveiling of the Memorial to the North Carolina Women of the Confederacy* (Raleigh: Edwards and Broughton, 1914), p. 14.

34. "The Monument Ready for the Unveiling," *Newton Enterprise*, August 15, 1907 (no page cited); *Statesville Landmark*, January 2, 1906 (typed transcription from clipping file, Iredell Public Library, no page cited); "Burgaw Monument Defaced by Vandals," *Wilmington Star*, February 26, 1914 (no page cited) (from Reaves Collection, Burgaw, Wilmington Public Library).

35. "New Monument Unveiled" (photo), Unknown photocopy "Courthouse 78," Statesville Public Library clipping file; Unveiling materials were sometimes re-used. Following Chatham County's ceremony, Pittsboro's Daughters used "the red streamers that the monument was unveiled with" to "stripe" a quilt for their sponsored room at the Soldiers' Home, an idea "received joyously for we knew we would have a fine time making that quilt," according to the group's minutes. The women, however, could find no further use for the veil itself, concluding three months later, that it "could do us no good" and choosing to "sell it if possible.... Its cost was $2.90." "United Daughters of the Confederacy—Winnie Davis Chapter Records," North Carolina State Archives (ORG. 121) minutes; "Confederate Monument at Franklin, N.C.," *Confederate Veteran*, vol. XVII (November 1909): pp. 540–541.

36. "Confederate Monument at Henderson, N.C.," *Confederate Veteran*, vol. XIX (April 1911), pp. 170–171; G. W. F. Harper, *A Little History of the Monument in honor of the Confederate Veterans from Caldwell County, N.C.* (No publisher cited; 1910) unnumbered page. North Carolinians rarely used the "Stars and Bars," the first Confederate national flag (1861–1863), as a commemorative icon. However local resident Orren Randolph Smith, who also penned the Vance County monument's front inscription, is widely credited with designing the banner. Smith took part in the 1910 dedication ceremony, and his portrait is included in the *Veteran* article, perhaps explaining this uncommon image of the national flag.

37. Blanche Lucas Smith, *North Carolina's Confederate Monuments and Memorials* (Raleigh: N.C. Division, United Daughters of the Confederacy, 1941), pp. 91–92, 118.

38. Connor, p. 7.

39. Smith, pp. 125–128; "Confederate Monument Unveiled," *Winston-Salem Journal*, October 4, 1905, p. 1.

40. "Confederate Monument Unveiled," *Winston-Salem Journal*, October 4, 1905, p. 1.

41. "Randolph County's Unveiling Day," *Asheboro Courier*, September 7, 1911, p. 1.

42. "Unveiled Amid Inspiring Scenes," *Elizabeth City Tar Heel*, May 12, 1911, p. 1; "Confederate Monument at Franklin, N.C.," *Confederate Veteran*, vol. XVII (November 1909): pp. 540–541; "The Unveiling Yesterday," *Statesville Landmark*, May 11, 1906 (no page cited).

43. "Confederate Monument at Henderson, N.C.," *Confederate Veteran*, vol. XIX (April 1911): pp. 170–171; "Pender Unveils Confederate Shaft," *Wilmington Dispatch*, May 27, 1914, p. 7 (from Reaves Collection, Burgaw volume, Wilmington Public Library).

44. Smith, p. 128.

Chapter 10

1. Monument inscription; J. Randolph Smith, "Miss Anne Carter Lee," *Confederate Veteran* vol. XIV (July 1906): p. 325.

2. Ibid.

3. Ibid., pp. 325–326.

4. Ibid., p. 326.

5. Ibid.

6. Blanche Lucas Smith, *North Carolina's Confederate Monuments and Memorials* (Raleigh: NC Division, United Daughters of the Confederacy, 1941); Ralph Widener, *Confederate Monuments: Enduring Symbols of the South and the War Between the States* (Dallas: R. W. Widener, 1982).

7. Tom Vincent, "'Evidence of Womans Loyalty, Perseverance, and Fidelity': Confederate Soldiers' Monuments in North Carolina, 1865–1914," *The North Carolina Historical Review*, Vol. 83, No. 1 (January 2006), p. 69.

8. "United Daughters of the Confederacy—Winnie Davis Chapter Records," North Carolina State Archives (ORG. 121), signed contract; W. H. Mullins Company, *The Blue and the Gray* (Cleveland: Caxton, 1913), p. 30.

9. W. H. Mullins, *The Blue and the Gray*, pp. 24, 44–47.

10. Ibid., pp. 68–69.

11. "Warren's Tribute," *The* (Warren) *Record*, October 31, 1913, p. 4.

12. Ibid.

13. "Warren's Golden Day," *The* (Warren) *Record*, October 31, 1913, p. 6.

14. "Mr. C. G. Moore," *The* (Warren) *Record*, November 7, 1913, p. 4.

15. Ibid.

16. W. H. Mullins Company, *The Blue and the Gray* (Cleveland: Caxton Company, 1913), p. 14; "Unveiling of Confederate Monument," *The* (Warren) *Record*, October 24, 1913, p. 6.

17. Lewis Waldron Williams, II, *Commercially Produced Forms of American Civil War Monuments* (unpublished, University of Illinois, 1948), p. 2.

18. Ibid., pp. 31–32.

19. Ibid., pp. 28–29.

20. Ibid., pp. 29–30.

21. Ibid., pp. 33–35.

22. SIRIS-Smithsonian Institution Research Information System, http://siris-artinventories.si.edu/ipac20/ipac.jsp?session=1224013I72GK8.94384&profile= (accessed October 14, 2008). Sources cite various Northern commemorations as copies of O'Donovan's Wilmington figure, none of which are well-documented. Many figures are similar, as outlined by Carol A. Grissom, in *Zinc Sculpture in America: 1850–1950* (Newark: University of Delaware Press, 2009), and perhaps this leads to some confusion.

23. L. C. Vass, *Ladies' Memorial Association: Confederate Memorial Addresses, Monday May 11, 1885, New Bern, North* Carolina (Richmond, VA: Whittet and Shepperson, 1886), p. 6; North Carolina Civil War Trails sign, Oakdale Cemetery, Washington, North Carolina.

24. SIRIS-Smithsonian Institution Research Information System, http://siris-artinventories.si.edu/ipac20/ipac.jsp?session=E224P05218915.93887&profile= (accessed October 14, 2008); "Gaddess Collection," Maryland Historical Society, http://www.mdhs.org/findingaid/gaddess-collection-pp68 (accessed June 17, 2011); "Early Patriotic Organizations in Greensboro and Guilford County," *Greensboro Daily News* (undated clipping:

Greensboro Public Library: "Guilford File"); Carol A. Grissom, *Zinc Sculpture in America, 1850–1950* (Newark: University of Delaware Press, 2009), pp. 500, 534. Zinc was a popular, low-cost statuary metal widely used throughout the second half of the nineteenth century. "White Bronze," a proprietary treatment of cast zinc, was produced by the Monumental Bronze Company of Bridgeport, Connecticut, and its seven subsidiaries, including the Philadelphia White Bronze Monument Company, manufacturer of the Goldsboro infantryman. Cast pieces were soldered internally rather than externally to avoid visible seams that would require painting. The smooth outer surface would then be sandblasted to create a carved-stone appearance.

25. Williams, pp. 28–29.
26. "It Is Finished," *The News and Observer*, May 20, 1895, p. 1; SIRIS-Smithsonian Institution Research Information System, http://siris-artinventories.si.edu/ipac20/ipac.jsp?session=1224013I72GK8.94384&profile= (accessed October 14, 2008).
27. SIRIS-Smithsonian Institution Research Information System, http://siris-artinventories.si.edu/ipac20/ipac.jsp?session=Y2Q39968655E8.91572&profile= (accessed October 14, 2008).
28. By the late nineteenth century, middle-class Americans frequently owned reproductions and/or mass-produced art. Nearly 100,000 plaster statuettes by John Rogers were sold between 1860 and 1890, while Currier and Ives prints were displayed in homes throughout the nation. Grissom 17.
29. Williams, p. 42a.
30. Ibid.
31. As quoted by Williams, p. 100.
32. Williams, p. 100; http://www.ohioantiques.com/articles/Mullins/mullins.html (accessed February 9, 2010).
33. http://www.ohioantiques.com/articles/Mullins/mullins.html (accessed February 9, 2010); After Hurricane Hugo blew across North Carolina in 1989, ripping a Mullins statue from its granite pillar in Randolph County (Asheboro, 1911), restoration experts discovered that the stamped infantryman weighed just eighty pounds. Chip Womick, *Remembering Randolph County: Tales from the Center of the Tar Heel State* (Charleston: History, 2008), pp. 73–74.
34. Williams, p. 101.
35. Williams, pp. 101–102; W. H. Mullins Company, *The Blue and the Gray* (Cleveland: Caxton, 1913), pp. 54–71.
36. Williams, pp. 101–102; W. H. Mullins Company, *The Blue and the Gray* (Cleveland: Caxton, 1913), pp. 54–71.
37. Williams, p. 102.
38. As illustrated in Williams, p. 201.
39. Carol A. Grissom, *Zinc Sculpture in America, 1850–1950* (Newark: University of Delaware Press, 2009), pp. 534, 656; illustrations reproduced by Williams, pp. 195–197,208.
40. *Confederate Veteran*, vol. XVII (February 1909) p. 93; see also *Confederate Veteran*, Vol. XVII (March 1909, p. 141, April 1909, p. 189, June 1909, p. 258, July 1909, p. 364, and August 1909, p. 427.
41. Documented Mullins' statues are located in Chatham County (Pittsboro, 1907), Randolph County (Asheboro, 1911), Warren County (Warrenton, 1913), Pitt County (Greenville, 1914), Jackson County (Sylva, 1915), and Stanly County (Albemarle, 1925); American Bronze Foundry figures top monuments in Edgecombe County (Tarboro, 1904), Cleveland County (Shelby, 1907), Burke County (Morganton, 1918), and Caswell County (Yanceyville, 1921).
42. The attributed works are: New Hanover County (Wilmington, 1872 — O'Donovan), Wayne County (Goldsboro, 1883 — Philadelphia White Bronze Monument Company), Wake County (Raleigh, 1895 — von Miller), Tyrrell County (Columbia, 1902 — Monumental Bronze Co.), Cumberland County (Fayetteville, 1902 — I. W. Durham), Anson County (Wadesboro, 1906 — Scoggins), and Orange County (Chapel Hill, 1913 — Wilson). The four soldier figures executed by Italian marble carvers are in Craven County (New Bern, 1885), Macon County (Franklin, 1909), Alamance County (Graham, 1914), and Alexander County (Taylorsville, 1958). Although attribution has not been ascertained, Grissom notes that Bertie County's (Windsor, 1896) soldier statue is "identical" to a widely used Union figure manufactured by the Monumental Bronze Company, with the exception that a "CS" belt buckle has been substituted to denote Confederate allegiance. Grissom, p. 634.
43. "United Daughters of the Confederacy — Winnie Davis Chapter Records," North Carolina State Archives (ORG. 121), signed contract.
44. Grissom states that "Foundry inscriptions for the Monumental Bronze Co. are found only once on a Confederate soldier monument, compared with nearly a third of the company's statues in the North, perhaps because it was undesirable to draw attention to the statue's Northern provenance." Grissom, pp. 492, 529.
45. Williams, p. 2.
46. "The Tomb of the Unknowns," http://www.arlingtoncemetery.mil/VisitorInformation/TombofUnknowns.aspx (accessed October 29, 2012).

Chapter 11

1. "Confederate Monument at Franklin, N.C.," *Confederate Veteran*, vol. XVII (November 1909): pp. 540–541; Weymouth T. Jordan, Jr., *North Carolina Troops: 1861–1865, A Roster*, vol. VI (Raleigh: North Carolina Office of Archives and History, 1977), p. 74.
2. *Confederate Veteran*, vol. XVII (November 1909): pp. 540–541.
3. Ibid.
4. Ibid.; "2 Governors at Unveiling of Monument," Macon County Historical Society, http://www.maconnchistorical.org/rankin/ (accessed March 31, 2008).
5. *Confederate Veteran*, vol. XVII (November 1909): pp. 540–541.
6. Ibid.
7. Ibid.; McNeel's April 1909 advertisement in the *Confederate Veteran* lists thirty-seven monuments erected or under contract. The firm's next ad, in October 1909, added thirteen new commemorations including one in Franklin, N.C.
8. *Confederate Veteran*, vol. XVII (November 1909): pp. 540–541.
9. Ibid.
10. Ibid.
11. Ibid.
12. Ibid.
13. Ibid.
14. *Confederate Veteran*, vol. XVII (April 1909), p. 187.
15. Ibid.
16. Ibid.
17. *Confederate Veteran*, vol. XI (August 1903): p. 383; *Confederate Veteran*, vol. IV (April 1896): p. 136f.

18. *Confederate Veteran,* vol. XV (March 1907): p. 99; Carol A. Grissom, *Zinc Sculpture in America: 1850–1950* (Newark: University of Delaware Press, 2009), pp. 489, 647–648.
19. *Confederate Veteran,* vol. XV (May 1907): p. 240 x; *Confederate Veteran,* vol. XV (March 1907): p. 99.
20. *Confederate Veteran,* vol. XV (May 1907): p. 240 x; *Confederate Veteran,* vol. XV (February 1907): p. 51.
21. *Confederate Veteran,* vol. XX (February 1912): p. 50.
22. W. H. Mullins Company, *The Blue and the Gray: Statues in Stamped Copper and Bronze* (Cleveland: Caxton, 1913), p. 14; Raleigh Marble Works, *Some Work Erected by Raleigh Marble Works: Cooper Brothers, Proprietors, Raleigh, North Carolina* (Raleigh: Edwards and Broughton, undated — although UNC Library copy includes a handwritten notation "1900?" which, if accurate, would predate the two Warren County monuments).
23. Mullins pp. 22, 30.
24. *Confederate Veteran,* vol. XVII (October 1909): p. 528 (back cover).
25. Ibid.
26. *Confederate Veteran,* vol. XVIII (February 1910): p. 96 (back cover).
27. *Confederate Veteran,* vol. XVIII (August 1910): p. 400 (back cover).
28. *Confederate Veteran,* vol. XIX (February 1911): p. 96 (back cover); "M'Neel Marble Company, Marietta, Ga.," *Confederate Veteran,* vol. XVIII (May 1910): p. 252.
29. *Confederate Veteran,* vol. XIX (May 1911): p. 264 (back cover).
30. *Confederate Veteran,* vol. XIX (June 1911): p. 312 (back cover); *Confederate Veteran,* vol. XIX (August 1911): p. 408 (back cover).
31. *Confederate Veteran,* vol. XIX (October 1911): p. 504 (back cover); *Confederate Veteran,* vol. XIX (December 1911): p. 600 (back cover).
32. *Confederate Veteran,* vol. XX (February 1912): p. 96 (back cover).
33. *Confederate Veteran,* vol. XX (April 1912): p. 192 (back cover); *Confederate Veteran,* vol. XX (August 1912): p. 400 (back cover).
34. *Confederate Veteran,* vol. XX (October 1912): p. 492.
35. Quoted from Neal Willis, *Memories of a Lifetime,* by Mary Warshaw, "Beaufort, NC — The Town and Why It's Unique: Confederate Memorial Monument," http://beaufortartist.blogspot.com/2007/10/confederate-memorial-monument.html (accessed January 29, 2011).
36. "Accident Delays Work," *Asheville Weekly Citizen,* March 11, 1898 (Pack Library Clipping file — no page citation).
37. Ibid.
38. "Lee Celebration," *Newton Enterprise,* January 24, 1907 (no page listed).
39. "Locals," *Newton Enterprise,* August 1, 1907 (no page listed); "The Monument Here," *Newton Enterprise,* August 8, 1907 (no page listed).
40. "Locals," *Newton Enterprise,* August 8, 1907 (no page listed).
41. "The Monument Ready for the Unveiling," *Newton Enterprise,* August 15, 1907 (no page listed); "Locals," *Newton Enterprise,* August 8, 1907 (no page listed).
42. Mullins, p. 24; Chip Womick, *Remembering Randolph County: Tales from the Center of the Tar Heel State* (Charleston: History, 2008) pp. 73–74.
43. Quoted by Mac Lackey, Jr., in "Confederate Memorial Loses Grime of 84 Years in Chemical Cleansing," *Statesville Landmark* (Iredell Neighbors), November 8, 1989, p. 3.
44. Quoted from untitled typed document, Iredell County Public Library.
45. *Statesville Landmark,* December 29, 1905 (Quoted from untitled typed document, Iredell County Public Library).
46. Undated, framed postcard, Kinston Visitors Center, Kinston, North Carolina.
47. "McNeel Memorials" (company catalog) (Marietta, GA: McNeel, 1924), pp. 2–3.
48. "The Memorialist: The McNeel Creed Is Still Relevant Today," *The Valdosta Daily Times,* August 8, 2005, http://www.valdostamemorials.com/articles/McCreed.asp (accessed March 1, 2012).

Chapter 12

1. "The Confederate Monument Will Be Unveiled Wednesday, May 13th. Come and Bring Your Friends," *Franklin Times,* May 8, 1914, pp. 1, 7.
2. "Monument Fund Completed," *Franklin Times,* April 3, 1914, p. 1.
3. "U.D.C. Meeting," *Franklin Times,* April 10, 1914, p. 2; "Meeting of the U.D.C.," *Franklin Times,* April 17, 1914, p. 1; "Dinner by U.D.C.," *Franklin Times,* April 17, 1914, p. 7.
4. "Let Everybody Come," *Franklin Times,* April 24, 1914, p. 1; "The Monument," *Franklin Times,* April 24, 1914, p. 6.
5. Untitled notes, *Franklin Times,* May 1, 1914, p. 6.
6. "Confederate Monument Unveiled," *Franklin Times,* May 15, 1914, p. 1.
7. Ibid.; Bands played music as the floats passed. "Annie Laurie" was the musical accompaniment for the first float; "Tenting To-Night" for the second; "Lorena" accompanied the hospital scene; "Old Folks at Home" for the fourth; and "Home, Sweet Home" played as the last float passed. Mrs. C. D. Malone, "The Franklin County Monument," *Confederate Veteran,* vol. XXII (December 1914), p. 537.
8. Ibid.; J. E. Malone, "The First Money Contributed," *Franklin Times,* May 15, 1914, p. 12. At the *Times*' "request," J. E. Malone detailed this initial contribution in a letter published May 15, printed immediately following the newspaper's dedication-day report. Malone, likely a physician, wrote of a widow who had "lost her husband and three sons fighting in the last war." The woman had "an awful looking sore on the side of her face and neck," Malone stated, and "months of treatment" were required for a cure. When healed, the widow returned and "took out two much-used dollar bills" for payment. The physician refused, opting not to "charge her for anything ... because she had furnished too many of her people fighting for the South." She felt "mighty bad" and "began to cry," insisting on paying, Malone said. "Then I told her that the Confederate veterans had appointed me a committee of one to collect money with which to build a monument." The woman reluctantly assented, still preferring to pay the physician directly. Malone took "the two dollars and so appl[ied] it," and thirty years later, "the interest brought it up to five dollars and sixty cents."
9. "Confederate Monument Unveiled," *Franklin Times,* May 15, 1914, p. 1.
10. Ibid.
11. "The Confederate Monument," *Newton Enterprise,* August 15, 1907 (no page listed — from Catawba County Public Library, Newton, N.C., clipping file); "Confeder-

ate Monument Unveiled," *Franklin Times*, May 15, 1914, p. 1.

12. "Confederate Monument Unveiled," *Franklin Times*, May 15, 1914, p. 1.

13. *"The Legacy of the Confederacy* (Raleigh: Edwards and Broughton, 1914); "Confederate Monument Unveiled," *Franklin Times*, May 15, 1914, p. 1.

14. Mrs. C. D. Malone, "The Franklin County Monument," *Confederate Veteran*, vol. XXII (December 1914): p. 537.

15. Ibid.

16. Ibid.

17. "Confederate Monument Unveiled," *Franklin Times*, May 15, 1914, pp. 1, 12.

18. "United Daughters of the Confederacy—Winnie Davis Chapter Records," North Carolina State Archives (ORG. 121) minutes.

19. "Southron" is a nineteenth-century term for Southerner.

20. "Abram Joseph Ryan," Wikipedia, http://en.wikipedia.org/wiki/Abram_J._Ryan (accessed December 15, 2008).

21. "Catholic Encyclopedia (1913)/Father Abram J. Ryan," Wikisource, http://en.wikisource.org/wiki/Catholic_Encyclopedia_1913/Father_Abram_J._Ryan (accessed December 15, 2008).

22. In Asheville, two small unfurled flags are shown on the 1903 cemetery monument in Newton Academy Cemetery. There are, however, few prominent depictions of unfurled Confederate flags until the following decade. Pasquotank County's (Elizabeth City, 1911) monument features one of the earliest such images, a high-relief carving on the front panel showing the battle flag as though blowing in a breeze.

23. Ryan's original words read, "Who bore the flag of our People's trust." "The Poetry of Father Ryan," http://www.flatfenders.com/scv/goodreading.htm (accessed December 16, 2008).

24. These lines are from the middle of the poem's fourth stanza and accurately reflect Tarheel memorial themes. The stanza's other lines, however, include martial imagery—"Out of its scabbard" and "waved sword"—as well as praise of a single individual, "a chief like Lee," themes rarely part of the state's commemorative milieu. These lines are not included on any North Carolina monument.

25. Forsyth's inscription reads:
"Sleeping but glorious,
Dead in Fame's portal,
Dead but victorious,
Dead but immortal,
They gave us great glory,
What more could they give?
They left us a story,
A story to live,"

Blanch Lucas Smith, pp. 95–96; "Confederate Monument at Henderson, N.C., *Confederate Veteran*, vol. XIX (April 1911): pp. 170–171.

26. This quote first appeared in March 1894 and was used until the *Veteran's* final issue, December 1932. *Confederate Veteran*, vol. II #3 (March 1894): p. 65.

27. "The Franklin County Monument," *Confederate Veteran*, vol. XXII (December 1914): p. 537.

28. Ibid. Francis Tiernan, a well-known author, had written the passage for Salisbury's monument. Franklin County's usage, according to the *Confederate Veteran*, was "borrowed by permission of the Salisbury Chapter." A second Franklin County inscription, penned by John Steele Henderson, was also "borrowed by permission," from a similar use in Salisbury: "To the memory of the Confederate soldiers of Franklin County, that their heroic deeds and sublime self-sacrifice may never be forgotten."

29. This "reply" was inscribed contemporaneously with the other inscriptions, not added later. *Minutes of the Tenth Annual Meeting of the North Carolina and Historical Association*, p. 32.

30. The Goldsboro Rifles had erected two monuments prior to 1896—in Goldsboro's Willowdale Cemetery (1883) and on Bentonville Battlefield (1895). The Rifles, however, were a unit of the North Carolina State Guard, not a Confederate veterans' organization, according to Amy Crow, and although many members were "sons of war veterans," a Confederate lineage was not required for membership. Instead, men were selected based on their "wholehearted commitment to their roles as apostles of the New South." Amy Crow, "'In Memory of the Confederate Dead': Masculinity and the Politics of Memorial Work in Goldsboro, North Carolina, 1894–1895," *The North Carolina Historical Review*, vol. LXXXIII (January 2006): pp. 36–37.

31. Mary Louise Medley states, "Smith gave the monument to the Daughters of the Confederacy who placed it on the north lawn of the courthouse," although Medley may have been referring to Anson County's women's monument (1934), which includes an inscription as being from Smith. Mary Louise Medley, *History of Anson County, North Carolina, 1750–1976* (Charlotte: Anson County Historical Society/ Heritage, 1976) p. 218; William Alexander Smith was a wealthy Anson County businessman, farmer, historian, and author, penning, among other works, a 1914 history of the Anson Guards. In the Civil War, Smith held the rank of private before being severely wounded at Malvern Hill in 1862, injuries that required the use of crutches for the rest of his life. He received the title "General" through long service as commander of the North Carolina Division of the United Confederate Veterans; William Powell, *Dictionary of North Carolina Biography*, vol. 5 (Chapel Hill: University of North Carolina Press, 1994) pp. 389–390; Risden Tyler Bennett, an Anson County native, was an attorney who had served as superior court judge, state representative, and U.S. congressman. William Powell, *Dictionary of North Carolina Biography*, vol. 1 (Chapel Hill: University of North Carolina Press, 1979) p. 138; "The Monument Arrives," *Wadesboro Messenger and Intelligencer*, undated clipping, vertical file, Anson County Public Library; "Col. Bennett's Real Eloquence," *Wadesboro Messenger and Intelligencer*, January 20, 1906, p. 1.

32. "Have You Seen This Tombstone Without a Grave?" *Salisbury Post*, January 14, 1939 (clipping file "Salisbury—Cemeteries," Rowan Public Library (no page cited); "Here's Graveless Tombstone Info," *Salisbury Post*, January 15, 1939, p. 5; "The Story of the Graveless Stone Erected to Four Unknown Soldiers," *Salisbury Post*, January 17, 1939 (clipping file "Salisbury—Cemeteries," Rowan Public Library (no page cited). According to the January 15 article, Buis died "40 or more years ago," thereby dating this as a nineteenth-century monument.

33. "Here's Graveless Tombstone Info," *Salisbury Post*, January 15, 1939, p. 5.

Chapter 13

1. Colonel, as used by Horne, is likely a term of respect, a moniker widely used throughout the post–Civil

War South. Grimes was born in 1868, and no record of military service is cited by William Powell, *Dictionary of North Carolina Biography*, vol. 2 (Chapel Hill: University of North Carolina Press, 1986), p. 376; R. D. W. Connor, *Addresses at the Unveiling of the Memorial to the North Carolina Women of the Confederacy* (Raleigh: Edwards and Broughton, 1914), pp. 3–4.
   2. Connor, pp. 3–4.
   3. Ibid.
   4. Connor, pp. 1–4.
   5. Connor, p. 11.
   6. Ibid.
   7. Women apparently were not ashamed of such wartime labor. Hill quotes a "society belle" who wrote of "eleven ladies working in the field with me today," before adding, "I have myself recently hoed 2,500 hills of corn." Connor, pp. 14–19.
   8. Connor, p. 20.
   9. Connor, p. 25.
   10. Connor, pp. 25–26.
   11. Connor, p. 26.
   12. Ibid.
   13. Connor, 7; William Powell, *Dictionary of North Carolina Biography*, vol. 3 (Chapel Hill: University of North Carolina Press, 1988), p. 205.
   14. "Monument to Women of the Confederacy," *Confederate Veteran*, vol. XI (September 1903): p. 415.
   15. "Letter from Chairman Mann," *Confederate Veteran*, vol. XIII (November 1905), p. 493.
   16. "Views of Gen. C. Irvine Walker, Charleston, S.C.," *Confederate Veteran*, vol. XIII (November 1905): pp. 493–494.
   17. "Monument to Confederate Women," *Confederate Veteran*, vol. XVII (April 1909): p. 152.
   18. H. M. Hamill, "Confederate Women's Monument," *Confederate Veteran*, vol. XVII (April 1909): p. 150.
   19. Cynthia Mills, "Gratitude and Gender Wars: Monuments to the Women of the Sixties," *Monuments to the Lost Cause: Women, Art, and the Landscape of Southern Memory* (Knoxville: University of Tennessee Press, 2003), p. 189.
   20. South Carolina (1912), Arkansas (1913), North Carolina (1914), Florida (1915), and the non-seceding border state of Maryland (1918) all erected individually designed monuments to Confederate women. Cynthia Mills, "Gratitude and Gender Wars: Monuments to the Women of the Sixties," *Monuments to the Lost Cause: Women, Art, and the Landscape of Southern Memory* (Knoxville: University of Tennessee Press, 2003), pp. 189–197; William Powell, *Dictionary of North Carolina Biography*, vol. 3 (Chapel Hill: University of North Carolina Press, 1988), p. 205; Connor, p. 4.
   21. William Powell, *Dictionary of North Carolina Biography*, vol. 1 (Chapel Hill: University of North Carolina Press, 1979), pp. 278–279; neither Long nor Mrs. F. M. Williams is included in Powell's six-volume *Dictionary of North Carolina Biography*. Mrs. F.M. Williams of Newton, North Carolina, also used the name Fannie Ransom Williams in an open letter to the U.D.C published in the *Tarborough Southerner* in 1910, in which she urged "not only every chapter but of every Daughter" to answer "the appeal ... from the United Confederate Veterans to aid them in erecting a Monument to the Women of the Confederacy." "United Daughters of the Confederacy," *Tarborough Southerner*, October 20, 1910. Mrs. William's use of her maiden name, Ransom, emphasized her Confederate heritage, her father being Confederate Major General Robert Ransom and her uncle Confederate Brigadier General Matthew W. Ransom, both of North Carolina.

Alvin J. and Janet B. Seippel and Wilda Dellinger Council, *North Carolina Historical Roster 1897–1997: United Daughters of the Confederacy and their Confederate Ancestors of the War Between the States* (Chapel Hill: Chapel Hill Press 1998), pp. 1–2.
   22. "Augustus Lukeman," Wikipedia, http://en.wikipedia.org/wiki/Augustus_Lukeman (accessed December 4, 2011).
   23. Sculptural convention commonly relates a soldier's wartime fate through the horse's stance. According to tradition, when a horse is shown rearing, with both feet off the ground, the depicted soldier has been killed in battle. When a single leg is raised, the rider has been wounded, while a soldier atop a steed with all four feet touching the ground survived uninjured.
   24. Connor, p. 24.
   25. William Powell, *Dictionary of North Carolina Biography*, vol. 5 (Chapel Hill: University of North Carolina Press, 1994), pp. 389–390.
   26. Tara Marie Egan, "The Evolution of Post-World War II Civil War Commemoration: Intersections Between Race and Memory at Harpers Ferry," *Lethbridge Undergraduate Research Journal*, vol. 1, no. 2, 2007.

Chapter 14

   1. *Report of State Commission for Erection of Monument to Ninth New Jersey Volunteers at New Berne, North Carolina* (Published by Authority of the Commission, 1905), pp. 39–43.
   2. Ibid., pp. 43–44.
   3. Ibid., p. 45.
   4. Ibid., pp. 45–46.
   5. Ibid., pp. 46–48.
   6. Ibid., p. 49; William S. Powell, *North Carolina Through Four Centuries* (Chapel Hill: University of North Carolina Press, 1989), pp. 441–442.
   7. *Report of State Commission for Erection of Monument to Ninth New Jersey Volunteers at New Berne, North Carolina* (Published by Authority of the Commission, 1905), p. 51.
   8. Ibid., p. 54.
   9. Ibid., pp. 63–64.
   10. Ibid., p. 31.
   11. Ibid., pp. 63–64.
   12. Ibid., p. 64.
   13. Ibid., pp. 65–74.
   14. Ibid., p. 74.
   15. Ibid., pp. 19, 25–26.
   16. Ibid., pp. 25–26. The monument's cost, however, took the full $5,000.00 appropriation. After awarding the contract, the commission "discovered that there would not be sufficient funds ... to properly dedicate same [the monument] in the manner in which it should be done, it being the desire that the Governor of New Jersey and Staff should participate in the event, and entertain the Governor of North Carolina." Supplemental funding of $1,500.00 was requested and "promptly granted" by the New Jersey legislature. Ibid., p. 20.
   17. Ibid., pp. 77–79.
   18. Ibid., p. 79.
   19. Ibid., pp. 80–83.
   20. Ibid., pp. 83–84.
   21. Ibid., p. 84.
   22. "Historical Information," http://www.cem.va.gov/CEM/cems/nchp/salisbury.asp (accessed November 8, 2011).
   23. "Mt. Auburn Cemetery Reception House Land-

mark Report," http://www2.cambridgema.gov/historic/receptionhouse.html (accessed November 8, 2011); "Historical Information," http://www.cem.va.gov/CEM/cems/nchp/salisbury.asp (accessed November 8, 2011).

24. "Historical Information," http://www.cem.va.gov/CEM/cems/nchp/salisbury.asp (accessed November 8, 2011).

25. *Address of Senator O. H. Platt, of Meriden, Conn., To the Survivors of the Fifteenth Connecticut Volunteers, at the Dedication of Their Monument, at Newbern, N.C. November 14, 1894* (No publisher or date listed—University of North Carolina Library, North Carolina Collection), p. 3.

26. Ibid., pp. 2–5.
27. Ibid., p. 3.
28. Ibid., p. 4.
29. Ibid., pp. 6–7.

30. *Report of State Commission for Erection of Monument to Ninth New Jersey Volunteers at New Berne, North Carolina* (Published by Authority of the Commission, 1905); *Report of the Maine Commissioners on the Monument Erected at Salisbury, N.C., 1908* (Waterville: Sentinel, 1908); James B. Gardner, *Massachusetts Memorial to Her Soldiers and Sailors Who Died in the Department of No. Carolina, 1861*–1865 (Boston: Gardner and Taplin, 1909); *Ceremonies at the Dedication of the Memorial Erected by the Commonwealth of Pennsylvania in the National Cemetery at Salisbury, North* Carolina (C. E. Aughinbaugh, Printer to the State of Pennsylvania, 1912).

31. "Honor Maine's Dead," *Salisbury Post*, May 22, 1907 (no page cited, clipping file, Rowan County Public Library, Salisbury, North Carolina).

32. *Report of State Commission for Erection of Monument to Ninth New Jersey Volunteers at New Berne, North Carolina* (Published by Authority of the Commission, 1905), p. 54; "Monument Dedication Helped Bind Civil War Wounds," *Salisbury Post*, March 30, 1986 (no page cited, clipping file), Rowan County Public Library; *Ceremonies at the Dedication of the Memorial Erected by the Commonwealth of Pennsylvania in the National Cemetery at Salisbury, North* Carolina (C. E. Aughinbaugh, Printer to the State of Pennsylvania, 1912), p. 8.

33. Ibid., pp. 8–10.
34. Ibid., p. 10.
35. Ibid., pp. 8–9.
36. Ibid., pp. 28–29.
37. Ibid., pp. 10–11.
38. Ibid., p. 11.

39. *Report of State Commission for Erection of Monument to Ninth New Jersey Volunteers at New Berne, North Carolina* (Published by Authority of the Commission, 1905), p. 17; *Report of the Maine Commissioners on the Monument Erected at Salisbury, N.C., 1908* (Waterville: Sentinel, 1908), p. 29.

40. The Beaufort Plow Boys, ultimately assigned as Company B, Sixty-first Regiment North Carolina Troops, were recruited in October 1861 in Beaufort County, North Carolina, a jurisdiction adjoining Craven County (New Bern). Originally known as Captain Henry Harding's Independent Company, North Carolina Troops, the Plow Boys mustered into Confederate service at Washington, North Carolina, on November 9, 1861. Weymouth T. Jordan, Jr., *North Carolina Troops 1861–1865 A Roster*, vol. XIV (Raleigh: North Carolina Division of Archives and History, 1998), p. 662; *Report of State Commission for Erection of Monument to Ninth New Jersey Volunteers at New Berne, North Carolina* (Published by Authority of the Commission, 1905), p. 52.

41. *Report of State Commission for Erection of Monument to Ninth New Jersey Volunteers at New Berne, North Carolina* (Published by Authority of the Commission, 1905), p. 52.

42. Ibid., pp. 55–56.
43. Ibid., p. 56.

Chapter 15

1. "For Confederate Memorial," *Wilmington Morning Star*, January 16, 1915 (no page cited) (all Wilmington sources from Reaves Collection, New Hanover County Public Library).

2. The American Civil War Research Database, "Gabriel J. Boney," http://asp6new.alexanderstreet.com/cwdb/cwdb.object.details.aspx?handle=pereson&id=200190229 (accessed April 10, 2012).

3. Ibid.; "For Confederate Memorial," *Wilmington Morning Star*, January 16, 1915 (no page cited), Reaves Collection, New Hanover County Public Library.

4. "Leaves Funds For Monument," *Wilmington Dispatch*, January 21, 1915, no page cited.

5. Ibid.

6. Ann Hewlett Hutteman, "Confederate Mound," unpublished document from Oakdale Cemetery, Wilmington, NC.

7. Catherine W. Bishir, "Landmarks of Power," in W. Fitzhugh Brundage, *Where These Memories Grow: History, Memory, and Southern Identity* (Chapel Hill: University of North Carolina Press, 2000), pp. 142–143.

8. "Request Referred to City Planning Board for Action," *Wilmington Dispatch*, May 24, 1922, no page cited.

9. "Place Confederate Monument at Corner of Third and Dock," *Wilmington Dispatch*, October 6, 1922.

10. "Model of Monument to Confederates Here," *Wilmington Morning Star*, January 28, 1923 (no page cited); "Nearing Completion," *Wilmington Morning Star* September 23, 1923 (no page cited); "Confederate Monument," *Wilmington News-Dispatch* (article summary, part of Reaves Collection, New Hanover County Public Library), May 27, 1924.

11. "Boney Monument Unveiled Today," *Wilmington News-Dispatch*, November 6, 1924 (no page cited).

12. Memorial Monument Soon to Be Erected at Third and Dock," *Morning Star*, March 9, 1924, p. 16; "Boney Monument Unveiled Today," *Wilmington News-Dispatch*, November 6, 1924 (no page cited).

13. Letter dated November 5, 1976, from Leslie N. Boney to Ben Williams, North Carolina Museum of Art, Vertical file, New Hanover County Public Library.

14. "Boney Monument Accepted," *Wilmington Morning Star*, September 14, 1924 (no page cited); "Seeks Information," *Wilmington Morning Star*, September 8, 1924 (no page cited).

15. "Boney Monument Will Be Erected at Third and Dock," *Wilmington Morning Star*, August 29, 1923 (no page cited); "Great Crowd Will Attend Unveiling Memorial Stone," *Wilmington Morning Star* November 5, 1924 (no page cited); "Plans Perfected for Unveiling of Boney Monument," *Wilmington News-Dispatch*, October 30, 1924 (no page cited).

16. "Boney Monument Unveiled Stands a Lasting Tribute to Heroes of Confederacy," *Wilmington Morning Star*, November 7, 1924 (no page cited).

17. Ibid.

18. "General Boyden Urges Change in Pension Law," *Wilmington News-Dispatch*, November 6, 1924, pp. 1, 5.

19. Ibid.; "Boney Monument Unveiled Stands a Lasting Tribute to Heroes of Confederacy," *Wilmington Morning Star*, November 7, 1924 (no page cited).
20. William Powell, *North Carolina Through Four Centuries* (Chapel Hill: University of North Carolina Press, 1989), p. 442.
21. Ibid., p. 449.
22. "Commemorative Landscapes of North Carolina—Unity Monument at Bennett Place Historical Site, Durham," http://docsouth.unc.edu/commland/monument/44/ (accessed August 27, 2012).
23. "A Tribute to the South's Ideal Character, Robert Edward Lee," (Asheville) *Souvenir Magazine*, September 15–20, 1924 (Pack Library, Asheville, North Carolina).
24. "Marking the Dixie Highway," *Confederate Veteran* vol. XXXIV (May 1926), cover, and June 1926, pp. 205, 237; *Souvenir*, September 1924.
25. "Echoes of the Unveiling," (Raleigh) *News and Observer*, May 22, 1895, p. 1.
26. Tom Vincent, "'Evidence of Womans Loyalty, Perseverance, and Fidelity': Confederate Soldiers' Monuments in North Carolina, 1865–1914," *North Carolina Historical Review* vol. LXXXIII no. 1 (January 2006): p. 69.
27. McNeel Marble Company, *McNeel Memorials* (company catalog: no publisher or date).
28. "Unveil Monument Here on Monday," *Beaufort News*, May 6, 1926 (no page cited).
29. "Unveiling Ceremonies Were Attended by Many Veterans," *Durham Morning Herald*, May 11, 1924, p. 1.
30. Ibid.
31. "Confederate Monument Being Erected," *Roxboro Courier*, May 3, 1922, p. 1.
32. "Memorial to Confederate Soldiers Now Stands on Court House Grounds," *Beaufort News*, May 13, 1926, p. 1.
33. Ibid.
34. "Unveil Monument Here on Monday," *Beaufort News*, May 6, 1926 (no page cited); William Powell, *Dictionary of North Carolina Biography*, vol. 2 (Chapel Hill: University of North Carolina Press, 1986), pp. 326–327; "Memorial to Confederate Soldiers Now Stands on Court House Grounds," *Beaufort News*, May 13, 1926, p. 1.
35. "Memorial to Confederate Soldiers Now Stands on Court House Grounds," *Beaufort News*, May 13, 1926, p. 1.

Chapter 16

1. "Forest to Be Memorial to Men of Confederacy," *Asheville Citizen-Times*, July 5, 1942, no page cited (File Folder 285, Pack Memorial Library, Asheville, North Carolina). Unless otherwise noted, all Asheville citations in this chapter are from the Pack Memorial Library, Asheville, North Carolina.
2. "Summary of Cooperative Agreement between the NORTH CAROLINA DIVISION of the UNITED DAUGHTERS of the CONFEDERACY and the FOREST SERVICE, U.S. DEPARTMENT of AGRICULTURE," North Carolina State Archives.
3. Ibid.
4. "Forest to Be Memorial to Men of Confederacy," *Asheville Citizen-Times*, July 5, 1942, no page cited.
5. Ibid.
6. "Memorial Forest to Confederates Will Be Dedicated Sunday," *Asheville Times*, July 7, 1942, no page cited (File Folder 285, Pack Memorial Library, Asheville, North Carolina; "Forest to Be Memorial to Men of Confederacy," *Asheville Citizen-Times*, July 5, 1942, no page cited.
7. "Forest Is Dedicated to N.C. Men of Confederacy," *Asheville Citizen*, July 13, 1942, pp. 1, 3.
8. "Forest Is Dedicated to N.C. Men of Confederacy," *Asheville Citizen*, July 13, 1942, pp. 1, 3; "Memorial Forest to Confederates Will Be Dedicated Sunday," *Asheville Times*, July 7, 1942, no page cited.
9. "Miscegenation Endorsed," (Raleigh) *News and Observer*, February 22, 1895, p. 4; "Forest Is Dedicated to N.C. Men of Confederacy," *Asheville Citizen*, July 13, 1942, pp. 1, 3.
10. "Memorial Forest to Confederates Will Be Dedicated Sunday," *Asheville Times*, July 7, 1942, no page cited.
11. Ibid.; "Forest to Be Memorial to Men of Confederacy," *Asheville Citizen-Times*, July 5, 1942, no page cited.
12. "Forest Is Dedicated to N.C. Men of Confederacy," *Asheville Citizen*, July 13, 1942, p. 1, 3; "Beech Gap Marker Dedicated," *Asheville Citizen-Times*, August 12, 1956, no page cited (File Folder 285, Pack Memorial Library, Asheville, North Carolina).
13. Personal communication, Jackie Holt, museum curator, Blue Ridge Parkway Archives.
14. Bronze plaques were significantly less expensive than earlier monuments. The two "large granite and bronze markers" that denoted North Carolina's borders along the Jefferson Davis Highway cost $200.00 each, according to Smith, while in Halifax County (Halifax, 1929), an ornate courthouse-lawn bronze "plate" honoring Confederate General Junius Daniel, erected by the U.D.C. in cooperation with the State Historical Commission, cost $300.00. Blanche Lucas Smith, *North Carolina's Confederate Monuments and Memorials* (Raleigh: North Carolina Division, United Daughters of the Confederacy, 1941), pp. 17, 90.
15. "Distinctive Tablets in Bronze" (advertisement), *Confederate Veteran*, vol. XX (May 1912): pp. 256, xi; "Woodland Bronze Works," (advertisement), *Confederate Veteran*, vol. XX (July 1912): p. 350; "Bronze Memorial Tablets" (advertisements), *Confederate Veteran*, vol. XX (October 1912): p. 492.
16. Blanche Lucas Smith, *North Carolina's Confederate Monuments and Memorials* (Raleigh: North Carolina Division, United Daughters of the Confederacy, 1941), pp. 112–113.
17. Ibid., p. 12.
18. "U.D.C. Will Unveil Monument June 3," *Forest City Courier*, May 19, 1932, p. 1; "Unveil Monument Here June 3," *Forest City Courier*, May 26, 1932, p. 1; "U.D.C. Chapter to Dedicate Marker Here Friday P.M.," *Forest City Courier*, June 2, 1932, p. 1.
19. "'Burnt Chimney' Men First to Leave in 1861," *Forest City Courier*, June 2, 1932, no page cited.
20. Ibid.
21. "Dedicate Monument in Impressive Ceremony," *Forest City Courier*, June 9, 1932, p. 5.
22. Ibid.
23. Ibid.
24. Blanche Lucas Smith, *North Carolina's Confederate Monuments and Memorials* (Raleigh: North Carolina Division, United Daughters of the Confederacy, 1941), pp. 121–122.
25. Ibid., p. 19.
26. Ibid., p. 36.
27. *History of the Wake County Ladies' Memorial Association* (Raleigh: n.p., 1938), p. 15.
28. Ibid., pp. 32–43. Two other Civil War–related plaques detail North Carolina's contribution of "127,000 to this war from a military population of 115,369" and

the state's efforts "In the Last Year of the War" to provision its troops and feed "General Lee's Army." The other plaques commemorate "North Carolina soldiers and sailors living and dead," and their role in all wars; two commemorate the American Revolution; a fourth memorializes "Soldiers and Sailors who laid down their lives" in the War of 1812, the Mexican War, and the Spanish-American War; one is titled "North Carolina in the World War;" while another is "To the Mothers" of Tarheel troops.

29. Five additional names are inscribed across the bottom of the monument. These five names, like the other eighty-nine, are inscribed without further identification and may represent veterans' names omitted during the initial carving or members of the monument committee.

30. "Marker in Honor of Cherokee Indian Soldiers to Be Unveiled Today," *Asheville Citizen-Times*, September 29, 1935, no page listed (from clipping file, Pack Memorial Public Library, Asheville, North Carolina).

31. Blanche Lucas Smith, *North Carolina's Confederate Monuments and Memorials* (Raleigh: North Carolina Division, United Daughters of the Confederacy, 1941), pp. 72–75; "Marker in Honor of Cherokee Indian Soldiers to Be Unveiled Today," *Asheville Citizen-Times*, September 29, 1935, no page listed; William Powell, *Dictionary of North Carolina Biography*, vol. 6 (Chapel Hill: University of North Carolina Press, 1996), p. 25; "The Civil War: Little Will's Cherokee Legion," *Our State*, September 2012, p. 71.

32. "First District North Carolina Division United Daughters of the Confederacy," Annual Meeting Program (from clipping file, Pack Memorial Public Library, Asheville, North Carolina); "The Civil War: Little Will's Cherokee Legion," *Our State*, September 2012, pp. 61–72; William Powell, *Dictionary of North Carolina Biography*, vol. 6 (Chapel Hill: University of North Carolina Press, 1996), p. 25.

33. Blanche Lucas Smith, *North Carolina's Confederate Monuments and Memorials* (Raleigh: North Carolina Division, United Daughters of the Confederacy, 1941), pp. 72–75; "Marker in Honor of Cherokee Indian Soldiers to Be Unveiled Today," *Asheville Citizen-Times*, September 29, 1935, no page listed.

34. "The Civil War: Little Will's Cherokee Legion," *Our State*, September 2012, p. 72.

35. "Fort Fisher Monument Bill Surprises U.D.C.," *Wilmington Star*, April 10, 1930, no page cited (all Wilmington newspapers from Reaves Collection, New Hanover County Public Library); "Marker Planned for Ft. Fisher," *Wilmington News*, May 6, 1930, no page cited.

36. William Powell, *Dictionary of North Carolina Biography*, vol. 5 (Chapel Hill: University of North Carolina Press, 1994), p. 347.

37. "Ft. Fisher Memorial Marker Design Approved by U.D.C.," *Wilmington News*, October 15, 1931, no page cited; "Work on Marker to Start Soon," *Wilmington News*, November 23, 1931 (no page cited). The *News* may have been using some hyperbole. Johnson might have physically constructed the Gettysburg monument, but the bronze figures were executed by Gutzon Borglum, one of the nation's most-renowned sculptors whose works include the bronze of Henry Lawson Wyatt on the North Carolina Capitol grounds in Raleigh and the presidential likenesses at Mount Rushmore.

38. "Urges Carolina Granite Be Used in Monument," *Wilmington Star*, December 7, 1931 (no page cited); "Memorial Shaft Work Is Started," *Wilmington News*, December 16, 1931 (no page cited).

39. "May Dedicate Marker June 3," *Wilmington News*, March 8, 1932 (no page cited); "Work Started on Monument," *Wilmington News*, April 28, 1932 (no page cited).

40. "Visitors Here for Program at Fort," *Wilmington Star*, June 1, 1932 (no page cited); "Unveiling of Fort Fisher Monument June 2, 1932," event program (no publication information listed), from the North Carolina Collection, University of North Carolina Library, Chapel Hill, North Carolina.

41. The *News* reported that "the Star Spangled Banner" opened the ceremony, however two other sources, the official program and the *Star*, report that "America" was the opening number. "Heroic Work of Defenders Lauded in Stirring Talks by Gardner and Mrs. Long," *Wilmington News*, June 2, 1932, pp. 1, 9; "Fall of Fort Fisher Fatal Blow to the Confederate Commissariat, Governor Gardner Says in Address," *Wilmington News*, June 2, 1932, no page cited; "Spirit of Dixie Prevails as U.D.C. Unveil Shaft to Heroic Ft. Fisher Dead," *Wilmington Star*, June 3, 1932, no page cited.

42. "Mrs. Long Extolls Spirit of Defenders," *Wilmington News*, June 2, 1932, no page cited; "South's Numerous Monuments Cited," *Wilmington Star*, June 3, 1932, no page cited.

43. "Staunch Rebels," *Wilmington Star*, June 3, 1932, no page cited.

Chapter 17

1. From bronze plaque on Alexander County Confederate monument, Taylorsville, North Carolina. Full text reads: "The young man who adorns this pedestal was killed at Gettysburg, July 3, 1863. Perhaps his dying lips were murmuring: 'Oh, fate of the just, thou gavest me this bitter cup, and I bow to thy behest and drink it up.' He was a lad of 'the Old South' whose name is known but to me. 'How bravely her sons can say farewell.'" Additional details from "Confederate Monument Graces Courthouse Lawn," *Taylorsville Times*, October 1, 1959 (no page cited).

2. Personal communication, Danny Lentz, Taylorsville, North Carolina.

3. "Confederate Monument Graces Courthouse Lawn," *Taylorsville Times*, October 1, 1959 (no page cited).

4. "North Carolina — Presidential Election Returns — 1860," http://members.aol.com/jweaver303/nc/prezlec.htm (accessed May 3, 2007).

5. "Confederate Monument Graces Courthouse Lawn," *Taylorsville Times*, October 1, 1959 (no page cited).

6. Ibid.

7. Michael Hardy, *Remembering North Carolina's Confederates* (Charleston, SC: Arcadia, 2006), p. 25; also from the plaque under the cannon which reads, "Picket's [sic] Charge. At 2:00 o'clock P.M. the belch and roar of this Jones six-pounder ceased and out of the grove on Seminary Ridge, Gettysburg, marched the bravest body of infantry that ever careered the fields of battle, to hurl itself against the Union batteries on Cemetery Ridge, only to be annihilated in a blaze of glory that will glow undimmed throughout the rolling flood of endless ages." Decades later a vertical granite slab was added west of the cannon. The south face is inscribed, "Remembering the 'Alexander County Boys' 1861–1865 These Men Gave Their All." "HONOR" and "VALOR," with letters placed vertically, adorn the narrow sides, while names of more than three hundred Alexander County Confederate dead fill the north face.

8. Personal communication, Danny Lentz, Taylors-

ville, North Carolina, based in part on excerpts from *Lentz Heritage*, by John Paul Lentz.

9. Weymouth T. Jordan, Jr., *North Carolina Troops: 1861–1865, A Roster*, vol. VIII (Raleigh: North Carolina Office of Archives and History, 1981), p. 242.

10. Ibid.; personal communication, Danny Lentz, Taylorsville, North Carolina, based in part on excerpts from *Lentz Heritage*, by John Paul Lentz.

11. Personal communication, Stratton Murrell, Onslow County Historical Society.

12. "Mrs. Long Extolls Spirit of Defenders," *Wilmington News*, June 2, 1932, no page cited (from Reaves Collection, New Hanover County Public Library, Wilmington, North Carolina).

Bibliography

Address and Poem: Delivered at the Unveiling of the Monument Erected to the Memory of the Confederate Dead of Warren County, North Carolina, August 27, 1903. Raleigh: Edwards and Broughton, 1906.

Address of Senator O. H. Platt, of Meriden, Conn., to the Survivors of the Fifteenth Connecticut Volunteers, at the Dedication of their Monument, at Newbern, N.C. November 14, 1894. N.p., n.d.

Arnett, Ethel Stephens. *Greensboro North Carolina: The County Seat of Guilford.* Chapel Hill: University of North Carolina Press, 1955.

Ashe, Samuel A'Court. *History of North Carolina: Volume I from 1584 to 1783.* Greensboro: Charles L. Van Noppen, 1908.

Ashe, Samuel A'Court. *History of North Carolina: Volume II from 1783 to 1925.* Raleigh: Edwards and Broughton, 1925.

Bagley, Dudley. *The Joseph Knapp I Knew.* Unpublished manuscript, 1964. Currituck County Library.

Behan, Mrs. William J. *History of the Confederated Memorial Associations of the South.* New Orleans: Graham, 1904.

Bishir, Catherine W. "'A Strong Force of Ladies': Women, Politics, and Confederate Memorial Associations in Nineteenth-Century Raleigh." *The North Carolina Historical Review,* Vol. 77, No. 4 (October 2000): 455–491.

Blair, William A. *Cities of the Dead: Contesting the Memory of the Civil War in the South, 1865–1914.* Chapel Hill: University of North Carolina Press, 2004.

Blight, David W. *Race and Reunion: The Civil War in American Memory.* Cambridge, MA: Harvard University Press, 2001.

Brundage, W. Fitzhugh, ed. *Where These Memories Grow: History, Memory, and Southern Identity.* Chapel Hill: University of North Carolina Press, 2000.

Burwell, Armistead. *The Ideal Confederate Soldier: Address by Judge Armistead Burwell; Unveiling Confederate Monument.* Cornelius, N.C.: N.p., 1910.

Caldwell County, N.C. In the Great War of 1861–5 On the Occasion of the Unveiling of the Monument to the Confederate Soldiers from Caldwell County at Lenoir, June 3, 1910. Hickory, NC: Clay, 1910.

Censer, Jane Turner. *The Reconstruction of White Southern Womanhood, 1865–1900.* Baton Rouge: Louisiana State University Press, 2003.

Ceremonies at the Dedication of the Memorial: Erected by the Commonwealth of Pennsylvania in the National Cemetery at Salisbury, North Carolina, 1910. C.E. Aughinbaugh, Printer to the State of Pennsylvania, 1912.

Clark, Walter. *Address by Walter Clark About Randolph County Soldiers in the Great War 1861–1865.* No publication information listed.

_____, editor. *Histories of the Several Regiments and Battalions from North Carolina in the Great War 1861–'65.* (Five volumes). Raleigh: E. M. Uzzell, 1901.

Cobb, William T., Joseph L. Small, and Thomas G. Libby. *Report of the Maine Commissioners on the Monument Erected at Salisbury, N.C., 1908.* Waterville, ME: Sentinel, 1908.

Confederate Veteran. Volumes I–XL, 1893–1932.

Conner, R. D. W. *Addresses at the Unveiling of the Memorial to the North Carolina Women of the Confederacy.* Raleigh: Edwards and Broughton, 1914.

_____. *North Carolina: Rebuilding an Ancient Commonwealth, 1584–1925.* (Four volumes) Chicago and New York: American Historical Society, 1929.

Cooper Brothers. *Some Work Erected by Raleigh Marble Works: Cooper Brothers, Proprietors, Raleigh, North Carolina.* Raleigh: Edwards and Broughton, n.d.

Corbitt, David Leroy. D. L. Corbitt Papers. North Carolina State Archives, Raleigh.

_____. *The Formation of the North Carolina Counties 1663–1943.* Raleigh: North Carolina Division of Archives and History, 1987.

Cornerstone of Confederate Monument Laid. Oxford, NC: Granville Grays Chapter, United Daughters of the Confederacy, 1909.

Cox, Karen L. *Dixie's Daughters: The United Daughters of the Confederacy and the Preservation of Confederate Culture.* Gainesville: University of Florida Press, 2003.

Craig, Locke. *The Legacy of the Confederacy: Speech delivered by Governor Locke Craig, accepting the Monument to the Women of the Confederacy, on the occasion of the unveiling at Raleigh, North Carolina, June 10, 1914.* Raleigh: Edwards and Broughton, 1914.

Crawford, Martin. *Ashe County's Civil War: Community and Society in the Appalachian South.* Charlottesville: University Press of Virginia, 2001.

Crow, Amy. "'In Memory of the Confederate Dead': Masculinity and the Politics of Memorial Work in Goldsboro, North Carolina, 1894–1895." *The North Carolina Historical Review,* Vol. 83, No. 1 (January 2006): 31–60.

Davis, Stephen. "Empty Eyes, Marble Hand: The Confederate Monument and the South." *Journal of Popular Culture* 16:3: 2–21.

Egan, Tara Marie. "The Evolution of Post–World War II

Civil War Commemoration: Intersections Between Race and Memory at Harper's Ferry," *Lethbridge Undergraduate Research Journal*, vol. 1, no. 2, 2007.

Emerson, Mrs. B. A. C. *Historic Southern Monuments: Representative Memorials of the Heroic Dead of the Southern Confederacy*. New York: Neale, 1911.

Foster, Gaines M. *Ghosts of the Confederacy: Defeat, the Lost Cause, and the Emergence of the New South, 1865–1913*. New York: Oxford University Press, 1987.

Fuzzlebug, Fritz. *Prison Life During the Rebellion: The Miseries and Sufferings of Six Hundred Confederate Prisoners*. Singer's Glen, VA: Joseph Funk's Sons, 1869.

Gardner, James Brown. *Massachusetts Memorial to Her Soldiers and Sailors Who Died in the Department of No. Carolina 1861–1865*. Boston: Gardner and Taplin, 1909.

Grissom, Carol A. *Zinc Sculpture in America: 1850–1950*. Newark: University of Delaware Press, 2009.

Hardy, Michael. *Remembering North Carolina's Confederates*. Charleston, SC: Arcadia, 2006.

Hardy, Michael C. *A Short History of Watauga County*. Boone, NC: Parkway, 2005.

History of the Wake County Ladies Memorial Association. Raleigh: n.p., 1938.

Horwitz, Tony. *Confederates in the Attic: Dispatches from the Unfinished Civil War*. New York: Pantheon, 1998.

Inscoe, John C., and Gordon B. McKinney. *The Heart of Confederate Appalachia: Western North Carolina in the Civil War*. Chapel Hill: University of North Carolina Press, 2000.

Janney, Caroline E. *Burying the Dead but Not the Past: Ladies' Memorial Associations and the Lost Cause*. Chapel Hill: University of North Carolina Press, 2008.

Jordan, Weymouth T. *North Carolina Troops 1861–1865 A Roster*. (Seventeen volumes) Raleigh: Office of Archives and History, 1979–2003.

A Little History of the Monument in Honor of the Confederate Veterans from Caldwell County, N.C. Unveiled at Lenoir, June 3, 1910. N.p., n.d.

Mason, T. W. *Address of Hon. T. W. Mason, before the Ladies' Memorial Association, at the Laying of the Corner-stone of the Confederate Monument, Raleigh, N.C., May 20, 1895*. Raleigh: E. M. Uzzell, 1898.

McLeod, R. A. *Historical Sketch of Long Street Presbyterian Church 1756 to 1923*. Fort Bragg Archaeology Division (courtesy of Linda Carnes-McNaughton, Ph.D.).

McNeel Marble Company. *McNeel Memorials*. (Company catalog) Marietta, GA: N.p., 1924.

Medley, Mary Louise. *History of Anson County, North Carolina, 1750–1976*. Charlotte: Anson County Historical Society/Heritage, 1976.

Mills, Cynthia, and Pamela H. Simpson, eds. *Monuments to the Lost Cause: Women, Art, and the Landscapes of Southern Memory*. Knoxville: University of Tennessee Press, 2003.

Minutes of the Eleventh Annual Meeting of the United Daughters of the Confederacy, Held in St. Louis, Mo., October 4–8, 1904. Nashville: Press of Foster and Webb, 1905.

Minutes of the Tenth Annual Meeting of the United Daughters of the Confederacy, Held in Charleston, S.C., November 11–14, 1903. Nashville: Press of Foster and Webb, 1904.

North Carolina Civil War Monuments. 2011 http//www.ncmonuments.ncdcr.gov/.

Pinnix, Frank M. *Corner Stone of Confederate Monument Laid*. Oxford, NC: Orphanage, n.d.

Powell, William S. *North Carolina Through Four Centuries*. Chapel Hill: University of North Carolina Press, 1989.

_____, ed. *Dictionary of North Carolina Biography*. (Six volumes) Chapel Hill: University of North Carolina Press, 1979–1996.

_____, ed. *Encyclopedia of North Carolina*. Chapel Hill: University of North Carolina Press, 2006.

Programme at the Unveiling of North Carolina's Monument at Appomattox, April 10, 1905. No publication information listed.

Report of State Commission for Erection of Monument to Ninth New Jersey Volunteers at New Berne, North Carolina. Philadelphia: International, 1905.

Report of the Maine Commissioners on the Monument Erected at Salisbury, N.C., 1908. Waterville: Sentinel, 1908.

Report of the New Bern Monument Commission made to the General Assembly at its January Session, 1910. Providence: E.L. Freeman, 1910.

Rosenberg, R. B. *Living Monuments: Confederate Soldiers' Homes in the New South*. Chapel Hill: University of North Carolina Press, 1993.

Savage, Kirk. *Standing Soldiers, Kneeling Slaves: Race, War, and Monument in Nineteenth-Century America*. Princeton: Princeton University Press, 1997.

Seippel, Alvin J. and Janet B., and Wilda Dellinger Council. *North Carolina Historical Roster 1897–1997: United Daughters of the Confederacy and their Confederate Ancestors of the War Between the States*. Chapel Hill: Chapel Hill Press, 1998.

SIRIS-Smithsonian Institution Research Information System. 2008 http://www.siris-artinventories.si.edu/.

Smith, Blanche Lucas. *North Carolina's Confederate Monuments and Memorials*. Raleigh: NC Division, United Daughters of the Confederacy, 1941.

Trotter, William R. *Bushwhackers! The Civil War in North Carolina: Vol. II The Mountains*. Greensboro, NC: Signal Research, 1988.

Unveiling of Fort Fisher Monument June 2, 1932. No publication information listed.

Vass, L. C. *Ladies' Memorial Association: Confederate Memorial Addresses, Monday May 11, 1885, New Bern, North Carolina*. Richmond, VA: Whittet and Shepperson, 1886.

Vincent, Tom. "'Evidence of Womans Loyalty, Perseverance, and Fidelity': Confederate Soldiers' Monuments in North Carolina, 1865–1914." *The North Carolina Historical Review*, Vol. 83, No. 1 (January 2006): 61–90.

W. H. Mullins Company. *The Blue and the Gray: Statues in Stamped Copper and Bronze*. Cleveland: Caxton, 1913.

Waddell, Alfred Moore. *Address at the Unveiling of the Confederate Monument, at Raleigh, N.C., May 20th, 1895*. Wilmington, NC: LeGwin Bros., 1895.

Walker, James D. *Ceremonies at the Dedication of the Memorial Erected by the Commonwealth of Pennsylvania in the National Cemetery at Salisbury, North Carolina*. Pennsylvania State Printer: C. E. Aughinbaugh, 1912.

Warner, Ezra J. *Generals in Gray: Lives of the Confederate Commanders*. Baton Rouge: Louisiana State University Press, 1959.

Widdemer, Margaret. *The Monument to the Women of the Confederacy*. No publisher, 1914.

Widener, Ralph W. *Confederate Monuments: Enduring Symbols of the South and the War Between the States*. Dallas: R. W. Widener, 1982.

Williams, Lewis Waldron, II. *Commercially Produced Forms of American Civil War Monuments*. Unpublished master's thesis, University of Illinois, 1948.

Winberry, John J. "'Lest We Forget' The Confederate Monument and the Southern Townscape." *Southeastern Geographer* 31 (November 1983): 107–121.

Index

Page numbers in **_bold italics_** indicate illustrations.

African American soldiers' monument *see* United States Colored Troops monument
African Americans 3, 11, 24, 47–49, 95, 123, 174, 195, 218; faithful slaves 122–123, **_164_**, 174; memory 20, 28; United States Colored Troops monument 2, **_186_**, 230
Alamance County 118, 122, **_148_**–149, 159, 222
Albemarle **_106_**, 159, 162, 225; *see also* Stanly County
Alexander County 213, **_214–215_**, 218, 222, 235
Alford, Captain G. B. 53–54, 195–**_196_**, 203, 226
Alleghany County 52, 235
Allen, Captain Thomas M. 33–**_35_**, 36–40; *see also* Immortal 600
Amateis, Louis 169–170
"America" (song) 69, 119, 130, 142, 201, 204, 206, 209, 211, 217, 248
American Bronze Foundry (Chicago) 84, **_108_**, **_138_**–139, 196, 242
Anson County: soldiers' monument **_132_**, 164, 173, 222; women's monument 160, **_172–173_**, 174, 206, 222
Anson Guards (Co. C, Fourteenth North Carolina Regiment) 72, 164, **_173_**–174, 206
Appomattox (North Carolina monument) 237
Arlington National Cemetery 91, 140, 157
Army of Northern Virginia 63, 77, 186, 189
Ashe, Samuel A. 78
Ashe County 59–60, 235
Asheboro **_116_**, 118, 129, **_139_**, 150, 162, 225, 242; *see also* Randolph County
Asheville 57–58, 60–61, 63–66, 69, 71–72, 84, 104, 119, 193, 200–202, 209, 222; Creasman monument 68–69, **_73_**, 76; Creasman monument 68–69, 76; Monumental Day 58, 66–**_67_**, **_69_**–71, 76–77, 119, 164, 222; Vance monument 57–58, 149, 153; *see also* Buncombe County
Asheville Chapter, United Daughters of the Confederacy 62–63, 66, **_68_**
Ashford-Sillers Chapter, United Daughters of the Confederacy **_125_**
Averasboro: battle 17; monument 15–**_16_**, 19, 24, 147, 223
Avery, A. C. 78–79
Avery County 235
Aycock, Gov. Charles 82–83

Bacon, Henry 167, 172, 189–191
Barbee, W. G. 12
Barbee House (High Point, NC) 12
Barre (VT) Granite 149, 151, 177
"The Battle of Alexandria" (poem) 162
Battle of Bentonville Chapter, United Daughters of the Confederacy **_208_**
Bayboro 64, **_205_**, 224; *see also* Pamlico County
Beaufort 149, 196, **_199_**, 222; *see also* Carteret County
Beaufort County 1888 soldiers' monument 33–**_34_**, **_35_**, 36, 50, 134, 202, 222; 1905 COC monument **_93_**–94, 202, 222
Beaufort Plow Boys (Co. B, Sixty-first North Carolina Regiment) 72, 186–187, 246
Beckham, Virgil Gustavius "Gus" 213–215, 218, 222
Beecher, Henry Ward 11, 46
Bennett, Col. Risden Tyler 164, 222, 244
Bennett Place: monument 193; surrender site 5, 7, 14; Unity Gate 193
Bentonville, battle of 4, 13, 27, 31, **_38_**, 67, 69, 160, 175, 188, 224, 227
Bertie County 40, 85, **_157_**, 164, 222, 236, 239, 242
Bethel Baptist Church Cemetery (Buncombe County, Creasman monument) **_76_**

Bickett, Gov. Thomas W. 153–154, 156, 224–225
Biltmore House 61
"Bivouac of the Dead" (poem) 9, 32, 157, 159
"black mammy" 154, 173–174; proposed statue 174
Bladen County 236
Blandford Church (Petersburg, VA) 12, 72
Blue Pearl Granite Company (Winston-Salem, NC) 150, 225
Blue Ridge Parkway 200–**_201_**, 223
Bolivar, Tennessee (monument) 29
Bond, William R. 78
Bond School House 60
Boney, James Gabriel 188–192, 224
"The Bonnie Blue Flag" (song) 119
Boone 104; *see also* Watauga County
Borglum, Gutzon 77, 248
Bourne, Judge Henry Clay 80–83
Boyden, A. H. 184–185, 191–192, 224
Branch, Gen. Lawrence O'Bryan 13, 42, 234
Branch, Mrs. Lawrence O'Bryan (Nancy Haywood Blount Branch) 13, 17, 42, 48
Brunswick County 236, 239
Buis, John 165, 225
Buncombe County 57, 70–72, 164, 239; Clingman monument **_73_**; Co. I Twenty-fifth North Carolina Regiment monument (Thrash monument) **_59_**, 164, 222; Creasman monument **_76_**; Newton Academy Cemetery monument 62–**_63_**, 222; Sixtieth North Carolina Regiment monument; 66, **_67–68_**, **_69_**, 70 164; 222; Vance monument 57–58, 66, 149, 193
Burgaw: Co. K monument **_156_**, 225; soldiers' monument 121, **_123_**, 125–126, 224; *see also* Pender County
Burgywn, H. S. 170
Burke County 60, 72, 106–**_108_**, 119, 124, 131, 158, 165, 222, 238–240, 242

Burnt Chimney *see* Forest City
Butler, Marion 47–48, 54

Cabarrus County **40**, 90, 222, 239
"The Cadets at New Market" (poem) 161
Caldwell County 60, 104, 120–***121***, 123–126, 147, 160, 222, 235, 239
Calvary Episcopal Church (Fletcher, NC) 193
Camden County 236
Cape Fear Camp, United Confederate Veterans 188, 190
Cape Fear Chapter, United Daughters of the Confederacy 189, 191, 239
"Carolina" (song) 130
Carolina Marble and Granite Company (Statesville, NC) 100, 150–151, 224
Carr, Gov. Elias 42, 48, 53
Carr, Julian S. 53, 82–83, 85, 166, 197, 223–225
Carrara Marble **8**, 21, ***23***, 134, 139
Carteret County 149, 196–***199***, 222, 236
Caswell County ***138***, 161, 196, 222, 242
Catawba County 116–***118***, 119, 122–123, 125, 149, 159, 222, 235, 239
Cedar Grove Cemetery (New Bern) 12, 14, 21–***22***, 177
Chapel Hill 8, ***140***, 224; *see also* Orange County
"Charge of the Light Brigade" (poem) 155, 161
Charles L. Robinson Camp, United Confederate Veterans 141–***142***
Charlotte ***30***, 32, 58, 61, 84, 210, 224; *see also* Mecklenburg County
Charlotte Ladies' Memorial Association 30, 32
Chatham County 91–92, 99–***101***, 102–***103***, 121, 123, 125, 156, 157, 159, 222, 239, 241
Cheraw, South Carolina (monument) 29, 39–40
Cherokee County 235
Cherokee Indians 208–209; monument 205, 208–***210***, 225
Cherokee Marble Works 68, ***70***–71, 222
Chicora Cemetery 15–***16***, 19; *see also* Averasboro
Children of the Confederacy 68, 71, 73, 77, 118, 146, 191, 198–199, 202–203, 207, 238; founding 93–94
Chowan County 64, ***86***, 99, 103, 162, 222, 227, 236, 239
Christian, Judge George L. 78
Christian, Julia Jackson 42, 54
Clark, Gov. Henry T. 81, 83
Clark, Chief Justice Walter 78, 108, 120–122, 222, 224–225
Clay County 74, 235
Cleveland County 64, 124, ***162***, 222, 235, 239, 242
Clingman, Gen. Thomas 13, 68, 70, 72, 170; monument 68–69 ***73***, 76

Clinton ***125***, ***137***, 199, 225; *see also* Sampson County
Cockade Marble Works (Petersburg, VA) 80, 223
Coke, Captain Octavius 44
collective memory 24–29, 40, 78, 218–219
Columbia (NC) 85, ***144***–145, ***164***, 172, 174, 225, 239, 242; *see also* Tyrrell County
Columbus (NC) 60; *see also* Polk County
Columbus County ***218***, 222, 236
Columbus (GA) Ladies' Memorial Association 14
Concord ***40***, 90, 222, 239; *see also* Cabarrus County
Confederate regimental battle flags 21, 23, 141; repatriation of 88, 182
Confederate Veteran: history of 88–90
Confederate Women's monument (Raleigh) 166–***168***, 169–172
Confederate Women's monument (Wadesboro) 160, ***172***–***173***, 174, 206, 222
Connecticut monument (New Bern National Cemetery) 177, 180–***181***, 182, 230
Connor, R. D. W. 166, 170
"The Conquered Banner" (poem) 118, 141, 143, 158, 208
Cooper Brothers 128, 145, 224–226
Coulter, George E. (monument builder) 149, 222
county appropriations (for monument building) 106–107, 141
Cox, Gen. Albert 197, 223, 226
Cox, Gen. William R. 42, 72, 83
Craig, Gov. Locke 71, 118, 122, 136, 153, 155, 168, 171–172, 222–223, 225
Craven County ***23***, 50, 91, 134, 222, 230, 236, 242, 246; *see also* New Bern
Creasman, Col. William B. 68–69, ***76***
Cross Creek Cemetery (Fayetteville) 7–***8***, ***9***, 15, 40, 57
Cumberland County **8**, 15, ***133***, 135, 159, 162, 223, 232, 239, 242; *see also* Fayetteville
Cunningham, Sumner Archibald 88–90
Currituck 64, ***110***, 223; *see also* Currituck County
Currituck County 52, 64, ***110***, 223, 238; monument construction first phase 108–109; monument construction, second phase 109–111

D. A. R. *see* Daughters of the American Revolution
D. H. Hill Chapter, United Daughters of the Confederacy 109
Daniels, Josephus 47, 54, 57, 122, 197, 201–202, 223, 225
Dare County 236

Darst, Bishop Thomas C. 203, 211, 223
Daughters of the American Revolution 194, 203, 226
Daves, Mrs. E. B. 22–24
Davidson County ***160***–161, 223
Davie County 235
Davis, George (Confederate Attorney General) 76; monument 189–190
Davis, President Jefferson 10, 57, 74–76, 81, 91, 206, 211, 232
Davis-Dickerson-Mills Chapter, United Daughters of the Confederacy 89
Dimitry, John 160
"dishonored graves" 11, 46, 84, 181, 217
"Dixie" (song) 57, 82–83, 108, 115, 119, 130, 142, 153, 202, 204, 217
Dixie-Lee Chapter, Children of the Confederacy (Tarboro) 77
Dixie-Lee Highway 193, 203, 235
Douglass, Frederick 49–50
Duplin County 91, 188, 207, 236; Faison monument 165, ***206***, 223
Durham 3, 14, 53, 76, 100, 145, 166, 185, 193, 201; monument ***151***–152, 196–197, 223; *see also* Durham County
Durham, I. W. 135, 223
Durham County ***151***–152, 196–197, 223
Durham Marble Works 129, 145–146, 222

Eclectic Club (Greensboro) 13, 30–31
Edenton 64, ***86***, 99, 103 162, 222, 227, 239; *see also* Chowan County
Edgecombe County 42, 236; cemetery gate ***96***, 223; soldiers' statue 64, 80–***81***, 82–***83***, 84, 99, 124, 162, 223, 239, 242; Wyatt fountain 77, 238
"Elegy Written in a Country Churchyard" (poem) 163, 203
Elizabeth City 110, 121–***122***, 125, 147, 224; *see also* Pasquotank County
Ellis, Gov. John W. 74, 82, 165
Elmwood Cemetery (Charlotte) ***30***, 32
Elmwood Cemetery (Enfield) 195
Enfield 159, 194–***195***, 223

Faison 165, 206–***207***, 223, 236, 239; *see also* Duplin County
Fayetteville 4, 7, 11, 15–16, 48, 76, 239; civic-space monument ***133***, 135–136, 159, 162, 223, 242; Cross Creek Cemetery monument 7, ***8***–***9***, 10–11, 15, 32, 40, 57, 64, 157, 160, 223; *see also* Cumberland County
Federal monument (Salisbury National Cemetery) 24, 179–***180***, 210, 230
Fifteenth Connecticut Volunteer Regiment *see* Connecticut monument

Index

Fifty-eighth North Carolina Regiment 78
Fifty-third North Carolina Regiment 120, 166
flag (as symbol) 62–63, 123–124, 158, 241
Foraker Bill 182, 186
Forest City 204; monument 203–**204**, 205, 225
Forsyth County: monument and its dedication 64, 112–**113**, 114–118, 124–125, 160–161, 223, 235–236, 239, 244
Fort Macon Chapter, United Daughters of the Confederacy 198
Fortieth North Carolina Regiment 188, **190**
Forty-eighth North Carolina Regiment 21
Forty-first North Carolina Regiment 44
Fourteenth North Carolina Regiment 72, 164
Fourth North Carolina Infantry 33, 167
Fowle, Gov. Daniel 33, 222
Frank M. Parker Chapter, United Daughters of the Confederacy 159, 194
Franklin 85, 116, 118, 123, 125, 141–**142**, 164, 224, 239; *see also* Macon County
Franklin County: courthouse fountain (Orren Randolph Smith) 76; cemetery monument (Justice) **98**; Louisburg soldiers' monument 153–**154**, 156, 161, 163, 223
frock coat (as artistic convention) 19, 37, 50
Fuller, Thomas C. 16
Fusionist political movement 47–50

G. W. Sellers and Sons (Newport, TN) 62, 222
Gaddess Brothers Steam Marble Works (Baltimore, MD) 31, 134, 226
Gardner, Gov. O. Max 211
Gaston County **146**, **158**, 223, 235, 239
Gastonia 146, 158, 223; *see also* Gaston County
Gates County **124**, 165, 223, 236, 237, 239
Gatesville **124**, 165, 223; *see also* Gates County
General James Johnston Pettigrew Chapter, United Daughters of the Confederacy 207
General William D. Pender Chapter, United Daughters of the Confederacy 80, 82
Gettysburg: battle 13, 17, 33, 47, 70, 75, 77–78, 80, 121, 124, 130, 179, 191, 214; national cemetery 10–11; North Carolina monument 206, 210, 248
Glenn, Gov. Robert B. 66, 69–71, 76, 119, 121–123, 130, 175, 178–179, 185–187, 222, 224–226
"God Bless old North Carolina" 45, 72, 160
Goldsboro 7, **25**, **28**, 31–32, 50, 91, 134, 159–160, 175–176, 202, 226, 242; *see also* Wayne County
Goldsboro Rifles 31–32, **38**, 159–160, 176, 224, 244
Goodlet, Caroline Meriwether 85–86, 88
Gordon, Gen. John B. 58, 88
Gorham Manufacturing Co. (NY) 77, 140, 149, 203, 224
Grady, Judge Henry A. 197, 199, 222
Graham 118, 122, **148**, 159, 222; *see also* Alamance County
Graham County 235
Grant, Gen. Ulysses S. 5, 178–179, 199, 214
Granville County 50, **117**, 223, 239
Gray, Thomas (poet) 162–163, 203
Green Hill Cemetery (Greensboro) **27**, 31
Greene County 162–163, **203**, 223, 236
Greene County Chapter, United Daughters of the Confederacy 162, 203
Greensboro 13, **27**, 30–31, 36, 50, 84, 91, 104–105, 120, 129, 134, 166, 178, 210, 223, 239; *see also* Guilford County
Greensboro Ladies' Memorial Association 13, 31
Greenview Cemetery (Reidsville) **216**–217, 225
Greenville 64, 83, **136**, 161, 225, 242; *see also* Pitt County
grief 40, 78, 216–218
Grimes, Gen. Bryan 166
Grimes, Sec. of State J. Bryan 78, 166–167, 170, 245
Gudger, Mrs. James Madison, Jr. 193
Guilford County 91, 104–106; Green Hill Cemetery monument (Greensboro) **21**, 31, 50, 134, 223; Oakwood Cemetery monument (High Point) 12, **37**, 223

Hale, Edward J. 78, 223
Halifax 76; *see also* Halifax County
Halifax County 236; Enfield fountain 159, 194–**195**, 223; General Junius Daniel courthouse marker 76; Jefferson Davis Highway marker 247; Weldon Burying Ground marker **109**; Weldon soldiers' monument **104**
Hampton, Gen. Wade 38, 76, 224
Harnett County **16**, 223, 232
Haywood County 49, 235; Confederate Memorial Forest 200–**201**, 202, 223; courthouse soldiers' monument 205–**206**, 223; "Last Shot" pyramid 193
Henderson 123, 125, **161**, 225; *see also* Vance County
Henderson, John Steele 155, 244
Henderson County 239; Dixie-Lee Highway plaque 193; Etowah Union monument 60, 235; soldiers' monument 55–**56**, 57–61, 224, 235, 239
Hendersonville: Dixie-Lee Highway plaque 193; soldiers' monument 55–**56**, 57–61; *see also* Henderson County
Hertford: Confederate monument **147**, 225; United States Colored Troops monument **186**, 230; *see also* Perquimans County
Hertford County **91**, 224, 236, 239
Hertford County Chapter, United Daughters of the Confederacy 91
Hibriten Guards (Co. F Twenty-sixth North Carolina Regiment) 121
High Point 12–13, **37**, 104, 202, 223; *see also* Guilford County
Hill, Gen. Daniel Harvey (D. H.) 122, 167–168
Hill, Daniel Harvey (D. H.), Jr. 121–122, 167, 224–225
Hill, Mrs. Daniel Harvey (D. H.) 42
historical memory *see* collective memory
Hoey, Gov. Clyde 224
Hoke, Gen. Robert 94, 191–192
Hoke County **15**, 224
Holden, William Woods 75
Holly Springs 165, 195–**196**, 203, 226; *see also* Wake County
Holly Springs United Methodist Church (Holly Springs, NC) 165, 195–**196**, 203, 226; *see also* Alford, G. B.
Hope, James Barron (poet) 127, 129–130, 161, 244
Horne, Ashley 42, 124, 166–172, 225; *see also* Confederate Women's monument (Raleigh)
House of Memory (Oakwood Cemetery, Raleigh) 207–208
Hulin, C. J. 100–102, 129, 146; *see also* Durham Marble Works
CSS *Hunley* (monument) 17
Huske, Dr. Joseph 7, 11, 223
Hyde County 49, 236

Immortal 600 33–36; Battery Wagner 33; Fort Pulaski 34; *see also* Allen, Captain Thomas M.
Iredell County: Mooresville monument **208**, 224; Statesville monument 47, **119**, 120, 123, 125, 150–151, 159, 162, 224, 235, 236, 239

J. L. Mott Iron Works 138
Jackson, Gen. Thomas J. "Stonewall" 14, 19, 29, 54, 76, 178, 213–214, 237
Jackson, Mrs. Thomas J. "Stonewall" 42, 54, 94
Jackson County 106, **139**, 172, 224, 235, 239, 242
Jacksonville 162, **217**–218, 224; *see also* Onslow County

James B. Gordon Chapter, United Daughters of the Confederacy 112, 114–115
Jeff Davis Mountaineers (Co. A, Twenty-sixth North Carolina Regiment) 72
Jefferson Davis Chapter, United Daughters of the Confederacy *218*
Jefferson Davis Highway 193, 203, 235, 247
Jim Crow segregation 24, 195, 218–219
John W. Dunham Chapter, United Daughters of the Confederacy 194
Johnson, Charles C. (monument builder) 210–211, 224, 248
Johnston, Gen. Joseph 3, 7, 14, 166, 178
Johnston County: Bentonville monument *26*, *38*, 42, 160, 170, 224; Riverside Cemetery monument 26, 32, 39, 224
Jonathan Williams, Inc. (NY) 138–139, 149, 203
Jones, Mrs. Nancy Branch 48, 234
Jones County 64, 218–*219*, 224, 236
Joseph J. Davis Chapter, United Daughters of the Confederacy 123
Junior Order United American Mechanics *37*
Junius Daniel Chapter, United Daughters of the Confederacy *104*

Keith, Lt. Col. James A. 59, 235
Kenansville 91; *see also* Duplin County
Kilmer, Joyce (poet) 195
Kincaid, Captain W. J. 107–*108*, 222
King and Whitelaw (marble company) 17, 225
Kinney, Belle 170–171
Kinston 21, 176, 181; Maplewood Cemetery monument *31*–32, 224; soldiers' monument *150*–151, 196, 224; *see also* Lenoir County
Kipling, Rudyard (poet) 128, 162
Kitchin, Gov. W. W. 94, 143, 185, 223–225
Knapp, Joseph P. 109–111, 223

Ladies' Memorial Association of Washington, North Carolina 33; Call, Secretary Margaret 36; Sparrow, Major Thomas J. 36
Ladies' Memorial Associations 11–12, 14–19, 21–24, 29–32, 42, 44
Lauder, George 8–9
Laurinburg *105*, 158–159, 225; *see also* Scotland County
Lee, Anne Carter 127–128, 130
Lee, Gen. Fitzhugh 88, 138, 176
Lee, Gen. Robert E. 3–4, 19, 29, 31, 45, 71–72, 76, 81, 92, 99, 105, 127, 160, 164, 166, 178–179, 189, 193, 199, 213–214
Lee County 237
Lee-Eaves-McDaniel Chapter, United Daughters of the Confederacy 203–204
Lenoir 60, 120–*121*, 126, 147, 160, 222, 239; *see also* Caldwell County
Lenoir County 236; civic-space monument *150*–152, 196–197, 224, 236; Maplewood Cemetery monument *31*–32, 224
Lexington *160*–161, 223, 239; *see also* Davidson County
Lincoln, President Abraham 4–5, 57–58, 72–74
Lincoln County *94*, 106, 224, 235, 259
Lincolnton *94*, 224; *see also* Lincoln County
Littleton 206–*207*, 226
LMA *see* Ladies' Memorial Associations
London, Henry A. 79, 99–100, 122, 170, 222
London, Mrs. Henry A. (UDC state president) 54, 99–*103*, 115, 119, 129, 156, 239
Long, Mrs. Glenn (UDC state president) 202, 204, 212, 218
Long, James A. 170
Long Street Presbyterian Church Cemetery (monument) *15*
Louisburg 76, 153–*154*, 155, 161, 163, 223, 239; *see also* Franklin County
Lukeman, Augustus 167, 171–173, 225
Lumberton *87*, 143, 158, 160, 225; *see also* Robeson County

M. C. Lyons' Son (Camden, NJ) 178, 230
Macon County 66, 116, 141–*142*, 143, 146, 164, 224, 235, 239, 242
Madison County 58–59, 193, 235
Maine monument (Salisbury National Cemetery) 183–*184*, 185–186, 230
Maplewood Cemetery (Kinston) *31*–32
Maplewood Cemetery (Wilson) *120*, 194
"The March of the Deathless Dead" (poem) 46–47, 158–159, 194
Marion 208–*209*, 224; *see also* McDowell County
Marshall 58, 235; *see also* Madison County
Martin, Gen. James G. 3
Martin County 91, 236
"Maryland, My Maryland" (song) 119
Mason, Thomas W. 46–49, 54, 64, 222, 245
Massachusetts monument (New Bern National Cemetery) *182*–183, 230
McClammy, Maj. Charles W. 19
McDonald, Alexander 180, 230
McDowell County 208–*209*, 224, 235

McNeel Marble Company (Marietta, GA) *142*–144, 146, *147*–*148*, 149, *150*–*151*, 152, 197, 222–226
Mecklenburg County 114; Charlotte Elmwood Cemetery monument 30, 224; Cornelius monument *163*, 224
Mecklenburg Declaration of Independence 44, 63, 69, 233, 235–236
Memminger, Christopher G. 55, 60
Memorial Day (Confederate) 232; origin of 14–15, 232
Methodist Church Cemetery (Ashe Street, Greensboro, NC) 13, 31
Milmore, Martin 133–134
Mitchell County 49, 74, 235
Mocksville 235; *see also* Davie County
Monroe *92*, 225; *see also* Union County
Montgomery, James (poet) 162
Montgomery, Walter A. 78, 226
Montgomery County 173, 195–*197*, 224
Montmorenci United Methodist Church (Candler, NC) *59*, 61
Monument Avenue (Richmond, VA) 29
Monumental Bronze Company (Bridgeport, CT) 144–145, 225
Mooresville *208*, 224
Mordecai, Henry 13
Morehead, Col. James T. 120
Morganton 60, 107–*108*, 119, 124, 131, 158, 165, 222, 240, 242; *see also* Burke County
Morrison, Gov. Cameron 197, 205–206, 224–225
Mount Airy (NC) Granite 102, 150, 184
Mount Zion United Methodist Church (Cornelius, NC) *163*
Muldoon Monument Company (Louisville, KY) 144, 225
Murdock-Reed Company (Boston, MA) 202–203
Murphy 208; *see also* Cherokee County
"My Country 'Tis of Thee" (song) 119

Nash County 119, 124, *134*–*135*, 224, 239
National Association of the Daughters of the Confederacy 86–88; *see also* United Daughters of the Confederacy
National Fine Art Foundry (NY) 18, 134
NCMA *see* North Carolina Monumental Association
Neuse Chapter, United Daughters of the Confederacy 205
New Bern 4, 14, 24, 75, 91; Confederate monument 12, 21, *22*–*23*, 24, 39, 50, 134, 139, 157, 222; *see also* Craven County, New Bern National Cemetery
New Bern Academy 21–22

New Bern Ladies' Memorial Association 12, 21–*22*, *23*–24
New Bern National Cemetery: Connecticut monument 180–*181*, 182, 230; Massachusetts monument *182*–183, 230; New Jersey monument 176, *177*–179, 183, 186–187, 230; Rhode Island monument *183*, 230
New Hanover County 236; Boney monument *189*–192, 209, 224; Fort Fisher monument 210–*211*, 212, 224; Oakdale Cemetery monument *20*, 50, 224, 242
New Jersey monument (New Bern National Cemetery) 175–176, *177*–179, 183, 185–187, 230
Newton *118*–119, 122–123, 149, 159, 204, 222, 239; see also Catawba County
Newton Academy Cemetery (Asheville) *62*–*63*, 66, 244
Ninth New Jersey Volunteer Regiment 176–*177*, 178, 185–187, 230
Norfleet Camp, United Confederate Veterans 114
North Carolina Confederate Women's Home 92
North Carolina Historical Commission 78, 170, 193, 203, 235, 247
North Carolina Monumental Association 44, 46, 48
North Carolina "Rebel Boast" 45, 70–71, 77–79, 207, 237
North Carolina Soldiers' Home 90, 92, 241
North Carolina state monument 42–*43*, 44–*45*, 46–50, *51*–*52*, 53–54, 225, 242; funding 48–50
Northampton County 46, 54, *104*, 239

Oakdale Cemetery (Mt. Airy, NC) 215–*216*
Oakdale Cemetery (Washington, NC) *34*, *35*, 40, *93*, 202
Oakdale Cemetery (Wilmington) 12, 18–*20*, 189
Oakwood Cemetery (High Point, NC) 12, *37*
Oakwood Cemetery (Raleigh, NC) 13–14, 17–*18*, 44, 48, *97*, 160, 207
"Ode Sung on the Occasion of Decorating the Graves of the Confederate Dead" (poem) 160–161
O'Donovan, William Rudolph (sculptor) 19, 134
O'Hara, Theodore 9, 32, 157, 159–160
Old English Cemetery (Salisbury, NC) *165*, 225
"The Old North State" (song) 48, 82, 142
Onslow County 106, 162, *217*–218, 224, 236
Onslow Guards Chapter, United Daughters of the Confederacy 217–218

Orange County 106, *140*, 224, 242
Oxford *117*, 223; see also Granville County

Packer, Francis H. 189–191, 224
Pamlico County 64, *205*, 224, 236
Panic of 1873 24
Parsley, Eliza (UDC state president) 88, 91, 189
Pasquotank County 121–*122*, 125, 147, 224, 236
Pender, Gen. William Dorsey 80–83, *123*, 236
Pender County: Co. K monument *156*, 225; soldiers' monument 121, *123*, 125–126, 224, 236
Pennsylvania monument (Salisbury National Cemetery) 183–*185*, 186, 230
Perquimans County: African American monument *186*, 230; Confederate monument *147*, 225, 236, 239
Person County 122, 196–*198*, 225
Pettigrew, General James Johnston 21, 78, 213
Pettigrew Hospital (Raleigh) 12
Philadelphia White Bronze Monument Company *25*, 134, 138, 242
Pickens, Sidney Vance 55, 57–58, 60, 64, 224
Pitt County 64, *136*, 161, 225, 236, 239, 242
Pittsboro 91–92, 99–*101*, 102–*103*, 115, 123, 129, 140; see also Chatham County
Platt, Sen. Orville H. 181–182, 230
Plymouth 4, 75; see also Washington County
political divisions in western North Carolina 58–60, 71–76
Polk, Mrs. Lucy 128, 145
Polk County 60, 235, 239
Power, Maurice J. 18, 19, 134
public memory see collective memory

Quakers 4, 75

R. E. Lee Chapter, Children of the Confederacy (Asheville) 68, 73
Raines, Anna Davenport 85–86, 88, 93
Raleigh 2–4, 7, 12–13, 64–71, 75–77, 84, 90, 128, 145, 185, 200, 206–207; Confederate Women's monument 121–122, 124, 155, *167*–*168*, 173, 225; Henry Wyatt monument 77; Ladies' Memorial Association 12–15, 17, 42, 44, 107, 189; Oakwood Cemetery arch *97*; Oakwood Cemetery monument 17–*18*, 160, 225; state monument 41–*43*, 44–50, *52*–54, 66, 84, 114, 131, 144, 189, 225; see also Wake County
Raleigh Marble Works see Cooper Brothers
Randolph County *116*, 118, 120–121, 125, 129, 150, 162, 225, 239, 242

Ransom, Gen. Matthew 91, 226
Ransom, Gen. Robert 47
Ray, Col. James M. 68–69, 71, 236
Rebel yell 82, 119, 125
"Recessional" (poem) 162
Reconstruction 14, 24, 48, 85, 169, 179–180, 202, 216, 218
Redemption (political) 24
Reidsville: civic-space monument 72, *95*, 98, 160–161, 225, 239; Greenview Cemetery monument *216*–217, 225; see also Rockingham County
Rhode Island monument (New Bern National Cemetery) *183*, 230
Richmond County 106, 162, 205–*206*, 225
Ricks, Robert 124, *134*, 165, 224
Riverside Cemetery (Asheville) *73*
Riverside Cemetery (Smithfield) *26*, 32
Roanoke Island 70, 75, 177
Roanoke Minute Men Chapter, United Daughters of the Confederacy 206
Robbins, Maj. W. M. 90, 222
Roberts, Gen. William P. 165
Roberts Marble Co. 224
Robeson County *87*, 158, 160, 225, 239
Robinson, Joseph 175
Rock Quarry Cemetery (Raleigh) 12–14, 17
Rockingham 162, 205–*206*, 225; see also Richmond County
Rockingham County: civic-space monument 72, *95*, 98, 160, 225, 239; Greenview Cemetery monument *216*–217, 225
Rocky Mount 119, 124, *134*–*135*, 165, 224, 239; see also Nash County
Rogers, Randolph 133–134
Rowan County: civic-space Confederate monument 106–*107*, 114, 151, 155, 163–164, 225, 239; Old English Cemetery Confederate monument *165*, 225; see also federal monument (Salisbury National Cemetery); Maine monument (Salisbury National Cemetery); Pennsylvania monument (Salisbury National Cemetery)
Roxboro 122, 196–*198*, 225; see also Person County
Ruckstuhl, Frederick *107*, 170, 225
Rutherford County 235; Forest City monument 203–*204*, 205, 225; Rutherfordton courthouse monument *89*, 147, 172, 225, 239
Rutherfordton: courthouse monument *89*, 147, 172; see also Rutherford County
Ryan, Father Joseph A. 46, 99, 101–102, 128, 141, 157–160, 194, 208

Salisbury 35, 155, 186, 191; Confederate monument *107*, 155, 163, 170, 225, 239, 244; Old English

Cemetery monument *165*, 225; *see also* Rowan County; Salisbury National Cemetery
Salisbury National Cemetery: federal monument 24, 179–*180*, 210, 230; Maine monument 183, 184–186, 230; Pennsylvania monument 183–*185*, 186, 230
Sampson County *125*, *137*, 225, 236, 239
Sanford 237; *see also* Lee County
Scotland County *105*, 158–159, 225
sculptural uniform distinctions 19, 36–38, 136, 198
Sharpe, T. O. (monument builder) 197–198, 225
Shelby 64, 124, *162*, 222, 239, 242; *see also* Cleveland County
Shelton Laurel killings 58–59, 235
Shephard, Heyward: monument (Harpers Ferry, WV) 174
Sherman, Gen. William T. 3–5, 7, 15, 67, 76, 166
"Silent Sam" *see* University of North Carolina Confederate statue
Sixteenth North Carolina Regiment 204
Sixtieth North Carolina Regiment *67*–70, 78, 164
Sixty-first North Carolina Regiment 72, 246
Sixty-fourth North Carolina Regiment 58–60, 235; Company E marker 61
Sixty-ninth North Carolina Regiment 208
Sixty-seventh North Carolina Regiment 21
Smith, Gen. Edmund Kirby 3
Smith, Orren Randolph 76, *161*, 241
Smith, William Alexander 164, *172*, *173*–174, 222, 244
Smithfield 21; monument *26*, 32, 39, 224; *see also* Johnston County
Smithville Memorial Association 15–17, 19
Snow Hill 162–163, *203*, 223; *see also* Greene County
soldier statue: "parade rest" form 18, 129, 136–139, 144, 151–152, 178, 184; "skirmisher" form *133*, 136–137, *138*–139, 196
Soldiers' Aid Associations 7, 11, 85
South Carolina state monument 29, 39, 46
Southern Cross of Honor 66, 71, 82, 91–93, 116, 119, 155
Southern Marble and Granite Company 146, 223
Spanish-American War 176, 182; monuments 173, 195–197; soldier statues 137–138
Stanly County *106*, 159, 162, 196–197, 225
"The Star-Spangled Banner" 108, 119, 130, 192, 201, 205, 217, 248
"Stars and Bars" 62, 123, 187, 241; *see also* Orren Randolph Smith

State Literary and Historical Association 78, 202
Statesville 47, 100, *119*–120, 123, 125, 149–151, 159, 162, 224, 236; *see also* Iredell County
Stewart, Gen. James, Jr. 177–178, 183, 230
Stokes, (NJ) Gov. Edward C. 121, 178, 186
Stokes County 165, 235
Stoneman, Gen. George 3–4
Suffolk Marble Works (Suffolk, VA) 153, 223–225
Sunset Hill Cemetery (Littleton) 206–*207*, 226; *see also* Warren County
Surry County 49, 215–*216*, 225, 235
Swain County *210*, 225, 235; *see also* Cherokee Indian monument
"The Sword of Robert E. Lee" (poem) 158–159
Sylva *139*, 172, 201, 224; *see also* Jackson County
symbolism 38–39, 136; "empty sleeve" 52–53; flag 62–63, 123–124, 158, 241; frock coat 19, 37

T. F. McGann and Sons Company (Boston, MA) 138–139
Tarboro 8; cemetery arch *96*, 223; monument 64, 77, 80–*81*, 82–*83*, 84, 99, 124, 162, 223; *see also* Edgecombe County
Taylorsville 213–*214*, *215*, 222; *see also* Alexander County
Tennyson, Alfred, Lord 155–156, 161
"Tenting on the Old Campground" (song) 22, 57, 119, 240
"Tenting Tonight" (song) 199, 243
Thomas, William Holland 208–*210*
Thrash, Captain Augustus Buckingham 61–62, 65, 164, 222
Tiernan, Frances Fisher 155, 163, 244
Timrod, Henry (poet) 160–161
Transylvania County 60, 74, 235
Trenton 64, 218–*219*, 224; *see also* Jones County
Troy 173, 195–*197*, 224; *see also* Montgomery County
Twentieth North Carolina Regiment 206
Twenty-ninth North Carolina Regiment 68, 215
Twenty-sixth North Carolina Regiment 13, 72, 75, 121, 167
Tyrrell County 85, *144*, *164*, 172, 174, 225, 236–237, 239, 242
Tyrrell Monument Association 85, 164, 225

Union County *92*, 225, 239
Unionists (in North Carolina) 4, 11, 28, 44, 58, 60, 72–75, 115
United Confederate Veterans: founding 85, 87–88, 90; women's monument 166, 169

United Daughters of the Confederacy: founding 55, 85–88, 90–93
United Daughters of Veterans 186
United States Colored Troops monument 11, *186*, 230
University of North Carolina Confederate statue *140*, 224, 239, 242
USCT *see* United States Colored Troops

Vance, Gen. Robert B. 70
Vance, Zebulon B. 24, 31, 57–58, 70, 72, 74–76, 235; monument (Asheville) 57–58, 66, 149, 193; monument (Raleigh) 76
Vance County 123–125, *161*, 170, 225, 239, 241
Vanderbilt, George W. 61
Vass, Rev. L. C. 22–23, 222
Virgil L. Fuller (manufacturer) 145
von Miller, Ferdinand, II 50, *51*–*52*, 135, 225, 242

W. H. Mullins Company (Salem, OH) *106*, 128–129, *130*–*131*, *136*, 137–*139*, 145–146, 150, 197, 222, 224–226, 242
Waddell, Col. Alfred Moore 42–46, 54, 64, 114–115, 189, 223–224, 226
Wadesboro: soldiers' monument *132*, 164, 222, 242; women's monument 160, *172*–*173*, 174, 206, 222; *see also* Anson County
Wake County 90, 239; Holly Springs monument 165, 195–*196*, 203, 226; Oakwood Cemetery arch 97; Oakwood Cemetery commemorative wall 207; Oakwood Cemetery monument 12–13, 17–*18*, 225; state monument 42–*43*, 44–*45*, 46–*51*, *52*–54, 225, 242
Wake County Ladies' Memorial Association 12, 14, 17–*18*, 42, 44, 107
Warren County 239; Anne Lee monument 127–128; courthouse monument *129*–*130*, 131, 159, 162, 226, 242; Fairview Cemetery monument 128, *145*, 226; Littleton monument 206–*207*, 226
Warrenton: courthouse monument *129*–*130*, 159, 226; Fairview Cemetery monument 128, *145*, 226; *see also* Warren County
Washington (NC) 33, 75; Children of Confederacy monument *93*–94, 202, 222; soldiers' statue 33–*34*, *35*, 36–40, 50, 134, 222; *see also* Beaufort County
Washington County 236
Washington Gray Chapter, Children of the Confederacy 94
Watauga County 103–105, 235
Wayne County *25*, *28*, 31–32, 50, 91, 134, 226, 236, 242
Waynesville 60; courthouse soldiers' monument 205–*206*, 223; "Last Shot" pyramid 193; *see also* Haywood County

Webb, C. B. (monument builder) 149–150, 222
Weldon: Confederate Burying Ground marker **109**; soldiers' monument **104**
Wentworth 239; *see also* Rockingham County
Wheeler, Gen. Joseph 58, 88, 176
Whiteville **218**, 222; *see also* Columbus County
Whiting, Capt. George M. 13, 17, 160
Wilkes County 114, 235
Williams, Fannie Ransom *see* Mrs. F. M. Williams
Williams, Mrs. F. M. (UDC state president) 170, 245
Williams, Mrs. Marshall (UDC state president) 154–155
Williamston 91; *see also* Martin County
Willowdale Cemetery (Goldsboro) **25**, **28**, 31–32
Wilmington 8, 12, 42, 44, 76, 84, 115, 188, 210–212, 223–224, 239; Boney monument 188–**189**, **190**–192, 196–197, 224; Oakdale Cemetery monument 15, 18–**20**, 24, 50, 134, 224, 237, 242; *see also* New Hanover County
Wilmington Ladies' Memorial Association 18–19
Wilmington race riot (1898) 189
Wilson 202; courthouse monument **194**, 203, 226; Maplewood Cemetery monument **120**, 194, 226; *see also* Wilson County
Wilson, Lt. Isaac 60
Wilson, John (sculptor) 140, 224, 242
Wilson County 236; Maplewood Cemetery monument **120**, 194, 226; courthouse monument **194**, 203, 226
Windsor 40, 85, **157**, 164, 222; *see also* Bertie County
Winnie Davis Chapter, United Daughters of the Confederacy 91, 99–**101**, 102–**103**, 123, 156
Winston, Francis D. 81, 115
Winston-Salem 60, 64, 112–**113**, 114–115, 119, 124–125, 150, 160, 223, 236; *see also* Forsyth County
Winton **91**, 224; *see also* Hertford County
Wolfenden, J. J. 176
"Women of Cumberland" 135, 159; *see also* Cumberland County
Woodland Bronze Works (Newburyport, MA) 203
World War I 103, 140, 172, 190, 192–193, 202–203, 214–215, 217; monuments 110, 173, 193, **195**–**196**, 209, 248; soldier statues 173, 196, **197**–**198**
Worth, Gov. Jonathan 99
Wyatt, Henry Lawson 77, 82; Capitol-grounds monument (Raleigh) 77, 248; Tarboro fountain 77, 238

Yadkin County 60, 235
Yancey County 235
Yanceyville **138**, 196, 222, 242; *see also* Caswell County

www.ingramcontent.com/pod-product-compliance
Ingram Content Group UK Ltd.
Pitfield, Milton Keynes, MK11 3LW, UK
UKHW050537150426
5217IPUK00026B/1977

9 780786 468560